DECOLONIZING HINDUISM

DECOLONIZING HINDUISM

Exposing Shallow Attempts That Destroyed and Divided Dharma

Shubham G. Deore

Copyright © 2024 Shubham G. Deore

Shubham G. Deore has asserted his rights under the Indian Copyright Act to be identified as the author of this work.

All rights reserved under the copyright conventions. No part of this publication may be reproduced or transmitted in any form or by any means, electronic or mechanical, including photocopying, recording or any information storage or retrieval system, without the prior permission in writing from the publisher.

This book is solely the responsibility of the author(s) and the publisher has had no role in the creation of the content and does not have responsibility for anything defamatory or libellous or objectionable.

BluOne Ink Pvt. Ltd does not have any control over, or responsibility for, any third-party websites referred to in this book. All internet addresses given in this book were correct at the time of going to press. The author and publisher regret any inconvenience caused if addresses have changed or sites have ceased to exist, but can accept no responsibility for any such changes.

The arguments in this book carry the weight of experiential knowledge and do not necessarily reflect objective reality. Examples given in it are purely hypothetical and should not be related to real persons or incidences. The author does not intend to hurt the feeling of any community, caste, race, religion, nation, country, or authority.

ISBN: 978-93-92209-92-5

First published in India 2024
This edition published 2024

BluOne Ink Pvt. Ltd
A-76, 2nd Floor, Sector 136, Noida
Uttar Pradesh 201301
www.bluone.ink
publisher@bluone.ink

Kali, Occam and BluPrint are all trademarks of BluOne Ink Pvt. Ltd.

Contents

Preface	vii
Acknowledgements	xi
∞Kāla Bhairava: Father of Artificial Intelligence	xiii

Part I: Shaping of the Reader's Mind

1.	The Cold War Within: Atheism Invasion Theory	3
2.	Macaulay's Formula of Brand Building	16
3.	Religion, Laïcité, Secularism, and Conflicts	29
4.	Multilayer Data Science: Hindu Society	55
5.	Neutral History Books before Saffaronization	77

Part II: Reality of Society, Economy, and Polity

6.	Humanity: The Lowest Value of the Universe	103
7.	Blockchain Technology: Jati, Caste, and Brahmins	119
8.	Human Capital versus Institutional Efforts	159

Part III: Untouchability with Hinduism

9.	Why I Am Not Hindu?	181
10.	Opium of Marxist Mythology	205

Part IV: Demystifying Popular Narratives

11.	Scriptures versus Scripture: One Scripture	233
12.	It's Terrorism, but For You	245

Part V: Going Back to the Roots

13.	No God to Many Gods, Many Gods to One God	265
14.	Quantum Physics: It's Entanglement with Paramātmā	283
15.	Three-Dimensional Buddha	308
16.	The Conqueror	324

Part VI: Personality, Responsibility, and Vision

17.	Bramhacarya: Going Closer to Bramha	331
18.	Dvanva to Dvaita	336
19.	The Real 'Fake God'	346
20.	Why Rituals Are Always Meaningless?	367
21.	God of Baseless Colonizers	384
∞	Kāla Bhairava: The Singularity of Artificial Intelligence	395

Appendix A   401
Appendix B   419
Appendix C   426
Appendix D   428
Notes   429
About the Author   447

Preface

The Purna Swaraj declaration promulgated by the Indian National Congress (supposedly drafted by Mahatma Gandhi) on 26 January 1930 said:

> The British government in Bhārat has not only deprived the Bhārtiya people of their freedom but has based itself on the exploitation of the masses, and has ruined Bhārat economically, politically, culturally and spiritually.

But How?

We are still carrying some colonial hangover in our mind, tongue, and behaviour, which are reflected in our cultural, social, political, and economic choices. In addition, most of our books were inspired by the British and twisted around expected political outcomes. So, this book is about decolonizing mindset, especially of Hindus. In Kashmir, Pakistan existed as a 'deep state' (invisible existence in the masses as a soft or hard corner). Similarly, Hinduism was shaped/molded in the form of Western religions, society, and philosophy; initially, it seems that we are reading about Hinduism, but it's actually 'western drink' in Indian bottles, which is an ideological level 'deep state'. That is why it's important to be legitimate and explain truth in the form of decolonization.

You are either taught all religions are the same and teach love and peace, or when violence happens, it's the people who have wrongly interpreted it; if someone is communist, then from time to time, brainwashing is done to convince them that 'religion is opium', but you are never taught what is religion and Hinduism, etc. You are always kept with an empty brain through shallow love or hate towards religion. After reading this book, you will know 'how they broke the backbone' of our cultural, geographical, political, and economic identity through narrative building.

Culprit and Victim

The only thing they did was never attack directly, like invasions, but the British destroyed Hinduism conceptually. Everyone knows colonial masters did 'divide and rule'. But how? This book gives an account of how. This book exposes Hinduphobic propaganda promoted through history books as well as 'popular Hinduphobic narrative' on the tongue of Hindus and rebels, which they never recognize. This book is not about what the policy of Hindus is for others, but about what others are doing to Hinduism and Bhārat. It lets you know the real culprit and victim.

Purpose

The purpose of writing this book is to eliminate all doubts and confusion about religion, secularism, communism, capitalism, spirituality, economy, society, ecology, festivals, and philosophy and start the journey of people in various aspects of life spirituality, or Mukti/liberation, and the right path of life. I don't claim this book is complete, but some sense of completeness and certainty is there. Hinduism is famous for its acceptance even without questioning anyone's faith, but when people start using liberalism or secularism as a battlefield against Hinduism, then it becomes necessary to stand on the battlefield. My goal is to take people out of the binary of hate–love, tolerance–intolerance, and religion–atheism because these binaries are based on two fixed standpoints, where debate is done to prove oneself right rather than journeying from darkness to light.

Nationalism

This book does not promote cute attempts to prove every citizen as national or antinational, with some values like brotherhood, love, and secularism and nationalistic poems, which have wide acceptance because they release intellectual stress and responsibility from the brain to hold nations sovereignty. This stress-less life is an ocean of joy for intellectually lethargic people. This book gives sharp content based on facts and references rather than emotionally appealing or polarizing sentences.

This book is not about questioning anyone's nationalism because nationalism belongs to the citizens, not ideologies and ways; this nation exists because of those people who chose nationalism irrespective of their ideology and religion. Every person has fundamentalism, liberalism, and nationalism with a varied percentage; from person to person, it changes. Even though I have discussed fundamentalism, it is not the complete reality of people, but some people follow it. At the same time, discussion of fundamentalism and concepts is always suppressed by tagging them with tags like extremism and non-secular, but without understanding them, how are we going to solve those issues? That is why, rather than tagging someone as national or anti-national on certain identity criteria, let's discuss the concepts that form these criteria.

This book is about strategic existence, dynamic reality, and conscious being, all of which indicate the same truth at the political, societal, and yogic levels, respectively.

Why Should One Read This Book?

This book is about authentic Hinduism and also enlightens about attempts that tried to eliminate Hinduism and create Abrahamic equivalents within Hinduism. When a common man tries to figure out which book should he choose to study religion and all other things because there are so many books in the market, the consumer always looks for a shortcut in the format of 'moral of the story'. Unfortunately, what the reader gets in the name of the moral of the story is 'love, humanity, peace'. This book goes beyond all these things.

Politicians generally explain the culture of Bhārat in terms of:
1. Melting pot
2. Diverse culture (without being motivated by religious fundamentalism)
3. Never giving data of diversity and roots and diverse concept
4. Multiculturalism (Ganga–Jamuni tehzeeb)
5. Celebrating diversity without knowing fundamentalism

Politicians use the above terms to keep factors like anonymity and confusion alive so that the common man never studies scriptures and concept, accepts religion in emotional terms of 'love, mutual respect, unity', and never uses intellect or critical thinking. So that his brain is uplifted to the level of expected social engineering equations for the next election, he is never introduced to what is actually written in religious books.

What is a unique thing that you will never find anywhere else? Many people have said dharma is not a religion, but they have failed to define it. I have given the best possible definition with which everyone will agree. Many Hindu terms and their authentic meanings and translations are mentioned and explained in this book.

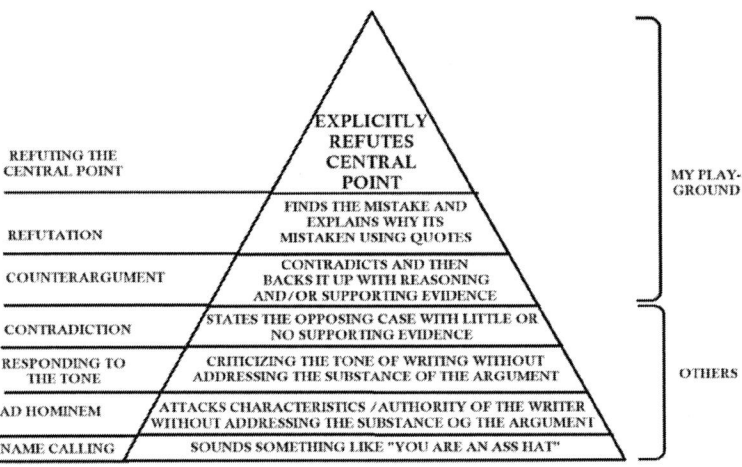

Fig. Graham's hierarchy of disagreement

Acknowledgements

Thanks to all my ancestors and parents who kept Sanatan Hindu Dharma alive in the form of 'sanskara, traditions, practice' and showered that knowledge on me directly or indirectly. Special thanks to Shri Chandrashekharacharya Saraswati (1907–94, Kanchi Peetham, Tamil Nadu) for his excellent book *Vedas*, which inspired me.

श्री महादेव

श्री तुळजाभवानी

शिवनृप रूपेणोर्वीमय

तीर्णोयःस्वयं प्रभु विष्णूः

एषा तदिय मुद्रा

भुबळ्यस्याभयप्रदा जयति।।

∞Kāla Bhairava: Father of Artificial Intelligence

Bhairava (MahāKāla Bhairava) is a Shaivite devata worshipped by Hindus. In the Trika system, Bhairava represents supreme reality, synonymous with *ParaBrahman*. It originates from the word *bhīru*, which means 'fearsome'. Hence, Bhairava means 'terribly fearsome form'. It is also known as one who destroys fear or one who is beyond fear. One interpretation is that he protects his devotees from dreadful enemies, greed, lust, and anger. Bhairava protects his devotees from these enemies. He is also called Dandapāni, as he holds a rod or danda to punish sinners. I am not going to discuss him in the context of devotee and devata, but 'Kāla Bhairava' as time travel on the cycle of 'karma' rather than the useless terms 'dreams, plans, motivation'.

Kāla is a word that is used for both time and space, or it is perceived as the unity of them. This time graph of Kāla Bhairava says that 'future is past and past is future'. When I use the words past and future, they are used in context and in reference to the present.[1]

Past Is Future
This is a method where one can determine 'cause' (past) through reverse engineering, i.e., finding cause from effect (future). Rather than random guesses, we find out the cause from effect. This is how karma functions. For example, you can know the breed of seed from a mango.

Future Is Past

In this case, we find out the effect from the cause. Effect (future) is not what you are dreaming or planning, but effect (future) is what karma you are doing in the present (the present is the past in relation to the future).

Both the things are based on content or karma and not on any marketing strategy, random guess, motivation, imagination, etc.

Artificial intelligence works on the same logic; it creates results on two bases:

1. From analysis of existing data inputs, it finds out something from the existing data set (finds out cause from effect). For example, Chat GPT generates information as per your demand from an existing online data set.
2. As per our demand, it generates a new data set (creative/generative artificial intelligence) which predicts future effect from cause. For example, if you search t-shirt on Amazon, then after some time, it will show related advertisements on every social media site you use.

Application of Kāla Bhairava

You might be wondering: What's its relation to history, religion, or civilization? By sowing fake, wrong seeds, you can create expected results. Which can turn in multiple ways, just like AI also gives multiple outputs. The only thing is how the reader perceives it; it also decides the outcomes, which can be a game changer. History books become important aspects to sow seeds of future society, political tone, and nation. Whatever seeds you sow yields a result. For example, if a communist fundamentalist writes history, they will promote 'atheism' as philosophy, impose 'communism' on ancient society, etc., i.e., using history books to sow seeds of communism.

This mechanism works in four ways:

1. What is sown as seed culminates in a plant. For example, women were limited to 'chulha chowka' (kitchen), so through a history book, women are told to remain limited to chulha chowka; they perceive it as a motivation and so limit themselves to chulha chowka (chapter 10).

2. Whatever vacuum is created in history, a new product is introduced to compensate for that. For example, women and vulnerable sections were limited to 'chulha chowka', no education, no skills, no entrepreneurship, and were considered inferior to men, so in the present and future, people will start feminist movements, reservations, etc., or vote bank for left-inclined politics (chapters 8 and 10).
3. Imposing a new product directly into history. For example, the imposition of the Western model of society and atheism directly in history so that Hindus never understand their true ancient society. So that a Hindu thinks communism is history, as a tradition, his psychology will vote for communism (chapter 4).
4. Don't mention anything in history so that people don't have awareness of what they have lost. It is like deleting search history or cookies from the web so that it never culminates in a choice. The greatness and archaeological value of temples are not glorified in books, so people don't pay attention to their maintenance.

Just like artificial intelligence has algorithmic biases, history also has ideological biases. This book decodes all those narratives, just like those that are set in our minds through history books and other influencing media platforms, that function in us, and that we manifest at the socio-economic and political levels but we remain unaware of it.

PART I
SHAPING OF THE READER'S MIND

1

The Cold War Within: Atheism Invasion Theory

If you observe the world map, all the subcontinents and continents are divided into multiple countries, for example, South America, North America, Europe, and Africa. But the Bhārtiya subcontinent belongs to one nation that is Bhārat. So, this is the biggest pain for the whole world, and that is why I always say third-world countries got freedom, but boundaries were drawn by colonial masters. So, separating southern Bhārat from northern Bhārat was the main goal. We cannot directly accuse colonial masters, but their hand in creating such a secessionist movement cannot be denied.

Why Separate Southern Bhārat?

1. Formation of second Pakistan troubles Bhārat such that the nation spends on internal–external security, i.e., geopolitical clash, rather than development.
2. Southern Bhārat is Bhārat's 20 per cent area (approximately) of the total area, so separating 20 per cent means a big loss.
3. The sovereignty of Bhārat over the Indian Ocean and challenges to Bhārat–Sri Lanka. A new naval power is in southern Bhārat; if it's separated from Bhārat, then it will definitely be against the nation, just like Pakistan.[1]
4. Creating political pressure on Bhārat through:
    a. voting against Bhārat in an international institution (Neo-Pakistan)
    b. cultural genocide of Hinduism in a new country by promoting 'foreign religions' and communism (rebels+ external interference)

5. Even if a new country (Dravidanadu) doesn't form, then work as a pressure group within Bhārat with a utopian state model against every nationalist policy,[2] and implement all of the above without a separate country status. For example, the Kudankulam plan.
6. Way to divide the country. Whenever you want to divide the land, the most important point is to divide the people at psychological, social, and cultural levels so that the people are convinced and they themselves will demand a separate nation. Biased media bombarding hate, atrocity, injustice, and crime reporting with the particular community so that it feels uncomfortable to be with mainstream and moves out of the nation as a separate nation.
   a) majority vs. minority
   b) religion vs. religion
   c) ethnicity vs. ethnicity
   d) language vs. language
   e) political ideology vs. political ideology

All these factors were absent in Bhārat; in addition, there were many uniting factors:
1. All were Hindus.
2. Uniform jati system and hierarchy all over Bhārat.
3. All cultural, psychological, and social patterns of Hindus are the same
4. Contribution of people in the south in Hindu culture: Alwars, Nayanaras, Ādi Śaṅkarācāryaḥ.
5. Absence of foreign religions with an expansionist policy for majority–minority division.

So colonial masters did an assessment of all five points and inserted seeds of the separatist movement through communal history writing, which is the modern way of conquering land. In ancient times, if someone wanted land, direct conquest was the way; in the mediaeval age, conversion; and in modern times, creating separatist movements through identity politics. So, they planted seeds in the '5-point agenda' to make it successful. Hinduism vs. six non-inclusive players (first read pp. 177–180 for better understanding).³

Post-1930s world started getting divided into a bipolar world order, the Marshall Plan, and the Warsaw Pact. So, division of Bhārat was an unavoidable scenario, as we saw in other cases during the Cold War.

1. Bhārtiya leadership started showing socialist inclinedness, so they adjusted 'right-wing' Pakistan in two socialist countries (USSR and Bhārat).
2. North Korea had a border with China, so it became communist, so South Korea was backed by the USA (right-wing or capitalist).
3. West Germany is capitalist, and East Germany is communist.
4. North and South Vietnam.
5. Within Bhārat also we find division and polarization. For instance, the south is generally more inclined to left politics and against Hinduism, upholding an atheistic identity, which often comes up against religion and culture that existed here for more than 3,000 years. Unfortunately, the story of a 'Second Pakistan', for example Dravida Nādu, is unpopular.⁴

Table 1.1 Making of Dravida Nādu

	Before Aryan invasion/original Dravidians	Aryan invasion event	After Aryan invasion
Narrative in history book	Atheists	Polytheism, caste system, rituals, Brahmins were introduced	Buddhism, Jainism, Carvaka, Samkhya, Vampan`th Ajivika, were marketed as atheists
Social base of movement	Southern part of Bhārat + marginalized varna/jati		Marginalized varna/jati of Bhārat

	Before Aryan invasion/original Dravidians	Aryan invasion event	After Aryan invasion
Impact on modern Bhārat	Atheist Periyar started atheist movement to make society pre-Aryan or atheist again, i.e., Tamils are not Hindus.⁵	Selective criticism/ cheap attacks/hate speech against Hinduism only. This left impact on government and judiciary that 'only' Hinduism is subjected to scrutiny, interference, and reforms.	He started an atheist movement to transform society to atheism, i.e., misinterpreted Buddhism.
Political Progress	Justice Party		Certain political party

China Model in Tamil Nadu

Communism is a political representation of atheism, so seeds of atheism were sown in history books, as shown in the Table 1.1, This then culminates in proper communism, which is actually separatism plus cultural genocide of Hinduism that can be carried out just like in China: targeting priests and monks, controlling monasteries, etc. Which exactly matches with Tamil Nadu, like the call for the exodus of Brahmins, controlling temples and weakening them financially, interference in rituals and infrastructure, properties and the land of temples.⁶

One more thing that matches with the Chinese policy is that they identify themselves as atheists/communists and promote it socially as an ideology, so they can't endorse capitalism and religion directly. But they do provide back-door entry to capitalism through market economy and to the indigenous religion under the garb of linguistic/regional culture with an atheistic filter/flavour. This contradictory nature of the Chinese policy nullifies each other and leads to confusion and conflicts but ensures short-term stability.

So, to launch atheism in history books, they introduced the concept of 'Aryan invasion theory', where Bhārat, pre and post Aryan invasion, looks atheist and people are pulled away from Hinduism in the name of eliminating Aryan/Brahmin colonialism. This is the only purpose that 'Aryan invasion theory' had. It's actually 'Atheism invasion theory'.

Dream of Tamil Country in History Books

The Bhārtiya subcontinent existed as a unified symbiosis of humanity and ecology; it existed as one system (explored in chapters 6 and 7). There were multiple empires established by various kingdoms. But no empire was based on language identity because a language-based state or nation is an 18th-century phenomenon. But many empires had their own official language, and you will never see language-based wars or clashes. All empires on the Bhārtiya subcontinent are identified as empires; only empires in the south are identified as 'nations' in our history books, i.e., Tamil country,[7] Maratha nationalism. The kind of history books shows the dream of a separate country, for instance Dravidanadu, in a latent form to 'reclaiming the ancient country in the name of linguistic identity'. Periyar turned the meaning of the words Aryan (high birth/nobel) and Dravidian (identification of land below Vindhyas) into linguistic racial theory to create more tensions among North vs. South, Brahmins vs. non-Brahmins (read A1.3, p. 402)

Table 1.2

Ideology	Atheism/materialism/communism
Identify themselves as	Misinterpreted Buddhism, original Dravidian (before invasions of Aryans/Brahmins), Adi Hindu
What they preach/Ends	Justice, liberty, equality, democracy rational for modern scientific society, and economy against authoritative Hinduism

What they actually practice/ Means	Cultural genocide and social boycott of Hinduism, cheap/ sexist interpretation of Hinduism, hate speech against Hinduism at ideological level, and expansion through proselytization (atheist also do proselytization).
Sources of their stand	Manipulated colonial history books by imposition of their ideology on history books
When means are 'unethical' and heavier than ends, then ends will be unethical. It doesn't matter how ethical your ends are, i.e., eliminating caste discrimination was the goal but ended up with 'Anti-Hindu' policy.	

Diagram 1.1

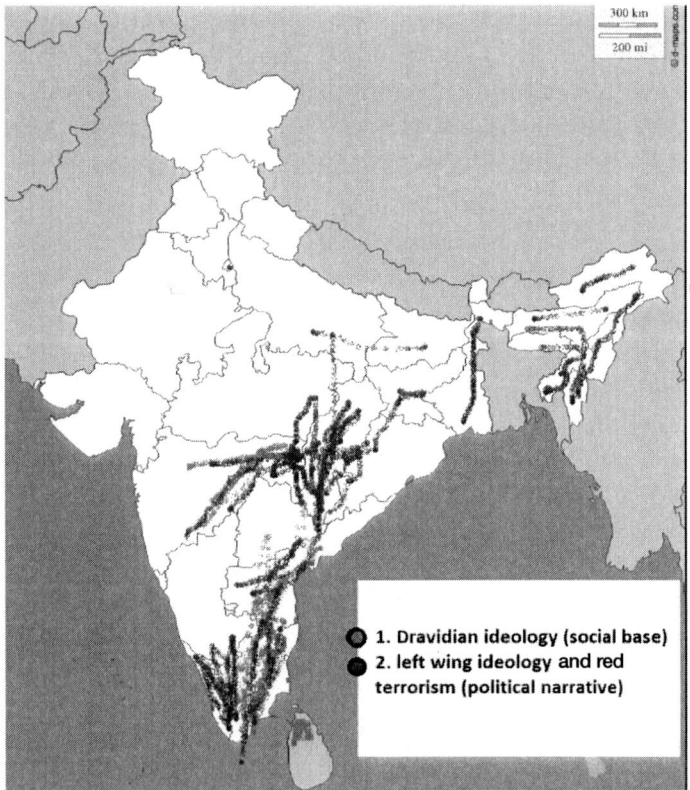

The Aryan invasion theory is fodder for every cult or community that wants to separate from Hinduism and Bhārat, now it's not limited to southern Bhārat. (We will learn more in chapter 9.) Today, in the northeast, sixteen separatist and militant organizations have united (ULFWSEA+CORCOM). They are not part of mainstream politics; if they become, they will create a separate northeast by using state machinery, just like Jinnah. Similarly, all Hinduphobic separatists are united at the political level; they do follow six non-inclusive ideologies as their philosophy. To hide their communal separatist tendencies, they accuse followers of Sanatan Hindu dharma of having negative attributes (read A1.1, p. 401). They have used the colonial social engineering equation of divide and rule.

Table 1.3

Ancient history in books	Aryan[8]	Dravidian (read A1.4, p. 402)
	Sanskrit	Tamil/non-Sanskrit
	North	South
	Brahmin[9]	Non-Brahmin
	Brahmins	Unprivileged class's
↓	White skin (Appendix A1.5)[10]	Dark skin
	Yajña culture	Dravidian temple
	Upper caste	Lower caste
	Vegetarian	Non vegetarian
	Capitalist	Labour class
Modern Politics	Indian National Congress (in British era) /Nationalist party (today)[11]	Left-inclined party (in British era)[12]

Once any social division gets a political touch, it becomes a political movement to create a separate state through the right to be recognized under a UN resolution. Just observe evolution from top to bottom. Aryan–Dravidian theory is the basis of separatism.[13] When you have divided society, taking a double standard for two different communities, policies, and political stands becomes an ideological compulsion. This is applicable to almost all six non-inclusive players.

The Dravidian Stock: Double Standard

1. They don't have their own new ideological contribution like Plato, Aristotle, etc., so content is weak and marketing is inclusivity, justice, and non-discrimination, but they practice untouchability with Hinduism by being selectively atheist against only Hinduism.
2. They are proud about Thiruvalluvar but do not mention the Hindu aspect of Tirukkural.
3. They are proud of Dravidian culture but do not recite any Āgamas—Tamil verses of Nayanars and Alwars.
4. They control temples under the government but do not enter them.
5. Temples are under state control, but industry, corporations, and education institutions owned by politicians are private property.
6. Idols of deities were destroyed by the leader, and followers created idols of the leader.
7. They condemn discrimination within Hinduism but never within other religions or by other religions with Hinduism.
8. Before the election, they market Hindu culture as Dravidian culture to get votes, but after the election, the same Dravidian culture/ideology is atheism or a cheap attack on Hinduism.
9. I am backward because my ancestors were Hindu, but the same ancestors had no cultural connection with Hinduism.
10. Idol worship is wrong because it is not mentioned in the scriptures (as per them), but the state will appoint priests to worship idols.
11. They speak highly of Tamil but have done nothing to promote classical Tamil, even when many words are not readable because of the loss of phonetics.[14] Oral tradition is most suitable because pronunciation helps to retain the originality of words; they don't change with the years.

12. They speak highly of Sangam literature, but an atheist politician will never tell you that *Pattupattu, Ettuthokai*, and several Tamil works of literature are full of Hindu content, right from mentions from events in the Mahābhārata to Hindu deities, e.g., *Silappathikaram* and *Manimekalai*. Chera king supplies food to Pandavas; *Manimekalai* also includes Kauravas and Pandavas. *Tirumantiram*, a Tamil work by Tirumular, speaks about the Srividya cult. They speak about the twin epics *Manimekalai* and *Silappathikaram* but limit it to the story of Kannagi.[15]
13. There are no significant efforts to revive tribal languages in states where linguistic regionalism is at their peak.
14. Many atheist politicians and voters would never have read any Tamil scripture. This is how anti-Hindu regional-linguistic politics works to appease those who are competing to become culturally non-indigenous.

In conclusion, we can say that the ideological war between Tamil-speaking atheists and Tamil-speaking Hindus is falsely being framed as south vs. north, Dravidian vs. Aryan, Non-Brahmin vs. Brahmin, Tamil vs. Hindi/Sanskrit, social justice vs. social injustice, and a clash between centre and state to encourage more and more people with multiple popular identities to fuel secessionist tendencies and communal disharmony, disturbing sociopolitical tendencies (Dravidanadu), etc., where, in fact, mostly Tamil-speaking atheist have secessionist tendencies, so they disassociate themselves from mainstream Hinduism, which contributes to the degradation of Hinduism. As a result, non-Tamil-speaking north Bhartiya Hindus can practise all the cultures/traditions of Tamil Nadu without hesitation but Tamil atheists, who claim to speak for Dravidian culture, strategically maintain distance from the same culture because of ideological exclusiveness like atheism.

To keep the atmosphere charged for separatism and secessionism, they use history books and write them in the same framework. Let's take a hypothetical example: Two toilets are found in excavation at archaeological sites, one in the north and the other in the south, so they will use the following terminologies.

Table 1.4

Aryan toilet	Dravidian toilet
Same binary used for all Hinduism vs. others marketing (refer to Table 9.4, p. 190)	
Only limited to the priestly class	Everyone can go inside
Dominance of the priestly class	More inclusive
Discriminatory, inequality, communal	secular in nature
Have to perform complex rituals before and after entering toilet	No rituals
Scriptural dominance, so orthodox toilet	Heterodox and liberal toilet
Mostly found in the north	Mostly found in south
Irrational, Brahminical patriarchy	Rational, right to choose
Have to chant Sanskrit mantras before and after	No chanting, but pride in the local language

The implication of this division

1. Division among Hindus created
   a. Brahmin vs. non-Brahmin social cleavage and contributed to the fall of Hinduism[16]
   b. north–south divide
   c. division between Hindus from different states

   Both contributed in
   a. weakening freedom movement
   b. weakening national integration
   c. scope for foreign religions to go for proselytization activity
   d. Brahmins becoming a bigger enemy than the British
2. The British tried to create a reservation quota for Marathas in Bombay province, again creating a new minority after Muslims, Christians, Anglo-Indian, scheduled castes, and scheduled tribes, so that Bhārtiya society remains politically divided, which reflects on a society level, but Marathas of Maharashtra didn't fall prey to British ideas.

To implement this ideology on the ground level, there is a need for human resources and leadership, so they themselves created ground-level leaders through biased history books.

Table 1.5

Factors	Maharashtra	Tamil Nadu	North Bhārat
Hero worship of a person by marketing them as 'non-Hindu'	Chhatrapati Shivaji Maharaj (himself is the reason that saved Hinduism)	Thiruvalluvar	No such person
Anti-Hindu ground-level leader projected as a reformer		well known (A1.1, p. 401)	No such person
Ideological tone	Anti-Brahmin, anti-Sanskrit idea of Dravidistan was applicable to entire Bhārat, since 'Brahminism' was a problem for the entire subcontinent[17]		
Driven, funded, and followed by	Six non-inclusive players[18]		
Status of Hinduism	Decline		Rise
Language politics	Marathi (against Hindi)	Tamil (against Hindi)	No
Language politics driven by	Both the states' 'language politics' initiated by 'left inclined' people initially		No
Presence of destroyers	Open attack on Hindus and Hinduism by the six non-inclusive players		
Anti-guru	Yes		
Important event		Warning to burn *Manusmriti* and *Rāmāyaṇa*[19]	No such event
Political tone	Even if a region's identity is predominantly indigenous or Hindu, it's projected as something different from Hinduism to break the social fabric of Bharat and divide the nation for political gains		

In this chart, you can observe the intensity of anti-Hindu politics and theories respectively. Intensity of Aryan invasion theory: Tamil Nadu > other south Bhārat > Maharashtra > rest of north Bhārat

This was created with a political motive: Dividing Majority (Hindus/Aryans) and Minority (atheists, hedonistics, Dravidians, misinterpreted Buddhism, Cārvāka), which culminates in 'right wing vs. left wing' politics.

This is how, in history books, certain sections were carved out of Bhārtiya society as 'vote bank' for left-inclined parties. This whole drama was created by colonial masters and their Bhārtiya slaves to divide and rule. Therefore, the problem of caste discrimination and the scientific and logical study of caste remain unexplored because of the politization of caste (Dravidian and misinterpreted Buddhism). This is how the social base of communism was built through history books.

Whether Aryans came or not is not controversial; what is controversial is whether the moto of 'cultural genocide' of left-inclined politics can survive or not. Two hundred years ago, there was no north–south divide and no Aryan–Dravidian politics in the minds and tongues of people. In history and even today, I don't find single upper caste, Brahmin, and north Bhārtiya calling oneself as 'Aryan'. This shows Dravidian identity and its localized one-side polarization.

Hindi Nationalism and Fear of Tamil

Nationalism can be built on geography, relative existence, belongingness, concept and constitution, and unity, but all these things are quite intellectual, so 'language' is the best thing to mobilize the masses because it's the most common and daily-used thing. Europe started building a language-based state before the two world wars, which were very quick and easy mobilization as a nation and in a few places, race-based nationalism was also observed. In the case of Bhārat, the same model was used, which is the promotion of 'one nation one language'. But nowadays, artificial intelligence is available that can translate texts and voices in any other language, whether government to government (Centre to state) or people to people, so language is no longer a barrier. If every type of load of a human being is taken by technology, then why not multiple languages? That is why today 'one nation, one language' or any type of monoculture for expansion or unification is an old-school idea. Kerala has gone one step ahead; they are providing education in 'tribal language', which is a very good combination of 'development and culture'.

This is how, without mentioning the Vedas, Upaniṣhas, Purāṇas, siddhas, Āgamas, Dharmaśāstra, festivals, char dham, common lifestyles of Hindus, 16 Saṃskāras, Yoga meditation, books on cosmology, Vedic math, science, astronomy, Ayurveda, economics, society, polity, *Kamasutra*, they completely destroyed Hinduism in southern Bharat and are being destroyed in northern Bhārat too. This has been achieved by the use of parallel terminologies of the colonial version of history of Bhārat without the essence of Bhārat; Aryan–Dravidian toilet is the best example (refer to A1.2, p. 401).

2

Macaulay's Formula of Brand Building

It was a huge target to conquer Bhārat completely and change the choice of Bhārtiya people to create an expected consumption pattern so that they stop consuming Bhārtiya products, food, culture, and thought, and they consume Western thought (brown in colour, English in taste). It becomes a two-way beneficiary for colonial masters; first Bhārtiya producers of food, culture, thought, and material products become unemployed, and that vacuum was captured by Western products that are manufactured in the West using raw materials from third-world countries. Please read the following column carefully. The table describes the terms that are associated with the respective area's culture, both tangible as well as intangible.

Table 2.1

European/ Western/ English [1]	Eastern / Hinduism / African /South American	European/ Western/ English	Eastern/ Hinduism/ African /South American
Unorthodox	Orthodox	Global	Local
Rational	Irrational	Scientific	Unscientific / dogmatic
Modern	Backwards	Ethical	Unethical
Literate	Illiterate	Inclusive	Exclusive
Rich	Poor	Urban	Rural
New	Old	Ruling class	Labour class

European/ Western/ English [1]	Eastern / Hinduism / African /South American	European/ Western/ English	Eastern/ Hinduism/ African /South American
Neutral	Biased	Dominant	Submissive
Moderate	Extremist	Employed	Unemployed
Proud	Shame	Secular	Conservative
Open /liberal	Communal	Atheists	Religious
		Logical	Illogical
Left means economically left		Left means venom against culture	

Who Implements This Formula?

Famous personalities include sports personalities, movie stars, movies, web series, and writers through their books, novels, television, newspapers, magazines, and history books, whether ancient, mediaeval, or modern Bhārat.

How Does the Formula Function?

1. Let's take an example. If any writer or director with a Macaulay stereotype wants to represent any Bhārtiya, he will project it as irrational, uneducated, poor, rural, orthodox, old fashion, backward, and communal; so that viewer of this phenomenon gives up his Bhārtiya-ness by shame, and to look modern, he adopts Western consumption patterns, cultures, and religions so that he looks scientific, moderate, the ruling class, rich, and educated.
2. Whatever quality they want to project in a character or product, they will first see in which column the quality exists, and according to that, they will choose a product or character. For example, if they want to project 'irrational, religious, uneducated, communal, poor, rural, orthodox, old fashion, backward', then they will choose a Bhārtiya person to represent this—i.e., a man or woman in Bhārtiya traditional attire speaking the local language. So, 'secular, scientific, moderate, ruling class, rich, and educated' will carry qualities of a Western man.

3. Any quality in that column doesn't exist in isolation; one quality is attached to another quality. For example, if the character is educated, they will be compulsorily 'modern, global, open urban, rational, moderate, atheist'. This means if a Bhārtiya is educated, he has to be 'modern, global, open, urban, rational, moderate, and atheist'.

Impact of This Formula

1. This is how an inferiority complex was created in the Bhārtiya people so that they gave up their culture, consumption pattern, and language and became consumers of Western products. This has created a sense of artificial guilt and suffocation because the term 'conservative' is in the Bhārtiya column.
2. Those who are Bhārtiya automatically developed one thing in mind, which is that if we are Bhārtiya or follow Bhārtiya culture, we will be unemployed (unemployed is in the Bhārtiya column). It was ensured by formula makers that whatever is Bhārtiya, it never takes the path of modernity, science, rationality, business, or the ruling class, so one must take the path of Western culture. This ensured people moved to the West to pursue education, modernity, and science causing brain drain.
3. Even though it seems as though it was urban vs. rural, rationality vs. irrationality, orthodoxy vs. liberalism, modernity vs. backwardness, somewhere it was a hidden war between Bhartiya and the West.
4. They wrote the whole of ancient, mediaeval, and modern history on these two column formulas. In short, I would say without mentioning Sanskrit terms from texts or texts (refer to pp. 59–60), they completely destroyed Hinduism and Bhārat with parallel terminologies.
5. According to this formula, we expected the rural population to achieve a Western consumption pattern in the name of urbanization and development, which created a vacuum of 'mechanization of agricultural sector' (refer to B1, p. 419) and also created mass migration, which created urban settlement

issues like slums, congestion, traffic, and excessive loads on land and resources.
6. Whoever opposed and exposed these two columns, the Bhārtiya sons and daughters of Macaulay tagged them with qualities of the Bhārtiya column plus, in addition to that, they were also termed right wing, extremists, or conservative, narrow minded, or orthodox (victim shaming). That is why Bhārtiya people never dared to oppose this formula. By avoiding criticism, they ensured their Western products maintained a monopoly in the market.
7. Branding Western culture and products as global, neutral, moderate, inclusive, and urban ensures geographical reach and global acceptance. Rational, unorthodox, literate, rich, dominant, and new ensures their products appeal to the transformation by consuming Western culture and products. Last but not least, 'ruling class, employed, proud, ethical' ensures financial security and class, which are essential for the middle class. This is how the Western column appeals to the transformation of Western culture (refer to B2, p. 419).
8. This formula was implemented by colonial masters through media, social media, newspapers, television, and movies; now this mission is taken by 'six non-inclusive players' to destroy Bhārtiya culture and Hinduism. Because they think being a Hinduphobic is equal to being scientific, liberal, educated, rich, literate, and rational. This means that by negating Hinduism, they attain mastery in every aspect of life, right from the economy and education to science and logic.
9. Bhārtiya entrepreneurs and industrialists don't keep the name of their product in Bhārtiya languages just to avoid that if it is kept, then people may perceive it as 'irrational, uneducated, poor, rural, orthodox, old fashion, backward, low quality, illogical'.
10. This narrative created by the West is superior; it created Bhārtiya psychology that is 'western means standard', so one must seek a certificate from the West for each and everything. So, they keep giving certificates on everything like secularism, freedom of religion, policies, and bills passed by parliament

through various sponsored NGO's and international reports (refer to B3, p. 419).
11. Bhārtiya people and their lifestyle are inferior narratives that also help them to impose non-tariff barriers on Bhārtiya exports.
12. All the international institutions and their meeting halls, justice organizations, and dispute-solving mechanisms are headquartered in the West, which is an indirect message to the East that justice, leadership, and resolution are the monopolies of the West; let's not go into details about the functioning and monopolies of Western countries (psychological warfare) (refer to B4, p. 420).
13. Western products, whose values are standard and universal, are an expansionist policy with the indirect message that 'you can use them anywhere in the world'. So that easterners never dare to create their own products, brands, or value systems. When the whole world is diverse, they will have products and values according to their diversity. If this Western universalist is given free hand in biotechnology, they will end up creating a universal genetic code that is free from all diseases and diversity with all humans with the same features. In the future, people will not only move towards knowing and experiencing diversity but will also contribute to maintaining it. Universal acceptance and practice—production, sale, and consumption—are the root causes of monoculture.
14. This formula created a vacuum of indigenousness and indigenous products, such as handicrafts (refer to B5, p. 420).
15. Men and women of Bhārat used to have a lot of jewellery and 'complex' fashion, which, in the name of modernization and simplicity, given up, which reduced their basic standard of living and richness of lifestyle and investment in gold through fashion and also created unemployment in the sector that produces and sells traditional fashion and lifestyle. This rebellion against the fashion of Bhārat is again supplemented by a new narrative: 'rebellion against Brahmanism, toxic masculinity, and orthodoxy' (refer to B6, p. 420).
16. Because of the narrative of the West being a symbol of peace, moderate, ethical, and inclusive and the East being extremist, the

East has always been a battlefield, for example, in West Asia or the South China Sea. Even though there are multiple factors, the West keeps fueling internal conflicts in South Asia.

17. When literacy, richness, and urbanization got attached to the term Western, all terms started being used interchangeably. Because of that achievement, the status of Western-urban life in the spheres of material life became a trend. This stopped innovation in Bhārtiya brains because success means achieving a Western lifestyle. Even the capitalists of Bhārat are victims of the Macaulay formula, as they don't make user-friendly products for rural and tribal areas, and these areas remain backward. They don't consider these people to be consumers as they are poor. Industrialists make products for urban people and wait for poor and rural people to become rich to become capable of consuming their products. Industrialists' must have products for everyone according to need, financial capacity, geography, etc. (refer to B7, p. 420).

18. As Western means class or benchmark, we are busy making exports for Western countries like the USA and trying to achieve that benchmark, which is nota wrong thing in itself. Are we considering Africa as our consumer? China is an exporter to every nation in the world because they are not suffering through this dogma and are now challenging the whole Western world.

Message to Hindus

1. Just replace the titles of the columns in Table 2.1, and the whole world market is yours. The branding of culture and products matters a lot; They sold whole Western products and culture under the umbrella of liberalism and secularism. Now, it's our time. Sell your products and culture by tagging them with global, rational, and secular. Secondly, westerners need to be criticized for their 'ethnocentric/closed-minded policy' that if something is secular or doesn't belong to any religion, then only they will purchase the product, e.g., yoga; otherwise, it shall be prohibited or boycotted as per monotheistic religious order.

2. Remove dogma from your mind and come out of guilt, shame, and suffocation. This Macaulay formula creates guilt and suffocation through 'wordplay' so that you don't rise as a global leader

World beyond East vs. West

Still, I would say one must come out of this East–West division because there is the Middle East too. There are various sections in the world: South America, North America, east, west and middle Europe, the Middle East and Bhārat–China, south-east Asia, Australia and Polynesia, and Africa, as divided according to resources and profits. If you observe the world map with every superpower, there are countries that are internally disturbed, either by terror or trafficking of drugs and humans, etc. This is to avoid competition in development from a neighbour, but if there is a factor of rivalry, then there is a serious issue. The existence of negative factors (country B) at the doorstep can be used by the country (country A) itself or its enemies (country C) through funding to keep them fighting with each other. If you see the case of Bhārat and China, both countries have a golden triangle and crescent, but at the same time, they have border issues too. If issues of terrorism, drug trafficking, and border disputes become an issue for every country in South Asia, then there will be a step to find a collective solution on one platform, and with that vision, Shanghai Cooperation Organization (SCO) appears, which may become the European Union of the future. As a geographic organization, the world will have the European Union, African Union, Arab League, SCO, and ASEAN. The issue with Africa is that it's divided in ethnicity and there is competition between Islam and Christianity. There is no single superpower in Africa that will at least create ground for competition for growth to tackle geopolitics. That is why Africa is still backward because internal rivalry is the main factor in increasing foreign interference. This helps big players loot the resources of Africa without creating or contributing to geopolitics, which makes Africa peaceful but vulnerable to the second wave of colonization.

Table 2.2

Super powers	Neighbouring internally disturbed countries	Rivalry
USA	Mexico and South America (hub of narcotic substance, crime, black money, round-tripping)	Border migration
Bhārat	Golden crescent and golden triangle of narcotic substances on both sides, Pakistan as terror hub	Border dispute, terrorism, black money, counterfeit currency, geopolitics
Saudi Arabia	Iraq–Syria terror of ISIS, Yemen	Nuclear weapons of Iran
Russia	A strong influence in countries which were part of USSR but with big brother attitude so no issues regarding border and neighbour disturbance, still it faces many temporary challenges from the West	
China	Golden crescent and golden triangle of narcotic substances on both sides, terrorism	Internal issues of Xinjiang
Europe	Settlers colonialism, refugee influx and riots	

That is why one must understand that the binary division of East vs. West by angle of business, market, and geopolitics is not a complete reality. One must go with the ground reality of resources, markets, production, etc.

The binary division right-wing vs. left-wing looks like the extreme opposite, but it's not. There are many leaders and countries that project themselves as right-wing but are left-wing, and there are many leaders and countries that project themselves as left-wing but are right-wing. These double standards are not just because of one or two people but also because of the nature and behaviour of the state, economy, and stakeholders (refer to Table 2.3, p. 24).

Even in the 21st century, why a theocratic state exists when democratic values like freedom, choice, and liberty are famous all

Table 2.3

Project themselves as right wing but are left wing	Project them as left wing but are right wing

1. Theocratic states, which control consumption patterns, society, and the economy according to books are implemented by the state; indirectly, everything is owned by the state.
2. Right-wing governments that do direct benefit transfers to poor sections or unemployed youth as policy rather than creating skillful mass employment schemes
	3. Left-wing leaders who function like dictators and make the state (government) private property and explore resources according to whims and fancy for personal benefit through 'illegal-informal' agents or shell companies
	4. A state that projects itself as a 'welfare state' but
	   a. corruption is very high in bureaucracy and politicians
	   b. direct taxpayers are very low (4–5%)

over the world? That is because these terms ensure political rights, not socio-economic rights. In a very crude way, for poor people, freedom is 'freedom of speech' and for rich people, freedom is 'purchasing power'. That is why theocratic states, which are mostly rich in resources, are still theocratic because citizens manifest their freedom in the form of 'consumerism', with some negative points about human rights and women's rights that exist in other countries too. Whether it's a theocratic state or a left-wing state, the dictator in a democracy does the same thing: centralization and state control.

Factor That Give Rise to Dictatorship

Bad economy, corruption, country out of control, bad governance, etc., are factors behind the rise to dictatorship. So somewhere in psychology, dilution of economy, rules, and loose control becomes a symbol of over decentralization, and demand or implementation appears like a dictatorship even though it's not.

Macaulay's Formula of Brand Building

The game of building the image of products and nations is the big challenge. I would like to introduce a concept from Hinduism.
1. What you are actually
2. What do the people around you think about you?
3. What do your enemies think about you?
4. What you project yourself in the market
(I would add the fifth one from my side for modern-day.)
5. Chewing gum or 'lower truth' of common people and the 'truth' of aristocracy

All five things are necessary to be applied to the product, resources, enemy's moves, and your moves in the market.

Why the World Has a Right-Wing World Order?

Capturing land and collecting resources is the main goal when it comes to the survival of the fittest. Over the period, modes changed, but the concept was always the same.
1. Early humans: evolution of hunter-gatherers and related species started small fights for food
2. Agriculture: agricultural settlements started fight for land
3. Empires: when agriculture got transformed into a huge society and organized way of life as civilization, then it shaped itself as an empire to expand.
4. Religion (mediaeval era colonization): to keep the empire stable, there was a need for a belief system that would connect all stakeholders and also be used to make new citizens from the captured area by conversion so that masses in the name of religion would remain united.
5. Modern colonization: created mass production and consumer chain to sell them the foreign market was needed. Religion was only about capturing resources and maintaining stability by converting/proselytizing the population. But modern colonization was about capturing resources, conversion through religion, selling manufactured products, having a colony as a market, creating a choice-shaping mechanism (Macaulay formula), memberships in clubs, companies, etc., shareholders, brand building, and marketing.

6. Artificial intelligence: AI captures past consumption patterns and shapes future consumption patterns.

Table 2.4

Issues	Reaction
Foreign empire and foreign religion	Protection of local empire and religion
Foreign big bulls who capture the market through colonization, AI	Protection of local market and local producers
Migration of masses	Protection of local masses and society
Climate change, terror, and other issue	Create feeling of fear which demands protection
Aggressive marketing by foreigners in spheres of products, religion, etc.	Local supply chains and producers need protection
Unequal distribution of industrialization	Demand for local production

Till the fifth wave of colonization or modern colonization, all strategies were made and applied at the social and physical level, either through religion, empire, etc.—what to eat, how to pray, what to consume, etc. Secondly, questioning colonization was suppressed by blasphemy laws, deterrence, terror, orthodoxy, customs, etc., but when the sixth wave of colonization, that is, AI came, the platform changed from sociophysical to individualistic digitization, where everyone has access to an ocean of information. Many people wrongly say this is the era of information; actually, this is the era of access to information because the information was always there, but you were denied access under sociocultural or orthodox parameters.

Today, a combination of indigenization (decolonization) + AI + production-led economy + export, can transform any third-world country into a superpower. All the old ways of colonization, mercantilism, religious expansion, communism, capitalism, and cold war are falling today. So all the old colonial masters are calling this combination the right wing, i.e., pot calling kettle black. This combination is just a level playing field.

Right-wing is always in support of freedom because it expresses power culminating in choice, and choice shapes consumerism, which is beneficial for capitalists. That is why, at the first stage, you will find three things: creativity, freedom of speech, and abusing old order; all three create demand for a new product. Religion, standardization, colonization, empire, mercantilism—all these philosophies were successful when physical boundaries had importance, but now, because of the digital platform, reach to the consumer has increased and it's much cheaper than previous technologies, so all philosophies that existed beyond 'country of origin' because of funding or other efforts are collapsing, whether it's religion, colonization, empire, mercantilism, etc. The world will now be reduced to production, supply, and consumption on a digital platform with a sense of responsibility.

Table 2.5

Three levels of truth	Capitalist logic
Prāthibhāsika satya (apparent truth)	Standardization of lifestyle
Vyāvahārika satya (truth to carry out business and alliance)	Ensuring consumer base beyond the geographic boundary
Pāramārthika satya (truth with supreme meaning)	Profit

Art of Controlling Third-World Countries or East

Still, the East is the slave of the West, that is because the Western world has set up 'judging power' in their hands. Through judging power, they interfere in internal matters in the eastern world and play with geopolitics and policies.

Table 2.6

Era	Judging power
200 years ago	West is superior because industrialization ensured that for consumer base the Western lifestyle is the standard one

100 years ago	Pulling Eastern slaves into the Western country to do labour or as militia to maintain strategic existence among Western world
50 years ago	1. Establishment of international institutions in Western countries (location also affects psychologically) and judging whole world on their standards through reports 2. Cult and attraction, brand building of Western educational institution
30 years ago	1. Various reports on social, cultural, economic spheres (biased) 2. Paid media to setup propaganda against the East

We, the people of the Eastern world, never thought to establish and create cults and brand building to set up and judge the world.
1. Creating big media houses that will judge the whole world
2. Reports and other mediums to judge the world
3. Establishing and brand building of big universities and institutions
4. Avoiding brain drain from east to west like the creation of Silicon Valley and other big tech areas in Asia itself

Time to take charge of the new world order!

Rather than using their platform of English and inviting them to the East, most of the Eastern countries first concentrated on localization of language. At least now, when artificial intelligence is there as a translator, we must focus on creating global reach and equality. The processes of globalization and deglobalization are merely political concepts. But digitally, we can expand anyway to the last mile of the world. If someone wants to buy anything, he will buy it online, only local policies will define tariffs. The problem is that the East is busy with theocratic orthodoxies, like Pakistan, dictatorships like China, low-moral countries, and mutual conflicts. I'm not saying they should be judged on Western parameters; now it's time to judge on Eastern parameters too.

3

Religion, Laïcité, Secularism, and Conflicts

Introduction

Europe was a rich civilization; the Romans were inspired by Greek civilization and the Greeks by Egyptian civilization. There are similarities between Hinduism and Egyptian culture in terms of philosophy, content, deities, and architecture. In all these civilizations, there were subjects that were at their best, for instance, civil engineering, medical science, technology, social science, humanities, literature, metaphysics, philosophies, economy, political setup, etc.; all these flourished because of diverse and flourished geography. On the other hand, compared to the geography of the Middle Eastern regions, which is non-diverse, or uniform, and un-flourished land because of the desert, despite that, in the early ages, civilizations such as Sumerian, Mesopotamian, and Naqada 1, 2, 3 (early Egypt) flourished over there.

Once the concept of one book for the whole of civilization or world was introduced as the word of God, it denied people access to knowledge; thus began the era of ignorance. This is the origin of all issues like science vs. religion and religion vs. political setup. Not only scientific development but also development in other subjects like civil engineering, medical science, technology, social science, humanities, literature, metaphysics, philosophies, and political concepts stopped. This can be seen when Europe believed the sun rotated around the earth, and a lot of such extraordinary claims by the priestly class were imposed by deterrence on the civilizations in the name of religion or God. This thing existed until the Renaissance happened. Once the Copernican revolution took place, and after that the French revolution, all the religious burden was brought down from the political setup and slowly from all aspects of society to develop consciousness and rationality. The French constitution introduced the word 'laïcité', which separated the religious head from the political setup and was limited to the church. Because Europe had a history of invasions and conversions where religion was merely the philosophy of empire to carry out demographic transformation in favour of a related empire, i.e., religion. Even one of the wars has been provoked by the popes with fiery speeches, so that land remains under their control.

The word 'religion' itself was drawn from Latin, to bind, and by the Romans it was used for general emotions like hesitation, caution, anxiety, and fear; feelings of being bound, restricted, or inhibited; and some Roman authors related the term 'superstitio', which meant too much fear, anxiety, or shame, to 'religio' at times. The classical explanation of the word, traced to Cicero himself, derives it from 're-v' (again) + 'lego' in the sense of 'choose', 'go over again', or 'consider carefully'. Modern scholars such as Tom Harpur and Joseph Campbell favour the derivation from ligo 'bind, connect', probably from a prefixed re-ligare, i.e., 're-' (again) + 'ligare' or 'to reconnect', which was made prominent by St Augustine, following the interpretation of Lactantius. This interpretation of 'to bind' became 'to bind or to unite people' over the period.[1]

When it came to the English language in 1200 AD, it got limited to 'God and his teachings'. That is why today religion is the diplomatic name of the 'European model of religion' because it is written in English. Just like we accepted English as the new normal, we also accepted the concept of their religion as a 'universal concept'.

Religion and Uniting World

Even before the birth of the 'exclusive religions' war and violence used to happen. Ghenghis Khan, after conquering, killed many people in a massacre, including civilians, but his empire's growth was in 'Ո' shape. He only appointed governors in provinces, and civilians never supported him because of his terror.

If invaded provinces are to be included in the main empire forever, then the most important thing is 'uniformity' in administration, economy, and society. To do this, imposing empires administration, economic, social, and culture on invaded provinces and destroying their existing structures of administration, economic, social and tangible and intangible culture is necessary so that all four never become a point of difference for secessionist movement by local people. So, all four things were packed in the 'religious book', and it was introduced as 'God's revelation'. 'Religion' was introduced so that people would accept invasion as a revolution. Even if all people don't convert, then those non-converted people who accept invasion under 'acceptance-multiculturalism or with discriminatory treatment by the state, e.g., religious tax or protection money (legal extortion)' is also conquering indigenous people. This 'proselytization' of culture, administration, and society is not only applicable in mediaeval or ancient kingdoms but also in democratic setups because 'number' decides everything, i.e., the unification or disintegration of a kingdom or country. In short, religion and colonization are a proxy of an empire.

Diplomatic terms Used by 'Expansionary and Exclusive Religions' (hypothetical example)

To unite people: To unite people means telling people you are divided because of diversity. Let us unite, indirectly promoting uniformity under a new identity, and I am your leader. Through identity, they create a new race-religion, i.e., empire. If you join us, then unity (administrative uniformity); otherwise, diversity is discrimination.

To promote equality: This concept of religion promoting equality is so superficial that a theocratic state can't ensure that everyone has equal wealth within the country or kingdom. Most people call non-discrimination and giving respect to others as equality. But what about income inequality? These people believe in equality until there is no cost to practicing it. What they call equality is either ethnocentrism or an attempt to create parallel and uniform society, economy, and polity.

Destroying tangible culture (idols, temples, etc.) and intangible culture of colonies (rituals, traditions, etc.): To close all the doors through which people can revive their ancient culture, which may become a political challenge for expanding empires or religions.

Even massacre is one of the elimination techniques to avoid political challenges, for example, anti-competitive practices.

To create a uniform work culture in all colonies to ensure unity: Changing their names, changing names of places, changing administrative language, and changing belief systems and customs.

Marketing strategy and foreign policy: In the modern world, value systems that have universal acceptance are 'truth, justice, equality, brotherhood, freedom, democracy, secularism, united against hate, peace, love, symbol of unity'. If anyone wants to expand religion or empire (unfit for the 21st century), they pack religion into the packet of these values so that it is a globally accepted proselytization activity without resistance. For example, X is the religion of peace, etc. That is why being non-violent doesn't mean he is for your welfare; he is there to introduce or impose his ideas or religion on you.

Proselytization techniques: Using marriage, social work, terror and power, health and education services, and mala fide debates to make non-followers as citizens of a utopian state.

Goals: Capturing geography and resources by hacking human capital, using converted citizens of the nation as a pressure group in policy-making, using them for destabilizing states, secessionist movements, and recruitment as physical training to create unrest. Resources that were completely belonging to the sovereign nation, after proselytization, they have to share with 'colonial masters'.

Motivation to expand empire: Certain religious theories promote xenophobia, ethnocentrism, anti-culturalism, anti-semitism, and chauvinism at a philosophical level, which is indirectly reflected in ethical and social behaviour which helps to motivate them to expand empire in the name of civilizing inferior or ignorant people. When it takes a physical form of violence, then it's just a manifestation of their intolerant philosophical theories, which you call terrorism or social conflict.

Table 3.1

Three levels of truth	Religion's logic
Prāthibhāsika satya (apparent truth)	Freedom of religion

Vyāvahārika satya (truth to carry out business and alliance)	My religion stands for peace, love, nationalism, and unity; respecting others' faith to avoid unnecessary friction helps in conducive seamless religious expansion
Pāramārthika satya (truth with supreme meaning)	I will expand my empire/utopian state in the name of religion

Table 3.2 Hypothetical framework of colonization

Proxy Identities	Actual Identities
Religion	Parallel empire, colonization, utopian state. Religion is like empires' shadow on heaven but projected vice versa.
Language of religion	State language of empire
Religious head/priest	King, representative of king/empire
Culture and festivals of religion	Strengthening cult of empire through celebration
Religious order, commandments	Order of king
The earth belongs to my God	The earth belongs to the king
Religious war to save religion	War to save the empire
Religious do's & don'ts	King's rule made for empire
Civil and criminal laws of religion	1. Law of the king/empire/kingdom 2. Civil and criminal laws of empire to keep colonies and religious diaspora under control 3. Controlling personal-social behaviour of diaspora of empire which is created through 'proselytization', which may further culminate into geopolitical gains

Proxy Identities	Actual Identities
	4. Making civil and criminal laws of empire active in others territory (colonies) through channel of religion
5. Exporting 'social evils' to new colonies (read A12.1, p. 414)
6. If there is 'day of judgement' after death where judge is God then why did he provided 'punishments' for violating laws in *Book of Religious Manifesto*?
Is it double jeopardy?
The religious brotherhood	1. Confidence building measure among group of citizens of the same empire
2. Identifying infidel who is subjected for proselytization discriminatory treatment or execution
3. Helps in staying away from other identities and related cultures, e.g., language, geography, region, nationality
This gives birth to xenophobia, ethnocentrism, anti-cultural, and chauvinism which is cause of social unrest globally
Organization of religious intergovernmental cooperation	1. The mechanism created by the capital of a kingdom to control completely colonized countries
2. Interfering in the internal issues of non-colonized countries in the name of 'religious interest of minorities'
This is how they control politically colonized and non-colonized countries through foreign policy, where 'kingdom' means a Central government and 'conquered territories' mean federal governments that are invited as members for religious unity in international groupings (i.e., religious version of British commonwealth organization)

Proxy Identities	Actual Identities
Holy book	The constitution of the empire or next emperor in book format
The holy place of religion	Headquarter or capital of the empire
Local religious places and shrine	1. Local decentralized offices to handle situation, proselytization or unification of followers 2. Franchise-based model
My God is one and formless and only my God exists	1. All other gods with body/form must be stereotyped, stigmatized, destroyed (anti-competitive practices/intolerance) 2. Created civil and criminal laws and marketed them as revelations from God; to avoid 'proof of existence of God' they made God 'formless' 3. A simple way of constructing a local branch/ franchisee of empire to maintain architectural uniformity without blending it with local cultural ethos
	4. Alter ego of founder = formless God, i.e., the shadow of the founder in heaven 5. Indirect call for the destruction of tangible and intangible cultures of other faiths 6. Only culture related to my God (revelation) has the right to exist
Followers vs. non-followers/infidels	Citizens vs. non-citizens
Don't kill any innocent	The culprit will be decided by them as per 'religious/empire's manifesto'
Remembrance of previous holy leaders	Remembering the tradition of emperors

Proxy Identities	Actual Identities
Proselytization	1. Granting citizenship 2. Route to enter in other nations internal issues and geopolitics by playing the minority victim card and religious interest 3. These countries never give citizenship to persecuted refugees or terror victims of other religions; they force them indirectly to settle in secular and non-colonized countries so that the creation of ghettos and colonies continue just as China has created dual-use villages for retired military personnel on its borders 4. If citizenship of the capital is granted, the spirit of colonialism will die because such move will force them to share the captial's resources with people from the Third World
My God is superior and rational than your God	I am superior and rational than you
Funding for proselytization	The initial investment to capture land and resources
My religion has a universal value system	The value system of my empire should be the value system of all countries (expansion through ideology)
Collectively bowing towards the capital at the same time	Daily routine in the form of 'roll call, inspection, commanding troops, allegiance to the crown, in defense of the realm of empire, oath of loyalty to the empire' by sounding loud bugle for a parade to impose colonial legacy (dress code, thinking, expansionism) on newly recruited/proselytized citizens from colonies. (Similar methodology was used by British Indian Army in Bharat)

Proxy Identities	Actual Identities
Religious tag to products	The parallel economy of the colonies is aligned with the brand name of the religion
Protection of religion	Protection of parallel empire and economy
Ghettos created by a group of religion	Land is occupied as a colony of the utopian empire, i.e., settlers colonialism
No-go zones (ghettos) created in the name of religion	Territories with unauthorized semi-autonomous status is created to implement parallel empire with own civil and criminal codes
Religious tax and donations as per religious manifesto	1. Investment returns after the consolidation of empire on foreign land because energy resources aren't permanent, i.e., sending tax to the central government, i.e., capital of religion (this will happen in future) 2. Utilizing money of new citizens (Third World) or investors for further expansion of empire (decentralize approach), i.e., indirect loot
My religion is borderless	My empire will break all boundaries
Boycotting or prohibiting 'practices of other faiths' by keeping them in negative list by declaring them irrational or wrong on 'God's command' (similar to the British discouraging Indian culture through legislations and policies)	1. Diplomatic way of avoiding mixing with others so that people don't develop belongingness outside community, and strategic separation is maintained which is necessary for 'us vs. them' 2. Social level separatism culminates in political level separation, indirectly capturing political setup to impose ideology of religion 3. Social level separatism also helps in building geographical separatism and challenging the sovereignty

Proxy Identities	Actual Identities
	4. Don't practice that which is going to be eliminated after some time, i.e., other religious practices, e.g., idol worship, etc. Marginalization is prior step to destruction
Protection money /tax on non-followers/ infidels	1. Economic exploitation until they convert 2. Extra tax on religious and business activities of infidels, e.g., discriminatory tariff practices to exploit colonies (similarly, the British also exempted tax of those who joined them, e.g., loyal princess, jamindars, landlords, troops, which contributed in the world wars')
Falsehood must be destroyed otherwise it will perish	List of falsehood = blacklist = negative list, which includes tangible and intangible cultures of other faiths, LGBTQ, cultural practices of infidels as per religious manifesto
Heaven	1. The absorbing concept of formless God is very difficult for people who live on earth and have material life, so another place better than earth is created so that people can easily relate with formless God 2. All entertainment mediums are banned according to 'religion' so that people don't divert from expansion of empire or utopian state implementation. To make that suffocating life without entertainment colourful, after-death heavenly fruit are created 3. Operant conditioning

Proxy Identities	Actual Identities
The rich will never go to heaven	Keeps colonized people poor and drains their wealth
Righteousness, honesty, sharing wealth are criteria to go to heaven	But righteousness and honesty are limited to religious worship and sharing wealth within religious ethnicity
Your culture is wrong	I want geography by converting you or offering you citizenship of my empire, but your culture is a hurdle, so it is wrong or irrational
Eliminate those who don't follow the right path	Right path = religious commandments
Everyone is born as a follower of my religion	Proselytization = going back to roots
If you accept my religion, all sins are forgiven by God	Encouraging criminals to do the sin and then join refuge of God and all sins washed by asking forgiveness
Religious school	Isolating kids from the mainstream and scientific study so that they don't get diverted from fairy tales of the utopian state as a goal
The biggest crime is keeping someone on an equal throne as my God because 'my God is greatest'	Anti-competitive practices to marginalize other faiths
Justifying every verse in 'religion' even if it's irrational	To avoid two things 1. As its God's revelation, if a single verse is wrong then other things can also be wrong so let's justify everything 2. To avoid truth 'either God is wrong' or to whom it was revealed was wrong 3. religion without criticism = seamless expansion

Proxy Identities	Actual Identities
Visiting holy places (even though God is formless)	1. To prove loyalty to Central government by visiting the capital 2. Medium of generating revenue for capital through religious tourism because there are no permanent resources. For example, communist countries promote 'red tourism' (places related to events of communist revolution, which is similar to court visits to pay respect to the British crown)
Extremist, fundamentalist, theocratic, exclusivist	The one who honestly follows 'religion'
Liberal, moderate, non-theocratic	One who follow 'religion' in a modified way as per time and era rather than direct criticism to avoid conflict
Creating a category of enemies as an infidel	1. The elimination process of non-followers becomes easy without discussing issues in detail which saves a lot of time. Just tag someone with that word (infidel) and eliminate. 2. Secondary citizen status to do discrimination (non-followers, ignorant, LGBTQ, atheist, irrational, uncivilized, sinners, idol worshipers, dishonest followers, non-followers of my God/faith, follower of the same religion but different sects)
Revelation by God	Content is not copied from anywhere else
Founder as the last messenger of God	1. Time to delete the existing or past system and accept a new, non-amendable religious-manifesto without the possibility of accepting new theories or books

Proxy Identities	Actual Identities
	2. Upgrade your system to avoid rebellion and resistance against existing power structures
	3. He is the first messenger, and his followers have a duty to promote his messages all over the world by becoming the second messenger; this expansionary policy helps them come out of the suffocative prison of religion but also avoids the introspection of exclusive religions
	4. God won't appear again as he has given the best and latest version, so don't ask 'why God doesn't appear in front of me?' ('divine kingship theory' of Georges Dumezil)

The technique used to divert people: The technique is used to confuse and divert people so that they don't understand the aforementioned terms (Table 3.2) and are unable to trace back the above practices to any scripture (hypothetical situation).

1. Its majority–minority politics and minority are always victims (generalizing issue)
2. Politicians spread hate and get votes by keeping the upcoming election in mind
3. Not all people are bad; there are bad/extremist people in every community
4. Religion has nothing to do with violence
5. All religions teach humanity, i.e., my book doesn't promote violence
6. Religion is misinterpreted by some people
7. Religion doesn't teach to hate; religion unites
8. Preacher of religion is preaching the wrong things
9. If someone exposes or gives a counterview, then he is spreading hate and disturbing communal harmony
10. Clean chit in history books for every crime

11. British and politicians used the 'divide and rule' strategy; otherwise, people are united
12. One who exposes is spreading negativity, hate, disturbing social harmony and fabric, secular, and multiculturalism in danger, or attaching a person to 'political party'/'organization' so that 'philosophical-historical-religious' debate can be diverted to political gains, i.e., win or lose elections and related economic interest
13. Attaching a prefix or suffix to the person who exposes them, e.g., divider-in-chief, master divider, hero of hatred, xenophobia, ethnocentrism, anti-culture, chauvinism, anti-freedom, ultra-nationalist, riding the hate wave (victim shaming)
14. It is interpreted out of context

Expansion is the main policy to procure resources because the original geography has no resources. To expand one thing is compulsory 'to identify enemy with name and unequal status', i.e., infidel, who remains with the clear motivation to expand the empire. If they give equal status to every human being, irrespective of faith, then there will be no motivation for expansion, which will hit them economically because they don't have resources. Here, discrimination is institutionalized to give unequal status to a non-citizen of the empire in the name of religious faith (infidel), which will exist until religion is followed, which is not amendable as it is marketed as a word of God.

In short, colonization which is packed in the cover of culture written in the form of practice and sold (funding) in the name of religion, which is kept alive through theologically racial invasions all over the world in the name of followers vs. infidels. This pattern is not only followed by religions nowadays but also by communism, capitalism (the crown took over India by sidelining its proxy the East India Company in 1858) and political ideologies, value systems, and even by democracy against dictatorship, ideologies, cults, NGO, organizational chain, business, atheists, franchisee models, etc. Prominent examples are the Warsaw pact, North Atlantic Treaty Organization (NATO), Molotov Plan, and Belt and Road Initiative (BRI). As a face value, all of them market their respective plans as 'developmental assistance and cooperation', but everyone knows the geopolitical aspect behind them. Similarly, exclusive or expansionist religions gain territory through 'proselytization' and officially pull colonization under the 'intergovernmental organization with religious theme (IOR)', i.e., just like the commonwealth organization of Britain.

That is why secularism is a disinfectant for this parallel empire/exclusivist religion in the modern world, which liberates humanity from all social evils. Sovereignty, republic, democracy, justice (own law and order), fraternity, and liberty (to think beyond religion) ensure that the other aspects of a parallel empire also dissolve. At the same time, we all say 'religion should not be mixed with politics', but when it should be, we will understand that religion (colonization) itself is a political setup to remain in competition with country itself. Let's say some state is a secular state and the institutions of government are separate from religious influence, but what if people's minds are radicalized by theocratic policy? What is the use of such a secular state? From the table, it's clear that exclusivist religion itself is a racist concept because it doesn't offer equality and freedom; it offers citizenship in the name of conversion and interferes with internal matters through demographic identities plus the import of social evils (read A12.1, p. 414). That is why religious racism vs. freedom of religion is a nonsensical debate.

Plato, Aristotle, and millions of other writers wrote books on God, politics, justice, republic, truth, and the ideal state, but nothing created issues in the world because they never had an expansionary policy with a utopian state model in the name of religion. Spinoza once said to read the Bible as a text, which is the best way to remain rational and treat any religious text just like other texts, which will bring down all extreme emotional and irrational drama.

I don't understand there are thousands of things we can know in the world and gather knowledge or do research about, but few people on the planet are just busy imposing 'religious book/religious manifesto' on their own and others' minds. The values of the French Revolution ensure that every human being flourishes like a flower; these values ensure equality, fraternity, justice, and freedom, not religion. If anyone believes in equality, then he should not have expansionary policies or conversion techniques. But even criticism of France is that they created colonies and their values were practiced within the country, even though they inspired multiple nations after Independence. That is why atheism is not merely denying God; it's about denying colonization, which was created in the name of religion.

Atheism is also a voice against intellectual suffocation; also it is denying social evils and irrational beliefs, which are protected under the nine-point agenda (refer to pp. 247–248). People are bored of fulfilling someone else's dreams in the name of expanding religion; people want to consume, contribute, and enhance life while helping other people to enhance life.

Expansion is a natural phenomenon, but those who don't choose to expand intellectually try to expand physically. Politicians or empires use religion to expand, but vice versa is also true, i.e., religion uses politics and empire to expand itself. At the same time, atheism also has limitations and has played an important role in carrying out cultural genocide of religions and civilizations.[2]

Either because of a shallow understanding or not knowing the value of culture, atheism does behave like a terror organization in theocratic countries. That is why Hindu civilization was kept in the mould of 'exclusivist/non-reformist/expansionary religion' by Hinduphobic historians so that it could be eliminated by 'atheism'.

Laïcité and Secularism

Chronology of secularism

You must be wondering why, even after mentioning the French Revolution, have I not even once uttered the word secularism. That is because the French Revolution happened on 5 May 1789, and the word 'secularism' was first coined by British writer George Holyoake in 1851.[3] This is what governments around the world and history books hide from you. George Jacob Holyoake was born in Birmingham. At eighteen, he began attending lectures at the Birmingham Mechanics' Institute, where he discovered the socialist writings of Robert Owen. He eventually became an assistant lecturer and decided to become a full-time teacher but was rejected for promotion because of his socialist views (which created anger about the religious right wing).

Holyoake joined Charles Southwell in dissenting from the official policy of Owen's that lecturers should take a religious oath to enable them to take collections on Sundays. Southwell had founded an atheist organization, Oracle of Reason, and was soon imprisoned on those grounds. Holyoake took over as editor, having moved to an atheist position (in Abrahamic faith, denying God is denying religion because a religious book is the word of God, it's not the case in Hinduism) as a result of his experiences. In 1842, Holyoake became one of the last persons convicted for blasphemy in a public lecture held in April 1842 at the Cheltenham Mechanics' Institute, though this had no theological character, and the incriminating words were merely a reply to a question addressed to him from the body of the meeting (this is the second incidence that initiated anger again about religion).[4]

In the religious spheres of the West, people were killed for merely questioning revelations of God. In 1842, Holyoake and socialist Emma Martin formed the Anti-Persecution Union to support free thinkers from the danger of arrest. Holyoake nevertheless underwent six months' imprisonment, and the editorship of the Oracle changed hands. After the Oracle closed at the end of 1843, Holyoake founded a more moderate paper, *The Movement*, which survived until 1845. He also established the *Reasoner*, where he developed the concept of secularism, and founded the *Secular Review* in August 1876. After an 1877 split with Charles Bradlaugh and Annie Besant, leaders of the National Secular Society (NSS), Holyoake, Charles Watts, and Harriet Law founded the British Secular Union, which remained active until 1884. On 6 March 1881, Holyoake was one of the speakers at the opening of the Leicester Secular Society's new Secular Hall in Humberstone Gate, Leicester. The other speakers were Harriet Law, Annie Besant, and Charles Bradlaugh. Holyoake chaired the Rationalist Press Association in 1899–1906. He retained his disbelief in God, but after the Oracle soon came to regard 'atheism' as a negative word, he preferred 'secularism', i.e., atheism = secularism.[5]

This scenario itself explains two things: first, Annie Besant was the outcome of the atheist movement, and she projected herself in Bhārat as an outcome of theosophical society to revive Hinduism. Annie Besant left Holyoake in 1877, then joined (or may have been recruited by the British) in theosophical society in 1899, which was founded in the USA in 1875. In 1893, she came to Bhārat to revive Hinduism. Let's clap for her journey from the atheist Christian movement to the Hinduism revival movement, that too without converting even after being inspired by Hinduism.

Introduction to Hinduism

In Hinduism, there are six subjects that are necessary and compulsory to learn the Vedas as a primary condition, which are known as *Vedāṅga* (parts of the Vedas), in which there are again four Upavedas.

Table 3.3

Vedāṅga (parts of Vedas)[6]	4 Upavedas
1. Śikṣā/phonetics or pronunciation	1. Ayurveda (health, medicine)
2. Kalpa or ritual	2. Dhanur-veda (archery)
3. Vyakarana or grammar	3. Sthapatya veda (construction and architecture)
4. Nirukta or etymology	4. Gāndharva veda (music, art, dance)
5. Chandas or poetic metre	
6. Jyotiṣa or astronomy	

When you learn these six subjects and four Upavedas, then interpretation of the Vedas and Purāṇas is at different level. For example, for the common man, it will be a merely mythological story with a message, but for one who has learned *Vedāṅga* and Upavedas the same thing will be astrology, human anatomy, climate, environment, dance, art, music, grammer, and enlightenment, etc.

Then there are six ways of cognition of the supreme reality, which include:
1. Nyāya (logic and verification)
2. Sāṅkhya (classification of reality necessary for liberation)

3. Yoga (process of liberation),
4. Vaiśeṣika (classification/particularity) of reality
5. Pūrva Mīmāṃsā (rituals)
6. Uttara Mīmāṃsā (metaphysical discussion oriented towards liberation)

All these schools criticize each other on the interpretation of the Vedas, the method of liberation and reality and its classification, but the philosophy of all is the same, i.e., 'seeking liberation'. Those who say these are six schools of philosophy haven't read either of them.[7] All are necessary vidya, which sharpens your brain to understand 'liberation/enlightenment' through multiple aspects, acts as a safety valve against each other.

Colonial-era intellectuals declared these six ways of cognition as six schools of philosophy, in addition to Yoga, Vedanta, Shaivism, Vaishnavism, Buddhism, and Jainism. Everything was termed philosophy by them. As I said, all these schools used to criticize each other, so theosophical society used that criticism to fit it into the Western framework of philosophical debate. So, they supported the school with no rituals as best against the school with rituals. Westerns called rituals as complex rituals and no rituals as a simple way, then they transformed modern Hindus into ritual-less Hindus in the name of simplifying religion.

This popularizing concept of no ritual from Uttara Mīmāṃsā (also known as Vedanta) from so-called philosophy, which gave rise to Vedanta in modern Bhārat. So Hindus first got stuck in six philosophy schools as the highest knowledge, even though it was just a way to interpret the Vedas or the same Vedic truth of enlightenment. Then they got limited to Vedanta or the Uttara Mīmāṃsā school.

As philosophy was the highest knowledge in the West, so the six ways of interpretation sidelined the real highest knowledge of Hinduism, which is learning the Vedas from Hindu minds, which became a great opportunity for Western thinkers to misinterpret the Vedas to create civil war in the name of Aryan–Dravidian theory to divide Hindus and make them vulnerable for conversion. This anti-Hindu propaganda of declaring six schools of cognition to learn the Vedas, Vedanta, Buddhism, Jainism, and Cārvāka as philosophy is also accepted as Bhārtiya philosophy. Today's Hindus have missed the bus of real Hinduism (refer to pp. 15, 59, 60, 166, 167, 269–271). The Vedas can't be part of it because religion should be separated from the state.

As Hinduism and its teachings expanded over the years, I thought it would be better to consolidate, decode, and bring back the 'one-stop solution' through this book. Its expansion goes like this from the Vedas to the Puranas.

1. Sutra: $(a+b)^2$
2. Bhashya: $a^2+2ab+b^2$
3. Vartika: $a^2+ab+ab+b^2$
4. Tika: $a \times a + 2 \times a \times b + b \times b$
5. I explain the same thing in diagrammatic form (Diagram 3.1) so that, without unnecessary expansion, people get to know the same concept through a diagram.

Diagram 3.1

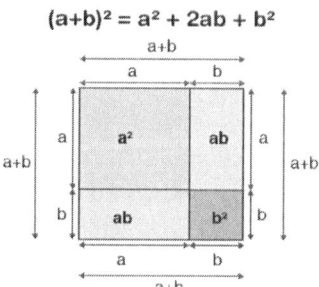

Conflicts

Misuse of secularism in Bharat

Holyoake's journey is secularism, which is not a political affidavit between state and church, just like laïcité. Secularism is another name for atheism against religion and the church. It is a social movement started by Holyoake that transformed itself into 'insecticide' to end the existence of religion in every sphere of life, right from politics, society, culture, and philosophy to everything. This insecticide behaviour gave birth to the binary division dividing society: religion vs. secular (modern format of infidel vs. religion).

Once Hinduism was baptized or abrahmized in the name of religion, the same tool (secularism) was used to divide Bhārtiya history in the binary format of secularism and religion. In one of the art and culture books widely used for civil services written by Nitin Singhania (IAS), you will find terms like secular love, secular book/literature, secular songs, secular architecture, secular paintings, and secular dance.[8] Justice N. Anand Venkatesh said in Seshammal and Others vs. State of Tamil Nadu (1972) that the appointment of an *archaka* to a temple would be a secular function, and only the performance of religious service by those priests would be an integral part of the religion. In that verdict, the apex court clearly differentiated between a secular and religious function. For example, in Bhārat, people have a habit of using the word secularism like salt, so whatever debates come, people pull secularism into them.

In the modern world, when concept of nation got developed, it was clear that the world is going to have solid boundaries and there will be new rules—regulation of settlement and migration—that the modern world is about the formalization (paperwork) of everything. Still, there are people who use the word secularism to accept illegal migrants. For example, even if a Hindu guy and a Muslim guy are in queue at the public toilet, these pseudo-intellectuals will use 'secularism' to express their emergency condition, even if both of them refuse to identify themselves with religion. Secularism is used as a replacement for the term 'belongingness' of two or more communities.

A Western world that follows either of the exclusivist religions and if Bhārat has to teach them yoga first Bhārat has to forcefully keep 'yoga' in the category of secularism to convince them it's not part of religion; otherwise, yoga belongs to neither of the categories. But this shows the backward mentality of the Western world. Even if 'yoga' is a part of any religion, they don't have the value of acceptance, even if it's useful for physical and mental health, because of the conservative, ethnocentric value system inspired by exclusivist religious value system.

This extreme use of 'secularism' you will find only in Bhārat. This is because most of the historians are paid to sprinkle this like an insecticide so that Bhārtiya history gets divided into this, and then you will find the major of history in the religion column and the minor in the secular column. Mediocre historians are already successful in convincing Bhārtiya people that whatever comes under religion is complex, biased, orthodox, communal, and the slavery of priests so that people run away from a major part of the past. Bhārtiya people are told Western secularism is laïcité and Bhārtiya secularism is multiculturalism. Most Bhārtiya people believe Western secularism as an interpretation of Bhārtiya constitution and in their subconscious mind that insecticide kills majority of things, which are in religions column. Which ultimately, in the conscious mind, creates the thought, 'Bhārat was nothing before 1947 or before British'.

Bhārtiya secularism is multicultulairsm, which means the state support all religions and cultures equally. Many people misinterpret it as citizen have special responsibility to follow all culture/religion or to maintain communal harmony. In the interpretation of Bhārtiya secularism, citizens have no role; it is actually about the state's role and its relation with religion. If anyone identifies himself/herself as 'secular', it is completely a meaningless and misinterpreted statement. At the same time, the contract between state and religion, that is, secularism/laicite is silent about 'social reforms' and the role of judiciary. So we need new terminologies, such as people, state, judiciary, and religious experts, in the contract.

In Raja Bira Kishore vs. State of Orissa case, the Supreme Court said that doing puja for the deity is a secular act and deciding who will be pujari of the temple by the state is also a secular function. In one of the books on internal security, there is a secular approach to 'recruitment of gang members' in the underworld.[9] I somewhere feel many people in Bhārat lack 'word power or vocabulary', which is why they use the word secularism to express every human relation. That is why it's important to use various words to express diversity of relationship and not everything needs to be accepted in the culture in terms of secularism. You can use words like 'belongingness, humanity, love, bonding, invasion, acceptance, forceful relation, non-discrimination, discrimination, foreigner, xenophobia, ethnocentrism, brotherhood, unity, multi-religious, multi-ethnic, cordial relation, communal harmony, conservative, liberal, treaty, and agreement' to express human relationships. It's not at all necessary to use the word secularism every time, which is a 'political' term to separate state and religion. The term that expresses separation is used to express bonding in Bhārat; that's the irony. Historians welcomed 'invasion, holocaust, human rights violation, atrocity, rapes, human trafficking, slavery, prisoners of war, physical torcher' as a symbol of secularism just to make you habit of welcoming present 'illegal migration, infiltration' through neighbouring countries in the name of secularism; if you speak against it, you are communal (culprit is given clean chit even though he has violated law). Even if you give invasive species of plants and animals to secularists, they will accept Bhārtiya land as a symbol of secularism and it's true there is no awareness about invasive species of plants and animals in Bhārtiya masses as using the word invasion is prohibited.

Mr X is an eminent writer in Bhārat, Muslim by birth and atheist by choice, and has written devotional songs on Hindu deities. If our secularist is asked to keep Mr X in the category of secularism or religion, it would be a very difficult job. Mr X can be religious because he is writing devotional songs, but he himself is an atheist. But the fact that a Muslim guy is writing songs on Hindu deities means there is a chance of playing the card of misinterpreted secularism.

In my childhood, during the Ganpati festival, I used to invite all my colleagues for celebrations, irrespective of religion. At that time, while inviting them, I never categorized them according to the religion. They were Christians and Muslims, and even during the celebration, we never mentioned our religion and played the card of secularism because we all didn't have that discriminatory power in our eyes to divide Bhārat in various religions and then unite them with a thread of bad secularism. Even our colleagues, who were Muslims and Christians (both non-fundamentalists), treated us in the same way. There was not only a positive incidence but also a negative incidence, where Hindu–Muslim riots happened in my area and one Muslim family moved to another city. They were our friends, and we were invited to their house for lunch when the riots were happening, and we safely took them and dropped them off at their houses once riots were over, but we never played the card of so-called secularism on social media.

The credit for this humanistic behaviour goes to my parents, not me. Even in my case, I once played the character of a 'pathan', who was a cook in the Mughal army at the school's annual function and got killed by Chatrapati Shivaji Maharaj, but I never played card of secularism, it was pure acting or art. That is why the division of Bhārat and its culture into terms of secularism and religion is a completely nonsensical thing. Where secularism started and see how we are using it in Bhārat. It's like once we bought a new branded three-piece suit from a foreign company and when it reached our home, we tore it into pieces and started using it for cleaning the floor, to fix the leakage of the pipe, to clean the kitchen, to make collage work, and to patch the old cloths. The time has come to limit the use of 'secularism' to specific contexts only..

Political Correctness

Non-secular liberalism

This extreme positive marketing of secularism never allows us to appreciate 'non-secular' approaches to life even if they are liberal. For example, even if a country has 'religion' as a constitution, if it also ensures freedom and liberty, we don't appreciate it. When geography is strategic and volatile and the masses are religiously motivated and radicalized, then launching 'secularism/state and religion are separate' becomes an extreme situation that may make the nation politically unstable. Such 'non-secular liberal' state (secularism in spirit but not in letter) then ensures the elimination of social evils and brings liberalism into its foreign policy based on its interests rather than 'anti-infidel' foreign policy. State-sponsored, non-secular liberalism is the best option in such a situation.

Religion, Laïcité, Secularism, and Conflicts 53

Akbar's secularism

The Mughal Empire was an Islamic empire, as priests were part of their court, and their policies were inspired by Islam. But historians concealed this and termed the Mughal Empire a symbol of secularism. Akbar himself established Din-e Ilahi, which means the state had a religion; then it's no more secularism. To hide this, our beloved historians started marketing of Din-e Ilahi, as I mentioned earlier, as a 'symbol of unity, love, secularism, and Hindu–Muslim unity'. This is how the religious state itself is given clean chit and termed secular. Akbar killed 30,000 Hindu civilians. He manifested or sowed seeds of fundamentalism and played the card of secularism in his court to get the support of Rajputs to expand the empire (read p. 86–87). This 'opium of political secularism' is given to us to give clean chit to the Mughals (refer to A3.2, p. 403).[10]

Is Bhārat a Secular or Religious/Theocratic Country?

Bhārat is a thematically diverse celebrational country with an emotion of oneness. By stopping the rampant and random use of secularism and religion, we must liberate ourselves from all such binary divisions so that not only we Hindus but all Bhārtiya people can survive in a multifaced, multiway world view; we shall explore unexplored dimensions of life. But at the same time, secularism in the constitution protects Bhārat from foreign media and NGOs, which generally target non-secular countries on five points: women rights, human rights, extremity, minority rights, and violence. When you don't have science as inspiration in your past, it becomes very difficult to create a science-based future. History books became merely appeasement policies while coining the term secularism multiple times because mediocre historians were mostly from the socialist background and had colonial influence. which influenced politics when political leadership read this mediocre history, they only wasted their time in secularism and religion appeasement to maintain Bhārtiya identity of multiculturalism and failed to promote actual content 'Ayurveda, yoga', Vedic maths etc.

As Ravindra Nath Tagore said, 'nationalism is not wrong, but the definition of it may change from nation to nation.' I interpret it as 'there can be different value systems and formats from country to country', which is a matter of research and a challenge to new-age political philosophers to create new terms. May be the secular word can be replaced with 'Laïcité' in the constitution as a contract between the state and any ideology (religion, culture, language, communism, capitalism, caste, and all such terms mentioned in chapter 10) so that no one imposes his ideology on the nation irrationally or discriminates on the basis of these terms, but the state can support a few services like ASI, the cultural ministry, and the Ministry of Ayush.

4

Multilayer Data Science: Hindu Society

Society is not just about the classification of human capital; it is about the complete picture or panoramic view (Rāmāyaṇa and Mahābhārata are one point access). It can be easily equated with modern-day 'multilayer data science', which integrates multiple data sets into one single picture, which helps you in decision-making by considering all the factors that help improve governance and service delivery.

Value, moral, and ethics are the ones that ultimately become the basis of laws, rules, regulation, economy, classification, duty, and responsibility. Values and morals must be backed by legislation (code of conduct: dharma shatsra), but if they don't have 'power' backup, they are dead books (letters without spirit). Values lose their value in time and space as they go away from power or even if anything becomes in excess, there will be a point where excessiveness is lost and equilibrium is achieved again. So, this cycle keeps on going.

Diagram 4.1

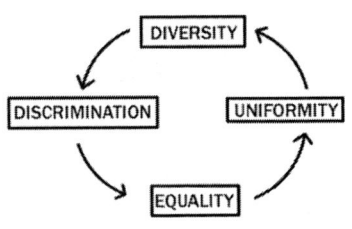

From Diagram 4.1, we can infer that when any value becomes in excess, it automatically culminates in or creates demand for the next value, and time and space roll on this cycle. Similarly, Hinduism has four cyclical phases, which we call yuga. In each yuga on a time scale to restore the value benchmark (dharma), power backup incarnates/descends (avatar) from time to time. On a space scale, power backup is a decentralized model that represents central power (the decentralized model of Bhārtiya democracy). The number of years and complex calculations given shall not be taken literally as scientific calculations (geologic time scale: era, eon, epoch), but they have some philosophical and semi-scientific significance (refer to A4.6, p. 409). In Hinduism, numerology plays a very important role. A single number reminds you of multiple concepts like 3, 4, 5, 6, 7, 8, 14, 21, 18, 108, etc.

Avatars of Vishnu have already been mentioned in *Shatapatha Brahmana* during 600 BC, in case you believe Vishnu was a post-Buddhist creation of Brahmins to counter Buddhism.[2] Avatars of Vishnu are the evolution story of human beings from marine life to full-fledged humans, divided into four yugas. Philosophy is described in numerological framework so that the remembrance of one reminds you other. That is why you will see the number of sages, seven, is fixed, but the sages keep varying in various texts. Similarly, framework of the Ikshwaku dynasty is fixed; names keep changing across texts and traditions.[3] The reason of telling you this is because even the varna system changes in every era/yuga as you move from idealism to chaos (refer to pp. 123–124). Hindu society is not merely a pyramidical varna hierarchy as many scholars draw. Just like human evolution, socio-economic (varna system) evolution also takes place. It's not like a framework where God revealed something and imposed it from the respective date onwards.

Are Rāmāyaṇa, Mahābhārata, *Manusmriti* Real?

In philosophy, we have two branches: descriptive and revisionary metaphysics. In descriptive metaphysics, the existing model is described, and in revisionary, a better/ideal model is suggested in theory. Hindu texts are a combination of both; they reflect social structure, economic structure, etc., plus the writer, from his side, adds his own innovation (revisionary) and integrates it into one story that matches the core/ideal Hindu philosophy. The most unique part about Mahābhārata doesn't exist in isolation; from the Vedas, Puranas, Upanishads, grammar books, Buddhism, and Jainism, everyone talks about characters, stories, and the content of Mahābhārata (refer to A4.2, pp. 404–405). The structure of the lineage plays an important role in understanding philosophy and the historicity of texts. In general, 'oneness (Brahman) - deity (Bramha) - rishi - current generation', as mentioned in Table

Table 4.1

Yuga	Satyuga	Tretayuga	Dwaparyuga	Kaliyuga
Years	Human/divine 3.456 million/ 4800	1.728 million/ 2400	1.728 million/ 2400	432,000/ 1200
Historical	Matsya Avatar saves Vaivasvata Manu (carried 7 sages + Vedas in a boat as a seed bank) from a great flood, with the help of fish (Matsya), i.e., the glacier melt that initiated the Holocene epoch.	Ikshwaku, 1st King of Bhārat after the Holocene epoch, 9500 BCE (but in Hinduism, he comes in Satyuga); Ram born in 5116 BCE	3101 BCE[1] when Mahābhārata finished (but in Hinduism, Mahābhārata happens in Trayuga) and Kaliyuga started.	We the people of the current generation
Value system	Values are in letter and spirit both	Values in letter but no spirit	Values are neither in letters nor in spirit	No values complete; chaos and anarchy
Hindu parallel	Ideal model free from sorrows.	Unethical people like Ravana (Rāmāyaṇa)	Unethical behaviour within family (Mahābhārata)	Values collapsed within
Avatars, his-story	Matsya, Kurma, Varaha, Narasimha	Vaman, Ram, Parshuram (Active in war)	Krishna (Passive in war)	Kalki
Spiritual	Dynasty starts from Bramha (Sushumna–Bramha Nadi)	Suryavanshi (Pingala–Surya Nadi Active)	Chandravanshi (Ida–Chandra Nadi Passive)	Our body

All four yugas are interweaved into one system by connecting everyone through lineage, starting from Satyuga to Kaliyuga (refer to A4.1, p. 404)

4.1, lineage gets divided into four yugas (refer to Table 8.2, p.166, which has a similar lineage structure).

1. Scripture or lineage supreme being (refer to the 3rd diagram of 19.1, p. 350) is a thread, which integrates whole existence into a single system, just like thread weaves to form cloth. This existence itself has an extension as 'oneness' descends itself and diversity is created (refer to A4.1, p. 404, the theory of creation, pp. 274–276).
2.
   A. Then the supreme being will incarnate on earth in the form of a deity/Bramha (a personality notion of Bramhan/Oneness). Knowledge is passed to sages, and then sages will pass knowledge on to their further generations. Ultimately the author will identify himself as the successor of that tradition of sages. This is called smriti: carried as memory from one generation to another. These are the stories or history that existed in masses as folklore and got institutionalized later (Rāmāyaṇa, Mahābhārata, Puranas, dharma shastras).
   Examples:
   a. Tamil grammer/language is revealed by Lord Shiva to Agastya.
   b. The *Manusmriti* was written around 200 CE. Its origin has been attributed to the creator Brahma, who is then said to have passed it on to the first human, Manu. The text was further shared with Bhrigu, the first teacher, who later passed it on to many other sages.
   c. Vyasa and Valmiki make themselves part of the Rāmāyaṇa and Mahābhārata, e.g., movie director is also doing a cameo role, but in reality, he is the director only. Vicitravirya is the father of Dritrashtra, not Vyasa.[4]
   B. Direct audio reveals it to the sage as a direct revelation by supreme oneness (shruti). Related to the science of enlightenment, rituals were created by rishis through contemplation in a meditative state. For instance, the Vedas and Upanishads.

Even though verses of the Vedas are contributed by various sages, the Vedas are authorless as they are revealed to sages by supreme oneness (*apauruṣeya*) in a meditative state. This division cannot be taken as watertight because Shruti and Smriti also have overlapping data.

Multilayer Data Science: Hindu Society

The content of the Hindu literature, especially Itihasa (Puranas, Rāmāyaṇa, Mahābhārata), is 'multilayer data science', which gives a panoramic view of multiple dimensions, which are as follows: If you choose atheism, then you are choosing destruction and deny the following dimensions. Most leftist and non-Hindu historians have missed all these dimensions because of ideological limitations (as mentioned in chapters 3 and 10), which is reflected in history books, and the same points are missing in education policy, especially among youth.

1. Polity
2. Economy
3. Diplomacy skills
4. Society and social structure
5. History, archaeology
6. Spiritual aspects: Shiva, Vishnu
7. Theories of cosmos
8. War: methods and types of war
9. Job diversity
10. Manufactured products
11. Beauty, cosmetics
12. Integration of country: various groups and geography integrated into one civilization in scriptures
13. Coins, medium of exchange, barter system
14. Education or gurukul system
15. Ancestry and lineage of present generations
16. Vehicles
17. Astronomical data
18. Sports, music, dance, entertainment industry
19. Calendar and its own timeline
20. Ayurveda, medicine
21. Mention/list of yogi/ rishi
22. Science and technology of that time
23. Biodiversity, cropping pattern
24. Food and cuisine
25. Traditions, philosophy
26. Family, relationships
27. Geography: rivers, mountains, etc.

28. Yoga, meditation, siddhi/Shakti
29. Weapons
30. Theories of creation of universe
31. Dynasties (across Bhārat of various periods)
32. Language art, tangible and intangible art and culture
33. Law, rules, regulation, justice system (refer to A4.5, pp. 408–409)

Many aspects of ancient Bhārat were overlooked due to a lack of understanding of Hinduism, which was reflected in policy-making and education policy. You will find the following points missing in both of them:

> 'Yoga, meditation, sports as a profession and lifestyle, Environment & ecology, Music, art, dance as a profession and lifestyle, Science and technology as lifestyle & profession, Financial literacy and economy, Job diversity in urban and rural Industry and MSME, Leadership, Disaster and its management, Research center and laboratory, Archeology' (refer to B11, p. 423).

History books try to impose a modern-age model of society on Hinduism, and they end by imposing the following structure on Hindu society, which actually looks like (refer to Diagram 7.1, p.124).

Today's structure of society Imposed models on Hinduism.

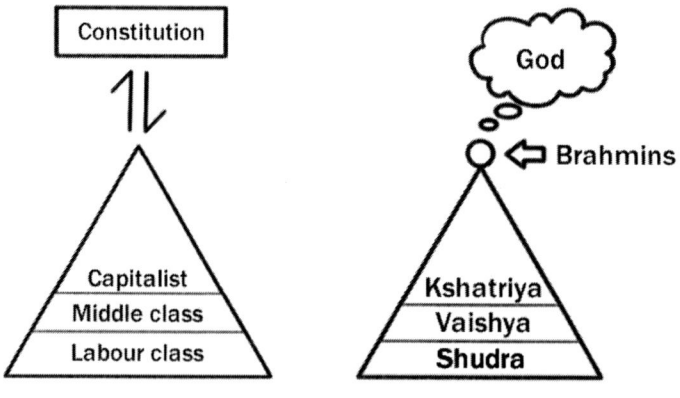

Capitalist model   *Hinduism in capitalist model*

Diagram 4.2

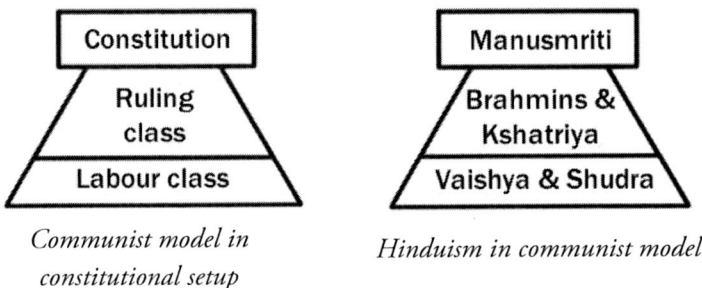

Communist model in constitutional setup

Hinduism in communist model

After imposing their model on Hindu society, capitalists and communists keep dividing society into modern classifications, i.e., general, OBS, SC, ST, etc., in these pyramidical hierarchy models. Then they run a parallel universe narrative: SC and ST suffered for 5,000 years. Marxists try to fit every society into caste, conflict, and exploited vs. exploiters, so you will see multiple dimensions and subjective studies of each society, but Marxists actually impose their ideas on each society to create a vote bank out of it.[5]

Diagram 4.3 Social engineering model of communists

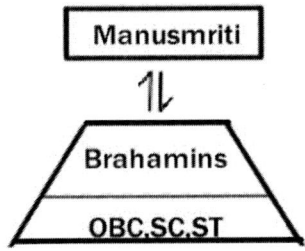

The varna system, which was created to institutionalize jati with the aim of a rule-based order of economy, is now marketed as 'division and discrimination' only (explained in later chapters). These parallel structures help them to maintain their vote bank eternally in favour, so they project Hindu society as eternally privileged or eternally discriminatory for respective jati or categories rather than evolution.

Plus, this pyramidical hierarchy helps you explain the modern secular state. To fit Hindu society into that, the pyramidical hierarchy helps you a lot.

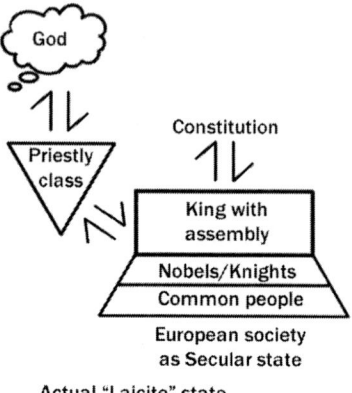

Laïcité, even though it's about a watertight separation between state and religion, is not possible. Because thinking, vocabulary, phrases, etc., are part and parcel of history, carried forward by state and individual as heritage or tradition. Like Britain, a state that supports the church and provides representation to the church is still 'secular'.

Biased History Writing

History books were written by colonial masters intentionally or unintentionally to suppress and finish the indigenous culture. The same legacy was carried out by communists because 'religion is the opium of the masses', which needs to be sublimated, i.e., cultural genocide (China model).[6]

In Bhārtiya context blueprint of communist/atheistic framework was as per (refer to Table 1.1, p. 5). Where pre-Aryan invasion culture and history need to be projected as atheistic. So to satisfy this condition, they denied all the cultural and religious aspects found in Bhārat before the Aryan invasion so that Hinduism could be projected as 'Aryan/Brahmin colonialism'.

Things they denied from the Indus valley that are directly related to Hinduism include:

Multilayer Data Science: Hindu Society 63

1. Gold: Archaeological proof of gold and other precious pearls (5000 BCE), which find their mention either in Rāmāyaṇa or Mahābhārata, which dates to 3101 bce and 5114 bce.[7]
2. Copper: Which is generally traced back to 2500 BCE is actually 5000–6000 BCE old; most of the locations where it is found are places that are mentioned in the Rāmāyaṇa. Myth, which is promoted by historians like R.S. Sharma, was that the trading community (Vaishya) dominated in the Indus valley, but copper arrows are found in places mentioned in the Rāmāyaṇa, which dates back to 5000 BCE. In post-Vedic period, Kshatriyas became strong enough to deny the historicity of Rāmāyaṇa and Mahābhārata.[8]
3. Iron: Iron was also found in Asia, dating back to 5000 BCE to 7000 BCE. Because the Rāmāyaṇa mentions Sri Lanka had a presense of irron, so iron is shown post-copper finding around 1300 BCE. Harappans knew iron.[9]
4. Firepits: Firepits, which are used to perform yajña, are found in Kalibangan. If this is accepted, then all the details related to yajña, their types, design, complex geometry of construction of firepits, types of rituals, everything would get focused,[10] then how will they convince them that in 1500 BC Aryan invaded and imposed rituals and polytheism.
5. Types of seals and religious/cultural interpretation:
   a. Bull seal: It shows the importance of cows and bulls in the Indus valley; some also trace it as a totem of Rishbhnath in Jainism. The bull and the cow have extreme importance in Hinduism.[11]
   b. Seal of Yamalaarjuna:[12] There is a story in the *Bhagavad Purana* where Krishna uproots a tree and two human beings come out of it who are Gandharvas, and Krishna liberates them from a curse. We find a seal that depicts this story on the seal. Which gives two or three conclusions: Indus valley people knew Krishna; stories or history from Puranas are not post-Buddhist or post-Vedic. They might be the outcome of folklore later, which got institutionalized and updated. This proves again the claim that Puranas were launched by Brahmins to counter Buddhism. Puranas mentioned

in *Chandogya Upanishad, Atharvaveda,* and *Sathapatha Brahmana.*

c. Pashupati seal:[13] Pashupati seal is not just proto-Shiva but also the deity. In Mahābhārata, there is dialogue between Duryodhana and others where there is mention that 'Pashupati (the deity) has allotted this land to us'.

d. Phallus worship:[14] The meaning of Shivalinga is: 'It is a combination of linga and yoni behind which Muldhara chakra exists.' The coiled snake at the bottom is a symbol of Kundalini, which exists in coiled format at Muldhara chakra. The same coiled snake goes above Shiva linga and poses like Umbrella, which is an enlightened state where the seventh chakra is out of body. Linga, yoni, the earth goddess, yoga, snake worship, and dice are found in Harappa. If Shivalinga is found in the Indus valley, it means they knew the science of enlightenment. Phallus worship is found globally across all civilizations, but no one is able to tell its meaning, which shows Hinduism is the mother of all civilizations.

e. Shubha Ashubha Swastika seal:[15] Both left- and right-handed Swastika are found in the Indus valley civilization.

f. Peepal tree seal:[16]

It has two significances:
- The importance of peepal tree and peepal worship in Hinduism
- Seven major leaves of the tree, form a brain-like structure and two dragon-like unicorns facing each other might be symbols of seven stages of kundalini and the two unicorns, Ida and Pingala.

g. Matrika seal:[17] Female deities with ritual sacrifice, you will know the importance of the number '7' in (refer to p. 288) of chapter 14, which is common in the Shakta cult.

h. Horse:[18] There is mention in the Rāmāyaṇa that Gandhara area, nearby Pakistan–Afghanistan, used to be a market of horses. Horse remains are also found in archaeology in Sinoli.

i. Astronomy: In the Indus valley civilization, people knew the 'astronomy' in great detail, and it was transferred to other

civilizations with misinterpretations. But as we are Origin, we know concepts in great detail and reason[19]
6. Professions/employment: Various professions from the Indus valley are not mentioned so that *Manusmriti* can be marketed as the origin of the jati/varna system, e.g., artisans and craftsmen, builders, carpenters, metalworkers, leatherworkers, weavers, and farmers.
7. The Indus valley people also knew Ayurveda in great detail.[20]
8. International connection: Hinduism is the mother of all civilizations. Many stories, concepts, architecture, and exports were exported to other countries, either through trade or after the great flood as seed bank. As these concepts are live and authentically practiced in Hinduism till today, we can infer that Bhārat is the mother of all civilizations. Other civilizations are also as old as 3000–4000 BCE, especially Egypt, so we can infer history, stories, and folklore from Puranas, Rāmāyaṇa, and Mahābhārata were exported around 3000 BCE, which is ground-breaking proof against those who try to prove Hinduism as myth or imported myth from Aryans. Proofs are attached in the appendix. Even Iran's society was based on the Hindu varna system, priests, warriors, agriculture, artisans, and caste (read A4.3, pp. 405–408).
9. Places mentioned in Rāmāyaṇa and Mahābhārata go back to Harappan or pre-Harappan era—Harappan sites in Kurukshetra, Indraprastha, and Mathrua.[21]
10. Stories like Urvashi and Purvaras, on which Kalidas wrote the book, are mentioned in the Vedas.[22]

As a conclusion, we can say that the Indus valley civilization is a full-fledged Hindu civilization based on Vedic philosophy. This was deliberately done so that people never understand that 'Hinduism' is only 'standalone' civilization or culture and rest of the civilizations/religions are inspired by or imported from Hinduism (read pp. 121–122 and 286–287). But we were not told that these things make Hinduism a culture that is

a. rootless in archaeology (mythical)
b. imported/colonial (Aryan invasion)

c. inspired by Buddhism (idol worship, Mahayana)
d. not original (modified Buddhism and launched as the bhakti movement)
e. unorganized, scattered, anonymous, unknown, inconsistent, ambiguous, vague, and fragmented rather continuous, streamlined, patterned, and inherent to the land
f. existed before other religions/sects existed

Points 'a' and 'b' are explained in this chapter, whereas 'c', 'd', and 'e' will be discussed later (in chapters 7, 8, 14, 15, and 19) once Hinduism and Enlightenment are explained with their Vedic roots. You will find the roots of atheism specifically mentioned in history books, but not Hinduism. This is the biggest tragedy (refer to Table 1.1, p. 5). This created Hindus at the social-level unorganized, scattered, and fragmented in caste, language, regional, and sectarian social cleavages. People started rebelling against Hinduism or ignored it because of a void rather than carrying it out as a 'legacy'.

If I were to represent Hinduism in mathematical equations, they would look something like this:

a. Archeology – Hinduism = Indus valley civilization (fodder for Dravidian movement)
b. Buddhism, Jainism, Sikhism, etc., – Hinduism = separate religion status or separate country, e.g., Khalistan
c. Medieval Bharat – Hindu kingdoms = Islamic Bharat
d. Tamil literature – Hinduism = anti-Hindu linguistic politics
e. Colonial era/post-independence – Hindu interest = formation of Pakistan, minority appeasement, pro minority legislations, administrative bodies, minority ministry, minority commission

Narrative War

1. Myth of Aryan invasion or Atheist invasion theory: How can the Aryan invasion kill 5 million people (population of Indus valley), which is almost equal to how much Joseph Stalin killed during his era, directly or indirectly (state- sponsored famine) and more than twice as many Jews who were killed by Hitler. The drying of Saraswati can be the only possible reason why Hindus

from Harappa migrated in three directions: Iraq, the Gangetic Valley, and southern Bhārat.[23] In the Vedas and Rāmāyaṇa, in both cases, Saraswati is shown alive. To strengthen this myth of 'Aryan invasion/atheism invasion', further terms like Indo-Aryan architecture and Indo-Aryan language were introduced, so that through etymology they tell you Indo and Aryan were two different things.

2. If Hinduism is Brahminical literature, then why not [24]
   - Islam is Mulla literature
   - Buddhism is Bhikku literature
   - Sikhism is Mahant literature
   - Christianity is Popeic literature
   - Jain literature as Muni literature

   So Hinduism also deserves to be expressed in a dignified language as other religions, such as, the origin of Abrahamic religions, so also the origin of religion in other traditions, are associated with their respective prophets.

3. And what about that Hindu literature written by Brahmins and non-Brahmins in non-Sanskrit language? What about the literature written on science by Hindu Brahmins? Are Vedic maths, Ayurveda, and astronomy also Brahmanical/Aryan conspiracy? This Brahminical literature myth is created just to tell you, 'Give up the rituals of Hinduism, which are the imposition of Brahmins created to loot money from non-Brahmins,' so that Hindus can be made vulnerable to conversion.

4. History books are also silent about Gurukul system, where people from almost all varna used to learn. This was not mentioned deliberately to tell Bhārtiya people that you were illiterate before the entry of British and British-sponsored social reformers.

5. What were varna and jati of transgenders? There is uncertainty in the continuity of vansh/genealogy in transgenders. In that case, allocating any profession to them was not possible because transferring skills, infrastructure, and supply chains was hereditary in the jati system. So, my assumption is that they were not given any jati or varna status, as both were related to professions. Transgenders had another mechanism to earn bread that was

collecting donations at the events where they were invited, e.g., sixteen samskara's: birth, marriage, etc. Generally, happy-mood events and, in return, their blessings were considered auspicious. British historians were motivated by their own ideas of religions (mostly third-gender exclusive fundamentalism), so they don't mention transgenders in history books. Till today, transgenders are not part of the mainstream economy, which is an irony of Bhārtiya society. Even though there have been various examples of LGBTQ physical relationships in ancient Bhārat, but biased leftist historians don't mention them, so 'void' in the history books becomes fodder for the anti-Hindu LGBTQ movement. That is why it's important to make history books more inclusive.

6. Many folklores from the Bhārtiya subcontinent, including Assam, Arunachal Pradesh, Polynesia (near Australia), Indonesia, Cambodia, and Nagaland, are very similar to Hinduism and Egyptian civilization. But just to satisfy the ideological framework of projecting the pre-Aryan world as atheistic, they didn't mention stories or folklores of deities prior to the date of the Aryan invasion (read A4.4, p. 408, i.e., stories from northeast Bharat). So much so that it seems that local folklore from the Bhārtiya subcontinent (including the northeast) got institutionalized as Hinduism. Atheist (Aryan) invasion theory caused marginalization or a feeling of alienation in the northeast, which created insurgency and militancy in the region.

Social Engineering: Majority, Minority, Nationalism, Regionalism

If two or more communities are working together, it's not always because of secularism, love, belongingness, or compassion; there can be multiple reasons.

1. Common past, future, and present
2. Common identity religion, caste, sect, region, language
3. Family alliance, i.e., relationship, marriage
4. One-to-one personal friendship
5. Ideology
6. Hiring skills
7. Common goal

8. Personality cult
9. Leader and follower relation
10. Value system marketing: truth, multiculturalism, justice, acceptance
11. Forced labour, surrender by the enemy
12. Functioning as a 'sleeper cell' under enemy
13. Working together in a discriminatory way, i.e., Rajputs under Aurangzeb but he is destroying temples, Jizya etc.
14. Seeking political support from enemies to save their own identity
15. Use of money and power to purchase support from other party
16. Use of threats and dominance to get support from the opposite party
17. Small stories for the common man: not everyone understands the Vedas, so Puranas must be there to keep connected to supreme truth
18. Some people are not your friends, they are just scared to be your enemy
19. Treaty, alliance, etc.
20. It's better that people of enemy identity also work with you, so the chances of 'over the ground workers' of enemy don't work against you increases, i.e., minimizing sleeper cells
21. Not mentioning invasion, exodus, and human rights violations also makes history books secular or multicultural

If one wants to know ideology of a state, it can be known directly or indirectly through their practices, seals, thoughts, literature, things which are unsaid sometimes, and policies. You have to interpret that through symbolism. So one must interpret the ideology and purpose of the Sikh Empire and Hindavi Swaraj in light of the above points. Satish Chandra in his book[25] clearly says the Haldighati war wasn't a Hindu–Muslim war; it was a mere political struggle because 'Rana Pratap + Afghani Pathans + Bhils vs. Akbar + Mansingh I'. Ultimately, what matters is that 'before the war', you must have maximum numbers, irrespective of identity. It was between Hindus and Muslims because it was a struggle between Hindu political leaders and Muslim political leaders, which makes a difference because 'treatment of infidels, religious tax, destruction of religious places, conversion'—all these things do happen under particular political power or empire and not under 'Hindu' political power because there is no backup of religious fundamentalism to these activities in Hinduism.

Does democracy, secularism, multiculturalism, and universal brotherhood exist because Hindus are the majority in Bhārat? Or how can Hindus/Hinduism be in danger if they are the majority? No, it is a partial view, not a complete reality as it projects only case D and case H (refer to Table 4.2, pp. 71–73).

What Were Hindus Doing?

They were busy taking 'destruction, exodus, massacre' as 'small/regional identity' rather than Hinduism, e.g., Tamils in Lanka, Kashmiri pandits, Nepali in Bhutan, Bengali Hindus in Bangladesh, Hindus and sub-traditions in Pakistan and Afghanistan, Sindhi in Pakistan, and Rohingya in Myanmar. If Hindus would have taken this entire exodus from South Asia as 'elimination of Hinduism', then 100 crore people would have stood together. Once it was removed from South Asia, it was then removed from border areas in Kerala (communist), Kashmir, Bengal, Tamil Nadu, etc. So, it is a twin-circle problem. On the circumference of Bhārat (border countries) and the circumcircle of Bhārat (border states), both Hindus and Hinduism are eliminated so that Bhārat's soft power can be reduced, and these areas are indirectly reduced to non-Hindu religions or atheism—where Bhārat is ultimately reduced to Madhya Pradesh.

Hindus identified with them with language, jati, varna, etc. The narrative of the majority is always safe, secure, or always anti-minority, which pushes Hindus on the backfoot. During that period, Hindus were eliminated from Bhutan, Sri Lanka, Pakistan, and Afghanistan. Many people say the Sri Lanka issue is linguistic, not religious. This myth is promoted by leftists so that Tamil Hindus don't identify themselves as Hindus and protect themselves from Sri Lankan Buddhists, which can become a threat for Dravidian (atheist) politics in Tamil Nadu, which is equally destroying Hinduism.[28]

Table 4.2

	When someone is 'ruling class'	When someone is not 'ruling class'
When one chooses to expand their own ideology', i.e., religion (colonialism), political ideology, etc. — **When in minority**	Case A Enforcing ideology by using institution e.g., 1. Mughal era 2. British era 3. ICHR (the things which this book exposes) 4. Waqf board[26] 5. Influencing media. In all 5 cases, Hindus were/are in the majority.	Case E 1. Terrorism, deterrence, atrocities on others, violence, crime, parallel crime ghettos (no go zones) 2. Minority victim card 3. Minority interest 4. Projecting self as 'minority' even when one is the second largest majority 5. Influencing media 6. Parallel economy, polity, parallel world/underworld 7. Quick and strong appreciation if anyone works in favour of religion to make him habit of appeasement 8. Support from international human rights institution + minority supporters 9. Illegal migration from neighbouring countries to change 'demographic' 10. Organized crime—terror chain nexus 11. Separate country demand—Pakistan

	When someone is 'ruling class'	When someone is not 'ruling class'

When in majority
 	
When one chooses to expand their own ideology', i.e., religion (colonialism), political ideology, etc.
	Case B
	Directly turning the state into theocratic state and enforcing theocratic discriminatory laws on infidels,
	e.g., Pakistan
		Case F
		Massacre and exodus of infidels and minority[27]
		e.g.,
		1. Pakistan, Bangladesh, Afghanistan
		2. Colonies cum ghettos of non-Hindu religions are in majority; Kashmiri Hindus
		3. Massacre and exodus created by Buddhist country
		   a. Sri-Lanka – Tamil Hindus
		   b. Myanmar – Rohingya Hindu
		   c. Bhutan – Nepali Hindus
		(Buddha is a symbol of peace-marketing strategy (see chapter 3)

When in minority When one believes in 'democracy, secularism, multiculturalism, universal brotherhood'	**Case C** Using power to promote secularism, multiculturalism, etc.	**Case G** Peaceful coexistence, e.g., Jews and Parsi, Hindu community

	When someone is 'ruling class'	When someone is not 'ruling class'
When in majority When one believes in 'democracy, secularism, multiculturalism, universal brotherhood'	**Case D** Believer and enforcing constitutional values, e.g., governments from 1947 till today with exceptional cases, the way history books are written itself is proof of it	**Case H** Believer in 'democracy, secularism, multiculturalism, universal brotherhood', e.g., all the people who don't mix their ideology with politics whether left, right, centre, etc. and vote only on development, national security, and sovereignty.

Why Are Hindus Divided?

Hindus are kept divided by political narratives with the ideology that 'not all eggs should be kept in one basket' or 'too big to fail'. In Bhārat, communal riots happen, issues of tribal people, issues of vulnerable sections, Maoism, extremism in certain border areas, Hindu exodus at various places. Certain people think if any identity is united at the pan-Bhārat level, then instability created by riots in certain areas may spread all over Bhārat. This pan-Bhārat spread of any issue may create pressure on the government, and political instability may take place. So issues like riots are limited to that particular area, community, etc., so that the approach of keeping all eggs in the same basket (unified diversity) is avoided. As a result, keeping all eggs in multiple baskets (scattered diversity) is done. But this rule is applicable to Hindus only. For this, they kept all Hindu culture scattered in 'regional/linguistic baskets'. This is to weaken Hindu unity, e.g., all indigenous new years fall on the same day (ecological-cosmic aspect), but they are kept in regional/linguistic basket, not 'Hindu new year'. In further chapters, you will see the nature of Hindu culture (read pp. 111–112, festivals). Plus, to absorb/mainstream the non-Hindus who usually can't participate in Hindu culture because of the 'exclusive policy,' so they are brought under the same culture through the 'linguistic/regional identity' channel. So that everyone votes for the 'extreme regionalist' political setup. Whichever way you market Hindu culture, whether as Hindu, linguistic/regional culture, secular version of culture (removing Hindu symbols), in any of the case 'exclusivist religions' can't cross their lines for social harmony because its violation of their fundamentalism, e.g., dance, music, etc.

But ultimately, after all these scenarios, who is paying the cost? What is the loss calculation for Hindus in terms of numbers, land, property, etc.

Is Bhārat Facing Hindu Majoritarianism?

If and when Jews and Parsis start feeling a sense of being persecuted by Hindus, then it will be a point of serious thinking.

Table 4.3

Ideology	Pan-Bhārat and global movement, events
Non-Hindu religions	Allowed and accepted as general practice so not subjected to any criticism
Communism, atheism	
Misinterpreted Buddhism, rebels within Hinduism	
Caste politics	
Constitution = nation/nationalism and marketing it as something which has nothing to do with ethos of Bhārat	
Hinduism	Majoritarianism and extremism, fascism, expansionary, totalitarian, absolutism

Trikalabadhit satya (evergreen truth) of federalism narrative

Table 4.4

	While in power	Out of power
National political Party	National unity, national integration, national uniting cultural aspects to ensure all Bhārat hold of party for long term stability of party. Allegation on state party: a. of being anti-national b. danger to unity of nation	Will demand: 1. decentralization 2. federalism To give challenge or weaken ruling party at the Centre, by strengthening local identity and localized politics. Allegation on Central ruling party: a. anti-federal, undemocratic b. centralized, dictatorial

	While in power	**Out of power**
Regional political party	Marketing of being: 1. pro-federal 2. democratic 3. decentralized To keep Central political party out of power in state	Social activities like: 1. pro-state activity 2. celebrating state-level culture 3. Centre is anti-state 4. Centre is anti-state language

This thing keeps on happening, but the thing is, this game of centralization–decentralization is real, and it is to concentrate or curb each other's power, which may lead to separatist or expansionist movements, including violent acts (covered in chapter 9). All identities of caste, sub-caste, varna, and language are somehow tried to be fixed in Table 4.4, which ultimately causes division among Hindus. Social engineering to maintain the federal character or centralization is definitely not in favour of the Hindu masses.

5

Neutral History Books before Saffaronization

In 2016, a Christian family came from Qatar to celebrate Christmas with their parents (our neighbours), and I was discussing many things with them, and that uncle said, 'Our country has such a glorious history and great warriors and empires, and we are not taught that'. I thought he must be feeling homesick, as he used to visit Bhārat on Christmas only. But after many years, I realized the same thing: even though I am part of this nation and live in this nation and culture, I also feel homesick. I started finding out the reason, and the reason was the same as he said: 'We are not taught history of the past, even if taught, it is in a discriminatory manner.'

The way you divide the historical eras shapes the minds of people, which becomes beneficial for getting expected political results. The British divided Bhārtiya history into three parts: Hindu, Muslim, and British, which helped them in divide and rule politics. But the second aspect of this history is telling Hindus that first you were following the Imported Hinduism (Aryan invasion), then Muslims came, and now we came; it's our time, so you should accept our imposition as you have a habit. To make this more familiar, they made the Aryan invasion theory that we came earlier as Aryan, now this is the second colonial wave. History is divided into the following periods (see Table 5.1); I am also mentioning eras and narratives.

Table 5.1

Name of era	Politics behind naming
Prehistory	Suppressed to avoid scientific study of human evolution (as seen in previous chapters)
Indus civilization	River and some random findings
Vedic period	Book and inequalities, caste discrimination
Post-Vedic/ Brahmin age	Book written by Brahmin community, some philosophical anti-ritualistic things
Buddhism, Jainism	Personality cult and value system
Mauryan age	Only empire of that era
Post-Mauryan age	Empire
Gupta period	Empire
Post-Gupta period	Empire
Sangam	Literature
Rajputs, Marathas, Sikhs, Chola, Vijayanagar, Pandya, Pallava, Kashmir, Kerlaputras, etc.	Hardly mentioned (Was this to discourage or curb regionalism? Then why was the Mughal Empire glorified?)
Delhi sultanate	Empire and personality cult, art culture, infrastructure
Mughal Empire	Empire and personality cult, art culture, infrastructure
Early British Bhārat	Era of renaissance
Northeast	Not covered at all. Separated from the rest of the Bhārat in history book only, this alienation created a secessionist movement, strengthening local communist-Maoist politics and kept away the northeast from the mainstream.

Neutral History Books before Saffaronization

Observation from Table 5.1 is that we want neutral history books where all dimensions of society are mentioned and tested (refer to pp. 59 and 60).

History of Europe and the entering of Christianity in Europe and the pope's control over Europe are seen as 'era of darkness' in Europe, and this is accepted by themselves only and as a worldwide truth. But a similar 'era of darkness' in mediaeval and modern Bhārat is shown as a cultural renaissance and era of secularism. Cathrine Nixey has written the book *The Darkening Age*; if someone writes such a book in Bhārat, he will be termed extremist, right wing, and barbarian. The message she conveyed in her book, are applicable to Bhārat too. Sometimes I feel Sikh warriors made a mistake by taking swords in the hand because today's generation has forgotten their sacrifice against the 'era of darkness'.

Table 5.2

Hinduism	Brahmin and scriptural supremacy with complex ritual and jati, caste problems (deliberately not discussing value systems and personality cults), cultural infrastructure, the only origin of social evils
Buddhism and Jainism	Personality cult and value system
Islam	Infrastructure, art and culture, Sufism (for attracting masses), personality cult, and the era of secularism, but its origin, value system, internal sectoral divides are not discussed, plus what Hindus lost under the Islamic era is not discussed
Judaism, Zoroastrianism, Bahaism	Hardly mentioned
Christianity	Origin, how it entered Bhārat, and its expansion deliberately not discussed anything just to keep activities underground from the eyes of Hindus

Table 5.3

Dimension of Bhārtiya society	Characters
Spiritual heads, Philosophers	Buddhism, Jainism in ancient Bhārat; Sufism in mediaeval Bhārat
Kshatriya or warriors and Kingdoms	Ashoka the Great (Buddhist), Akbar the Great (Muslim/Mughal)
Vaishya or business	British as traders
Shudra	The outcome of the Hindu caste system
Where is the share of Hinduism?	

Prehistory Myth

They call it prehistory because the aim of Western historians is to eliminate most ancient history as much as possible so that the richness of history lowered and Christianity and the era after can be glorified. So they try to push all history back 5,000 years before Christ because earth formed approximately around 5000 BC. Even though China has 29,000-year-old pottery, Iran has a 10,000-year-old civilization, and Egypt is almost 10,000 years old—somewhere all civilizations are inspired by Hinduism. Unfortunately, all those countries don't much care about this biased history writing because they don't connect themselves with history because of today's political and religious ideology.

Prehistory (Great oxygenation event) and human evolution from apes to sapiens are not taught in detail, because if they are taught, then all people irrespective of caste and religion will feel superior over the past. By eliminating prehistory, we create 'victims of the caste system' in the history books rather than 'advantageous people over apes and animals', so that these historical victims are either used to create political turmoil, pressure group, appeasement, rebels, or communist vote bank.

Origin of human beings in Africa (African replacement theory) according to archaeology and research has the capacity to prove all humans are outcomes of Africa, then it would have been a big challenge to establish the Aryan invasion vs. Sons of Soil concept. Even ethnocentric religion's preachers never discuss 'human evolution' and deny 'Darwin's theory' to prove their God created earth, and our history books indirectly convey the same thing without mentioning God. It's very important to find out the names of history book writers who indirectly created theocratic brains in school.

Indus Valley Vedic Age

Indus valley civilization is divided into Early Harappa, Later Harappa, Early Vedic, and Later Vedic. This division is the biggest fraud, as we have seen in chapter 4.

Indus valley civilization is one of the biggest frauds; naming it Indus valley or Harappa–Mohenjo-Daro itself is created with some political motive that is telling Bhārtiya people indirectly that 'civilization exists on the northwest of you'. From this period to the next 3,000–4,000 years, we are told that you always received invaders as guests without any war, so Britishers must be welcomed in the same way and let them loot just like others did; you accept their cultural imposition as adding sugar to multiculturalism just like you did always.

Mauryan Age

Before the Mauryan age or during the Mauryan age, they don't mention any era with the empire's name. This is an indirect message to Hindus: if you follow Buddhism, then only you will rise as an empire. They don't mention details of any other empire of that era; they make that era Maurya-centric. We see its result in modern Bhārat, someone who converted to Buddhism with the masses to become 'a ruling class with religious zeal' to make the country Buddhist.

Gupta Period

The Gupta period is termed as the golden period only on the basis of the economic boom, but doesn't see 'out casting of people'.

Sangam Age

The Sangam age goes back to 600 BC, but no one is ready to accept. Another thing is that Sangam is the only age named after 'language-based literature', which has all Hindu aspects.

Rajput History

Table 5.4

Topics	Impact on the psychology of Hindus	Political intentions after independence	The way they are taught in history books with sweet poison
Those Hindu kingdoms who joined hands with the Mughals are covered in history books	Accept our supremacy	The dominance of the national party at the federal level too by curbing regionalism	Mughals were secular they gave job to Hindus too, but they don't mention those who didn't accept their supremacy were crushed (my way or highway logic)
Those who challenged Mughals are hardly mentioned or not covered in history books	'We are forever unchallenged' and 'we will be unchallenged' E.g., excluding the 5th to 11th centuries glory of Rajput empires, who defended Bharat from Arabs; partially teaching wars fought by Rana Pratap, who abruptly stopped history at the Haldighati war; Amar Singh (son of Rana Pratap); and the rebellion by Durgadas Rathod	No one can challenge the national or Central party in states	Mentioned as a merely small revolt in one line

Science of alliance and application of Table 5.4

Islamic rulers attacked Delhi and established the Delhi sultanate. They were merely looters with no vision, so they didn't last long. Mughals did come into an alliance with Hindu kings and used Hindu kings to expand their empire. But when you expand an empire only on the basis of alliances without establishing bravery/*purusharth*, then that also doesn't last long because alliances can break at any time. Can you compare the conditions of Babur, Aurangzeb, and FarrukhsSiyar? Just in 200 years, the whole game turned the other way.

But history books never mentioned this, and even if it was mentioned, credit is given to the Sayyid brothers rather than the warriors who attacked Delhi. A mistake that all Hindu kings made was placing Mughal royal blood always on the throne rather than capturing and sitting on it directly and starting Hindu rule. This might be because of the psychological supremacy created by the Mughals: 'We are made for the throne; we are unchallenged.'

Some things should be there while expanding or maintaining an empire, and one should use either of them or their combination according to the situation, time, space, and political wave. One should not take a stand permanently.

1. Going on the mission with full preparation directly as 'personality/ideology/plans' to prove bravery and power, e.g., the direct game of Afzal Khan and the surgical strike on Shaista Khan.
2. Sending someone else on a mission
   a. subordinates, e.g., Rajputs sent to Maharashtra by Mughals
   b. alliances, e.g., Chhatrapati Shivaji Maharaj (refer to A5.1, pp. 410–411) did alliances with Mughals and Adilshah on different occasions to create a fight between two foreign-origin empires. Siding with either of them, this avoided uniting two foreign powers against Chhatrapati Shivaji Maharaj (infidel).
3. Becoming kingmaker, e.g., Shahaji Maharaj changing teams under Adil Shahi, Nijam Shahi, and Mughals so that Bhārat never comes under a single umbrella; otherwise, it would have been difficult to uproot all invaders, so make them fight among themselves. If he had declared himself king, then all three would have united to kill an infidel.

4. Becoming king, e.g., crowning ceremony of Chhatrapati Shivaji Maharaj gave confidence to Hindus that we are not only politically alive somewhere but also established an empire so that others would also join the alliance.
5. If all the above options are not possible, then work under establishment, don't do anything against establishment socially, politically, or culturally, but maintain uniqueness with separatism under establishments, e.g., Shahaji Maharaj went to Bangalore, never worked against Adil Shahi, expanded Adil Shahi under expenditure of Adil Shahi, and never supported his own son, Shivaji Maharaj, directly. Once Chhatrapati Shivaji Maharaj became powerful, he expanded his empire till Thanjavur because his brother Vyankoji Raje succeeded as son of Shahaji Maharaj in the south.
6. When nothing is possible, then stay out of power and build a social base to uproot the existing empire, e.g., bhakti yogi Eknath Maharaj awareness through literature, Ramdas Swami constructed gyms and through literature, now-a-days non-Hindu religion, and communists in Bhārat.

Through history books, they created 'Mughalian interest' as mainstream interest, whereas the interests of indigenous people and their culture was sidelined. This is how 'Hindu interest' became sub-nationalism in modern Bhārat and Mughalian interest got satisfied, which was considered 'mainstream' or 'neutral'.

Every social evil related to Hindu society, like women's condition, the condition of Shudras, etc., was or is properly traced to Hindu books like *Manusmriti* and *Yagyavalakya smriti*, which creates the background for reservation for certain sections.

But following the things that happened to all Hindus, who will trace back injustice to the respective scriptures?
1. Concept infidel
2. Massacre of and atrocities on Hindus
3. Destruction of tangible and intangible culture of Hindus (cultural genocide)
4. Rapes, loots, kidnapping, sex slaves
5. Imposing tax on infidels

6. Curbing Hindu practices[1]
7. Forced state-sponsored proselytization of Hindus

My question to readers is, what is a more heinous crime? Caste discrimination, gender discrimination, lack of freedom to profess any religion, or crimes mentioned in the aforementioned list? Then why only caste became the basis for reservation?

In addition, 'safety valve' of negationism (damage control) is created so that no one tries to find a common theological pattern So that no one traces it back to any scripture.
1. Don't accept it happened
2. Don't mention it in history books
3. The army and administration were full of multi-religious people
4. There are also other temples that existed then and now
5. Mention but in lighter form (it was merely intolerance)
6. They also made some contribution in culture and nation
7. Accept it but limit it to personality, not motivated by 'religious teachings'
8. Accept it but in the mild form, e.g., few temples were destroyed, few people were killed or converted (small number)
9. Promoting falsehood: idol worship is wrong according to Hinduism itself
10. It was merely political clash or class conflict
11. Collateral damage (came to loot temple, not to destroy idol)
12. Struggle against regime and injustice
13. It was done to liberate Hindus from Brahminical control and Brahminical patriarchy, or to punish corrupt Brahmins
14. It was done because someone else invited to invade, loot, and destroy
15. It was destroyed or invaded because someone else provoked
16. It was done because someone else invited in alliance
17. It was done to crush rebels
18. Convincing Hindus to ignore the aforementioned crimes by imposing values like tolerance, inclusive, and acceptance on them by teaching them to tolerate/accept theologically motivated crimes even though no invaders inquired before invading whether their foreign policy is inclusive or exclusive (a sophisticated way of victim shaming).

This gives multiple gains.
1. Uncompromised expansion and no criticism. This is done so that no one traces a common pattern that is rooted in fundamentalism, so that Hinduism/civilization can be destroyed in a salami-slicing or decentralized way
2. Accepting mistakes gives space for two things: reforms and compensation for losses or reclaims for losses (reconstruction of temples). Delaying court procedure and reconstruction of temples (refer to A5.2, p. 411).
3. Silent support to culprits so that it can be repeated (see chapter 4 ending), i.e., team A will do crime and team B will justify, hide, and clean sins (whitewash by historians and media).[2]
4. Creating human capital that is merciless and justifies 'genocide and cultural genocide' with no sorrow, no grief, no repentance, no regret

Generally, while consolidating empires or converting others, people practice liberal belongingness (Akbar's way), and after consolidation, they apply fundamentalism (Aurangzeb's way). In a democracy, practice 'belongingness' when you are in the minority or are politically weak, but once you become the majority or politically strong, then fundamentalism is a reality. The problem is 'rather than focusing on integrated strategy, we tag people as liberal or orthodox'.

Table 5.5

Era	Liberalism and belongingness	Fundamentalism[3]
11th to 13th century AD	Sufism 1. Chishti silsila (khwaja Nizamuddin 1238–1325) 2. Suharavardi silsila (1097–1168)	After consolidation empires, discriminatory law imposed by state or kings 1. Religious tax on infidels 2. Pilgrimage tax 3. Destroying religious infrastructure

Era	Liberalism and belongingness	Fundamentalism[3]
15th to 17th century	Akbar promoted art, culture, music, and consolidated empire through alliances	Aurangzeb imposed discriminatory law 1. Religious tax 2. Pilgrimage tax 3. Destroying religious infrastructure of infidels
18th to 19th century	Mohammad Shah Rangila and his liberal activities and Mirza Ghalib	Rise and establishment of exclusive religion's schools of thought in north Bhārat, which promoted 'go back to fundamentals'
First half of the 20th century	Mohammad Ali Jinnah became symbol of Hindu–Muslim unity in 1920s	Formation of Pakistan in the 20th century, direct action day-fiery speeches which caused the death of more than 5,000 people (16 August 1946) 1. Huseyn Shaheed Suhrawardy 2. Khwaja Nizamuddin
Second half of the 21st century	Expanding religion in various continents in local languages through heavy funding	Eliminating local culture and making colony's culture same as the empire's capital's culture for better administration and uniform work culture
21st century in the world	Liberalism to get funds and to adjust self in world order	Fundamentalists are used to creating instability by various stakeholders for geopolitical gains
Pakistan	All citizens are equal with freedom of religion—M.A. Jinnah	After consolidation of nation, all minorities were eliminated including religious places

What people generally do is 'they are attracted towards belongingness and hate fundamentalism', but both are merely tools to achieve goals; what one must concentrate on is political tone, direction, and future.

Maratha History or Hindavi Swaraj

The same thing happened with 'Hindavi Swaraj' by Chhatrapati Shivaji Maharaja and Sikhs. Shivaji Maharaja's empire is termed the Maratha empire, which is actually 'Hindavi Swaraj', which ultimately culminated through a policy of reserving seats for Maratha in Bombay province just to create another minority pressure group, but Marathas never picked up a biscuit thrown by the British. It's a myth that Hindavi Swaraj and Mughals had no enmity against Islamic forces and Hinduism, respectively, because they also had an internal conflict, so it was only politics: Hindu vs. Hindu, Hindu vs. Muslim, and Muslim vs. Muslim, i.e., random political alliances and enmities. This 'myth' of random political alliances or enmities was told so that no one reached the 'fundamental truth', i.e., concept of infidel, the treatment to be given to infidel, and tangible/intangible culture.

This means that if Bhārat has internal conflicts, Pakistan and China are not enemies. It is just politics: Bhārtiya vs. Bhārtiya, China vs. Bhārat, Pakistan vs. Bhārat, etc. It has nothing to do with the sovereignty of the nation or the protection of constitutional supremacy. So, let's have a sweet policy with China and Pakistan because we have internal conflict, even though China is showing aggression.

When Chhatrapati Shivaji Maharaj's ancestry was proved right and confirmed by historians as 'Kshatriya' and his family tree was drawn, communists promoted a fake agenda—that, 'to declare him as king, contemporary Brahmins gave him fake ancestry, but actually, he was Shudra'—so that Marathas develop a sense of 'victimhood' and vote for communists. They only proved Chhatrapati Shivaji Maharaj a Shudra. What about other Marathas? Shinde, Pawar, Shisodiya, and Suryavanshi are surnames common in both Marathas and Rajputs, which means they are Kshatriya from different geographical locations.

Table 5.6

	Conversion of Marathas to communism from Hinduism	
Step 1	Projecting Chhatrapati Shivaji as a mere 'rebel'	

	Conversion of Marathas to communism from Hinduism	
Step 2	It was merely the Maratha empire, not Hindavi Swaraj.	
Step 3	Chhatrapati Shivaji Maharaj was not Kshatriya, he was a Shudra according to Brahmins. a. Genealogical records maintained by Brahmins (independent Bhatt), b. genealogy maintained by Rajput kingdoms. c. The genealogy mentioned in Puranas solar and lunar dynasties (Suryavanshi and Chandravanshi). All mention that his kula (family) was Kshatriya and all written by Brahmins. But Brahmins were pulled into conflict to create an 'anti-Brahmin' notion to transform Maratha into step 12.	2013
Step 4	Chhatrapati Shivaji Maharaj's empire was not for saving Hindus, he was secular because there were Muslims in his army, which means if you have Muslims around you then you can't/should not practice Hinduism.[4]	2014
Step 5	Chhatrapti Shivaji Maharaj's Hindavi Swaraj has nothing to do with an independent Hindu state.	2015
Step 6	Chhatrapati-. Shivajiraje's crowning ceremony was according to Buddhism (fake narrative on social media).	2016
Step 7	All Brahmins were against him by ignoring that Sawant (Maratha of Vadi), More (Maratha of Jawli), Mambaji Bhosle (Chhatrapti Shivaji Maharaj's cousin), Naikji Kate, and Ghadgesarkar were also against him even though they were Hindus. He was surrounded by almost 16 empires. But he was projected as anti-Brahmin or Brahmins as 'anti-Chhatrapati Shivaji' so that Marathas remain united and become a puppet to anti-Brahmin ideology for political gains in the current political scenario.	2017
Step 8	Chhatrapati Shivaji Maharaj ensured farmers' welfare, but communists never mention that he created shipbuilding industry, ammunition and arms industry, and 300 forts infrastructure in 50 years, because this creates a capitalist inclined image of Shivaji Maharaj so communist avoid this fact.	2018

	Conversion of Marathas to communism from Hinduism	
Step 8	Chhatrapati Shivaji Maharaj was projected as 'secular' even though he appointed Panditrao as 1/8 minister to see the affairs related to Hinduism. This is completely opposite of 'pope and state should be separate'. Shivaji Maharaj's model was 'non-secular liberalism' (see chapter 3). From 'Jai Bhawani Jai Shivaji', Marathas themselves eliminated Jai Bhawani.	2019
Step 9	Rich Marathas were the enemies of poor Marathas. Rich vs. poor divide gave a touch of 2-level communist model and made Marathas fight among one another.	2020
Step 10	Direct offer to Marathas by Maoist to join hands with communism and take arms in hand if you don't get a reservation (demand of reservation is right of every Bhārtiya, but this table is about how Marathas, the saviour of Hinduism, were turned into 'communist')[5]	2021
Step 11	Marathas are not Hindus, just like Sikhs are not Hindus, Tamils are not Hindus, etc.[6]	2023
Step 12	Marathas change religion to either 'misinterpreted Buddhism' and communism, so that all the income of Marathas goes as political funding to these two.	2025

Just as 'missionaries' project their god in various skin colours, facial features, and clothing as per local culture for mass acceptance, the 'manifesto of religion' remains constant. Similarly, communists choose local culture, local heros, and local leadership for user-friendly mass support. Ultimately what remains constant is 'communism'. This is what I call the 'Great Transformation: Chhatrapati Shivajiraje Bhonsle to Comrade Shivaji'—the saviour of Hinduism to the communist leader.[7] A successful experiment where the 'conversion' of a late leader will lead to the conversion of present followers. This also happened in the case of Carvaka, Buddhism, and Samkhya, as they were projected as atheists. Just like Buddhism was used as a social base by communists, a similar thing happening with Marathas. All this was easily convinced because Marathas lost connection with history and culture related to 96 kula (family).

When the history of Hinduism and other allied sects is taught, it should be taught as a civilization because it is a reality, and when Islam and Christianity come, they should be taught as motivated by the book because it is a reality. But unfortunately, it's taught the completely opposite way in history books, with ideologies dividing the majority and uniting the minority. The history of Bhārat should not be written about any empire or book; it should horizontally cover all areas and vertically cover all time with no bias.

Table 5.7

Factors	Hinduism	Islam	Misinterpreted Buddhism	Communists
Leader or king in history books		Islamic kings, Sufi saints	Ashoka and Buddha	Karl Marx's *Communist Manifesto* (Table 1.1, p. 5)
Ideology/philosophy	Social hierarchy based on caste society and post-Buddhist bhakti movement	Teaching through religious books or institutions	Teachings of Buddhism taught in history books	Ideology through history books
Social base	Discriminatory caste system	Religious brotherhood, equality, peace, Sufism	Social base united under him	Union of all victims, weaker sections, labour, minority
Social issues	Identified and being solved (this is how only Hindus were made tolerant through criticism)	They are perfect no social issues and freedom of religion is there	They are perfect, no social issues, and freedom of religion is there	They are super perfect

One group deliberately was made 'progressive attitude, tolerance, compromise, etc.' and other 'intolerant, uncompromised'. This influences judiciary and law implementing agencies to interfere in the issues/practices, civil and criminal laws, resource exploitation of only tolerant community to avoid violence.[8] In terms of psychology, this is called as 'guilt tripping'. Every religion has its territory; if Hinduism is criticized then battlefield will be 'Hindu land'. Territory of other religions will never be interfered in.

So that Hindus are cheated, and they start a separatist movement in Bhārat, which actually happened. Why will Hindus feel proud when there is nothing in history to feel proud about; this is how Hindus were made intellectually impotent. Others were loaded with motivation to establish their theocracy, as mentioned in the book according to the Table 5.8.

This created the invisibilization of the umbrella identity Hinduism and hyper visibilization of foreign faiths, sub-sects-castes within Hinduism as rebels against Hinduism that Hinduism is orthodox and sub-sects are heterodox (refer to Table 1.1, p. 5). We never questioned it because Hinduism was projected passively as 'pessimistic' and rest of the heterodox schools and non-Hindu faiths as 'optimistic' in history books. This culminated into 'preferential treatment' to 'heterodox and non-Hindu faiths' in the spheres of political representation, human rights, institutionalization, International institution, ethnocentric development indicators, etc.

Hinduphobic Social Engineering in History Books

History books are not about evolution of civilization but about 'dissolution', where pre-Aryan atheists (original Dravidians), Buddhism, Jainism, Charvaka, Ajivika, Bhakti Yoga, Sikhism, lower caste, everyone is shown as a rebel against autocratic, authoritative, casteist, or polytheistic Vedas and leaving Hinduism one by one. Rather than teaching their own philosophy, these sects were taught as 'anti-caste, monotheistic, or atheistic morality' up against Hinduism. The same division is reflected at the political, social, and geopolitical level as secessionist tendencies (refer to p. 184). You have seen seen this play out at the time of Independence as Dalit–Muslim unity against upper-caste Brahmin Congress leaders in colonial period (Hindu equals Brahmin, according to them).[9, 10]

Jews–Muslim–Christian and Hinduism–Buddhism–Jainism–Sikhism should be two groups on the basis of geographic evolution, but in my school history books, Islam–Buddhism–Jainism were taught one after the another in a single chapter in medieval history book but Hinduism was not covered either in ancient or medieval history holistically.[11] (Dividing the majority and shifting faiths from the basket of Hinduism to that of foreign religions). It is clearly visible that history books were used as a medium to create 'anti Hindu' mindset and social-engineering setup for anti-Hindu left-inclined politics. Today, it is clearly visible that all these social groups are represented by anti-Hindu political setup, where Hinduism is the culprit and the rest of the people have moral, religious, and ideological obligations to fight with it.

Discriminatory Appreciation of Architecture

This appeasement politics of supporting minority against majority didn't stop throwing light on historical records discriminately. But also in case of appreciating the architecture of Bhārat by international institutions that are in the hands of the West. In the case of Islamic architecture in Bhārat, it is architecture, which is explained with details and heritage site status, but in the case of Hindu temples, it is expressed in terms like:
1. Dravidian temple
2. Temple with the name of deity
3. Temple with the name of the king who constructed it
4. Temple identified with little architectural details
5. Temples' list state wise
6. No entry to particular jati (nothing wrong in criticizing it but sectorial divides of other religions not mentioned regarding entry in religious places)
7. Way of wealth collection by Brahmins
8. Nagara-style temple, etc.

The term 'Hindu' is hardly used to refer to temple.

Table 5.8

Hindu temples include following things which are carved on rock and are never or generally not told in history books in any detail	Pietra Dura
3D carving of humans and animals (any carving can be done no limitations)	It is a method of 2D carving

Hindu temples include following things which are carved on rock and are never or generally not told in history books in any detail	Pietra Dura
With minute expression, emotions, activities	Flowers and leaves are the only things that are created
Proper spherical and cylindrical shapes with complete symmetry	The above two points are repeated on a large scale with not much diversity, so symmetry is obvious outcome; spherical shape, multi-diameter cylinders are hardly found
Jewelry, micro holes, minute details on body, also in 3D	No minute or micro details as compared to temples, not even in 2D
The way the temple is constructed, through reverse engineering, creates a question in mind what tools they used to carve it. As atheism, anti-temple, idol worship is wrong, the temple is a business of Brahmins. This discourages the carving profession and eliminates the community from mainstream economy.	Today also Pietra Dura can be done 'art of making is alive'
Things carved on temple are subjected to deep decoding, not all temples are merely multiple deities carved on the temple; there are many things that are subjected to decoding	No detailed decoding is required only flowers, leaves, and some objects
Many temples have such wonders like, e.g., a. Panchganga in Mahabaleshwar where 5 rivers' water enters in temples after 12 years (approximately) and no one knows how? b. There is one temple where the flame comes from underground, i.e., Jwaladevi temple. c. Rajput forts and some personal areas of forts have 'precious stones'. d. Golden temple of Amritsar and Lakshmi Narayani temple of Tamil Nadu, itself has taken bath in gold.	It includes putting 'precious stones' in the carving only no other geographical, science-based mystery included like the Panchaganga and Jwaladevi temples.

Hindu temples include following things which are carved on rock and are never or generally not told in history books in any detail	Pietra Dura
Types of temples: a. The whole temple is carved out as a monolith. b. The complete uniform colour of all rocks in temples even when it's not a monolith. c. Underground temples, cave temples, and underwater temples.	a. There is no monolith. b. Multiple rocks used of same category do not have uniform colour (multiple shades of white which looks like overnight architecture). c. No underground, underwater, caves made
This difference is never compared because temples and Pietra Dura are taught on different technical points so that comparison never takes place. This is how with complete political approach 'Pietra Dura' is made a heritage site and given wonder status.	
Solution 1. There is a need to measure architecture with various new criteria in terms of quality and quantity, diversity, uniformity, etc. 2. According to the new criteria, a ranking should be given. 3. Need to create our own list of the heritage sites in Bhārat, which will not only give heritage status to Bhārtiya architecture but to other countries' architecture too. Such a list needs to be created in Bhārat as well as international platforms like SAARC, ASIAN, SCO, BIMSTEC, BRICS, etc. We need to create an unbiased attitude towards architecture because Western countries do appeasement politics in the case of history and culture so that Bhārat's identity politics are under their control.	

Bhārtiya history must look like the rise of civilization, not empire, books, or personality. Students of history will only have the impact of these three things. Only history goes much beyond that. The liberal view is required in history, not the British agenda, which is carried forward by the many 'Indians'.

Discrimination with Titles

They say suffix and prefix titles should not be used when the king is mentioned so that equality is maintained and bias is removed towards anyone. Let's see the implementation.

Table 5.9

Real names	Name with titles/ popularly known as/ titles	Name in history books
Zahir-ud-din Muhammad	Babur (tiger in Persian)	Babur
Abu'l-Fath Jalal-ud-din Muhammad	Akbar (supreme king)	Akbar
Mirza Nasirud-din Baig Muhammad Khan	Humayun (blessed/ auspicious)	Humayun
Mirza Nur-ud-din Beig Mohammad Khan Salim	Jahangir (universe king)	Jahangir
A'la Azad Abul Muzaffar Shahabud-Din Mohammad	Shah Jahan (king of the world)	Shah Jahan
Abdul Muzaffar Muhi-ud-Din Mohammad	Aurangzeb (ornament of the throne)	Aurangzeb
British viceroy, governor, commissioner	Sir, lord	Lord Minto
Shivajiraje Shahajiraje Bhosle (Raje is a hereditary family title not artificially given)	Chhatrapati (crowned king on the throne) Shivaji Maharaj.[12]	Shivaji (this might have been done so that in the future 'comrade' can be used as a prefix)
Sambhajiraje, Shivajiraje Bhosle	Chhatrapati (crowned king throne) Sambhaji Maharaj	Sambhaji

Real names	Name with titles/ popularly known as/ titles	Name in history books
Śaṅkarā	Ādi Śaṅkarācārya	Śaṅkarā[13]
Siddhartha Gautama	Buddha	Buddha[14]

They just don't accept that these were 'crowned king' (Chhatrapti Shivajiraje and Ch. Sambhajiraje); they just say these were small rebels. This is a British trick to declare someone an illegitimate king so that his throne and empire can be finished (the doctrine of lapse). Now this is being applied to Chhatrapti Shivaji Maharaja in history books. Chhatrapti Sambhaji Maharaja was that man whose presence and absence both finished the Mughal empire. In chapters 8, 14, and 19, you will find the contribution of Ādi Śaṅkarācāryaḥ (dialogue and debate, critical questioning) rather than monologue/sermon to followers. Yet, Hinduism is marketed as a Brahminical imposition, autocratic, and authoritative rule; on the other hand, monologues, sermons, and revelations (i.e., unidirectional lectures) were marketed as democratic. This is how stereotypes about the 'sociopolitical space' of Hinduism/Hindus are created in a latent form in history books. This kind of history books, where there is no level-playing field for Hindus, are called 'neutral history books before saffronization'.

Foundation of Khalistan in Culture Books

In art culture book, which is widely used for civil services examinations, the writer (Nitin Singhania, IAS) writes:
1. Guru Nanak gave an organized fight/opposition to Hindu religion.
2. Initially, Mughal–Sikh relations were very cordial, but the execution of Guru Arjan Dev on Jahangir's orders became a cause of dispute.[15]

The reality is that Guru Nanak never organized a fight against Hindu religion, i.e., Sikhs were not organized initially as they were organized as Khalsa under Guru Gobind Singh. Guru Nanak went to all religious places Hindu and Muslim in Tibet, Bhārat, Pakistan, and Baghdad. He spent time with yogis who invited him to sadhana and siddhi prāpti; he refused that because he was of the opinion that in lowlands people are suffering and one must serve humanity. Even if Hindus and Sikhs were extremely exploited and physically tortured, Hindus and Sikhs never introduced the concept of infidel in their respective books; they always kept 'universal brotherhood' as an eternal value. Guru Nanak called Babur as Jabar (invader, exploiter). Sikh had no cordial relations with the Mughals, the whole Sikh tradition is a symbol of sacrificing life to save the land from the injustice of the Mughals and establish an empire of justice, truth, and universal brotherhood. Such a fake allegation on Sikh gurus who were badly tortured and killed is a shameful thing, even when most of the people who joined Khalsa were Hindus, i.e., Banda Bahadur was a yogi who turned into a warrior. Therefore, one must not project Hinduism and Sikhism as separated by strict walls of religion (Abrahamic pentagon). Nitin Singhania teaches Sikhism as a separate religion, even when the constitution includes Sikhs under the Hindu tradition because of its historic evolution and the content of the Guru Granth Sahib being based on enlightenment, where most of the terminologies are from Hinduism.

So the whole propaganda is hiding the reality of 'destroying infidels and their culture' and creating an artificial picture of 'Hindus vs. Why I am not Hindu', so that Hindus fight among themselves. But those two allegations or passive propaganda somewhere conveys that Sikhs should go away or fight with Hindus and go close towards Islam, even though Guru Granth Sahib includes many Sanskrit and Hindu terms like moksha. So the journey of Sikhs starts from the Hindu majority state (Bhārat) to the Muslim majority state (Pakistan), i.e., Khalistan propaganda of Pakistan.

The common man of this country, irrespective of religion, is very innocent; he avoids communalism most of the time (only if he is a non-fundamentalist), but the so-called liberal historians create 'discriminatory history' with political goals that are according to blueprints given by colonial masters. Weaken the majority psychologically, numerically, socially, and culturally, and unite the minority on the same basis. Race to become non-indigenous.

God save this country from the Rwandan episode.

PART II
REALITY OF SOCIETY, ECONOMY, AND POLITY

6

Humanity: The Lowest Value of the Universe

There are two types of societies: anthropocentrism (human are at the centre, and the interests of humanity are highest; it's not ecology but resources are made for humans) and biocentrism (humans and other creatures share ecology equally).

Figure 6.1

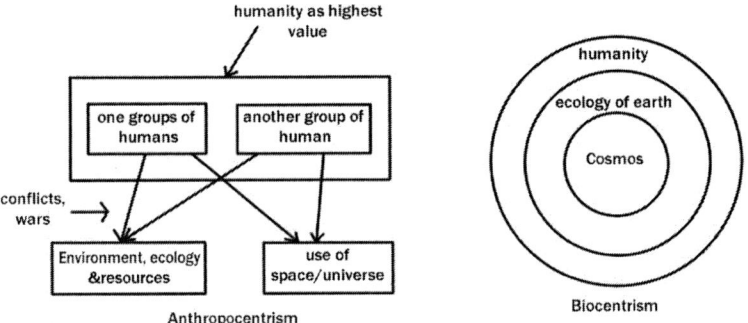

When I saw the sustainable development goals (SDG) of the United Nations, there were sustainable from no angle because sustainability itself means goals that lead to sensible use of resources while developing. The name of the SDG must be changed to 'exploitation of resources by keeping distributive justice in mind'. Out of seventeen SDGs, only goals 7, 11, 12, 13, 14, and 15 somewhere speak about sustainability. The remaining eleven goals are challenges within humanity; they have nothing to do with life beyond humans, i.e., animals, insects, plants, ecology, space, and the universe.

Table 6.1

Examples of anthropocentricism (shallow ecology)		Examples of biocentrism (deep ecology)	
Philosophy	Reasons	Philosophy	Reasons
Exclusive/ ethnocentric religions with poor natural resources	1. Rebel from previous and contemporary cultures so their existence is relative to each other (faith-based differences in human society) 2. Expansionary policy because of 'poor natural resources' background so philosophy promotes capturing resources as they are created by God for followers	Hinduism, few tribal cultures, indigenous survival practices	They have arranged themselves as per existing ecology and they live in a symbiosis with ecology rather than superior exploitative over ecology
1. Humanism 2. Democracy is the political name of humanism (fundamental rights of only humans, not ecology)	Rebel from exploitative teachings of religion by keeping 'human-centric approach'	Ecuador, Bolivia	Rights of nature in the constitution
Capitalism	Humans are consumers of their products so by nature capitalism is human-centric	The city of Pittsburgh, Pennsylvania, Municipality of USA	Rights of nature recognized
Communism	Distributive justice among humans	Economic model	At present, there is no think tank that will think about new eco-economic world order
Few tribal cultures	Zoom farming		

Examples of anthropocentricism (shallow ecology)		Examples of biocentrism (deep ecology)	
Philosophy	Reasons	Philosophy	Reasons
Science and technology	Developed according to industry and consumer needs	Eco-science and technology (my innovation)	Manufacturing of product according to consumer need by keeping 'carbon footprint' and effect on the environment
Climate change		No danger of climate change	

The package of SDG looks like the new year budget of the nation with 65 per cent budget allocation for the development of citizens and 35 per cent budget for collateral damage, while development and government call it sustainable development. The United Nations is also bound by the dogma of anthropocentrism.

Bhārat is gifted with diversity of ecology and fertile land, which is why there is diversity of resources, and because of that, there are various professions to make use of that, which is reflected in terms of the jati system. Even with this much diversity, Hinduism never turned that system into haphazard and random use, which may reflect climate change. That is because Hinduism created a belief system that is based on collectivism rather than individualism, avoiding multiple infrastructures for the same person with multiple identities, which ultimately culminates in minimum consumerism. The best teaching of the Bhārtiya subcontinent was 'Greed is bad habit', which ultimately ended up being 'consume according to need and maximum use with modification so that new product or resource exploitation is avoided' (in modern terms, 'right to repair').

When I said 'avoiding multiple resource infrastructure and resources for the same person with multiple identities' what does it actually mean?

In Hinduism, professional life, family life, protocol to be followed in profession, protocol to be followed in family life and society, infrastructure of family or personal life, infrastructure of professional life, dress code in official and unofficial life—all these multiple identities and multiple aspects are reflected just by one word, which is jati, by avoiding multiplicity or duplication of efforts. Hindu human capital exists as a synthesis of personal and professional life.

The modern-world system is the outcome of the consumeristic value system, which is the outcome of capitalism. Those are individualism and duplication/triplication of all aspects of life in terms of official and unofficial just to increase consumerism for profits. Material life, code of conduct, infrastructure, hierarchy of systems, language, value systems—all these are separate in the Western, modern, or capitalist model to promote consumerism. This multiplicity culminates in a modern democratic political system that expands horizontally as bicameralism and vertically as a decentralized political setup. When we overdo it, it culminates in duplication of efforts.

Western modern systems of society are divided into two categories: professional and personal. Personal lifestyle is defined in a generalized way, e.g., liberty, fraternity, justice, fundamental rights etc., and professional life is defined separately in a specification and specialist way. In Hinduism, there was no separate distinction between personal and professional life; it was one and the same as defined by jati and varna. The only deliberate mistake historians made was that they never promoted Hinduism's personal universalist value system of the Upaniṣhads and Vedas and the rights of women and men as per the Shastra's but only showed how Hinduism promotes discrimination. For example, 'Sarve Sukhina Bhavantu' (let peace and prosperity belong to everyone). Appreciation of the right things and criticism of the wrong things must go hand in hand.

Table 6.2 A Western model of the duplication of efforts

This separation is origin of capitalism, communism, democracy	Professional/ official life/ economic life	Personal/ unofficial life/ social life
Material life and fashion	✓	✓
Family relation	-	✓
Profession relation	✓	-

Code of conducts	✓	Liberty
Infrastructure	✓	✓
Hierarchy of system	✓	Equality
Tone of language	✓	Fraternity
Value system	Professional ethics	Humanity
Political stand	✓	Different than professional
Skill development, trade union, arbitration	✓	-
Social security	✓	-
Social status and hierarchy	✓	Equal as mentioned by respective constitution
Economic status	✓	✓

Table 6.3 The Hindu system of society

Integrated approach no doubling of efforts	Professional and personal life same = jati/socio-economic life
Material life and fashion	✓
Family and profession relation	✓ same as jati
Infrastructure	✓
Hierarchy of system	✓
Language	✓
Value system	✓
Political stand	✓
Skill development	✓ hereditary
Trade union and social security	✓ jati wise
Arbitration or dispute resolution	✓ 5 heads body of jati
Social and economic status are one and the same	✓

From Table 6.3, you will know why dharma shastra or Hindu society has the following things:
1. Why will one only get married into his jati (endogamy)?
2. Why can one's jati interfere in personal life because professional and personal life are one and the same?
3. Why are there strict protocols of separation between two jatis because their personal and professional lives are one and the same?
4. Why does a person with a particular jati have a particular dress code?
5. Why does a person of a particular jati have a separate devata and culture, festival, e.g., farmers celebrate harvest festivals, and so do the other communities according to geography. You need to know that Hindus only celebrate three things as festivals: ecological, cosmological, and economical changes. Why does every jati have separate meetings and celebrations—party, dinner?
6. Why does jati have a dispute resolution body?[1]
7. Why does the jat panchayat pass orders on personal issues?

To disgrace Hinduism, mediocre historians mention it as Hinduism based on hierarchy and has a code of conduct according to that which is against equality and humanity, but they don't mention its role as a profession or avoiding duplication of resources. By avoiding duplication of resources, followers of Hinduism never faced ethical dilemmas or conflicts of interest; this is how the value system is coded in the jati system. That is why for Modern corporates 9 to 5 is a job, not life, because their personal value system of liberty, fraternity, freedom, and equality gets destroyed by hierarchy and a code of conduct. Many people also enjoy integrating themselves with the organization. But in Hinduism, there is no such duplication. But as of today, there is no jati system in urban areas because Bhārat is on the path of capitalism. The economic value of jati vanishes because people are choosing modern jobs in industry, so jati is only a social identity, and that is also becoming faded as there is no economic rationale to follow it. Rural and tribal areas are not industrialized, which is why the old system of running economies still exists in many places. That is why the jati system exists in rural and tribal areas.

Consumeristic and Conservative

The consumeristic model of society, even though it separates personal and professional life, still has inequality in various forms, like income inequality, the glass ceiling for women, overtime, disturbances to the biological clock, etc. So those who say that by accepting French Revolution values and a modern constitution, they got liberation from the old discriminatory system are having opium for the Western bookish value system. People do face new inequalities and problems at their place of profession. Even though there is liberalism by breaking the limits of endogamy, 'new endogamy' is also evolving somewhere as per the modern profession, which we cannot deny.

If we want to create a modern society and they want to boost GDP by transforming into an organized sector with high tax collection, they should follow the models of consumerism and multiplier effect. If the world wants to move towards an eco-friendly lifestyle, then follow the Hindu way of avoiding duplication in cases like infrastructure and material life wherever possible. I know it's not always possible to work from home, but an excess of digitization and a city in one building concept can lead to minimizing the use of resources.

The Myth of Ultimate Truth

Hinduism never claims it has a set of values that are universal and ultimate because such branding is needed for those religions whose teachings don't have technical scientific soundness, so they avoid criticism and debate by calling it universal or ultimate truth. What they actually do is 'give a set of rules and teachings under the heading of ultimate truth so that followers follow them without questioning', but they don't know what truth is or what the process of reaching the truth is. That is why when the modern judiciary gives judgement on religious cases, religious sentiments are hurt because what they believe is the ultimate truth is merely religious teaching without a critical approach. How can the truth be one? Two or three? Case-by-case, the truth changes in court. That is why what religions brand as the ultimate truth is merely their teachings.

Hinduism has inbuilt multiple methods of reaching truth or processes of defining truth. These methods are used to verify texts, definitions of oneness, arguments given, or even can be used in the modern non-conservative world.

First method: pramanas
1. Pratyakṣa (perception)
2. Anumāṇa (inference)
3. Upamāṇa (comparison and analogy)
4. Arthāpatti (postulation, derivation)
5. Anupalabdi (void or absence)
6. Śabda (reliable testimony)

Six pramanas are like six judges on the Supreme Court's bench, which give judgement with one pramana representing each judge. Cārvāka represents 'Pratyaksha', but unfortunately, politically biased history books equate him with 'contempt of court' rather than judge with dissenting opinion, i.e., rebel against establishment to create an 'atheistic/ materialistic parallel' in ancient society (Table 1.1), which will motivate the reader to 'rebel' against their own culture.[2] Cārvāka does not deny other pramanas, he just says everything shall be verified by Pratyaksha pramana. But reality is that many times Pratyaksha pramana also fails, so all pramanas exist as safety valves for each other. Role of Cārvāka/ Pratyaksa pramana is verifying authenticity of the Vedas/journey of liberation, but 'Cārvāka' (the one who chews) is projected as ISIS/ Taliban terrorist who destroys every tangible or intangible culture existed before him by keeping him in basket of heterodox school of Western framework of binary, orthodox (God and religion) and heterodox (atheists and rebels against religion).[3] As reforms are not possible in those religions as everything is revelation of god, so deny the god (Atheism) so you deny revelations. (Refer Table 1.1)

Second method: theory of error[4]
Almost all the Mimamsa, Advaita, etc., have this theory to confirm and verify the nature of oneness and the material world. They question, argue about perceptions, etc.

Third method: pramanyavād [5]
To verify knowledge through internal and external verification.

Fourth methor: verification criteria of mantra
a. ūpakrama – beginning
b. ūpasamhara – conclusion
c. abhyāsa – repetitive things
d. āpoorvata – not mentioned earlier
e. phala – consequent result
f. arthavāda – core of the matter

It's like whether a mantra satisfies structure or not. This safety valve or self-improving, checks and balance, critical inquiry-inbuilt model of Hinduism helps Hindus transform as per time and adopt a scientifically and practically correct lifestyle that culminates in an inclusive, eco-friendly, shared interest-based lifestyle.

Table 6.4

	Manifestation of anthropocentrism religion	Manifestation of biocentrism approach
Actual product	Calendars, festivals, and all other dimensions based on 'personality cult' rather than season, atmosphere, ecology, and science	All festivals, calendars and dimensions are 'ecology and cosmos' based. (200 years back Irrespective of Jati, people knew Cosmic Calendar)
Marketed as	Humanity is the highest value, revelation by God, message given by personality, teachings given by personality	Unfortunately, no marketing strategy

Factors that Decide the Celebration of Festivals in Hinduism/Biocentrism (Integrated Multilayer Data Science)

1. Sowing, crop growth, irrigation, rainfall, harvesting, selling, high tide, low tide—all activities are celebrated in Hinduism, e.g., Diwali, Holi, Pongal, Onam, Bihu, and Makar Sankranti (all harvesting festivals).

2. Changes in atmosphere and seasons are celebrated in Hinduism, e.g., Makar Sankranti, Shravan, Sharad Purnima, Diwali, and Narli Purnima (all festivals mark changes in atmosphere and season where people change their consumption patterns according to the season, which ensures health and crop diversity and gives time to animals for breeding).
3. Celebrating change in cosmic patterns (rotation, location, and constellations) and their formations, especially those which reflect changes in the earth's atmosphere and climate.
4. Ecological observation: the bearing of new foliage, animal breeding, and other such indicators were used as indications that a festival was coming.
5. Convergence/conducive point of spirituality: a point where one can experience oneness, e.g., Mahashivratri and upavas on certain occasion.[6]
6. Puranas, Rāmāyaṇa, Mahābhārata, Upanishads, and Vedas: all the stories and history from these books are associated with every festival, which gives it a cultural and philosophical touch.

That's why if Hindus lose geography, they lose Hinduism, and geography is being lost through 'demography alteration' or conversion. There are some anti-Hindus who market Hinduism as Brahmin colonialism/Brahminism and demand further decolonization by eliminating Hinduism. What will they eliminate, 'Ganga, Himalaya, atmosphere, climate, constellation, Ayurveda, and biology'? At the same time, there are also people who keep Hindu festivals, etc., in the basket of their regional or linguistic identity. From the above six points, you can infer that there is no linguistic or regionalist factor.

What linguistic extremism and regionalism has given you? Fights between national and regional parties, tolerance towards proselytization of Hindus, and alienation from Hinduism and other states?

Application of Biocentrism

Hindu civilization arranged our books, lifestyle, multiple personalities, and their stories (not personality cults) according to ecology and the cosmos. Even while planning the smallest things of life like birth and marriage to the biggest things like infrastructure building, wars, and buying products, Hindus follow festivals and cosmic calculations (astronomy). This ensures consumption patterns are in a pattern according to ecology and the cosmos, which also brings certainty to the economy, especially if you are a producer. All Hindus will buy products on the same day today, which brings a sense of cultural, social, and political unity too. This culture is followed by all Hindus, related sects, or pseudo-rebels. Not only humans but even infrastructures are built on the same logic; if you see certain temples in Bhārat like Kolhapur Ambabai Temple, only on a particular day every year will sunlight fall on her feet. Because of climate change, seasons are changing and other things are not happening at the right time, so failure of the mechanism of ecology can be observed through these festivals, especially by rural-traditional Hindus. Today, we have lost that traditional knowledge about ecology. Hindu festivals are indicators that draw the attention of the masses to changes in ecology (bio indicators) and its relation to cosmic patterns (astronomy).

Anthropocentrism and Its Application

Whereas religions arrange calendars, lifestyles, festivals that are based on a personality cult and their respective activities and events, ecology is merely a means and cosmology is ignored as seasons and atmosphere on earth happen irrespective of planetary position (according to them). If we seek God's blessings on festivals, then what does God do on other days? Unfortunately, many religions don't have technical soundness about value systems, so they forcefully make religions exist through the following nine points (refer to pp. 247–248).

Fixing Hinduism in the same framework as other religions is not technically correct as Hinduism has a completely different set of values in terms of ecology, astronomy, festivals, etc.

Does the Movement of Planets and Stars Affect Humans?

First of all, how is it possible that the motion and location of planets, natural satellites, and stars can create changes in tide, seasons, atmosphere, and temperature, but saying that it doesn't affect living beings means we are considering that living and non-living beings exist in isolation. Hinduism considers 'gravitational force' exerted by other planets and its effect on earth and calculates daily routine and events as per that whether it effects us or not; that's another part, but making that complex calculation as part of routine makes these concepts 'alive' and makes people enlightened about these deep concepts on a day-to-day basis. In the case of gravity, there is the possibility of 'certain patterns' like LaGrange's point or stable gravity. Maybe ancient masters have such calculations in mind because they were already aware of the rotation speed of planets. Life/ecology is the summation of all internal and external forces and factors, so considering it independent of all external factors, etc. doesn't sound sensible.

In Hinduism, people will tell when rain will happen by looking at the nakshtra, i.e., calculating or predicting ecological change by looking at the cosmos. When the Hindu economy and belief system are based on ecology, they are definitely connected to cosmology too.[7]

There are nine phenomena, which include stars, planets, and phases, which impact us by their position and gravitational force are taken in consideration.[8] Therefore, navagrahan ≠ 9 planets. The navagrahas actually include:

- Surya (Sun)
- Chandra (Moon)
- Mangala (Mars)
- Budh (Mercury)
- Brahaspati (Jupiter)
- Shukra (Venus)
- Shani (Saturn)
- Rahu (ascending node of the moon)
- Ketu (descending node of moon)

Each navagraga has been associated with a character or deity with the same name, and temples are also associated with it. You can learn Hindu concepts like solar and lunar calandars, the logic behind the calculation of days, muhurta, details of astronomy, and velocity of planets in short YouTube videos.[9]

Day Calculation

1/27,60,48,00,000 (1 Manvantara = 71* Yuga) = 1/1,55,52,00,000 (4 Yuga) = 1/129600 Dev varsha = 1/360 Devahoratra = 1 day = 3 prahara (8 each) = 30 muhurta = 2 ghaTyaH = kalAH = 30 KaShTHAH = 30 TatpaRAH = 100 trutiH whereas 1 turtiH is 29.6 microseconds.

As per our context, we use various micro and macro measurements, like classical singers using prahara to sing certain ragas, muhurta used for puja, etc. Doing particular things at a particular time and its effect can be experienced by great yogis. The logic behind calculating and doing something in a particular 'time frame' can be understood in the following way:

Table 6.5

To place an object or to carry out an event under stable condition			
1.	When both object/earth and celestial bodies are static	Only space is important to avoid attraction/repulsion towards any gravity	This is what non-believers of astrology believe because they don't consider relative existence; they think that we exist in uninfluenced isolation.
2.	One object moving and other static	Time is important while placing object in a particular position	Train passing on platform on which you are standing

To place an object or to carry out an event under stable condition			
3.	Both the objects are moving	Space + time = moment	This is what Hindu astronomy, or Panchanga, is based on, which gives events and dates at particular points. As all planets are moving, one has to carry some event on one particular alignment of planets. A planet or space remains constant for a small part of time which we call *muhurta*. Modern concepts like 'dynamic stability' are quite similar to this. I expect more research on this by space experts.

What Astrology Decides: Destiny?

Diagram 6.2

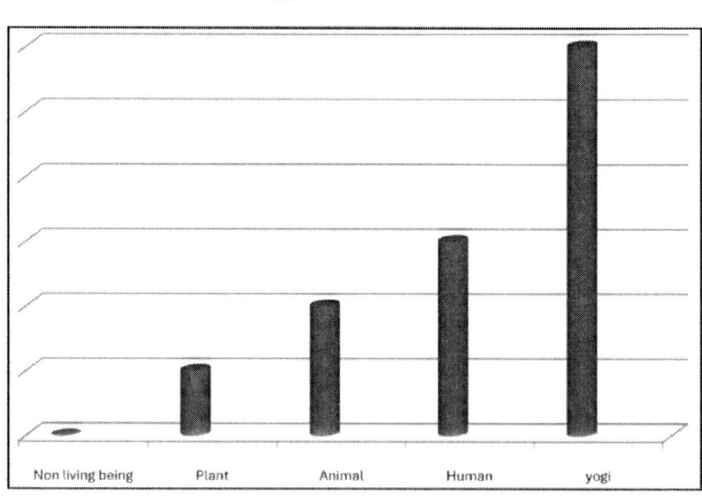

The level of consciousness is different in all things, as shown in Diagram 6.2. As the level of consciousness changes, the level of experiencing other factors, like cosmic events, also increases. Some astrologers do predict future and past events. People have multiple opinions.

Table 6.6

Objects	Ability	Functioning of ability	Implementation
Material	No consciousness	They don't react nor can oppose things happening to them	Destiny decision: material>plant>animal human> yogi The destiny of material is decided by all external factors, including gravity. As we move towards yogi, 'will' increases, which challenges destiny-decided natural factors. That is, 'development of consciousness within' increases 'will power'. That is why a yogi, who has only consciousness, can do anything. Independence is all about minimizing negative internal and external impact and maximizing positive internal and external impact. Modern science tells us that coronal mass ejections, solar flares, geomagnetic storms, cosmic rays, which do affect activities on Earth. E.g., phases of high tide and low tide affect coastal communities.
Plant	Have little consciousness so they have little will	They change according to climate and atmosphere; they have adaption capacity but can't resist change	
Animal	They have more consciousness than plants so they have will and willpower	They react, adapt, change, and resist.	
Human	They have a consciousness so will and willpower are very natural	They react, adapt, change, resist, and challenge.	
Liberated yogi (siddhi achieved)	They have only consciousness and no material aspect. So, their will is will power and will power is real.	They change, react, resist, challenge, and manifest will irrespective of rules.	

Humanity-centric approach, exclusivist religions, capitalism, and communism, all together, are exploitative towards 'ecology' and ignorant towards the cosmos. Hinduism remains the only civilization to align itself as per cosmos and ecology, i.e., most scientific lifestyle.

Table 6.7

Conclusion of Hinduism		Why is 'circle' everywhere?
Approach towards	**Diagram**	'Synergetic approach, convergence, minimum resources, and maximum output, considering all stakeholders, integrated approach, seamless, unified approach, holistic approach, eco-friendly' etc., are satisfied by the only 'circle'. Circle/sphere has a minimum surface area and is most smooth in movement and functioning. That is why when anything is represented in a circular format, it adopts the qualities of a circle. E.g.: 1. Minimum surface area for maximum volume, i.e., minimum government, maximum governance. 2. All points are at equal distance from the centre, i.e., symmetric. Similarly, the hub-and-spoke model or point-to-point model are able to shape outcomes. (refer to p. 153).
Ecology	Circular Diagram 6.1	
Economy	Circular economy (100% waste recycle)	
	Circular diagram of Table 7.12	
	Self-sustaining village economy	
Society	Circular Diagram 7.2	
Philosophy	Circular Diagram 19.1 (third diagram)	
Mukti/ liberation	Circular Diagram 19.1	
Quantum nature of reality	Circular Diagram 14.2	
Concept of infinity	Represented by 'bindu'/circle/dot rather than '∞', which is dual in nature.	

7

Blockchain Technology: Jati, Caste, and Brahmins

Theories Given by Various Traditions (Top-Down Approach)

A. Theory of creation of jati varna in Hinduism.
1. Purusha sacrifices himself and creates four varnas from his mouth, hands, thighs, and legs.[1]
2. In Purusha medha yajña, Purusha (iswara = oneness) is requested to create four varnas.[2]
3. *Bhagavad Purana* says four varnas came out of Vishnu's various body parts (same as Purushsukta).
4. In *Vayu Purana*, Bramha divided people in four categories and created four varnas.
5. From Purusha's body, four varnas came out with the same sequence as per the *Manusmriti*.
6. The Bhagavad Gita says, '4-fold division of varna is created by Krishna.'[3]

B. Creation of jati varna in Jainism.
1. The creation of varna traces to the Bhārata legend. According to this legend, Bhārata performed an 'ahimsa-test' (test of non-violence), and those members of his community who refused to harm or hurt any living being were called the priestly varna in ancient Bhārat, and Bhārata called them dvija, twice born.[4] Jinasena states that those who are committed to ahimsa are deva-Brāhmaṇas (divine Brahmins).[5]
2. The text *Adi Purana* also discusses the relationship between varna and jati. According to Padmanabh Jaini, a professor of Indic studies,

Jainism, and Buddhism, the *Adi Purana* text states, 'there is only one jati called manusyajati or the human caste, but divisions arise on account of their different professions'.[6] The varna of Kshatriya arose when Rishabh (Rishabhnath) procured weapons to serve society and assumed the powers of a king, while the Vaishya and Shudra varna arose from different means of livelihood in which they specialized.

C. Theory of creation of jati/varna in Buddhism.
1. Buddhism, even though remains silent, it accepts everything is the outcome of past karmas, which is a very generalized comment, but it doesn't specifically exclude 'varna, jati' from outcome of karma.
2. Buddhism and terms related to Hindu society.[7]

Table 7.1

Terms for fortunate people	Terms for unfortunate people
mahabhoga kula	dalidda kula
sadhana	Adhana
sugata	Durgata

Mention of Slavery in Buddhism

The rules of Buddhist sangha mention that slaves could not join sangha until they were freed from their masters. *Vinaya Pitaka* mentions three types of slaves:
1. antojatako (offering women slaves)
2. dhanokitto (buying slave)
3. kara-mara anito (bought from another country)
   Digha Niakaya mentions a fourth slave too.
4. saman dasavayam upagato[8]

Conclusion

1. Hinduism, Buddhism, and Jainism all give credit to or devote creation of 'jati, varna' to that which they value most, i.e., Purusa/Vishnu/Yajña, karma, and ahimsa, respectively. This is just an effort to show everything is the outcome of that which they value

most; any of the theory cannot be taken seriously as a reason for the origin of the jati/varna system. Why Hinduism expresses varna as coming out of body parts rather than being created externally by deity will be explained in further chapters.

2. At the same time, it must be pointed out that over the years, we were told by history books fake narratives to create social cleavage between Hinduism and Jainism and Buddhism (refer Table1.1) to create majority vs. minority divide. Hinduism (Vedas) already had the following concepts in it, and Jainism and Buddhism adopted them with or without modification, but we are told Jains and Buddhists denied the authority of the Vedas.[9]

   a. Hinduism is theistic (polytheism), and Jainism and Buddhism are atheists, while Guru Nanak was a non-conformist.[10]
   b. Buddhism and Jainism were against the varna system, indirectly conveying the message that Hinduism is the origin of jati or varna, but the reality is that Buddha didn't deny the caste system.
   c. Buddhism and Jainism were limited to merely messages of morality, peace, and non-violence rather than 'theme to achieve liberation', i.e., kaivalya and nirvana. The unique feature of Bhārat is that it is the 'mother of the process of enlightenment', which originated in Hinduism and was carried forwarded by Jainism and Buddhism.
   d. Jainism and Buddhism were also projected as anti-ritualistic, and Hinduism as ritualistic by hiding the message of Hinduism of 'moksha' i.e., liberation, which originates in the Vedas, which includes yoga, meditation, and Ayurveda, all practices mentioned in chapter 14.
   e. Heads of tradition were projected as the founders, i.e., the creators of some new content indirectly denying the 'contribution' of Hinduism.
   f. All trace their ancestors back to Ikshwaku.[11]
   g. Concept of loka (cosmic plains)[12]
   h. Zodiac signs, solar/lunar calendar, time scale (yuga)[13]
   i. Etymology, numerology, script, rituals (yajña in Buddhism) of Jainism, Buddhism, and Hinduism are the same.

As Buddhism and Jainism were projected as separate and anti-Hindu (anti-caste), this ultimately convinced someone to convert to Buddhism in post-Independence to get rid of Hinduism and the caste system. While converting, he created the 'Buddhist Manifesto' exactly on these lines (colonial history narrative), which includes Buddhism as anti-caste, atheism, boycotting Hindu rituals, no aspect of enlightenment, and limited Buddhism to morality. To market Buddhism better than Hinduism, he went on equating Buddhism with French values justice, liberty, equality, democracy, and communism.[14] You will know about real Buddhism in further chapters.

At the same time, all these concepts are also present in Mesopotamian, Sumerian, Zoroastrian, Egyptian, Chinese, Japanese, Roman, Greek, Egyptian, African, and Mexican civilizations too. But history books never told us these aspects, so we never find the similarity and origin (Sanatan Hindu dharma) of these concepts. This technique of undermining the contribution of Hinduism in multiple faiths and traditions gave an indirect hint through history books to start subversive, fissiparous activity against the Hindu majority country (Bhārat). How are these artificial clashes created in history books by colonial masters different from the Abrahamic clashes (refer to p. 182) Do such historical writings promote communal harmony or subversive or fissiparous activities against Bhārat?

Additionally, Hindus created guilt in their own minds for creating a caste system, but everyone created theories for justification for jati or varna. People (including Muslim rulers and British) enjoyed taxes collected from every jati; they enjoyed goods and services given by other jati; they allowed the system where cleaning roads and dead bodies of animals were duties of a particular jati to continue—but still, the burden of guilt shall be on the shoulders of Hindus.

Reasons for the Formation of the Varna System (Bottom-Up Approach)

The evolution of the varna system in a scientific or anthropological way can be explained in the following ways:

Geography: diverse and fertile land with abundant natural resources
Phase 1: Hunting, shelter, and small fights for food
Phase 2: Agriculture and land distribution
Phase 3: Mass production and market

These happened because of innovation, mechanization, rise in population, and exports

Phase 4: Diversification of production and jobs

This created the need for organization of labour; jobs gave birth to systemization, i.e., the institutionalization of jati and rules (varna system)

Phase 5: Classification of multiple jatis into four varnas and codification of behaviour, protocol, and qualities according to jati might have become necessary because of the excess number of jati

Phase 6: Punished people for violating the code, not officially into the Hindu Economic Union, i.e., self-sustaining tribals, and formation of the fifth varna

Hinduism explains the same evolution of Hindu society in four phases on a time scale in a semi-scientific way, i.e., yuga. It talks about the evolution of society (but it doesn't match the timeline of Table 4.1 exactly).

1. Satyuga: Everyone is happy, free from all problems or sorrow, which shows the early phase of the evolution of Hindu society. No untouchability in the Vedas before seven castes; Purushsukta origin of varna but no hierarchy.[15]
2. Tretayuga: In the Rāmāyaṇa, Brahmin = status, Kshatriya = power, Vaishya = wealth, but Shudra were not undermined.[16] Varnashrama dharma existed in this era; people were given jobs as per their quality and karma by rishis. The economy was good, no poverty. Society was free from disease.[17]
3. Dwaparyuga: No varnashrama dharma means hereditary employment (episode of Karna). It is an era of hate, jealousy, and warfare.[18] But Dasa Shudra are not untouchables.[19] Mahābhārata includes fifth category vratya: many tribes—Andhaka, Licchavi, Magadha, Abhira, Malla, Suta, Yaksha, Gandharva, Pannaga, and Raksasa. Athravaveda says they were Vedic tribes' worshippers of Shiva and Shakti.[20]

This is a very important aspect of Hindu society. Shudra, ati-Shudra/avarna/vratya were not original Dravidians or Adi-Hindus who were atheist before Aryan invasion, as Periyar says, but they were part of same Hindu society but left behind in social strata, may be because 'Indus valley civilization' became urban civilization on strategic location boundary of Bhārat with river coast who were out of that urban civilization got fifth varna (one of the possible conclusion).

4. Kaliyuga: Full-fledged static caste system with some exceptions. According to *Matsya Purana*, moral degradation is a yuga feature, i.e., theft, hate, falsehood, which is very normal, drought, famine, and often climate change.[21]

The full-fledged model of Hindu society can be projected as follows:

Diagram 7.1

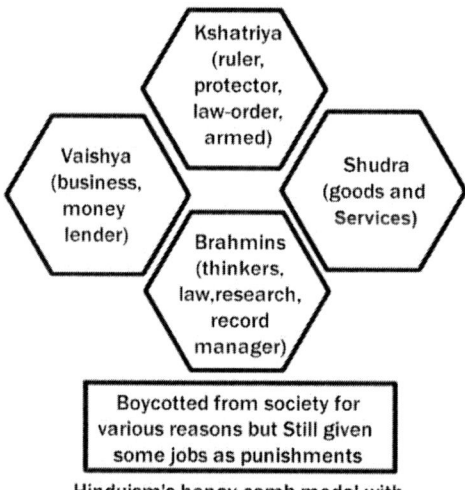

Hinduism's honey comb model with checks and balances separated from each other with professional protocols (discriminatory/non discriminatory both). Which were termed as Brahminism by Western scholars.

Myth about Hinduism Being a Varna System Not a Jati System

Hinduism as a text is the origin of the varna system, but as a society it is also the origin of the jati system. Even many texts contain a list of jatis.

1. *Yajurveda*: No static jati; already many jati came into existence[22]
2. Sub-jatis mentioned in *Shukla Yajurveda*: Sut, Shailush, Rathakar, Manikar, Kitav, Krishak, Dhivar, Vaidhya, Ganak[23]
3. Manu: 4 varnas and 57 jatis[24]

Manusmriti myth

The eighteen Smritis were written by eighteen Smritikaras, namely, 'Manu, Parasara, Yajnavalakya, Gautama, Harita, Yama, Vishnu, Sankha-Likhita, Brihaspati, Daksha, Angiras, Prachetas, Samvarta, Usana, Atri, Apastambha, and Satatapa'. Then who popularized the concept of 'Manusmriti' as the origin of the jati system?[25]

Table 7.2

Author	Time	Books	Conclusion of author to promote propaganda
William Jones	1784 AD	*Manusmriti, Shakuntala, Gita Govind*	*Manusmriti* as sole law book and Bhagavad Gita as 'root book' to adjust Hinduism in the Abrahamic mould
Charles Wilkins	1785 AD	*Bhagavad Gita, Hitopadesha*	Bhagavad Gita is about promoting monotheism from Vedic polytheism
Max Muller	1850s AD (approx)	*Biography of Words and the Home of the Aryas*	explained in this book
Vincent Arthur Smith	1904 AD	*Early History of Bhārat*	-
All these books were written or translated when no excavation of Harappa–Mohenjodaro was done.			

In the colonial era, a few books were translated and themselves popularized as *Manusmriti* and marketed as the origin of the varna system.

Table 7.3

People accept the following columns selectively as per political convenience.[26]	
Mechanisms created to strengthen the 'jati/varna' structure with discrimination	**Mechanisms that dilute the existing 'social structure'**
Inter-varna marriage as jati origin (then how did non-Brahmin jati receive skills? So these statements are written to create deterrence that if you do inter-varna marriage, your social status and suffering would be like the lowest varna/avarna)	Dharma sastras had provisions for taking up professions rather than hereditary.
Agni Purana: jati is outcome of inter-varna marriage (if u do inter-varna marriage your next generation will be candela)	
Varna system 3+1 No right of Upanayan to Shudra	Apada dharma (anybody can take up professions of lower varna in case of emergency/disaster)
Vedic age: discrimination in legal matters, punishment, freedom to choose bride	Shudas protected by law
Narada Purana: who eats cooked food by Shudra is sinner	*Vishnu Purana*: truthfulness, hard work, friendship, and cleanliness are the basic duties, if fails he can take rest of the varnas
Shiva and Vishnu idols shall not be touched by Shudras	Jati is decided by quality and ability by sages (varnashram dharma)

People accept the following columns selectively as per political convenience.[26]	
Mechanisms created to strengthen the 'jati/varna' structure with discrimination	**Mechanisms that dilute the existing 'social structure'**
Killing Brahmins is sin	*Garud Purana*: if duty is performed then each varna will go in prajapatya, indraloka, vayuloka, gandharvaloka
Yagyavalakya: 6 anuloma + 6 pratiloma, 24 jatis combination (trying to fit existing jati system into varna system by maintaining hierarchy)	*Padma Purana*: Brahmin can take up Kshatriya and Vaishya professions for livelihood
5th varna: varvara, kaivart, chandal	Details about varna-gotra and 7 generations do inter-varna marriage in same pattern
There is list of jatis that came out of inter-varna marriage system	Ambala vasi, Shagrid pesha, karan are some castes which recruit members from other castes
Discouraging pratiloma	
Akrita , krita (slaves) by Manu 7 types of slaves in Manusmriti: dhvajahrtah, bhaktadasa, grahaja, krita, datrima-dasa, paitrika dasa, and dadndadasa	

Conclusion

1. When the economy expands protocols in jati, organization becomes a need for smooth governance. But when the same organization and protocol are combined with wealth concentration or distribution, it gives birth to inequality.
2. When the same inequality exists in the same institution or organization over the years, irrespective of socio-economic changes, then it becomes 'institutionalized discrimination'.

This technical phenomenon is termed 'Brahminical society' by communist historians to create a binary war between Brahmins and non-Brahmins.
3. The tribal people in Bhārat don't have a large economy or mechanization so there is no proper organization, You will find almost zero discrimination based on profession/jati and gender, but they have ethnic fights. This difference in the economy is taught as 'tribal are not Hindus' to the tribal population, which leads to marginalisation of tribals and creates the issue of non-tribal vs. tribal so that 'Maoism rises in the nation. Multuple efforts are made to project Hinduism and nature worship have nothing to do with eachother which further intensified issue.[27]

Institutionalized discrimination and inequality are getting eliminated or will be eliminated because of industrialization and social-moral value change by giving up old codes of conduct. Which is a need of the hour because we face and suffer through the old protocols of jati, which is institutionalized discrimination.

Over the years, we have never questioned 'jati/varna' in a critical way except through the *Manusmriti*:
1. Financial role of jati in the economy in spheres of production, supply chain, production technology, import–export of products, currency, and self-sustaining village.
2. How can a couple married inter-varna produce the whole jati? And who ensured the infrastructure of production and related skills were given to that jati?
3. Why are jatis in the north and south similar as well as different? Why do material products produced by jatis change from north to south as per geography if all jatis are the origin of *Manusmriti* or related mythical theories.
4. Why is there so much uniformity in the jati and varna societies? i.e., four-fold varna in all over Bhārat.
5. Why are we not taught that tribal people were also part of the jati system? (Separate them in history books so that they remain separated in reality, whose isolation existence can be used for Maoism.)

6. Why was there no concept of changing jati? Why are some people kept forever out of the village? Or what was the mechanism for changing jati?
7. If Brahmins and Kshatriya maintained elite status by creating and maintaining jati, then why don't they have the skills of another jati if they have created it?

Diagram 7.2

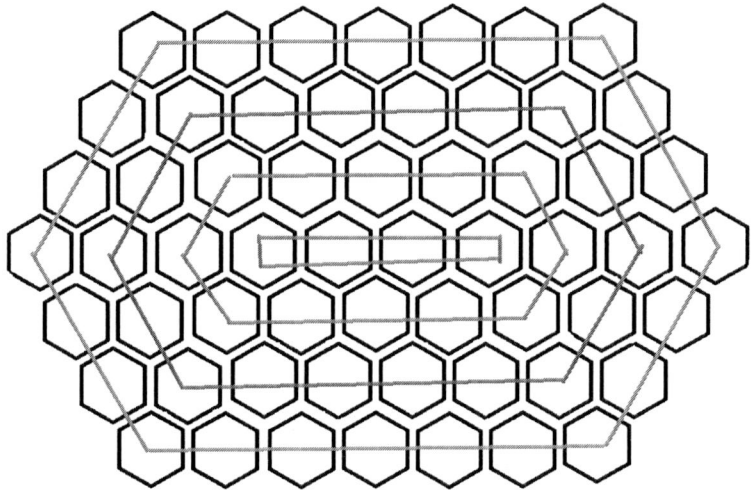

EACH HEXAGONAL BLOCK : 1 CLOSED SYSTEM
4 COLOUR LINES : UNITE ALL SUCH CLOSED SYSTEM

The following is how Bhārat will look when it is unified and integrated culturally, socially, and economically, i.e., with multilayer data integration.

The Village as an Economy Unit

A village economy is a self-sustaining economy with no imports except precious metals and materials and the export of products as per need or tax. The question is, if all villages are self-sustaining, then what is that factor that unites all villages (the four lines in Diagram 7.2) in a nation?

Those factors are:
1. Sixteen saṃskāras or way all get married, last rites, introduction to education, etc., are conducted the same way from north to south, and samskara is a big ceremony and event where the interest of every jati is satisfied through mass procurement or mass distribution, e.g., dinner or lunch to the whole village.
2. There are some jatis who move from one village to another to earn money, for example, entertainment industry, the cattle market once or twice in a year, animal grazing, or bhat (a man who carries information in written form about ancestry). These people take liquidity and wealth from one village to other, earning from one village and spending in other villages.
3. All do char dham yatra and culturally significant temples.
4. The Rāmāyaṇa, Mahābhārata, Puranas, and Vedas connect the whole Bhārat in one epic. One can know all detailed geographical features through the Rāmāyaṇa, Mahābhārata, Puranas, Vedas, etc.
5. Villages were gifted for tax collection after losing war by the kings.
6. Hindu fashion, e.g., tilak, jewelry, dhoti, and saree, everything as common.
7. People from the same gotra, varna, jati, etc. from another village.
8. People of different jati united under the roof of the village deity or gram devata.
9. Temples of deities of the same gotra, varna, and jati.
10. People of the same ancestry.
11. Celebrating festivals according to the season change or bumper production of the economy at the time of harvesting. Many festivals are celebrated on the same day with different names. For example, Sankranti, Makar Sankranti, Pongal, etc.
12. Uniting at Kumbha Mela, irrespective of identity, after twelve years.
13. People from the same village have the same geographic background, so the same food consumption patterns are the same; even Diwali, Holi, and all other nationwide festivals boost consumerism on the same day, which also ensures 'unity' in consumerism and production.
14. In every temple, puja will be conducted in Sanskrit.

Jati as a Social Unit
Even after having the same or different jatis, what unites all such jatis are the following factors:
1. People from the same gotra, varna, jati, etc., from the same or another village.
2. Union-cum-arbitration councils of jatis.
3. Marriage within jati (endogamy) is only possible when the person is from another village or gotra.

Negative Points of This Model
1. Once any single hexagonal unit goes out of the system, then all stakeholders related to this system go out. For example, the conversion of one village means losing one geography; conversion of jati means losing one profession or gifting one profession or skilled force to another religion. This thing happened in the form of throwing someone out of jati for violation of the rule. Hinduism is the union of all these professions and their councils; all are equal stakeholders. That is why 'why am I not Hindu?' is an effort to remove people and their units from Hindu union.
2. If one has to bring back those people, then they must be brought back on the same basis, and ensuring their employment is a difficult thing as before.
3. Hindus were united with each other on basis of 'same' jati, varna, language, deity, etc., but at the same time, 'different' jati, varna, and deity became alienated, and alienation with each other started. Those who were punished and thrown outside the village remained in the same condition over the years, as everything was hereditary, including punishment.
4. There is no physical border for this system. Unification is based on psychological connections with multiple identities. Rough boundaries and groups of villages were boundaries that could go from one hand to another depending on the outcome of the war.
5. There is a lack of common foreign policy among all jatis, varna, avarna, etc., which means two jatis can't sit together, but the foreigner is welcomed as 'atithi devo bhava'. This destroyed Hinduism as internal alienation and rivalry were supported by

external players. It is true that vasudhaiv kutumbakam (the world is family) is a core value, but to become part of a family, one must have a healthy, physically unbroken body that is a nation.
6. No permanent capital or political setup in the form of infrastructure.

Diagram 7.3

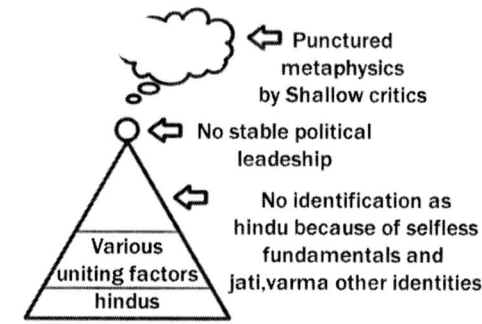

Real condition of hindu society

7. The inner core (refer to Diagrams 7.1 and 7.2, pp. 124–129) was protected from adversaries and attacks with discretionary social benefits, which culminated in discrimination in later days, and the elites were protected from external and intellectual attacks, but people from the outer periphery started leaving Hinduism because of internal inequality and external intervention. Discriminatory practices, jati-wise, must end in all formats.
8. Today, atrocities on weaker sections are again a challenge in Hindu society, but at the same time, atrocities and abuse by anti-Hindu forces on Hindus are not recognized as atrocities; they are merely seen as 'communal tension'.
9. There is no platform where all jatis' heads and cultural sect heads can have annual meetings or be members.
10. Discriminatory abusive language and attachment of particular qualities to particular jati, jati-varna superiority and cheapness attached to it, rituals and practices promoting Brahmins and other varnas superior over others, is another challenge or social evil.

11. Practicing untouchability is also an economic loss for the exploiter: Denying any service, goods, thoughts, atmosphere, or infrastructure related to Hinduism to anyone on basis of jati, varna, religion, or other discriminatory thoughts is denying its followers and consumers. In a market economy, only the number of consumers matters.

Today's Society Faces Multiple Problems

1. The problem of discrimination and inequality in the jati and caste systems.
2. Poverty and unemployment.
3. The fall of traditional industry and lack of development of the manufacturing sector.
4. Urban–rural, rural–tribal, and urban–tribal divides in modern society, which were absent before British colonized India.
5. Fall of old MSME because of British rule but not having a V-shaped recovery in MSME after Independence.
6. Only 2 per cent of Bhārtiya people get skill development, including vulnerable sections.

The biggest problem is that no one recognizes this sixfold problem; everyone thinks they are backward because of jati and Hindu texts.

Relation between Blockchain and Jati

If you refer to Diagram 7.2, p.129, you will discover the following common points between the blockchain technology model and Jati model:
1. Decentralized model yet integrated
2. Data is with every stakeholder
3. Altering data and interference in the system is very difficult
4. Every block is connected to the same string
5. A new block can be added

The difference between blockchain and jati systems is that 'jati system is purely honeycomb model, whereas blockchain isn't'. Another thing is that systems are being built on the 'blockchain model', i.e., 'polyversity', but democracy and related systems cannot be built on blockchain technology because of hierarchy, single control point, and interdependency. We can run away from old jati, but the varna system is taking on a new form.

Table 7.4

Old	New
Brahmin	Cloud computing and quantum computing
Kshatriya	Cyber security and cyber warfare
Vaishya	Artificial intelligence and e-commerce
Shudra	Machine learning and robotics

South American model[28] was repeated in Bhārat by our colonial masters, and 'he' was also in South America for studying. The Americas were divided into north and south, where it was supplemented by one more division, i.e., Black and White. So to create a 'parallel South American model', they introduced Aryan = Brahmin = Hinduism vs. Dravidian = non-brahmins = Buddhism. To create such a social clash, they carved out a parallel Abrahamic version of Buddhism out of Hinduism, as mentioned in chapter 9. This social clash is still going on.

Diagram 7.4

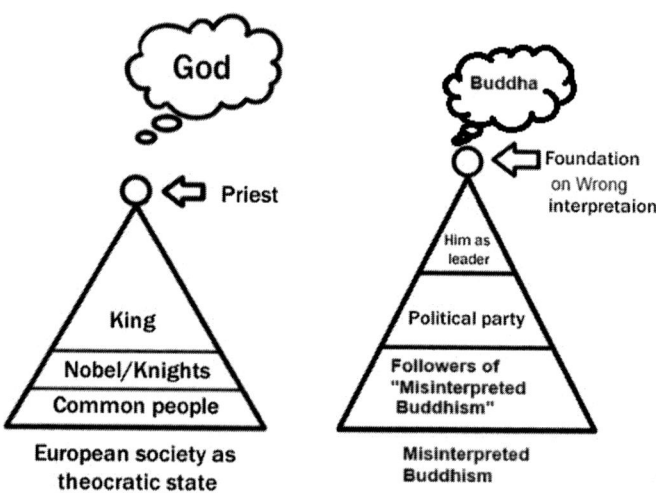

Table 7.5

South American caste system	Bhārtiya caste system[29]
Black vs. white	White Brahmins vs. Black non-Brahmins (even though colour division is illogical)
Anti-colonial	Anti-Brahmin
Colonial masters left American countries but left Christian colonization	Colonial masters left Bhārtiya subcontinent but left Brahmins (European Aryans)
Black Panther movement	Caste-based Panther movement[30]
Indigenous Black vs. colonial white	Indigenous (mulnivasi) vs. foreign Brahmin
Colonial masters left pope as an agent in the USA to handle mobs	Left pseudo-intellectuals in the name of rationality with ideology as agent to handle mobs; one in Tamil Nadu and the other two in Maharashtra
Colonial masters left Christianity and there was no need of creating local culture in Abrahamic form	Here left Christianity and 'misinterpreted Buddhism'
1917's anti-clericalism movement of Mexico where people rose against pope who was interfering in state's matter (which was the final goal of colonial masters through conversion)	The same model was implemented in Bhārat by colonial masters so that people are convinced against Brahmins and leave Hinduism

Building Up Anti-Brahmin Movement

The Western model was adopted in building up the anti-Brahmin movement.

Table 7.6

Western model	Bhārtiya model
Anti-priest vs. masses	Anti-Brahmin vs. non-Brahmins
Minority vs. masses	Hinduism vs. non-Hindus
Rebel against religious book	Anti-Manusmriti movement
Priest means gains without hard work vs. hardworking masses	Brahmins mean gains without hard work vs. hardworking masses
Priest as oppressor vs. suppressed masses	Brahmins as suppressor vs. oppressed masses

The British colonial administration began the codification of Hindu and Muslim laws in 1772 and continued through the next century, with emphasis on certain texts as the authentic 'sources' of the law and custom of Hindus and Muslims, which in fact devalued and retarded those dynamic social systems. The codification of complex and interdependent traditional systems froze certain aspects of the status of women, for instance, outside the context of constantly evolving social and economic relations, which in effect limited or restricted women's rights. The selectivity of the process, whereby colonial authorities sought the assistance of Hindu and Muslim religious elites in understanding the law, resulted in the Brahminization and Islamization of customary laws in British Bhārat. For example, the British orientalist scholar William Jones translated the key texts Al Sirjjiyah in 1792 as the Mohammedan Law of Inheritance and *Manusmriti* in 1794 as the Institutes of Hindu Law or the Ordinances of Manu. In short, British colonial administrators reduced centuries of vigorous development of total ethical, religious, and social systems to fit their own preconceived European notions of what Muslim and Hindu 'law' should be. These are words by Abdullahi Ahmed An-Na'im

Reservation on Jati Basis

There are 545 Lok Sabha seats and 5,000 total IAS, but there are 718 districts, 5,000+ jatis (orignal), 6,64,369 villages, 19,500 mother tongues, SC, ST, OBC, OPEN, capitalists, labourers,

46,000 jatis (fake), MSME, and 1,000s of such socio-cultural-economic identities. Everyone wants to see their representation rather than be satisfied with their interests. This non-acceptance of reality is the ground of caste politics in Bhārat. The only solution is that representatives should be inclusive, and even if they are not, then people should get their work done. Because reservation is to ensure representation, one considers colonial history books and socio-economic background for representation.

A possible solution is to make political representation of jatis in the Bhārtiya parliament a reality. For that we can create twenty jatis groupings of similar identities and give representations on a rotational basis for three years.

Brahmins

When colonial powers came to Bhārat, there were four varnas. They eliminated Kshatriya (Hindu and Muslim, both kingdoms) by the subsidiary alliance, the doctrine of lapse and direct conquest. They eliminated Vaishya through discriminatory tax systems, import duties, and parallel banking systems for money lending. They destroyed Shudra by introducing an alternative to modern production technology: mass production factories. Macaulay's policy was there to change consumption patterns. Only one varna that was safe from elimination was Brahmins. So, it was necessary to eliminate them also because the British feared that they may revive past culture and also because many Brahmins participated in anti-British activities and were popular freedom fighters. Brahmins didn't have arms, wealth, or production skills as per the jati system's strict rules, so the only way to eliminate them was an intellectual civil war. As the three varnas were eliminated by the British, so to avoid resistance from them, they promoted the philosophy 'you are backward because of Brahmins'; this saved the British from criticism and resistance from the other three varnas, which failed in the future because social reform came and the great leadership of Gandhi and many social reformers united Bhārat against the British. But after Independence again, this British-sponsored philosophy is popularized by Marxist historians to create vote bank.

So, the biggest challenge facing Western anti-Hindu powers was to eliminate customs, rituals, and conduct of life from day-to-day life so that common Hindus lose their daily connection with Hinduism. So, if an attack is made directly on these customs, then Hindus will give a strong reaction, just like they gave to Henry Louis Vivian Derozio (1809–31) in pre-Independence. It was obvious that a direct attack was not possible. So, the best way is to create a rebellion movement in the name of rationality and meaningless customs and to remove imposition and slavery and the modernization of Bhartiya society. When one of the options was imposition, it means there should be some imposer or dictator. So the plan was first to declare someone an imposer of customs, and in the second step, call customs the slavery of that community and give up customs to feel free from slavery. The answer is clear: those who conduct rituals occasionally declare them imposers of every custom and practice. The best option is purohits of Brahmin varna. But the word was used not purohit but Brahmin to include all Brahmins, so that with criticism of purohits, all other Brahmins are also declared imposers of customs, and all eliminated together.

Diagram 7.5

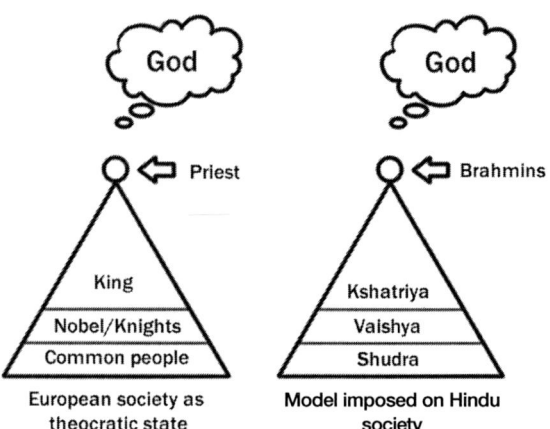

Once Brahmin was equated with priest, then, just like the anti-priest movement brought a revolution in theocratic states in the

West, the same model they wanted to bring to Hindu society. Because Brahmin is a very broad term in Hinduism that has various meanings, in terms of the jati system, there are various jatis, and in terms of varna, there are various types. So, every Hindu has multiple identities like jati/profession, varna, education status, gotra, etc. The same thing is applicable to Brahmins too. Western people wanted to create an anti-Brahmin movement so that they could eliminate the priest and his scriptures through this movement. So obviously, they were not interested in explaining the details and reasons how the Brahmins were. They just equated the word Brahmin with priest in religion and subjected Brahmins to the same criticism that was attracted by priests in Western religion, and work was done. The exact same pattern is used to destroy Hinduism by attacking priests.

Table 7.7

Priests in religion	Brahmins in Hindu civilization according to colonial masters
Guardians of religious infrastructure and teachings or hereditary owner	Guardians of temple or hereditary owner
Those who tell dos and don'ts	Those who tell dos and don'ts
Hurdle in liberal value	Hurdle in liberal value
Run parallel government in a secular state and absolute government in a theocratic state	Runs parallel government in secular state and absolute government in a theocratic state
Middleman/his word is word of God	Middleman/his word is word of God
Cunning man for vested interest	Cunning man for vested interest
Who loots people in the name of God as donation	Who loots and cheats people in the name of God as donation
Clergy abuse (general term used in foreign countries)	Clergy abuse in terms of self-styled Godman not as Brahmin

Priests in religion	Brahmins in Hindu civilization according to colonial masters
Hurdle to secular and democratic state	Hurdle to secular and democratic state
I will debunk all these myths	

The term 'Brahmin' absolutely translated as a human who has widened the boundaries of his mind or expanded his mind. In Harappa Mohenjo-Daro and post-period, it was like a common degree, as the jati system was not completely evolved as we see in the 18th-century AD. The jati system evolved and changed from time to time. Jati became hereditary, similarly in the case of Brahmins. When 25 per cent GDP of the world is from Bhārat, then per capita income must be healthy too. So, tag of poverty can't be attached to any of the jatis.

Table 7.8 Jatis and their classifications

Brahmin	Varna
Vedas	One of the 4 Vedas, dvivedi, Chaturvedi
Samhita or branch	While being a Taittirīya Kṛṣṇa Yajurvedin, you would be an Āpastambin Yajurvedin or a Baudhāyana Yajurvedin or so on, depending on what kalpasūtra you follow
Branch according to the so-called philosophy in colonial terms	Vaiṣṇava follower of Rāmānuja's Viśiṣṭadvaita, or a Vaiṣṇava, Mādhva's Dvaita.
Languages/region	Above Vindhya range gouda brahmin Below Vindhya range Dravidian brahmin
Gotra	1 out of 49 gotras
Sutra	1 sutra from branch

The reasons for creating so many multiple identities are:
1. The burden of the Vedas and philosophy is divided on multiple shoulders and remains in a decentralized way, which avoids 'too big to fail'.

2. Even if a Brahmin forgets one identity, he is connected to dharma through other identities.

All these things were relevant because, in those times, there was no computer or seed bank concept, so this human seed bank concept was quite practical. Nowadays, we have all these technologies, so these patterns are not very relevant.

In Brahmin varna, there are various types, like
1. Acharya: One who follows and teaches the same
2. Upadhyay: One who teaches some part of education
3. Sadhu: 'Sadhu' came from 'sadh', which, among other things, means 'to gain control over through relentless efforts'. Sadhus are in search of achieving liberation or 'moksha' to save themselves from the cycle of birth and rebirth
4. Muni: Manan shil, moun means don't have verbalization or talk
5. Rishi: Those who understand at their highest and don't have visualization; they only speak mantras; by sound, they will do what they want; by right pronounce, they will do what they want, for example: vak shakti, whatever they say will become truth at the ultimate level. Vipra: vidvan or learned many aspects of the Vedas
6. Mahrshi: Supreme among the rishi
7. Swami: A person who initiated a new monastic order
8. Yogi: One who practices yoga can be sadhu, sansyasi, or householder; if he is sannyāsi, then he goes into the category of Brahmins
9. Siddha: One who has achieved supernatural powers
10. Sannyāsi: One who has given up social and material life
11. Purohits: Those who conduct rituals and temple caretakers

Non-Hindu Terms
1. Baba: It is a Farsi word used for a father or priestly person; it has nothing to do with Hinduism.
2. Peer-fakir: Both have nothing to do with Hinduism.
3. Saint: Saint is a Christian expression, and it came from the Latin word 'Sanctus', which, among other things, means 'change to

holy', and therefore a saint is a holy person, and holy is 'that which has a likeness of God'.

Generally, all three terms are used for those who propagate the idea of their respective religion and convert (colonize) people.

Ancient texts describing community-oriented Vedic yajña rituals mention four to five purohits. The functions associated with Brahmins were:
1. The hotri recites invocations and litanies are drawn from the *Rigveda*.
2. The adhvaryu is the priest's assistant and is in charge of the physical details of the ritual, like measuring the ground and building the altar, as explained in the Yajurveda. The adhvaryu offers oblations.
3. The udgatri is the chanter of hymns set to melodies and music (sāman) drawn from the Samaveda. The udgatar, like the hotri, chants the introductory, accompanying, and benediction hymns.
4. The Brahmin recites from the Atharvaveda.
5. The ritvij is the chief operating Brahmin.

Other than the aforementioned tasks, Brahmins (non-hermit Brahmins) performed various tasks in society, which also became a medium of earning.
1. Vyasa Brahmins were masters in both knowledge and speaking. The name Vyasa was given to them because they were excellent at explaining the scriptures to common people. Vyasa means 'compiler' in Sanskrit and is the name of Vedavyasa, the writer of the Mahābhārata. Vyasa Brahmins are also known for their tradition, which keeps historical and non-historical accounts of culture in written form.
2. Ojha Brahmins in Uttar Pradesh and Nepal were regarded as healers because they possessed knowledge of many herbs that worked on the human immune system.
3. Some served as astrologers, political advisors to kings, some served as cooks in temples, as a cook on special festivals and

ceremonies, making multiple copies of the Vedas and shastras to keep them alive.
4. Many Brahmins were brilliant mathematicians and scientists (one must note that even non-Brahmins have written many books); some Brahmins have become Kshatriyas and kings too.

This is the depth, diversity, and living experience of Hinduism that are being destroyed by shallow attempts like the 'anti-Brahmin' movement. Keeping Sanskrit alive is also a challenge because Sanskrit survives on pronunciation. Now, just think: when Brahmin varna is equated with a priest, it is unjust, i.e., multiple books and research vs. one book (generally). That's why using word 'priest' for Brahmin is another attempt to 'Westernize' Hinduism.

What Is Diluting Jati System?
1. Values of the French Revolution: liberty, equality, and fraternity
2. Heavy industrialization and a new supply chain.
3. New kinds of jobs and their new protocols and new systems of hierarchy.
4. Digitization and the new cyber world are new platforms other than social platforms.
5. The radical approach of Periyar in Tamil Nadu reduced the unnecessary importance given to Brahmins in the modern world on the basis of ancient books, which is a valid point. But Periyar promoted many wrong things too, which challenged the sovereignty of the nation through fake history and a wrong interpretation of Hinduism.
6. The rise of pro-Hindu groups who are conserving Hinduism by working on the elimination of caste discrimination.
7. We eliminated the jati system from our minds without understanding, which diluted not only jati but also gender discrimination.

Problem of Bhārat's Economy
In the Western world, when philosophers came out after the Renaissance, they tried to show direction to the world through their

theories, which were written in an AC cabin and expected to be followed by the rest of the world who would be working in the hot sun. Meaning is imposing bookish models of society on diverse worlds and realities; trying to make society as per book. That is why there is no more renaissance; it's merely changed or jumped from one book to another. For example, consider capitalism, communism, and mixed economies.

Table 7.9

Top-down approach: Bookish division and format of society	Bottom-up approach: Society and economy in reality
Capitalism: Society: Capitalist, middle class, labourers. The capitalists will be decision-makers who hire intellectuals from the middle class and use labourers for production.	Agriculture, science and technology, writers, poets, jobs related to art and culture, gig economy, MSME, unorganized sector, disaster management, climate change investments, science and technology
Communists: Society: Capitalist and labour class	
Hinduism: Varna society: Brahmin, Vaishya, Kshatriya, Shudra	Jati system and its ground-level functioning, bureaucracy, and administration of kingdoms
Economy: Handling economy, inflation, unemployment through monetary policy of RBI, imposing 5-year plan on the nation without a goal-oriented approach	Creating Ministry of Skill Development (2015), promotion of MSME, startups, export led foreign policy

We are always taught to believe bookish theories of column 1 as an ideal or practical way to run an economy without considering the diversity or ground reality of column 2; imposing bookish column 1 on column 2; or making column 2 function and organized like column 1. Because of this, we kept jumping from communist to capitalist models. In the mediaeval age, 'exclusive' faiths started this cult-creating model in the book and imposed on society irrespective of social, economic, cultural, and geographical diversity. This exclusive psychology is being carried forward by this left, right, and centre ideologies, and no new models are coming. That is why naturally left, right, and centre are getting divided or diversified in the format of centre-right, centre-left, left-extremist, right-extremist, etc., but this change is still bookish because society is being run and will be run by column 1.

The same thing happened after Independence: Nehru was accused of being left inclined by the right wing and right inclined by the left-wing. The centrist said that he had a balanced view about left and right. But we never discuss Nehru and the post-Independence economy beyond left and right. Have we ever discussed:
1. What were the post-Independence policies and implementations for MSME?
2. What was the post-Independence policy for traditional industries?
3. What was the post-Independence policy for ecology and the environment?
4. What were the post-Independence policies for the unorganized sector and gig economy?

Because fifty years ago, these issues were never on the discussion table as all the people around the world were busy finding solutions to economic problems in political theories. As the varna system was considered an ideal theory of learning jati or caste system, that is why we never tried to study the traditional industries of Bhārat. We were busy in the bookish binary of theocratic state vs. secular, which is why we never tried to study Bhārat's ancient books and jobs related to Hinduism or the jati system. The British destroyed traditional handicrafts and industries, and we continued it by reading books written by them.

Problem of Stagnancy in the Economy

Mistrust theory

As many aspects of the economy and ground-level problems were ignored, that is why it is reflected in policy too. Bad governance was one of the reasons, but in addition, a policy that ignored various dimensions of society added fuel to bad governance. Today, the invisible anti-Bhārat hand is creating mistrust in psychology, which is reflected on the ground level. Mistrust is created by generalizing all bad qualities and mostly attaching them to professions so that people don't trust that profession, anymore especially leadership. The following tables explain and create ground for the 'total communist revolution'.

Table 7.10

Leadership	Qualities and tags
Politicians & bureaucrats (political leadership)	Cheaters, looters, wealth drainers, anti-poor, selfish
Religious leaders (religious leaders)	Fake, rapist, looters, cheaters
Doctors' other services (social leaders)	Wealth-making business, fake tests, costly products, anti-poor, cheaters
Industrialists (big bulls of the economy)	Cheaters, looters, wealth drainers, anti-poor, selfish

Mistrust is created in the people; people as consumers run away from consumerism because they are not sure that services will be worth it, and people as producers don't invest in the market and continue bad practices because everyone is doing it (generalization). Both don't trust the government while paying taxes because they are not sure about returns in the form of development. So as producers, people remain underground in unorganized or informal sectors to avoid legal framework, and as consumers, they don't ask for bills. Mistrust is just one word that is penetrated through various ways in the Bhārtiya mind which hurts economically from the production and consumer sides. Mistrust is responsible for most of the economic problems, irrespective of the political ideology of the government. Today, these 'Mistrust Theory' is getting defeated as we can see there were 3.36 crore taxpayers (2013–14), which has now jumped by 90 per cent, hitting 7.41 crore (2023). It takes 'extreme positivity' and counter narratives to defeat such a 'destructive mistrust theories'.[31]

Clashing theory

Clashing policies, which create binary opposition, cause economic stagnation. That is because finance and short-term gains (column 1 in the table) are dominating, but maintaining a balance between two is a practical solution.

Table 7.11

Column 1: Need for development	Column 2: Issue arising
Cement, aggregates (pro infrastructure policy)	Sand mining
Tribal and mountain area development	Environmental concern
Development and energy needs	Climate change
Packaging industry development	Plastic issue
Electronic material	E-waste
Strong foreign policy	Weak internal economy
Fight against black money	Source of FDI
Cleaning banking system	Capitalist on the back foot
Liberalization, FDI, ease of doing business	Import substitution, Atmanirbhar Bhārat, local for vocal
Gene editing, biotech, fertilizer, food processing	Traditional and organic farming
Liberalization and decentralization of economy	Centralization, good governance, fight against black money

This clashing effect is only the outcome of 'populism'. Better implement both things with balance and proper marketing to give the message to people and capitalists that government policy believes in growth-led sustainable development.

Risk avoiding theory
We Hindus were taking up ancestral jobs by acquiring skills with the same mindset they continued in the modern economy, i.e., the service sector, and because of a lack of capitalist values like creativity. They never subjected themselves to risk-taking abilities or market volatility. Even though we find proofs in the scriptures of the turning wheel of karma, time, or the 'volatile' nature of Indra, in reality, Hindus lack that. Our traditional value system of being averse to market forces combined with our education system never gave us the entrepreneurial push we needed. This created a situation where we had to make a leap from agriculture to service sector by skipping manufacturing altogether. But one thing people don't understand is that we can 'minimize volatility and risk through excessive planning and skills so that volatility becomes a certainty'.

Eliminating middleman theory: Unesthetic materialism
In Bhārat, there was a theory promoted in the masses by an invisible anti-Bhārat hand, i.e., because he is a middleman, he is corrupt or unnecessary.
1. Between God and spirituality, Brahmin or yogi/guru is the middleman.
2. Between bungalow and owner, the architect is the middleman.
3. Between furniture and the owner, the decorator is the middleman.
4. Between development and people, a politician is a middleman.
5. In financial management, a chartered accountant is a middleman.
6. Between consumer and producer, the supplier is the middleman.
7. In legal transactions, the concerned authority is the middleman.
8. In goal and target, the legal person or authority is the middleman.
9. In customer and bodybuilding, the gym trainer is the middleman.
10. In doctor and patient, the laboratory is the middleman.

This theory is created in such a way that it creates an illegal, unaesthetic way of working because all the people I mentioned as middlemen are experts and professionals in the field, which we call the quaternary sector. Their presence or support increases the asset value or aesthetic value of work. In the name of eliminating middlemen, what we are doing is lowering professionalism and aesthetic management. Today's biggest problem in the economy is that stakeholders are unconnected with each other. Even though there is potential for the economy to rise because of unconnected stakeholders, there is stagnancy because of the elimination of middlemen and not recognizing them as jobs. Digitization and artificial intelligence will eliminate many middlemen, but it cannot replace them. So, it's good to identify middlemen as jobs to promote employment and hire middlemen to multiply quantity and quality so that stagnancy is eliminated.

Isolation implementation

Giving a solution to a problem in isolation without considering multiple stakeholders doesn't solve the problem in the long term. The problem repeats itself from time to time. This recurring problem creates stagnancy. What points should be considered while solving a problem?

1. Is there any national or state-level policy?
2. Is there any international agreement?
3. Are there any international or national funds available?
4. Is there any institute, agency, or organization that solves the problem?
5. Is there any research institute or technological solution for this problem?
6. Is there any permanent data bank at the central or international level?
7. Who are the multiple stakeholders?
8. Which industries are related to problems?
9. Is there any real-time digital, GIS, and physical infrastructure available for implementation?
10. Who else is geographically facing problems?
11. What are government schemes?
12. Is an implementation plan available? Who solved the problem com\pletely?

Diagram 7.6

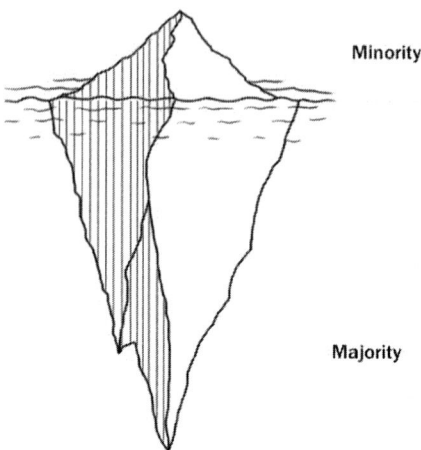

Iceberg effect

The 'iceberg effect' is an illusion created in psychology where 'majority' is projected as a base that can't be destroyed; otherwise, 'minority' will also get destroyed. Where minority can be equated with 'government law enforcement agencies, the formal economy, and organized sectors', and the majority can be equated with the 'informal sector, unorganized sector, informal economy, black money, and illegal activities'. This illusory effect is created so that 'right and justice, law enforcement agencies' never dare to eliminate 'informal sector, unorganized sector, informal economy, black money, and illegal activities'. This also includes social evils, human trafficking, and drugs.

This illusion becomes reality after a period of time because the 'formal economy and taxpayers, law enforcement agencies' are supported by law and constitution, so to counter that, 'informal and illegal players' create a new parallel power that is based on mutual coordination and strong unity.

The solution to this problem is slowly shifting people from majority to minority, i.e., from underwater to over-the-water (informal to formal) and collective upliftment of people and sectors with isolated digital efforts. I mean, at the individual level, through positive narratives, people should be moved towards trust and formal sector. Even sector-wise, there should be efforts to measure how much informal economy a particular sector has and how it can be shifted towards formal. Once 40 per cent economy, taxpayers, and labourers are formalized, then there will be a very fast revolution to turn the economy formal. That is why a major part of the economy of Bhārat is still illegal, informal, and unorganized. The only way to eliminate illegal, informal, and unorganized sectors is to make them practices of the masses by teaching them through the media so that once the masses face problems, through common and mutual consensus, they organize themselves and stop illegal activity for a win-win situation or to benefit every stakeholder.

Another effort that is done to curb the informal economy is 'privatization' where the iceberg above the sea is kept at a minimum and the iceberg below is increased. Where the iceberg above is government and the iceberg below is private sector, the government enforces laws strictly after 'privatization', which actually curbs 'illegal and informal' sectors. If the government fails to control the private sector after privatization, then extreme conditions of communism will arise, which may take the economy into more darkness. The government will again try to revive it by promoting the public sector, and the economy will collapse. That is why having control over industries and markets is important, whether they're in the public or private sector. 'Icebergs exist in binary form above and below sea level.' In reality, this binary of legal–illegal, formal–informal, and unorganized–organized doesn't exist as a binary; it exists as a whole, so that binary of legal vs. illegal is never created because once the binary is created, legal will eliminate illegal and justice will prevail.

This avoidance of binary division is created through various practices, which we call corruption, malpractices, mutual benefits, and self-interest. When such a situation exists in a country, the government becomes merely a legal platform to be used as a puppet by unorganized, informal, and illegal people. That is why the creation of a binary in legal vs. illegal matters is important (law enforcement), and this is the only way. This can only be created through influential mediums and platforms. A non-binary economy where legal–illegal, formal–informal, and organized–unorganized go hand in hand is termed 'nexus'. Law is binary (legal–illegal divides sharply), but enforcement is non-binary. Corruption exists as a parallel system.

There is another problem that is never identified in an economy: is 'formal but unorganized sector'. In this case, all the stakeholders are legal and formal, but they are not organized according to forward–backward linkages in the hierarchy of producer, distributer, and consumer. People from the same sector don't know each other. That is why there is a need for a digital revolution that will connect all stakeholders in the same sectors all over Bhārat.

We must unite all stakeholders and the forward and backward linkages of sectors, at least digitally. If at least informal sectors (both modern and traditional) are reflected on digital platforms, then these sectors can be pulled into the formal economy. Bringing certainty to consumption patterns and the willful upswing, downswing, and circulation of wealth is one of the solutions to running an economy.

Diagram 7.7

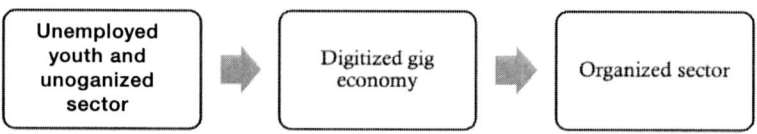

Who Will Solve Bad Governance?

Bad governance is promoted by the state or indirectly by not taking action on unethical practices, unjust practices, illegal practices, immoral practices, and adharma. People vote their candidate so that candidate will allow the voter to continue 'Malpractices'. Everyone has their own nexus but 'Good Governance' exist beyond this. Let's have a look.

Which model is better? Whichever model satisfies the current interests of society.

Table 7.12 Popular models of the budget, economy, and nation

Model 1	Model 2
Believes in uncalculated asymmetric constitution and governance	Constitutional symmetry + calculated asymmetric governance structure. They don't believe in majority and minority; they believe in individualism.
They believe in unorganized/ fragmented diversity which they market it as 'non-uniform'	Unique combination of uniformity and organized-harmonious diversity (hub and spoke model)
Their ideal model is 'point to point model' to create interdependency and checks and balance in democracy but planning in silos. Ultimate result is 'non-performing democracy'.	Their ideal model is 'hub and spoke' multidisciplinary organized approach. Plus, political structure is democratic for 'checks and balances'. Ultimate result is 'performing democracy' (service delivery)
They avoid unifying the system to avoid 'keeping all eggs in same basket' or 'too big to fail'. This makes the nation decentralized and stakeholders are multiple; in terms of polity which culminates into 'democracy', 'separation of power', balance between independent organization and dependency on government.	They eliminate doubling of efforts and move towards unified system to improve good governance to bring synergy, convergence, integrated approach, streamlined administration, uninterrupted approach, one stop solution (PM Ayushman Bhārat Digital Mission, One Health Mission of UN) in spheres of society, polity and economics, defence (Integrated Battle Groups), governance, schemes, and policy.

Model 1	Model 2
But it's time consuming, doubling of efforts, and friction in the opinions ultimately culminates into bad interrupted governance.	This culminates into 'one-stop solution' which ensures easy access, governance, user friendly. The danger of 'too big to fail' is always there. If it fails, then rectifying/simplifying problem is difficult because it is integrated.
They believe in decentralization and devolution of power because post-Independence it was difficult to reach to each and every individual so 'decentralization and devolution of power' was the only way. Devolution and separation of power culminates into non-seamless governance, i.e., Bhāratiya railway administration and infrastructure.	They believe in 'individualism' because reaching to each and every individual is possible because of technology so 'decentralization and devolution of power' automatically gets surpassed. Just like the private sector shows jobless growth because of technological intervention, government will also shrink because of technology. Which people wrongly identify as 'Fall of democracy'
They support the democratic approach checks and balance and interdependency which helps to avoid separatist movements originating from extreme independent approach. But if federal institutions and their leadership are empowered, it might also lead to separatist tendency. But this model is good only when human capital is trained-skilled, otherwise it culminates into unmotivated approach, lethargy, unenthusiastic, and non-adaptive for new best practices, which culminates into slow and bad governance (refer to p. 198).	A democratic approach in the background plus skilled governance. The philosophy of choosing this model is 'human capital of Bhārat is untrained-unskilled' so it's better that only skilled people get opportunity to run government, which would be quick, smooth, and quality work. For that they choose Integrated approach Minimum government Involvement of private sector because of professionalism Use of technology and digitization

Model 1	Model 2
They keep rural and agricultural economies under the government's umbrella to ensure their welfare because of the communist inclination. They consider farmers, labours etc. as victim and use compensatory model, e.g., MSP, loan waiver. (They have stereotype farmers are always victims and capitalism-innovation duo can't solve problem rather it will push farmer into risk). This mindset is colonial burden to keep people 'subordinate, inferior and passive' which was even continued by communists.	They consider farmer as supplier and vulnerable they use combine model. Compensation (MSP, loan waiver), Crop Bima, technological, innovation, mechanization, fertilizer, gene editing, digitization, market exposure. We can call this as 'Indian Socialism' or Fabianism. As there is no compensatory model, they encourage initiative, leadership, etc. In economy, its startup and entrepreneurship, to make people job creator rather than seeker.
They should appeal to urban consumers to maintain consumption patterns in such a way that promotes crop diversity, farmer's welfare, and nutrition through food culture change.	
No focus on consumer protection	New consumer protection act passed.
They make country economically strong for short term through undiversified rural empowerment but fail in long term because other aspects of the economy failed.	They believe in 'holistic' development, cover all aspects of economy.
They believe in passive political leadership but not weak.	They make country politically strong because of equal status to Bhārat and Bhārtiya culture at international level which West opposes.
They don't sell or liberalize public sector to keep maximum government to avoid right wing tilt, which ultimately ends up with bad governance.	They liberalize and privatize the public sector to make government minimum and governance maximum. So that it becomes compulsory for government to enforce the law strictly to prove its existence in market but enforcing law against private sector is another challenge.

Model 1	Model 2
Scientific development remains untapped because of ignorance.	They promote scientific development so that it culminates into industrialization, which makes the country export oriented with innovative solutions.
They believe in dialectical method as means and end. Dialectical method: Discussion and debate keeps on going. Their history writing, political ideology, and governance is limited to discussion and to keep that discussion alive forever they add 'confusion' in it. This culminates into negative liberty (refer to Table 10.2 (first row only), p. 222).	They believe in dialectical method as means and absolutism as end. Absolutism: Getting all concepts cleared, coming to a conclusion, and solving the issue. Knowing everything, no confusion, getting rid of all problems, and finding solutions whether in history, polity, or economy. This culminates into positive liberty (refer to Table 10.2 (first row only), p. 222).
Ideologically motivated or emotional decision. Even in case religion they do social engineering without knowing religious fundamentalism of either and promote the same.	Facts, data, reports, e.g., data driven governance.
They entertain everyone including fringe elements, separatist, unprofessional etc. in the name of democracy.	They only encourage and entertain mainstream, legal, national interest, professionalism.
No focus on urban development and urban areas, and no idea that tier 3 and tier 2 cities exist.	They focus on urban development. Concentrate on tier 3 and tier 2 cities too.
Bad governance, no technology intervention because digitization follows 'hub and spoke model', which is against their ideology or democratic setup.	They believe in corporate governance.

Model 1	Model 2
They don't control consumption patterns which is good for FDI but not for indigenous manufacturing, but bad in the ease of doing business	Tries to control consumption pattern, e.g., indigenization of 'local for vocal' which is contradictory to attract FDI. Still FDI comes because they compensate it by ensuring 'Ease of doing business'
No control on consumption pattern and CPI, WPI. High inflation lowers unemployment. They are able to lower unemployment through high inflation which is not a long-term solution.	They control I and WPI. Low inflation increases unemployment rate. They deal with unemployment separately by creating multiple schemes of skill development, encouraging entrepreneurship, job diversification.
They keep people away from 'foreign policy' and 'internal security challenge', which helps to keep people un-polarized and society and economy stable. But if people are unaware of the danger at social level, then it may create a long-term issue of unskilled-dumb human capital.	They create awareness in people about 'foreign policy' and 'internal security challenge', which helps to keep people aware of anti-national movements and ideologies. It creates nationalistic wave, which people wrongly identify as social instability.
They induce capitalism in policies very slowly and in mild ways to avoid tag of 'right-wing'.	They induce capitalism quickly to promote professionalism and quality.
Don't believe in diversification of the economy, no idea about proper management of resources of nation.	Believe in diversification of the economy and various resources, they utilize national resources at best.

Model 1	Model 2
E.g., Problem: textile sector is down.	E.g., Problem: textile sector is down.
Solution: turning victims into vote bank with populist promises, e.g., freebies	1. Tax incentive 2. Pushing up FDI limit in various sectors 3. DBT 4. Making liquidity available in market for existing and new MSME 5. Huge infrastructure projects related to various sectors 6. Skill development, innovation 7. Legislative-policy reforms 8. Production linked incentives
Need of Verghese Kurien for every sector who will unify primary production, laborers, technology, processing, marketing, market capturing, digitization, and infrastructure.	

Bharat is an emerging economy with a lot of potential. In 2024, we opened our gates to the future. If we identify our past mistakes and focus on innovative solutions, we can take the nation to the next level.

8

Human Capital versus Institutional Efforts

When the British came to Bhārat, Bhārat's economy contributed 25 per cent GDP to the world's economy. How it's possible that an economy with this size and scale has a 'useless or illiterate' human capital? But the narrative was built that the people of Bhārat are a waste. Education was the outcome of British efforts to start institutions and some social reformers. The only difference between the Western world and Asia in the 18th and 19th centuries was that the Western world had an industrial revolution and philosophy and psychology that supported capitalism and consumerism. Industrialization was supported by electricity, iron–coal chain reaction, and spinning wheel, and industry required machinery that was lacking in the East.

The difference between the modern world and the old world is that in the old world, everything was achieved without necessary formal efforts, which include land rights, paperwork, education, skill development, legal efforts, and institutionalization. Lack of understanding of this pushes Bhārat's economy on backfoot. Because people in government and the common man never recognized this point. A formal or legal way is still avoided in the name of being expensive or by tagging it as a middleman's income source. Which is one of the reasons why Bhārat's economy is still informal and many people don't have formal skill development certificates.

Human Capital

Skill development

In many of the cases we have seen in the last chapter, vocational skills became hereditary, and infrastructure and technology were also hereditary. Some experts say that at the time of the dharma shastra, there were a skill development institution. But if we look at the 18th century, at that time, skills were transferred from family as hereditary. It's quite common in the world that once a business or industry is established, the rights to run it become hereditary today as well. But as I have explained the artificial division of Brahmin vs. non-Brahmin, masses of Bhārat were made busy in saying, 'Why should the son of a Brahmin become a Brahmin? Or should the king's son become the king? Because of this, we never questioned why a man who is a businessman, or an industrialist becomes a businessman or an industrialist, respectively? The narrative was built to create an issue between 'outcasts vs. ruling Brahmins and kings'. Jati was not related to financial condition according to class because, at that time, there was no mechanism for measuring per capita income because there was no concept of per capita income as individualism.

The problem of the jati system is the monopoly on work and profession by that jati only; unfortunately, only Brahmins and Kshatriyas are targeted, but other varnas also maintain a monopoly, for example, fishermen, money lenders, businessmen, etc. Secondly, the complete eradication of the jati system would result in the loss of production of indigenous products and industries as well as skills and artisans. Thirdly, tribal culture is also protected under the constitution, so losing the jati system means losing distinct cultures related to every jati. A tradition that is carried forward by every jati, like Rajputs, is having palaces and antiquities. Who will protect them? Is there any mechanism that can connect the individual with every tradition? Is there any human being who will carry the responsibility of every culture? In Bhārat, jati is not only a profession, but they have their own culture, language, geography, lifestyle, fashion, food, deity, protocols, and festivals to be followed among various jatis; Hinduism is not a uniform pattern like 'one religion, one god, one pattern, one language for all'. Even if Bhārat were composed

only of Hindus, it will still be a 'diverse country' because Hinduism is inherently premised on internal cultural diversity; whereas colonialism, or religions with 'internally uniformity', imposes uniformity on others too and contributes to the destruction of diversity. Whenever someone wants to destroy diversity, they tag it with discrimination, and people of that diversity will give up cultural diversity to eliminate discrimination. That is why you will see two famous personalities from southern Bhārat giving slogans in the colonial era as follows:
- One religion, one God, one caste
- There are only two castes: men and women
- My religion/ideology has no 'caste system' like Hinduism
- I am only Hindu/Indian, I don't believe in caste/varna, etc.

These kinds of immature statements are given only because of a lack of understanding about Bhārat's job diversity and Bhārtiya production services. History and art-culture books and paid media generally use nice tricks; while explaining discrimination and atrocities, they use the word 'caste', and while explaining professions, skills, fashion, food, geography, rituals and festivals, housing construction, and deities of the same caste, they use the word 'community'. I don't understand this double standard approach. Either say directly diversity is fine but don't discriminate against each other. Endogamy and the code of separation/segregation were ways to keep alive jati practices. There were no artificial institutions in those days, and even if keeping that culture alive through institutional support may work as a seed bank, if not practised, such cultural practices are vulnerable to being transferred from temples to museums. To be sure, it took seventy-three years for the government to finally launch the PM Vishvakarma Scheme.

Personal responsibility towards dharma
The reason for the fall of Egyptian civilization, Greek civilization, etc., might be a lack of organized economies and skill-transferring mechanisms. Because only institutionalization or creating a seed bank in the form of a book or particular class makes the responsibility of civilization limited to itself, it never becomes a mass movement. In such a case the masses become vulnerable to anti-national ideologies

and enemies' efforts to convince them to accept new citizenship in the name of religion and atheism to weaken emotion about civilization.

The efforts to keep individuals and communities attached to dharma are reflected in the creation of a 'multilayered identity'. This system was applied to every individual of each jati. At the same time, it looks like individual responsibility, but it gives a sense of collective responsibility by mentioning kula, the capital of the empire, the flag, etc., as part of identity. In chapter 7, we have seen Brahmins and their common but differentiated responsibilities.

There used to be head Brahmins for an empire that used to have this lineage and multilayer identity details in written record (refer to p. 163). Even today, many Bhatt go from village to village to give an account of family, lineage, and all multilayer identity details so that it becomes an income source as well as enlightens people about their identity, which strengthens their faith towards Hinduism and their responsibility as drivers of Hinduism, and this also helps in the cessation or diversion of individuals from Hinduism. The same thing is termed 'identity pluralism' by Amartya Sen, which helps in curbing extremism and secessionist tendencies and the entry of sleeper cells/black ships, which can create security issues in a country. So this is also like a census, but we are told the British carried out the first census in 1871.

Whenever someone speaks about the education system in ancient Bhārat, then experts try to explain it by giving institutional examples like Nalanda, Takshashila, etc., or examples of Maitrayi or Gargi, but no one tells how common men were well trained as Hindus. So it is an obvious question: how common man remained Hindu and practiced Hinduism for 5,000+ years without breaking tradition or cult? We never think about these things, but at the same time, we are very proud to say we started getting an education when the British came to Bhārat.

Education of Hindus

1. Traditionally, from generation-to-generation tales of the Rāmāyaṇa and Mahābhārata, Hindu lifestyle is based on ecology and cosmology, so things like ecology, cosmology, psychology, calendar, plants, herbs, Ayurveda, philosophy, and politics were learned from parents.

Table 8.1 (Content may vary as per sources.)

वंश – सूर्यवंश	तंवर (तोमर) वंश – चंद्रवंशी
गोत्र – कश्यप	वंशकेगोत्र-प्रवरादि
वेद – यजुर्वेद	कुलदेवी – चिल्लायमाता
शाखा – वाजस्नेयी	शाखा – मधुनेक,वाजस्नेयी
प्रवर – कश्यप, अप्सार, नैधुव	गोत्र – अत्रि, व्यागर, गागर्य
कुलदेवी – चामुंडामाता	प्रवर – गागर्य,कौस्तुभ,माडषय
वरदेवी – गाजनमाता	शिखा – दाहिनी
कुलदेव – विष्णुभगवान	भेरू – गौरा
सूत्र – पारासर	शस्त्र – खड़ग
शिखा – दाहिनी	ध्वज – पंचरगा
कुलगुरु – वशिष्ट	पुरोहित – भिवाल
निकास – उत्तर	स्थान – पाटामानससरोवर
प्रमुखगादी – भीनमाल, मंडोर,कन्नोज	कुलवृक्ष – गुल्लर
ध्वज – लाल (सूर्यचिन्हयुक्त)	प्रणाम – जयगोपाल
वृक्ष – सिरस	निशान – कपि(चील),चन्द्रमा
पितर – नाहङराव, लूलरगोपालजी	ढोल – भंवर
नदी – सरस्वती	घोड़ा – श्वेते
तीर्थ – पुष्कररा ज	निकास – हस्तिनापुर
मन्त्र – गायत्रीजाप	प्रमुखगादी – इन्द्रप्रस्थ,दिल्ली
पक्षी – गरुड़	रंग – हरा
नगारा – रणजीत	नाई – क़ाला
चारण – लालस	चमार – भारीवाल
ढोली – सोनेलियालाखणियाविरद – गुजरेश्वर, राणा,	शंख – पिचारक
	वेद – यजुर्वेद
	देवता – शिव
	गुरु – सूर्य
	उपाधि – जावलानरेश.दिल्लीपति

2. Sixteen saṃskāras and day-to-day rituals ensured that they were one with dharma on a day-to-day basis.
3. Three varnas were allowed for the upanayana ceremony, which means they used to get education in dharma.

This is how jati's cultural common places made economic-political-social union of Bhārat and transformed Bhārat into one nation. But what kind of state and private sector relationship was there? There was no public sector enterprise; all businesses, industries, and supply chains were private, according to jatis and all were expected to pay taxes, but we do find references about artisans and artists being patronized by the state. To handle the situation, every village had a headman, five headmen of each jati, Brahmins as law and jurisprudence, etc.[1] Minimum state and market-driven economy with no habit of consumerism based on greed, which brought certainty in production and distribution. This stabilized the economy over the years. Changes in consumption patterns were according to changes in season, harvesting, festivals, ceremonies, etc.

Now just tell me that do multiple identities like gotra, jati, and varna 'only' promote discrimination, orthodoxy, backward–forward inequality, exploitation, something that should be compulsorily opposed, which divided Hindus?

Ādi Śaṅkarācāryaḥ

Ādi Śaṅkarā, the reviver and saviour of Hindu dharma, who was Advaita-Vedanti (explained in chapters 14 and 19), created a combination of human capital and institutional efforts to save Hinduism.

Combination of Human Capital, Institutionalization and Events By Ādi Śaṅkarācāryaḥ

First, he defeated many schools of thought, whether aligned with the Vedas or not, on the debate on Brahman, maya, and liberation. In that time, there were no egoistic people who continued following the wrong teachings of their sect just to maintain the useless egoistic unique identity of pantha (sect) or just 'freedom of religion'. Those people who lost the debate became followers of Ādi Śaṅkarācāryaḥ. Then Ādi Śaṅkarācāryaḥ created ten types of swamis according to Bhārat's geography so that 'Sanatana dharma' exists in the whole of Bhārat. He also established four mathas.

Dashnami sampradaya

A swami is one who renounces and seeks to achieve union (oneness) with the *swa* (self). In formally renouncing the world, he or she generally wears ochre, saffron, or orange-coloured robes as a symbol of non-attachment to worldly desires and may choose to roam independently or join an ashram or other organization cum school, typically in an ideal of selfless service. Upon initiation, which can only be done by another existing swami, the renunciate receives a new name (usually ending in 'ananda', meaning 'supreme bliss') and takes a title that formalizes his connection with one of the ten subdivisions of the Swami Order. A swami's name has a dual significance, representing the attainment of supreme bliss through some divine quality or state (i.e., love, wisdom, service, yoga) and through harmony with the infinite vastness of nature, expressed in one of the ten subdivision names: Dashanami Sampradaya, 'Tradition of Ten Names', is a Hindu monastic tradition of Ekadandi sannyasins (wandering renunciates carrying a single staff) generally associated with the Advaita Vedanta tradition.

1. Giri (mountain)
2. Puri (tract)
3. Bhāratī (land)
4. Vana (forest)
5. Āraṇya (forest)
6. Sagara (sea)
7. Āśrama (spiritual exertion)
8. Sarasvatī (wisdom of nature)
9. Tīrtha (place of pilgrimage)
10. Parvata (mountain)

Akharas

Sampradāya is translated as 'tradition/theme' with some theme. It relates to a succession of masters and disciples, which serves as a spiritual channel and provides a delicate network of relationships that lends stability to cultural identity. Sampradaya is a body of practices, views, and attitudes that are transmitted, redefined, and reviewed by each successive generation of followers.

A particular guru lineage is called parampara. By receiving diksha (initiation) into the guru–shishya traditional parampara of a living guru, one belongs to its proper sampradaya. One cannot become a member by birth, as is the case with gotra, a seminal, or hereditary, dynasty. In the traditional residential form of education, the shishya remains with his or her guru as a family member and gets the education as a true learner.

Sampradaya is a particular system of belief, and within it, a particular guru's lineage is called parampara. There are three distinct belief system sampradayas (Vaishnava, Shaivite, and Dashanami sampradayas), each of which follows one of three types (Deva, Rishi, and Manav parampara) of the guru–shishya parampara lineage. Each sampradaya parampara may have several akharas of shastradhari (intellectuals) or astradhari (warriors), and larger akharas may have one or more permanent mathas.

Table 8.2

Daiva paramparā (deities themselves are protectors of dharma)	• Nārāyaṇa • Sada Shiva • Padmabhuva (Brahmā)
Ṛiṣhi paramparā (rishis are protectors and carriers of dharma)	• Vaśiṣṭha • Śakti • Parāśara • Vyāsa • Śuka
Mānava paramparā (humans are protectors and carriers of dharma)	• Gauḍapāda • Govindabhagavatpāda • Śankarabhagavatpāda Then Ādi Śaṅkarācāryaḥ's four disciples • Padmapāda • Hastāmalaka • Toṭaka • Vārtikakāra (Sureśvara) and others

The three sampradayas are Vaishnava, Shavite, and Advaita.
1. Vaishnava sampradaya: It has four major guru–shishya traditional paramparas:
   a. Sri sampradaya parampara of guru Ramanujacharya
   b. Madhva sampradaya parampara of guru Madhvacharya

c. Rudra sampradaya parampara of guru Viṣṇusvāmī/ Vallabhacharya
   d. Kumara sampradaya parampara of guru Nimbarka
2. Shaivite sampradaya: It has six major guru–shishya traditional paramparas:
   a. Nandinatha sampradaya parampara of guru Tirumular (now known as Siddha sampradaya of Shaiva Siddhanta)
   b. Meykandar sampradaya parampara of guru Meykandar (now known as Saiva Adheenams of Shaiva Siddhanta in southern Bhārat)
   c. Adinath sampradaya parampara of gurus Matsyendranath and Gorakshanath (now known as Nath sampradaya of Siddha Siddhanta)
   d. Trika sampradaya (also known as Ragasya sampradaya and Trayambaka sampradaya) parampara of guru Durvasa and Vasugupta who follow Kashmir Shaivism
   e. Lingayat sampradaya parampara
   f. Srouta sampradaya parampara
3. Advaita sampradaya (also known as Ekadandis or, more recently, as Dashanami sampradaya): After the decline of Buddhism, a section of the Ekadandis was organized by Ādi Śaṅkarācāryaḥ in the 8th century in Bhārat to be associated with four maṭhas paramparas to provide a base for the growth of Hinduism.
   a. Bhogavala parampara of guru Padmapāda at Govardhana Pīṭhaṃ (Puri in Odisha)
   b. Bhūrivala parampara of guru Sureśvara at Sringeri Śārada Pīṭhaṃ (in Karnataka)
   c. Kitavala parampara of guru Hastāmalakācārya at Dvāraka Pīṭhaṃ (Dwaraka in Gujrat)
   d. Nandavala parampara of guru Toṭakācārya at Jyotirmaṭha Pīṭhaṃ (Jyotirmath in Uttrakhand)

Two types of swami or sadhus
1. Shastradhari (Sanskrit: शास्त्रधारी, scripture-bearers) intelligentsia.
2. Astradhari (Sanskrit: अस्त्रधारी, weapon-bearers) warriors. This refers to the Naga sadhus (a sub-set of Dashanami sampradaya),

an armed order created by Śaṅkarācāryaḥ to act as a Hindu army. These highly militant sadhus used to serve as mercenaries and were thus divided into akharas or regiments. Akhara evolved into the 'fighting martial force' of mendicants, likely as a reaction to the harsh and brutal treatment of Hindus by the Muslim rulers.[2] Akharas act of self-defence was turning into armed monasteries of mystics. Presently, Naga sadhu still carry weapons, but they rarely practice any form of fighting aside from wrestling.

While introducing one of the integral sects of the Sanatana Dharma, one of the Indian art and culture books explain that concept of 'this soldier saint' of certain sect was quite practical than Hinduism's concept of sannyāsi. As the history of Hinduism was suppressed deliberately, that is why there is no recognition of Ādi Śaṅkarācāryaḥ and his contribution. Even Kshatriyas are considered to have the knowledge of the four Vedas, six shahstras, and eighteen Puranas; isn't this astra + shaastra? In the case of Hindu sannyāsi, Naga sadhus are real saint soldiers because they never trouble anyone until Hinduism is attacked, and then they again become saints after the war. But some (Hindu-phobic) books mention that tradition, who was king, who had an empire, knew some philosophy, were progenitors of the 'saint soldier' concept. That tradition can be equated with Kshatriyas in Hinduism, not saint soldier.

Initially, there were only four akharas based on the sampradaya (sect), which have split into subsidiary akharas due to differences in leadership and expansion in followership. In January 2019, there were thirteen akharas that were allowed to participate in Prayagraj Kumbh Mela, and they formed the Akhil Bhāratiya Akhara Parishad with two representatives from each of the thirteen akharas to manage the akhara-related affairs across all kumbmelas and across the nations. All sadhus of akhara will meet in kumbhamela every six or twelve years to discuss strategy for Hindu dharma rather than just a 'secular form of meeting'. Kumbhamela happens only on certain occasions when celestial bodies are in a certain pattern.

Akharas

Sannyāsi akhara
These are the followers of Shiva. Examples of these akharas include:
1. Niranjani akhara and its subsidiary
2. Ananda akhara
3. Juna akhara and its subsidiaries
4. Avahan akhara
5. Agni akhara
6. Pari akhara, an exclusive akhara of female sadahavi (saints), was included in Prayagraj Kumbh for the first time starting in 2013 as a subsidiary akhara of one of the existing akharas.
7. Kinnar akhara, an exclusive akhara of transgender people, was included in Prayagraj Kumbh for the first time starting in 2019 as a subsidiary akhara of the Dashanami akhara.

Vairagi akhara/Bairagi akhara
These are the followers of Vishnu. Examples of such akharas include:
1. Mahanirvani akhara (or simply Nirvani) and its subsidiaries
2. Atal akhara
3. Nirmohi akhara
4. Digambar akhara
5. Khalsa akhara

Udasi akhara
These are the followers of Sikhism. Examples of such akharas is Nirmal akhara

Kalpwasis akhara
These are the followers of Brahma, generally ordinary people who are temporarily living the austere life during the Kumbh Mela to mimic Vanaprastha's 'retiring into a forest' stage of later life. In that sense, kalpwasis akhara is a temporary akhara with no fixed ongoing organization or leadership.

This much-organized Hinduism dates from ancient times in the spheres of economy, society, and culture, and we are taught how Hindus are divided because of diversity. There are many ancient cults and organizations, I have not mentioned because of a lack of knowledge. In the Kāla Bhairava chapter, I mentioned that the past is the future. So, when Hindus are divided, their brains were ready to become vulnerable for conversion or vote bank politics of jati, varna, language, culture, etc.

Non-Brahmin, Non-Kshatriya Effort

We are taught Brahmins and Kshatriyas conserved religion (not through history books but in the general narrative) and Shudras are permanent victims of the jati system, which confirms their communist inclination. But we are never told that many jatis in 'non-Brahmin non-Kshatriya' 'Hinduism kept alive in two ways'. First, they knew all philosophy, stories from the Puranas, Rāmāyaṇa, and Mahābhārata, and all customs and traditions that I have mentioned in chapter 20, which are the identity of trained human capital that kept alive dharma as a tradition. Second, they kept alive dharma through tangible and intangible traditions, i.e., temples, sculptures, and cave construction. Sculptures included deity and all stories from Rāmāyaṇa and Mahābhārata. Other than this, they kept dharma alive through arts like paintings, e.g., pattachitra, etc.; they kept it alive through traditional dance, music, both classical and folk; theatres of Bhārat in the local language and Sanskrit, which promoted dharma to the masses. Traditional Entertainment industry was lead particular Jatis as a business.

But we are never told of their efforts to keep Hindu tradition and teachings alive. We are always told Brahmins wrote books and Kshatriyas fought to save dharma, and few mentions of bhakti saints were from all jatis. But what goes beyond that? But if this effort is appreciated through history books, then the status of 'Shudras are permanent victims and suppressed' will go, and then how would they choose communism as a tool for 'total armed revolution'? To divide, create that binary of Brahmin–Kshatriya-Vaishya vs. Shudra-Ati Shudra, which is easy to translate into establishment vs. victims; communists never told the truth. Today also, many Brahmins and Kshatriya have gone away from dharma in the name of modernization and liberalism. Still, those jatis are performing traditional arts and keeping Hinduism alive, and we don't even have that humble attitude to thank them. Financing them for economic upliftment is way ahead. That is why communists removed the economy and cultural ethos related to Hinduism so that what remains is only the identity of someone established and someone victim, which is the best human capital with a social-political divide to play the card of communism.

Illiterate Non-Brahmins

There are thousands of proofs that Kshatriyas have written many kinds of literature, and many languages were known to them; they were well versed in Hindu dharma. But this doesn't fit in the narrative of 'Brahmins kept other castes illiterate'; the same is true about Vaishya because the business class must know multiple languages as Bhārat was an export-led economy. We just discussed Shudras too. We were never told the contribution of non-Brahmin jatis in Hinduism to create the Kāla Bhairava effect 'your ancestor never contributed in Hinduism, so you should not'. So anti-Hindu historians were successful in creating the narrative Brahmins = Hinduism and vice versa.

The best example is South Asia; Bhārat, China, Japan, Southeast Asia, and a few other countries like Brazil, etc., are the only countries that were colonies of European countries, but today they are in the race for superpowers or already have nuclear weapons. This is because these countries have kept the deep roots of indigenous culture alive, maintained their distinct identities, and combined it with modernization. See the countries of South America, Mexico, Africa, and a few countries from South Asia and Southeast Asia, which are colonies of major religions. Few are victims of opium and other drugs; remaining one's terrorism; in between, religion is shown as a way to come out of this problem, and again, they are pushed into colonialism.

The Challenge of Conserving Culture

The most difficult thing today is that Hinduism has multiple bodies, multiple sects, individual connections with Hinduism, efforts by sannyāsis, temples, maths, ashrams, etc., but everything collectively creates confusion and duplication of efforts. Ignorance about Hinduism among modern-day Hindus is one of the biggest challenge;

even if sleeper cell comes in saffron clothing, Hindus will go and worship him. Hindus don't know what our dharma is and what is not? They only celebrate festivals in their own liberal way and go to temples; other than this, they don't know anything else. Hindus are caught in a vicious circle of God, religion, followers, worship, peace, secularism, capitalism, communism, orthodox–liberal, Brahmanism, Aryan, Dravidian, etc. Secondly, exclusive religions are to be promoted and kept alive through a nine-point agenda (refer to page 247–248), but Hindu civilization is to be consumed to keep it alive.

Some jatis only have professions and skills that they adopted hereditarily and carry out as employment, whether they are potters, goldsmiths, ironsmith, artists, or artisans. Today, we have lost jatis or communities that had skills in constructing classical temples and forts and thousands of such skills. But the Kshatriya community (Rajputs, Marathas, Varmas, etc.), who (not all) still have a royal lifestyle in forts and lavish traditional houses, have the whole heritage of their ancestors with them, right from jewellery, clothes, utensils, war equipments, literature, lineage records, manuscripts, etc. Not only this, but many Kshatriyas were well versed in the Sanskrit Vedas, six shastras, eighteen Puranas, and various vidyas like music, archery, poetry, etc., e.g., Rajput kings, Chhatrapati Sambhaji Maharaj, are maintaining it as a hereditary tradition, not only of the king but even of the staff, just to ensure that the whole culture related to them remains safe. Today, in Rajasthan, traditional artists are supported by royal families through financial and infrastructural support so that tangible and intangible culture is kept alive.

Do we have a mechanism (under the government of Bhārat) to handle the tradition, tangible and intangible culture of this nation? Who will take responsibility for manufacturing traditional products, whether for cultural or daily use? Even if we create institutions and mechanisms, what guarantees that the way the hereditary system used to take care of tradition will be done with the same intensity and devotion? How will we attach the youth of this nation about our history, culture, and past traditions? Will youth study details about tangible and intangible culture in detail in the era of fast life and modernization? Is the government serious about maintaining manuscripts and digitization? What is the mechanism to transfer the responsibility of culture from one generation to another? What if the any sleeper cell enters in maintenance and destroys it? If some jatis don't want to institutionalize their art and skills so that their monopoly remains on them through hereditary means then how can we take this art to an international level?

Those who want to see a nation as individualism (Clean slate or themeless individual) with no collectivism of family, jati, village, tribal identity do they have answers to these questions of conserving culture. On the other hand, climate change and population explosions are leading nations to destruction. Have we ever thought about what will happen to this nation when resources are inadequate? And the country and its heritage will again fall.

That is why I deny terming 'Hinduism as religion' or Hinduism as Brahmins religion, because the responsibility of tangible and intangible culture is much bigger, which is not the responsibility of only Brahmins and Kshatriyas, nor do they have that much physical and intellectual capacity. How can Brahmins or Kshatriyas protect or revive the profession or art related to other jatis, if they don't know basics/skills; secondly, what is future of those jatis modernization, semi-modernization, the old system of the profession, rural to urban transformation, what is financial security and literacy of them? Giving reservations or representation and letting society take shape however it wants is making society more vulnerable to an unpredicted future. Hinduism should be taken as civilization, and the responsibility of civilization must be taken by civilization. But counterview to this is the 'freedom to choose any profession, the right to choose, personal liberty, caste discrimination', which is equally correct.

The Government Has Done Various Efforts
1. Indira Gandhi National Centre for Crafts
2. Nehru Memorial Museum and Library
3. Centre for Cultural Resources and Training
4. Indian Council for Cultural Relations
5. Indian Council for Historical Research
6. Indian National Trust for Art and Cultural Heritage

7. Sahitya Akademi
8. Sangeet Natak Akademi
9. Lalit Kala Akademi
10. Archaeological Survey of Bhārat
11. Crafts Council of Bhārat
12. National Archives of Bhārat
13. National Mission for Manuscripts
14. Schemes for Tribal and Traditional Industry SFURTI
15. Other private and government institutions are working on dance, music, martial arts, etc. but unrelated and duplicating efforts

Even after such institutional efforts, Hinduism, rather than saving or reviving it, still faces deterioration. Biased history books with anti-Hindu propaganda were written in such a way that common Hindus never feel connected with history or feel connected, and the outcome is guilt. Many places are not under ASI, but at the same time, only temples are under the control of state governments. Manuscripts are not digitized, and the biggest thing is that there is no uniform physical safe infrastructure where manuscripts can be kept; many manuscripts are kept at various universities and semi-government institutions. Many historical books are under the full control of specific universities. Most of the history books are written by north Bhārtiya people and northern universities with Delhi-centric history. The condition of conserving Hinduism is facing division, randomness, a scattered approach, and duplication of efforts.

Other than Hinduism, we have cultures of Buddhism, Indo-Islamic, Jainism, etc., which have contributed to the art and literature of nations, so conserving that art and literature is also a challenge. That is why uniting people and ending duplication of efforts, randomness, and uniformity is another challenge.

What We Need to Revive Today

1. Single organization and end of duplication of efforts.
2. Maintenance of physical assets like temples and matha.
3. Bringing spiritual legitimacy and depth in knowledge.

4. Events that match up according to tithi and astrology, like Kumbha Mela.
5. Uniform institution and uniform digital infrastructure and ending duplication of digital place.
6. Geographical reach and diversification.
7. Digitization of manuscripts and interpretation.
8. Translation of books in local language (not British one).
9. Explaining the importance of rituals, festivals, etc.
10. Taking Ayurveda, astrology, clothing all services to the common man.
11. Personal as well as community-level responsibility.
12. Uniform funding and collection and management of funds uniformly.
13. End of corruption, corrupt practices, corrupt babas.
14. Opening libraries that teach necessary basic education nearby temples.
15. Taking the science of liberation to the common man.
16. Temple-led development.
17. Reviving traditional industry and products.
18. Promoting eco-friendly life and climate change awareness.
19. Single publication house for Hindu books.
20. A branch that handles MSME sectors too for permanent funding and creating employment.
21. Eliminating political, religious, cultural, and social movements which have goal of a non-accepting tangible and intangible culture of Bhārat.

Fundamental duties and the directive principle of state policy add value to the country's composite culture and preserve the rich cultural heritage, including places of national importance such as monuments.

But how? And as a citizen, what are we doing?

PART III
UNTOUCHABILITY WITH HINDUISM

1. Exclusive religions whose fundamentals include:
   a. the existence of gods, deities, or tangible/intangible cultures of other faiths is denied, hence boycotted (marginalisation of others), e.g., commandments against idol worship
   b. concept and commandments against infidel
   c. non-participation, boycotting, or destroying tangible/intangible culture or culture beyond 'religion' as prescribed in the 'religion', i.e., sociocultural untouchability + music/dance completely banned
   d. I'm nationalist, but within the framework of my religion, i.e., if nationalism fits in religious framework, then I will follow it; otherwise, only religion; nationalism = citizenship to expand an empire (religion)
2. Communism
   a. denies and negates all religions
   b. mocking religion creates a social base for political gains
   c. avoid nationalism or project it as stigma
3. Misinterpreted Buddhism: combination of 1 and 2, exclusive oaths to boycott Hindu deities and practices
4. Language politics and regionalism (regionalism vs. Hinduism) which can't make you think beyond language; otherwise, polarized language-based population will lose concentration because of expansion (refer to p. 66)
5. Caste-based politics, limiting identity to caste as a caste leader without recognizing the cultural-economic heritage of caste

6. Nationalism = only constitution; eliminating or negating the whole Bhārat, its history and culture, before or beyond the constitution, i.e., exclusive religion's model, boycotting everything beyond 'book' [1]

For all six, citizenship is only proof of being Bhārtiya, which is why all of them become aggressively active when issues related to citizenship and census are on the table of discussion. That is because 'except citizenship' they don't have any proof to call themselves Bhārtiya or indigenous. Can we say that somewhere an intent reflects the will to carry out cultural genocide and disturb multicultural social fabric, causing communalism?

All these six non-inclusive players have a union at the psycho-philosophical level with a common think tank, which is a combination of all six, i.e., 'Why I am not Hindu'. So, all these things are symbols of 'non-acceptance, denial, non-inclusive, and negation'. When their ideology or religion has already divided the world into 'follower-infidel, follow-unfollow, world within our ideology-world beyond ideology', then following double standards, biasedness, and hypocrisy is an ideological necessity to maintain 'us vs. them' so that one day 'them' are eliminated. The origin of the ideology is 'relative', which makes them bully others.

In addition, all six ideologies have legal, unconstitutional, and institutional support under diplomatic terms: minority rights, representation, linguistic minority, secularism (atheism), etc. Plus, they have external support (foreign funding) from where their ideology originates, such as international institutions and universities. Politically, all are united as coming to power with non-inclusive politics is an impossible task. Even though they have conflicting values, double standards and hypocrisy help to unite two different systems simultaneously in a discriminatory way.

Now the effort is on to convince caste-reservation categories (sects of Hinduism) to join the union of 'Why I am not Hindu'. If they are given political power, then their ideology will culminate in the cultural genocide of Hinduism by creating policies, excluding Hinduism from history books, and giving free hand to their followers, which has already happened and is happening.

As ideology is non-inclusive plus poor or no content, the only way to survive is by promoting ethnocentrism, ethnocentric economy, ethnocentric polity, ethnocentric society-infrastructure-education institutions, and capturing political power to survive so that the one who questions poor, discriminatory, or irrational content can be threatened by number in ethnocentric parallel economy, parallel polity, parallel society, parallel infrastructure, parallel education institutions, so that fight becomes to protect number, which diverts from questioning irrational ideology or religion. Because if they leave 'ideology' in the lap of markets and rationality, their ideology will vanish. So they create 'stereotypes and stigmas' about Hinduism so that Hinduism fails without knowing it as mentioned in A1.1, p. 401. They are like big onions; if pilled off, you get nothing. One of the tools they use for their anti-Bhārat campaign is fake indices to measure socio-economic indicator.[2]

After creating a parallel nation within a nation, they want themselves to be 'mainstreamed' by mainstream society (the victim card). UN, World Bank, etc. calculate poverty, hunger, and illiteracy universally, but in Bhārat, it is separately calculated for the six non-inclusive players which helps to project them as 'non-mainstream'. They want their parallel world to be mainstreamed. All six non-inclusive players have always been united even before the independence of Bhārat with one common goal: 'anti-Hindu fascism'.[3] To hide their real face, i.e., the foreign origin of ideology and foreign funded or sponsorship, they strongly support Aryan invasion theory to make Hinduism look like a foreign religion or Brahmin colonialism, and six non-inclusive players identify themselves as Mulniwasi or indigenous people. They are given preferential treatment on international platforms[4] in terms of shaping opinions, human rights, cultural views, etc. If you practice any anti-social philosophies, the implementation of these destructive ideologies is so dangerous that it may welcome certain sections of IPC Articles 23, 24, 34, 35, 107, 121, 123, 124a, 126, 147, 153A, 157, 147, 141, 295, 297, 299, 354, 360, 369, 375, 376, 390, 396, 441, 463, 499, and 504. These sections are not a judgment against any ideology but are used only as a reference.

Best Example

At the outset, let me state that we fully agree that anti-Semitism, Islamophobia, and anti-Christian acts need to be condemned, and Bhārat firmly condemns such acts. However, UN resolutions on such important issues speak only of these three Abrahamic religions together, ignoring human rights and the voice of Hindus.

First secretary of Bhārat's permanent mission to the UN Ashish Sharma on 'Culture of Peace', 3 December 2020.

This shows how institutional/academic Hindu-phobia, which exists in Bhārat, is also reflected in international institutions like the UN.[5]

Diagram U.1 Untouchability with Hinduism

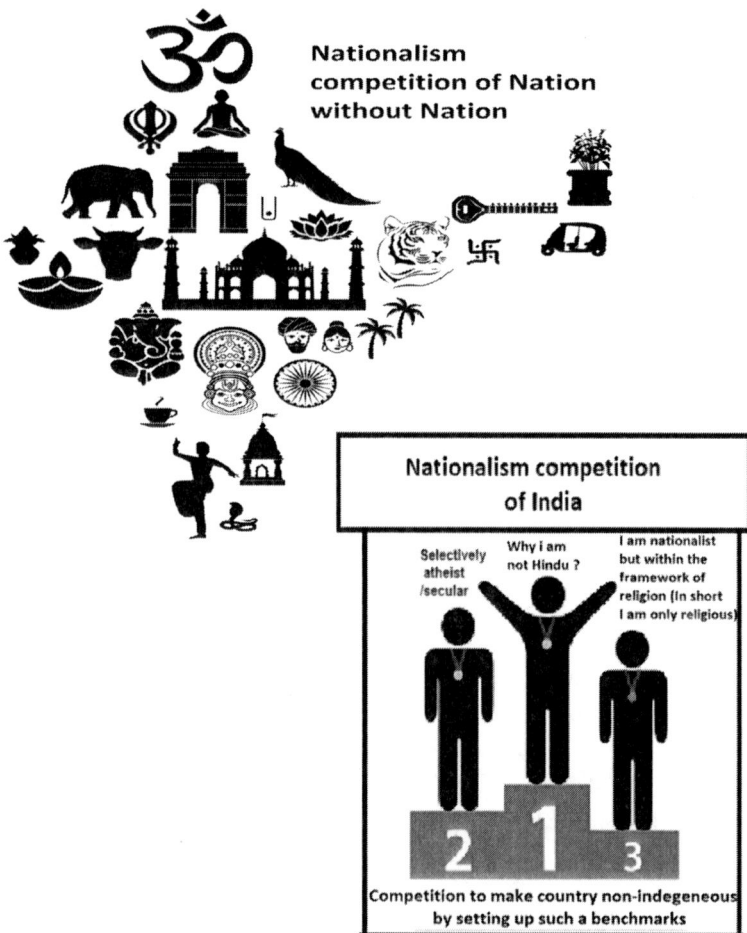

9

Why I Am Not Hindu

Shastra of 'Why I Am Not Hindu'

In the Abrahamic trilogy, Judaism and Christianity all have some common teachings, beliefs, stories, ancestry, etc. But the geography of all three religions is very strategic; if walls of separation fall, then East Asia and the Middle East/west asia will be connected, which will be beneficial for both of them. There is 'oil' in the Middle East, so everyone wants to control it. You can control someone only when he or she is internally disturbed, so the strategic wall of separation is to be maintained at the religion-based identity level so that it reflects strategic separation at the geographical level. This pentagon is successful because the teachings of religion (which may be misinterpreted) are supportive of maintaining strategic separation.[6]

1. Don't accept that religion is inspired or influenced by the previous common civilizational past.
2. Because of conservative/exclusivist fundamentalism, they don't participate in each other's religion, culture, or festivals, so that strategic separation is maintained.
3. They don't accept that their teachings, beliefs, and stories are influenced by previous religions, but they claim the same religious places and geography, which they even accept as evolution.

This chapter is about whether we want to make Bhārat's geography like Al-Aqsa mosque (Diagram 9.2) or we want unified intermingling diversity existing as a symbiosis with ecology and development, so according to that, we need to behave, speak, and support ideology. So 'why I am not Hindu' is the essence of the above three points to create the 'pentagon' within Bhārat.

Diagram 9.1

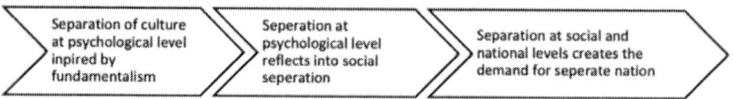

Diagram 9.2

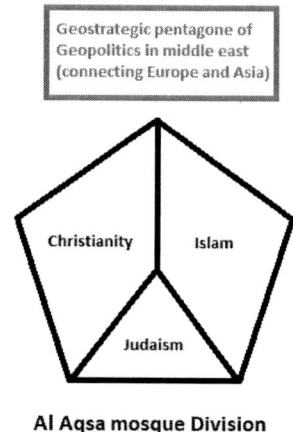

Al Aqsa mosque Division

Why I Am Not Hindu because I Am Abrahamic

The same pentagon pattern was shaped by our colonial masters to repeat in Bhārat so that water-tight separation takes place between Hindus and non-Hindus or within Hinduism. Plus, colonial masters carved out Buddhist, Jains, Sikhs[7], Cārvāka, etc., from the Hindu fold (the pattern of carving out explained on pp. 121–122). On the same basis mentioned in chapter 7, Sikhism was also carved out of the Hindu fold.[8]

When various sects and traditions within Hinduism itself are carved out and projected as separate from the Vedas or Hinduism or against them, then definitely followers of this sect will practice 'untouchability with Hinduism' and will walk on the paths of Diagrams 9.1 and 9.2. External enemies are there to fuel this by marketing 'majority' as a majoritarian regime, nationalism and sovereignty as hyper-nationalism, etc., and projecting the minority as the victim. One successful mission we have seen in the format of Pakistan, which is not a partition of Bhārat; it is actually a successful separatist movement carving out Muslim majority provinces from Bhārat. So the goal is to create an Abrahamic parallel within Bhārat by carving out multiple sects from Hinduism, as shown in Diagrams 9.1 and 9.2. So this people-led social movement of carving out certain sects out of Hinduism has some 'common content', which I call 'Why I am not Hindu?' and is divided into two categories.

a. Denying the contribution of Hinduism in these sects as content (refer to pp. 121–122) and removing all that content that is taken from Hinduism. By projecting the initiator of the sect as the 'founder' by denying his own foundations in Hinduism.
b. Aggressive, abusive verbal attacks on Hinduism to market the respective sect as a better option than Hinduism.

Both of these things cause alienation and separation from mainstream Hindu society, which helps in promoting secessionist and subversive activities.

Table 9.1

Rebels	Secessionist tendency	Reality
Dravida Nadu	Hinduism and Dravidian/ Tamil are separate, i.e., imposing atheism on Tamil literature	Sangam literature itself has mentions of Hindu deities, Ayurveda, stories from the Mahābhārata, and Siddha inspired by Ayurveda. Tamil grammer (Tolkapiyyam) is inspired by Sanskrit grammar rules.[9]
Khalistan	No contribution of Hindu scriptures and culture to religion	Hindu population adopted Sikhism because their gurus never practiced alienation and cultural untouchability with Hinduism. Etymology, cultural practices, and many other things are reflections of Hinduism itself.[10]

Rebels	Secessionist tendency	Reality
Buddhism, Jainism	Heterodox atheists against Hinduism	Explained on pp. 121–122
Cārvāka	Atheist, materialist	Explained on p. 110

Before British invasion, there was no such separatism and untouchability with Hinduism. The most important thing is that all these sects are practised in border areas where separatism is easy because of external interference. For example, Punjab (Sikh majority), Tamil Nadu (Tamil atheists vs. Tamil Hindu), Buddhism (Srilankan Sinhali Buddhist targeting Hindu Tamils), atheism–Maoism (Red Corridor in eastern Bhārat), for that they run narrative tribal are not Hindus.[11]

The following two diagrams are enough to tell you the flow of etymology, yoga, meditation, values, astronomy, time calculation, survival skills, Ayurveda, ancestry, philosophy, etc., vs. separatism.[12]

Diagram 9.3

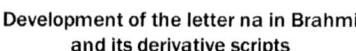

Development of the letter na in Brahmi and its derivative scripts

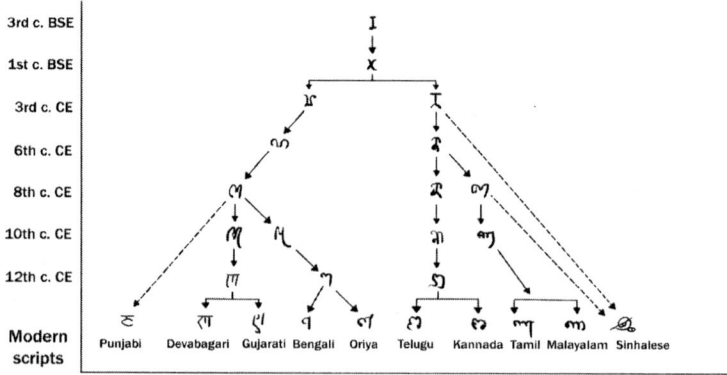

Diagram 9.4

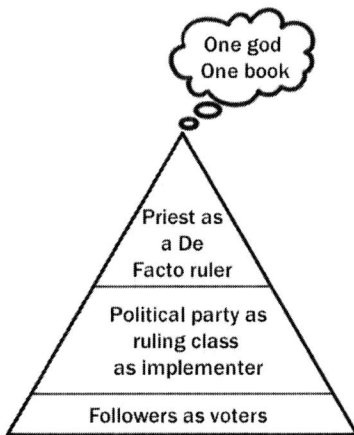

In the British era, Pakistan was a top priority because Afghanistan was not enough to stop the connection between the socialist Bhārat and the communist USSR in those times. So Jinnah was the best puppet, a Sunni Islamic country that is counter to Hindus on the east, Shias to the west, and communists to the north. Another secessionist movement was not given priority because the challenge was the USSR, but today Bhārat itself is a big challenge, which is why anti-Bhārat movements are a big challenge. So majority vs. minority is the best fit for creating violence or secessionist tendency, but if the minority gets support from 'Bibhishan/Why I am not Hindu', then it becomes double power.

If one is interested in holding national interests over and above everything, then he will accept religion as part of the evolution of humanity rather than an isolational existence. For such people, the contribution of a small and sweet story of 'brotherhood' is enough, even if it mismatches with fundamentalism, e.g., 'Kabuli Wala and the girl' in Rabindranath Tagore's writing. But the problem is that 'non-participation and non-contribution' is an intrinsic and institutionalized value of some exclusivist religions, but 'Kabuli Wala' incidents are neither religious nor institutionalized, and people in this nation experience such incidences on a day-to-day basis. There are thousands of examples that can take 'why I am

Table 9.2

Exclusive religions	Dravida Nadu	Khalistan	Misinterpreted Buddhism	Communists
One God	'No God' is God (sticking to atheism strongly)	Misinterpreted and manipulated scriptures	Buddha as God	'No God' is God
One book	*Thirukkural* (secular book according to them)	Misinterpreted, manipulated religion/scripture	Exclusive policy towards Hinduism	Critique of Hegel's philosophy of right
Better society dreams	Limited Hinduism to caste discrimination	Limited Hinduism to caste discrimination and 'Hindu' is an abusive word used by Arabs	Limited Hinduism to caste discrimination	Limited Hinduism to caste discrimination
Political party	Well known	Well known	Multiple parties with same model	Well known
Leader	Periyar	Well known	Him	Multiple leaders at multiple geographies

not Hindus' to their roots, but as they have taken a blind oath of separatism with rootless culture and blind hero worship (leader of separatist), how can my words convince them? I would not have written this chapter or this book if mainstream history books, government history books, and books used for civil services would not have promoted Hindu-phobia and fodder for separatism in their respective books.

Cultural separation creates a 'social base', which culminates in a political one and then a separate nation, as we saw in the case of Jinnah. He didn't demand the country directly.

1. We are not part of the majority (in the case of Bhārat and its Hindus).
2. We want special space in politics and bureaucracy.
3. We want special legal status for the community-dominated area.
4. We can't live together.
5. We want a separate country.

There were various Jinnahs (separatists) in Bhārat with Hindu names too. But these people remained unobserved. Pakistan was created out of a political movement. So we must vote for those who are in the national interest. Because there are many people who market 'national interest'. Bhārat allocated 1,03,927 crores in 2019–20 budget from 61,401 crores in 2014–15. All these issues cost us economically, and martyrs are priceless. I want to let you know how these separatist movements happened and their pattern. Just see Table 9.3, which is mostly observed and applicable to all separatist and expansionary policies. Compare it with all the separatist movements that happened in Bhārat and the world. To fit Bhārat in these left, right, and centre structures, atheism was imposed (refer to Table 1.1, p. 5), which becomes the central motivation to separate from Hinduism.

Table 9.3[13]

Ideology	Expansionary policy	Separatist policy
Right wing	Unification on common Culture background or capturing resources, e.g., east–west Germany	Different cultural backgrounds can't live together. Examples: Bhārat and Pakistan on basis of religion, eg. Khalistan, Dravida Nadu, Kashmir
Left wing	Federation of state, i.e., common socio-economic interest, e.g., never seen any successful example	Disintegration because of absence of unifying culture and merely federation. Examples: 1. Disintegration of USSR 2. The recent issue of misinterpretation (Bhārat is a union of state).
Centrist policy	Their expansion is unification of lands or ideology with a common interest. Unites country by uniting left and right under the umbrella of centrist unbiased policy. This nature of nationalism has a short life because of 'clashing values' but survives because of tolerance	They try to express diversity and depth of country with just few shallow Western terms like 'secularism, tolerance, and multiculturalism,' which again make nationalism non-indigenous or artificial so that no one feels connected to them.
Exclusivist religions	Cultural genocide of others with expansionist policy	They demand a separate country by boycotting the majority's culture, etc., which they market as a mismatch with fundamentalism.

Hindu-Phobic Content

Step 1: Now you will understand from Table 9.3 why Hinduism is criticized on these four points only, as the title of the book says shallow attempt, which is destroyed in depth.
1. Disrespect and denial of Hindu gods
2. Denial of Hindu scriptures and their cheap criticism
3. Criticism of the Hindu model of society
4. Criticism of the political space of Hindus

Step 2: An alternate model of society, psychology, and philosophy is provided in the format of a new utopian state, 'Why I am not Hindu', which creates a social base for separatism and is reflected or becomes visible on the ground once separatism starts or terror starts. That model is:
1. There is my God, who is better than your gods/only my God exist
2. My scripture is better than others
3. My model of society is better than yours, mostly based on universal value system of truth and justice (they never speak about income inequality)
4. My political space/umbrella is better than the discriminatory umbrella of Hinduism

Suppressing Hindu Pride

a. Macaulays' formula (chapter 2)
b. Discriminatory marketing (chapter 5)
c. Discriminatory approach towards Hinduism (refer to chapter 5)
d. Sexist interpretation and sexist comments on Hindu deities, e.g., Durga is a prostitute or Ganesha's trunk is Shiva's reproductive part (utilizing sexist Hinduphobic brains with user-friendly content)[14]
e. Not accepting Hinduism's actual contribution to humanity (refer to pp. 59–60, 269–271).
f. Positive marketing of players who failed to experience 'oneness' (refer to Table 14.7) against Hinduism/'origin of experiencing oneness'
g. Atheistic and social engineering-based interpretation of the bhakti movement (refer to Tables 19.1)

h. Terming rituals irrelevant by promoting them has no scriptural basis or logic
i. Interpreting or practicing freedom of religion in such a way that it always interpreted 'not following'/freedom to become atheist within Hinduism rather than following
j. Declaring stories and rituals from great epics as 'meaningless, unreal, or impractical' without making an effort to decode them

This is how six non-inclusive players are given the candy of 'why I am not Hindu?' just to convince them that they didn't make a mistake by taking up a new non-Hindu identity and that there is nothing to be guilty about in selling self-identity to a foreign ideology/religion. Learning Hinduism is not at all a goal. As everything is fair in love and war, it doesn't matter whether the attempt is shallow or deep; what matters is its impact through marketing. Their source of understanding Hinduism is 'trust me bro'.

If Hindus think that by remaining secular, liberal, or atheist, they can run away from these Hindu-phobic/anti-Hindu forces, then you are wrong. Once Hindus are eliminated, you (liberal/secular) are the target, as it happened in 'theocratic terrorism' in various neighbouring countries. Rather than attacking directly at Hinduism, enemies use diplomatic names and pseudo-identities, i.e., Trojan horse. So, this Hindu-phobic content is circulated in multiple communities to utilize existing or artificially created social cleavages to deteriorate Hinduism or to carry out cultural genocide.

Table 9.4

Brahmin	non-Brahmin
Orthodox	Heterodox
Upper caste	Lower caste
Manusmriti	Non-*Manusmriti*
Aryan	Dravidian
Sanskrit	Tamil
Hindu	6 non inclusive players

Religion	Secularism
Vedas	Non-Vedic
Orthodox	Liberal
Metaphysics	Materialism
Extremism	Moderate
Right wing	Left wing
Non-tribal	Tribal
Sanatani	Hindu[15]

Their goal was to divide a unified civilization into mainstream and non-mainstream so that non-mainstream can be carved out as separate nations as follows.

Diagram 9.5

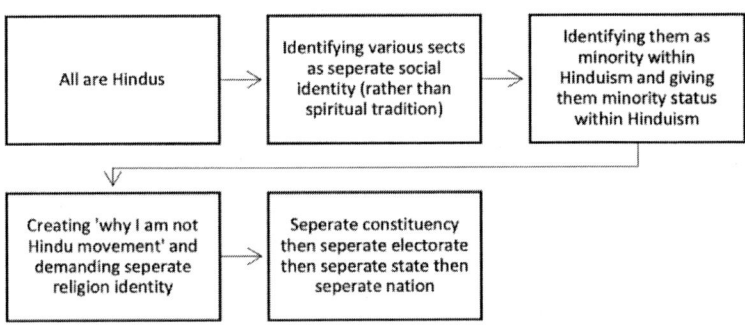

So they created non-mainstream sects with a multilayer approach: 'not keeping all eggs in the same basket', for example, theory of Kashmir, Dravida Nadu, theory of Khalsitan, Maoist theory of tribal, northeastern region theories, misinterpreted Buddhism, anti-Hindu communism, theory of Pakistan, and the theory of the Red Corridor, but one thing is common fodder in all: 'Atheism (Aryan) invasion theory, Hinduism = Brahmin colonialism'.

Today, 'why I am not Hindu' supporters have a louder argument than 'why I am Hindu' supporters. The illiteracy/ignorance about Hinduism among Hindus, which is systematically created, is the biggest reason for it. Even after so many attempts, why did they fail? I won't tell that secret.

A Case Study

The USSR was a communist regime, and a communist regime is an ideological one, and ideological regimes in certain cases are undemocratic as they focus on ideology. There were some factors that contributed to the disintegration of the USSR.

1. Diverse society and culture which are unrelated and unconnected to each other; in addition, 'religion/culture is opium', so there is a lack of cultural unity and unification.
2. Diversity and differences in culture created an identity crisis or strengthened identity of local areas, local cultures, etc.
3. The USSR was highly centralized and dictatorial, which created the 'capacitor effect', which is the charging of opposite plates with the same intensity but opposite charge, i.e., high centralization was opposed by separatism, which is a concentrated form of decentralization.

The same model was implemented in Bhārat; I don't know who was funding or supporting it or who carried out those things on the ground level and institutional level; better we focus on concepts rather than personalities. That is why you will see artificially few people give some prefix–suffix to Bhārat dictatorial regime, majoritarian regime, centralized power, etc., so that border states can be carved out in the name of democracy, peoples voice and whole country remains silent.

USSR model imposed on Bhārat

In multiple ways, Hinduphobic tones are being popularized by strengthening the rest of the identities that are exclusive to Hinduism (refer to p. 66). They are further strengthened in following ways,

1. Good achievements: Culture, festivals, scientists, personal achievements (e.g., first Marathi achiever, Marathi new year, etc.), even though writers and poets have written literature on Hindu deities, literature will still be kept in 'language/secular literature' rather than 'Hindu literature' to avoid decentralized Hinduism, e.g. *Thirukkular* is secular literature, Chola are Tamil kings (i.e., Tamils are not Hindus).
2. Negative achievements: Injustice, inequality, discrimination with our linguistic identity people
   Both of these things achieve two goals:
   A. Identity strengthening
   B. Partial truth (one has to pack propaganda in the cover of truth for mass acceptance of innocent people)

Further regional identity is strengthened for separatism with the 'Evergreen' formula:

Step 1: Declare Central government and leadership as dictatorial and fascist, and nationalism as hyper nationalism.

Step 2: Carry out anti-national activity or separatist activity in the name of freedom of speech and expression, fight against dictatorship, fight for democracy, fight for justice, fight for equality, and federalism.

How USSR Became Russia

The era of 1970–90 was the period when all the countries under the soft power of the USSR started seeing the rise of the 'right wing'. So that all neighbours of the USSR become busy fighting with internal security issues so that no one comes to support the USSR at the time of its disintegration.

Right-Wing Movements All over the World

1. Iraq–Iran war 1980 – two theocratic nations
2. Iraq invasion of Kuwait 1990 – two theocratic nations
3. Khalistan's demand of separate theocratic nation in 1980
4. LTTE – civil war in Sri Lanka in the 1980s
5. Rise of Taliban in Afghanistan in the 1980s
6. Kashmiri Pandit threw out from the Valley in 1990[16]
7. Extremist opposing revival of Ram temple in 1980s
8. Bulgaria gets first non-communist President in 1990
9. USSR – nineteen-month special powers to the leader to transform into market economy in 1990
10. Reunification of Germany and end of communism in 1990
11. Terror attack in Trinidad and Tobago in 1990
12. Uganda–Rwanda civil war in 1990
13. Fall of communism in Albania in 1990
14. The US troops enter Saudi Arabia to protect Saudi from Iraq in 1990
15. The rise of regional party on the basis of local identity (linguistic right wing in nature)
    A. Against the socialist policy of the Central ruling party

It was justified under two permanent stands, irrespective of time, space, and situation.
  i. Every national-level party is anti-state against regional culture and language
  ii. Regional parties, which are allies of national parties, are merely puppets of the Centre

Both i and ii are still the best cards to keep the national party out of regional politics so that extreme 'regionalism' can be promoted, which can culminate in secessionist tendencies.

All these issues are right wing in nature; this era is the peak point where communism started going out of the picture and the whole space in the media and minds of the people was captured by one or the other right-wing ideology. On the other hand, two big events happened that had the background of all fifteen events and failed the socialist economy.
1. The disintegration of the USSR in 1990
2. Liberalization in Bhārat in 1991

Once the goal (the fall of communism) was achieved, almost all fifteen points were diluted automatically because they were artificial in nature, but the poison of anti-social activity still exists in a dormant state.

What Ensures Russia's Internal Security and Safe Borders?

Deep state existence in former USSR states with positive or negative notions of soft power as a face value combined with the big brother role of state and leader.

Meanwhile, Hindus are busy celebrating Navratri, Ganeshotsav, Dahihandi, Pongal, and dancing on waves of music.

Nationalism

Colonial masters destroyed our cultural roots in history books, so the only thing left to us was to find the roots of nationalism in the freedom movement. The freedom movement is 'how we threw colonial masters out of the country with multiple efforts' so that we don't get colonized again. But what I found in history books are chapters on personality cults and movements that never clearly speak about action and reaction, i.e., moral of the story. Secondly, when we limit our nationalism to the 'freedom movement' then we are manufacturing 'watchmen and gatekeepers' who are either aware of gora masters as slaves or as resistance to avoid the second wave of colonialism. We definitely don't want only watchmen and gatekeepers in a free country; we have to train human capital that is civilized, cultured, and strong enough economically, socially, and politically. This can only happen when we 'decolonize' our minds, throw all white man's burden in the Indian Ocean, and create a nation on our roots and terms.

Even after looting and destroying Bhārat culturally, socially, economically, and politically, we see following debates and with no shame of atrocities, looting and leaving colonizing values. Their (colonial masters) history books are full of pride and here rather than opposing British colonialism. We still see debates like:
1. Should we be proud of the British Empire?
2. Did the British loot Bhārat or gifted systems, railway, and democracy?

Double standards are an indirect way of saying we belong to different races and classes. That is why standards are different. If someone's nature is double standard, then it's their duty to teach lessons until they come to a single standard, which is equality.

When we speak about culture, is it going to be copy of the West? Or only Bhārat's culture? It should be a mix of both or something new and innovative that has never been seen before, but with no 'inferiority complex', as Macaulay created. So, it's obvious that our cultural roots are deep. The cultural events, festivals, and national festivals themselves create a sense of belongingness. Which is the platform that unites all of us.

Nowadays, only 'why I am not Hindu?' forces have adopted qualities of exclusivist religions by boycotting, prohibiting, and non-participating by keeping Hinduism and national festivals in a negative list, e.g., religion is opium for the masses. Otherwise, culture itself was a uniting factor that gave people a platform to feel belongingness.

All the countries in the West of Bhārat don't have civilizational roots in their culture and nationalism because civilization is destroyed by exclusivist–expansionary religions. So, their nationalism is either religious, linguistic, or racial, and those shallow roots ensure that they remain unstable as a nation. In the case of Bhārat, it's neither the case, therefore civilizational culture can become part of nationalism. If we ask Western countries to adopt this model, those guys will say it's 'cultural nationalism', because in their nationalism, culture is not part because they have lost most of the unique culture. So it should not be a shame to accept culture as part of nationalism because it's our lifestyle, our ancestor, and we kept our culture alive by testing it with rationality. They (the West) didn't keep it alive; that's their problem.

'Cinco de Mayo' is a national festival where the Mexican army defeated the French army, which came there for colonization, and Mexican people celebrate by eating their traditional food, traditional music, and traditional festival; uprooting colonization should look like decolonization or promoting indigenous culture. That is why the six non-inclusive players are facing a 'battle for belongingness' because they are boycotting the indigenousness of this land under various names like 'Brahmin slavery', 'negative list of religion', 'unholy or sin', and 'opium of religion', respectively.

When they are twisted to prove belongingness, then they call it majoritarianism; they say 'my nationalism in my own way'. This idea of 'my nationalism in my own way' is fine when you have no goals like secessionist movements or expansionist policy. For example, three Muslim girls from Ladakh were singing nationalistic songs in their Balti language written by them. It was fine because it was pure love, innocence, and patriotism. But when someone with exclusive religion, the ideology of the secessionist movement, and an expansionist policy to destroy indigenous culture within a country is merely practicing their destructive setup in the name of nationalism, or 'my nationalism in my own way', they become nationalists to avoid the dissolution of citizenship so that they can carry out their expansionist and secessionist policies.

If nationalism fits in the framework of ideology, then it's fine. If a clash happens, then religion is supreme, which means religion is only belief because clashes can be created at any moment, so while preaching 'clash point' is mentioned, otherwise, in practice, every point is a clash point, which I called strategic separation from nationalism and indigenousness at the socio-cultural level, so that social separation in the future culminates in political and geographical separation, respectively.

Unity means people are somehow connected to each other and ensuring sovereignty and uniformity, means people are properly organized and connected to each other and ensuring sovereignty, but have we questioned both of these people about how much they know about each other and the diversity and depth of the nation in the sphere of knowledge? Even if they are organized or unorganized and maintaining sovereignty, in the long term, they are going to fail because shallow ideas will never ensure long-term sovereignty, irrespective of the strength of the social fabric. That is why understanding depth, diversity, strategy, and concepts in detail by every individual is the most important thing. We can switch strategies as per the situation, whether to remain organized masses in the name of uniformity or remain unorganized, unprofessional, and unplanned, but for that, we need 'trained human capital' to take calculated risks.

The percentage of unity and uniformity cannot be fixed. The problem starts when one believes in diversity but starts criticizing others. How can you criticize when you already believe in the non-uniform and diverse ways of nationalism? It's indirectly saying 'my way is a highway' with the name 'diversity'.

Politicians, social activists, or the government are only interested in whether people share the social fabric or not so that internal security threats are avoided and sovereignty is maintained, which is important for development or growth. They are not interested in discussing concepts, depth, and diversity of religion, civilization, Hinduism, etc., so one should not follow them if one wants to learn these things; otherwise, you will end up knowing every religion, civilization, and 5,000-year-old history merely as secularism, social fabric, unity, etc., and you will become an empty brain player in the unity vs. uniformity debate; once you get stuck in this binary, then there is no scope for learning (refer to p. 59).

Table 9.5

Value system	When manifested by policymakers it affects the following dimensions ((refer to B8, p. 421)
Unorganized	Economy (90% labour in unorganized sector)
Informal	Labour
Unprofessional	Attitude or unskilled labour (only 5% labour is skilled)
Unplanned	Urban and rural infrastructure growth
Unregulated	Institutions
Illegal	Immigrants and activity
Unsolved	Social issues, river disputes
Unconnected, non-cooperation, no-coordination	Society: urban–rural divide, upper–lower caste, tribal–non-tribal, forward–backwards linkages in economy and supply chains, plains–hilly area divide (northeast and other areas)
Non-accountable	Approach of people towards government
Irresponsible	Human capital without civic sense or deliberately kept 'unaware'
Non-uniform/ non-integrated	Efforts that contribute to duplication of efforts or untargeted approach

Many people support this 'anti-national' value system because they want to run away from the 'legal' fold of government, which brings them under:
1. Tax Base 2. Slowest working judiciary which may hamper their business. This gives 'space' to non-state actors and foreign states to shape Bhārat though parallel world/Underworld.

After reading Table 9.5, p. 60, you can understand the bad condition of Bhārtiya economy even today. From this, you can imagine how many post-Independence cabinet members who were founders of Bhārtiya economy were overrated, including multiple degree holders from the London School of Economics, Cambridge, and Harvard.
You can see India through English glasses but not Bhārat.

Table 9.5 is the reality of the picture of Bhārat, which is why the value system and right attitude of nationalism are very important; otherwise, they manifest in such a way. Liberalism is okay when you are not interested in taking responsibility for a nation. Celebrating it in the name of an unorganized, informal, unprofessional, unplanned, unregulated, illegal, unconnected, non-accountable, irresponsible, or non-uniform is okay, but claiming that this approach of 'civic nationalism' will help in building a nation is 'anti-nationalism' because it culminates in bad governance, killing your own country. This kind of behaviour is a hurdle to transforming Bhārat from a developing country to a developed country. This kind of civic nationalism means alienating oneself from the mainstream indigenous culture, which is the uniqueness of every country and region. This kind of civic nationalism, which limits nationalism to political rights, is merely setting up atheism as a benchmark of nationalism and undermining or suppressing cultural heritage and other dimensions like military power, scientific achievements, etc. We cannot limit nationalism to 'heaven of lawyers', i.e., civic nationalism.

Secondly, only identifying the British as colonizers is a biased view, i.e., 'why I am not Hindu' are also surviving on foreign funding. This means we, as gatekeepers, are ensuring the British will not colonize us, and then someone else will come and colonize us, and that's what happens. That is why there is a necessity for such nationalism, which creates citizens who are strategically awakened, culturally united, politically strong, and economically balanced.

What Unites Bhārat or What Is Our Nationalism?

1. Sense of multiculturalism
2. Defining nationalism in its own way, various writings, poems, etc.
3. Nationalism in the form of celebration or carnival
4. Relative nationalism (border disputes and strategic existence)
5. Common cultural habits, mostly inspired by Hinduism, exist in every religion
6. Digital connectivity and social media
7. Memes, jokes, humour, comedy shows, movies, and web series
8. The various organizations that promote nationalism and inclusivity

9. Common consumption patterns are traditional as well as modern (monoculture by capitalists)
10. National achievements in space and other sciences, etc.
11. The intrinsic nature of inclusivity and collectivism in Bhārat's society
12. Falling irrational barriers to jati
13. After doing all riots in public, the same public blames politicians for the riots and people again normalize the situation
14. People across all religions gave up fundamentalism and orthodoxy and chose humanism + capitalism + inclusive celebration
15. A political and economic unified system

This multilayer, diverse, complex type of nationalism is necessary because even if one layer or one type is destroyed, the other is there to save the nation's culture, sovereignty, etc. That is why one-nation-one-type nationalism should not be hardcore criteria, but definitely, to identify anti-nationals, there should be criteria; otherwise, we will awaken at that time when blood falls on the soil, which is against the value of peace.

The uniformity of nationalism can be expressed, shown, or ensured only when it takes physical form in the form of symbols, e.g., the national anthem, national song, national slogan, national flower, or national animal. Some self-styled intellectuals say my nationalism can be development, economy, justice, equality, etc. Why is there a need for slogans, songs, flags, and anthems? My counter to that is that when the British were there in Bhārat, there was an absence of all four things: development, economy, justice, and equality; we people of Bhārat only had the emotion of nationalism, slogans, symbols, and many unification symbols and factors that were breath of us and which kept us alive even when we were suppressed. In the 1857 war of independence, we didn't have these symbols, and we lost to the British. A recent example is Afghanistan, where there is no sense of nationalism and its uniformity. Everyone is defining nationalism in their own way; if the Taliban comes into power, it will turn into a theocratic state; if the secular government comes, it would be a semi-secular state; but at the ground level, masses would always be fighting with each other because their nationalism is limited to their community identity. That is why defining nationalism with some sense of uniformity and symbols of expression has a very important role in maintaining stability.

Diagram 9.6

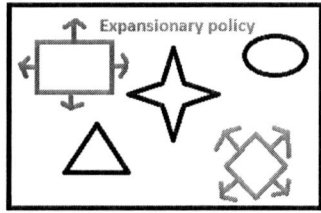

MY NATIONALISM IN MY OWN WAY, I RESPECT YOUR RELIGION OR NATIONALISM BUT I DONT WANT TO PARTICIPATE = causes alienation

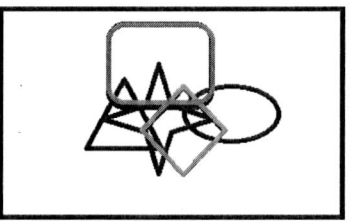

MY NATIONALISM AND SOME COMMON SET OF VALUES, PARTIALLY DIVERSE WITH MINUMUM UNIFORMITY

Which Model of Nationalism Do We Need?

We need neither of them; we need a mix model because Bhārat's topography is diverse; someone in plains, someone in mountains, and someone is desert. The problem is that you can't ask everyone to be part of something common, nor can you ask everyone to remain isolated. So according to condition, direction of tone of people and politics, space and time, both models should be applied. Accepting one model is denying another; in the case of nationalism, no model and no person should be denied; it's very necessary to include everyone and every model.

Bad Marketing of Hinduism

To welcome people from six different categories, some experts do marketing of Hinduism in the following way:
1. Pseudo liberal
2. Atheist
3. Non-Hindus
4. Why I am not Hindu
5. Materialist
6. Critics of Hinduism

Make Hinduism available for the above six categories in their format, i.e., the right to choose; whether you practice or don't practice Hinduism, you are still Hindu or practice as per your choice. This is like our bank has a 'zero balance account'. You can open an account in our bank; there is no compulsion to participate in financial activity or transactions. Which is a good policy in the first instance.

But Hinduism itself has so many services, like experiencing Shiva, Brahman, etc., festivals, astrology, jewellery, food, architecture, Ayurveda, fitness, yoga, Vedic math, traditional martial arts, music, dance, etc., and thousands of other services. If we have so many things, then why do we welcome new people with empty hands? We are the people who believe in '*atithi devo bhava*'. It's true that the constitution has given the 'right to choose', but the 'right to choose' is a consumer-side approach, but as a service provider, what are you giving to them? Those who have merely one book welcome people by giving them rice bags or by self-certifying own religion as a religion of peace. That is why 'the right to choose' is good as an introductory remark, but what beyond that? In addition, the right to choose in the case of Hinduism and its traditions is interpreted as the 'right to *not to* choose'. In case of other, it is 'right to choose', e.g., women's attire/fashion as per religion.

Zero balance account sometimes gives 'cobra effect'; whatever you do, it turns against you. When you allowed new customers to have a 'zero balance account', what if, after a few days, existing customers took out money and the bank faced a 'bank run' and crashed? This 'right to choose' is considered liberal Hinduism (empty packet).

Is There Someone Who Is More Bhārtiya than Other Bhārtiya People?

Yes, atheists, communists, and why I am not Hindu. Some of them created the narrative that it's not necessary to be Hindu to become nationalist, and they projected themselves as more nationalist, while Hindus were termed subnational. To become a nationalist, one must give up this culture. For example, they promoted popular lines like 'all other days we are Hindus, Muslims, and Christians', and on one day we are 'Bhārtiya people' either on Republic Day, during a cricket match, or on Independence Day. We ignorantly believed it. We are 365 days

Hindu and nationalist also. They actually created communism and atheism as benchmarks or litmus tests to become nationalist.

Those who follow ancient civilization and maintain Bhārat's unique identity are sub-nationalist, i.e., 'We are Indian first, then Hindu, Muslim, etc.' means when you are Hindu, you cannot be nationalist, so to become nationalist, one must dissociate from Hinduism and indirectly become atheist–communist to become nationalist. When someone exposes them, they ask, 'Are you a Hindu nationalist?' to reset atheism–communism as a benchmark of nationalism.

Conclusion

Imposing ideas on others, convincing others, hate others, achieving cheap interpretations of mythology, promoting falsehood, anger, grudges, boycotting other cultures or cultural untouchability (why I am not Hindu) is very easy; it doesn't require a brain but self-introspection, meditation, turning inwards, practicing universal love, forgiveness, kindness, becoming part of various cultures and sections of society, mercy, belongingness, acceptance, and a celebration with everyone requires a big heart or the art of living. I am lucky that I received an invitation for lunch on Holi, Diwali, Guru Purab, and Baisakhi from a Sikh family with no intention of playing the 'secularism' or 'communal harmony' card but with the background of the unspoken intrinsic umbrella culture (Hinduism) of all of us. This is the beauty of belongingness.

Table 9.6

Two futures of Bhārat	
Fundamentalism (6 non-inclusive)	**Belongingness**
Boycotting other religions' gods/deities and related culture, festivals, national festivals as intrinsic nature or extrinsic nature of religion or identity	Celebrating together (not as one side approach), celebrating doesn't mean following other religions, it is just participating in event to build harmony

Two futures of Bhārat	
Fundamentalism (6 non-inclusive)	**Belongingness**
Supporting either Israel or Palestine during their internal conflict	A Muslim family from 3 generations taking care of synagogue (Jewish temple) in Kolkata by keeping fundamentalism aside and giving this example to Middle Eastern conflict
Isolation existence	Togetherness, belongingness
Destroying tangible and intangible cultures of others	Contributing to our literature, culture, art, and infrastructure
Supporting social evils under religious umbrella	Liberal value system and support to uniform civil code
Involving in secessionist and subversive activities	Sacrificing life for the country irrespective of one's belief system
Separatism, extremism is ultimate reality	Believing in belongingness and and being liberal in attitude, e.g., the Kabuliwala story

Even though these two columns reflect two different approaches, both reflect the reality of the same society, and same people. What people do is practice only belongingness (secularism) or only fundamentalism.

This much is enough to teach you how religions and social-political ideologies carry out Hindu-phobic activities, which are the basic condition for creating separate identity and division so that geographical separatism can be carried out. Now you are capable of handling 'belongingness' with a sharp brain rather than with an empty one (calculated risk).

To maintain the sovereignty and the integrity of Bhārat, under the constitution of Bhārat, the following institutions are established:
1. National zonal council – 5 zones
2. National integration council
3. Rashtiyaekta divas – run for unity
4. Multiple security agencies
   What is our responsibility?

10

Opium of Marxist Mythology

When Karl Marx said 'religion is opium' he had an idea of the three Abrahamic faiths, which have similar socio-cultural structures. He didn't have any idea of civilization, history, archaeology, or spirituality (refer to p. 66 and A4.2, p. 404), especially Asia. Because religions took over civilizations and moulded them into 'religious mould' and control of society in the hands of priests, Abrahamic religions have a model of individualism that is suitable for capitalism, which is not the case in Bhārat, which has been a union of multiple groups of jatis, tribes, and ethnicity. Before taking individual decisions, we say, '*log kya kahenge*'. Whereas religion itself is political and expansionary in nature. So in the era of Marx, there were two things: dogmatic society or followers of religion, and other dogmatic society which was a critique of religion. Some people say the rich will never go to heaven, so the masses will automatically choose to remain poor with dreams of heaven. Maybe because of this, he would have said, 'Religion is the opium of the masses.' Colonial masters fixed Hindu society in the Abrahamic model, which later became a new punching bag for communists, who are still following the same model.

When he gave the communist manifesto, he divided society into two parts: capitalists, who have wealth, and labourers, who are hardworking poor. To eliminate poverty, he gave a simple formula: the transfer of wealth or power to the poor. According to me, Karl Marx was very uncreative as compared to other economists. Because in Bhārat thousands of saints were given solutions to donations/distribution of wealth and we had mechanisms of rotating wealth, Marx only added violence to it to transfer of wealth. We cannot compare Marx with an economist too because he wanted to create 'equal bank balance' (this should not be taken literally) and 'abolition of private property', so this can be seen as his imagination of society or one of the solutions. Marx and Indian social reformers (who supported 'income equality/wealth distribution') didn't know creating new businesses, scientific advancement, the art of budget-making, the role of governance, the role of corruption in weakening systems, the role of technology, shaping the economy, industrial policy, creative schemes, infrastructure, job creation, gig economy (artists, teachers, food stalls, drivers, etc., where the capitalist–labour relationship is not there). So this lack of diverse understanding and lack of creativity transforms into freebie culture (people think it's about appeasement, but it's actually about an incompetent ruler).[1]

Even the great capitalist economists (finance ministers) left everything on the market and limited themselves to monetary incentives. which is actually a Marxist model of wealth transfer or liquidity handling. All the six non-inclusive players never speak on this issue because they don't take any off from social engineering. If they start understanding all these aspects of the economy then they will identify where the government is lacking and where the problems actually are, and they will also participate in solving those problems and be part of the smooth functioning of society. But if this happens, how will they convince the masses that there is a need for a total revolution and the need to uproot existing establishment. That is why they only pick up social issues so that the masses can be collected as an army of total revolution and can be kept away from mainstream by not having a holistic approach deliberately. Candy of 'criticism of religion (only Hinduism in Bhārat)' is given to masses so they are somehow connected with movement and masses are mobilized for red terrorism.

Karl Marx and His Double-Standard Approach

1. If a stateless society is an ideal society and at the same time private property must be abolished, then who will own private property? If collectively owned, then it is a parallel state because land, business, and industries have expanded, plus they have became so complex that we need a professional approach, which creates a natural

demand for a full-fledged state. In the 21st century, believing in the Marxist model is the same as saying the the four-fold varna system is capable of running a nation socially, politically, and economically.
2. Religion is the opium of the masses, but all historical events are driven by only economic reasons and have no role for religion, culture, or ideologies at all. Even if terrorists justify terrorism by quoting their religious manifestos, Marxists will still not believe in him to satisfy their ideological egos.[2]

In this country, the masses are ignorant about the economy, schemes, and policies, so communism is a very user-friendly empty philosophy for empty brains. So, this poor vs. rich, religion vs. criticism, establishment vs. total revolution—all these binary options are very useful to attract empty brains without any discussion of issues and solutions. There is no understanding of strategic existence and trade calculation in foreign policy; what Marx and his kids believe is that 'labour-army and masses' should not be involved in war, irrespective of condition, time, and space, even if Bhārat recaptures the land that legally belongs to it.

Today on the MyGov app of the government of Bhārat, even students and kids give sector-wise creative solutions to the government of Bhārat that are way better creative than Marx. So to hide this partial and unholy approach, the Marxists create debates like 'religion vs. others' (thirteen debates in this chapter) so that followers of communism are connected on a day-to-day basis. For example, religion vs. economy, they will take two stands.
1. Religion is opium, which is a hurdle to development.
2. Development is not happening because of religion (e.g., infrastructure development is labour intensive job except for temple construction).

In this active and passive voice game 'communist and followers' are made busy, and they never discuss science, technology, financial literacy, infrastructure, budget, government policy, banking sector, and agriculture and its solutions (solution-oriented discussion is avoided because it may divert from communism). Even if they discuss this, they will mix criticism of religion with communism. Then they call this 'rationalism'.

These people find 'victims' or create 'victims' so that it fits into their political ideology because mere labour can't ensure that the Marxists will come to power because 70 per cent of the labour force in in the informal sector. In Bhārat, as communists don't have economic vision, they create mythology where some group is the victim. To justify this, they write biased history and biased interpretations of mythology so that it reflects victim vs. ruling class, which somehow is connected with today's political population dynamics. The British created a majority–minority issue, and in minority category, many religions, castes, and ideologies were kept. So that they can be used for political gains under the umbrella scheme 'minority are always correct, and they are always the victim'. A similar social engineering was continued post-Independence.

Communist's Mythology Is of Three Types

1. Imposing a communist model in a history book will create a communist vote bank.
2. Interpretation of stories from the epics and finding victim community (e.g., Karna was not allowed by upper caste to be involved in Mahābhārata, but forget to identify Karna was allowed to fight by people of the same so-called upper caste; this is how communists create vote banks through Hindu mythology).
3. Religion vs. xyx debates so that with anti-religion policy people are charged as communist vote bank 'religion can't be taught in school but criticism of religion can be taught' culminates into 'religion can't be part of politics but criticism of religion can be'; this is how biasedness happens.

Just like various 'brands' in the market to lure lazy, ignorant consumers who don't read the 'content', brand owners launch advertisements, and marketing strategies. Ideologies use the same technique.

1. Event (communism through films or stories)[3]
2. Book (interpreting the constitution in such a way that it promotes 'communist' ideology)
3. Stories from the Rāmāyaṇa and Mahābhārata (certain section were exploited)
4. Nature of rule or government (they will never mention there is an ASI or ministry of culture to convey state and religion are separate)
5. Political–non-political values (e.g., secularism = atheism/communism)
6. History (e.g., history concludes that the communist model is the ideal one)
7. Personality (projecting Mahatma Gandhi, Pandit Nehru, and Thiruvalluvar as left inclined or secular)

Table 10.1

Opinion of Periyar (who was atheist and communist) about Thiruvalluvar	*Thirukkural* (book by Thiruvalluvar)
1. People are talking highly of Thiruvalluvar, but in practice, they do not respect his teachings; they act against him and disregard him.[4] 2. When the purpose of clearly exposing the differences between the Aryan and the Tamil culture, civilization, conduct, and creed of *Thirukkural* was written. 3. In the *Kural*, there is a chapter on the invocation to God. But there is no place in it for the principle of idol worship.[5]	1. In Kadavul Vaazhthu itself, Valluvar pays respects to the Tri Murthis (Brahma, Vishnu, and Shiva).[6] 2. Hindus don't believe in one formless god, so idols or physical features are the only things that differentiate Bramha, Vishnu, and Shiva

The conclusion of all these seven points of marketing is that 'product is good' or certified by their respective personalities and great literature. You will also find some people projecting French values (liberty, fraternity, equality), communism, and democracy as part of 'Buddhism' to make it acceptable.

Thirteen debates against 'religion' are beneficial for communists to keep masses charged against religion and existing social order to bring armed revolution through consistent polarization by stereotyping Religion especially Hinduism.

1. Religion vs. science and technology
2. Religion vs. rationality
3. Religion vs. liberty
4. Religion vs. modernity
5. Religion vs. economy
6. Religion vs. environment (only exists in Bhārat)
7. Religion vs. nationality
8. Religion vs. human rights
9. Religion vs. feminism
10. Religion vs. secularism
11. Religion vs. poverty
12. Religion vs. development
13. Religion vs. atheism and materialism

All these debates are relevant in Western society because it was needed in their society as renaissance. As we have seen, Hinduism was moulded in the Abrahamic framework by the colonial masters, which atheists and communists later started using, supposing it to be the original Hinduism. We think that this is merely done to get votes, but slowly degradation of Hinduism happens because social movement culminates into political ideology. Even if it loses in politics, it is still continuous as social movement. Which creates ignorance towards the content of Hinduism, which is mentioned on page 66, but Marxists ignore this and project religion (Hinduism in our case) as a 'medium of exploitation of the masses', which is a tool of capitalists.

Artificial Debates

Religion vs. Economy
Bhārat's GDP in the Mughal era was around 25 per cent of global.[7] I am not sure about the size of the economy. That economy was a Hindu economy; as an outcome of the jati system, the Mughals only collected taxes and looted. I do not know why the Mughals are given credit for that. Hinduism has so much content (p. 66) that it only contributed to the economy. Yet rather than holding the constitution and government accountable for poverty, Marxists deliberately target Hindu temples. Whatever wealth temples have, that's an internal matter for Hindus. If that's the case, atheists shall not have excessive wealth and shall donate everything to the poor, including political party funds, which are based on Marxist and atheist values (refer to B9, p. 422). British looted 45 trillion dollars from Bhārat and told us, you are poor because of your culture.

Religion vs. economy debate was created to inject the idea 'one has to give up religion for economy' so that when missionaries come to convert by offering money, they can take it and give up Hinduism. How is this model different from the Ziziya tax? Give up Hinduism or pay us, i.e, religion vs. economy.

Mughals looted, British looted, atheists looted temples, but Hindus never gave up Hinduism, that is why this propaganda was created.

Religion vs. Rationality
Hinduism is full of dialogue, discussion, debate and, conveying messages through stories rather than forceful imposition. There are many safty valves and scrutinizing mechanisms that are created that scrutinize every book, things beyond books, etc. (refer to pp. 110–111).

Atheism, communism, and criticism of religion ≠ rationalism; it is just atheism, communism, and criticism of religion. Rationalism is kept in a basket of atheism and communism, just like God's stamp on a 'religious book' is ensured as 'revealed by God' so that people follow it without questioning.

Religion vs. Modernity

Hinduism itself is evolving civilization but transition from one phase to another is not always smooth, but even this is accepted in scriptures. i.e., disaster (pralaya) will happen when you move to the next yuga cycle. The four yuga cycle, and every time he takes over by new Bramha, old Bramha Vishnu Mahesh dissolves itself into Paramtama. The so-called modernization or transition is now limited to consumerism and excessive pleasure-seeking mechanisms from material, which is culminating in climate change. We do need a balanced approach, e.g., the Mission LIFE of the government of Bhārat.

Religion vs. Feminism

Their idea of feminism only arises on Hindu female deity festivals because that's the point where religion vs. feminism spikes, which appeals a lot. Otherwise, for 364 days, they don't have any sense about women's empowerment, the policies of the government related to women, women in entrepreneurship, etc. because entrepreneurship will be anti-left as she will become Capitalist.

What do Hindu books say? In Atharvaveda, it's clearly written that before marriage, women must get education. Hymns in the *Rigveda* are written by females like Lopmudra, Viswavara, Ghosa, and Sikatanivarari. Yagyavalakya lost the debate to Gargi. Brahmavedin were the women who used to pursue higher and deeper education. Kasakritsna contributed and created a branch within Mīmāṃsā. If you read stories in our Hindu texts, women are an integral part of it that exist beyond motherhood; otherwise, you will find religions where all stories are male-centric or only male characters, male prophets, and male dieties are there.

Arjuna is kidnapped by a beautiful woman to get married. Arjuna was asked by Urvashi (apsara) to establish a physical relationship. Female deities or devi's are shown to be more powerful than male deities (refer to A10.2, pp. 412–413) to solve the problems; sometimes they become so powerful and uncontrollable that their husbands have to lie down in front of them to stop the anger (Shiva–Durga). There are various examples where not only devi but common women have taken arms in their hands to fight. There have been rights for women in holding property, especially in the case of the widow.

Not only this in Khajuraho temples, sex with animals is there, but critics must see this as a wild, unconventional imagination rather than motivation or ideal of Hindu society, just like in masses there are phrases like 'it is better to marry a tree rather than marrying third time with women', i.e., Dashrath's (Rama's father) third wife created a political issue on succession of thrown, so don't have more wives (not that trees are better than women for marriage).

When colonial masters came to Bhārat, they were shocked by seeing Kali, who is unclothed, sexually active, killer, blood drinker, and more powerful than men because colonial masters were followers of cultures where these things from women were unaccepted, where women are completely suppressed, weak, subordinate, or limited to motherhood and household work. So they almost eliminated Kali from books on Hinduism that were written by them, and when they mentioned her, they projected her negatively. Shakta parampara is a symbol of Hindu philosophy, but in mainstream books it is never considered; it is projected as occult. Which was the first step to eliminating tantra-yantra and related rituals.

Common Hindu women: We are always told that women in Bhārat were limited to 'chulha chowka' (cooking and household work). As I have mentioned in chapters 7 and 8, training human capital in spheres of economy, culture, tradition, psychology, survival techniques, i.e., concepts of Hinduism, etc. Similarly, Hindu women were also trained in all these aspects. There used to be sixty-four arts in ancient Bhārat, and women used to be considered as suitable brides who had the most arts out of sixty-four. If you go to a village area, women work as equal as men. Females have been sannyāsins; they have taken leadership in many akharas established by Śaṅkarācāryaḥ, Other than this, there have been n number of female rulers and warriors too. Even in the modern world, many countries prohibit women from voting, and we never thought about this once.

External reasons for suppressing women: In Nepal and northeast Bhārat, women have the same or higher status as men. If both are

following Hinduism or indigenous culture as we do, then what is the reason those have equal status as men?
1. Women should not come into the hall when guests are in the house.
2. Women should tie their hair; hair should not be open at all.
3. Women should cover their heads.
4. Her body parts must be covered completely.
5. She cannot go outside without her male companion.

All these discriminatory rules don't originate in Hinduism but belong to some other religion; colonial masters imposed them on Hindus, which degraded women's liberty and freedom.

Otherwise, when in mediaeval Europe, the picture of Monalisa was revolutionary; here in ancient Bhārat, we had apsaras almost nude sculptures on caves and temples; if you see Khajuraho temples, complete romance is projected. But this doesn't give Hinduism immunity from criticism. At the same time, we must accept the reality that certain misogynistic laws in Hinduism were limited to that time and space.

Why was chulha-chowka logic imposed?
1. To give 'weak personality' as motivation from history so that women don't grow or dream big
2. Creating a union of weak women or a social base to launch feminism, one of the branches of left-inclined politics
3. Giving credit for 'women empowerment' for making women 'zero to hero' only to the 'constitution, pre-Independence rationalists, social reformers'. For that, projecting 'women as zero' is a precondition. For example, in ancient times, there were scholars like Lopamudra, Ghosha, and Sikta plus traditional Hindu women knew Rāmāyaṇa and Mahābhārata, so what makes you say, 'Some person opened girls' school in the 17, 18, and 19th centuries?' Because traditional schools were running in the 18th century and government records are available for that, many women were taking education. But unfortunately, just to prove someone as an 'initiator of women's education', because he was a thinker who promoted a manipulated version of Hinduism, the data from

prior to 1850 regarding women's education was hidden from us. For that, they projected women as zero, completely illiterate, or suppressed by society from taking education.[8]

There were many jatis who used to move from one place to another, which were nomadic in nature because their profession was like that: selling of animals, grazing of animals, entertainment industry, etc. Communities in the group used to move together. Then how can one say women were limited to chowakat (boundary of house)? When so much information is available about women, how easily do they limit women to chulha-chowka in history books. The goal is to prove that before the entry of the British, there was 'zero' literacy and 'zero' labour force participation.

Modern world and women: Modern education was new to both women and men; modern economy and job were new to both women and men; and migration was new to both men and women. Because in the Hindu economy, villages have a self-sustaining model. So there is no need for migration except in business communities. Sexual harassment at the workplace is also a new phenomenon in Bhārat. So in the new modern world, gender inequality is a challenge, and women in entrepreneurship and political representation are also challenges. You cannot impose the failure of women's empowerment solely on Hinduism by ignoring modern-day factors and challenges.

A Hindu version of social feminism: Many religious books and philosophers have given women a discriminatory status, and 'gender hierarchy' was created by these people. Male is the first gender, and then women and transgenders are out of consideration. The most important thing is removing guilt and derogatory remarks attached to women. In Hinduism, there are temples of devi (the female deity) where purohits wear female clothes and makeup and do puja on some auspicious day. The celebration of women's menstrual cycle is celebrated in Assam in the ambubachi mela. In some temples, only women can enter, and men are prohibited. In many folk dances and traditional theatres, men play the role of women. On the occasion of Holi, men are beaten by women with a stick known as lath mari Holi. In southern Bhārat, the first menstrual cycle is celebrated by inviting people for dinner so that girl doesn't feel

guilt or discomfort about her body to give the indirect message that this is as common as 'upanayan' sanskara. Sannyāsi can only touch the feet of their mother, not of anyone else. In Hinduism, atma changes body just like body changes clothes, and atma may take the body of women, which is popular and very common in Hindu psychology.[9]
This entire story conveys five things:
a. Nothing wrong with being a woman.
b. Being a woman is not secondary.
c. There is nothing to be guilty of about being a woman.
d. Dissolve your toxic masculinity, which is anti-women.
e. This is how it feels to be a woman.

That is why the elimination of gender hierarchy should be the foundation of feminism. But what we see is a measurement of women's consumption-led approach. So, both things are important.

Now, people are becoming more aware of the third-gender LGBTQ. In the case of Hinduism, the Rāmāyaṇa and Mahābhārata have multiple examples of LGBTQ being part of society, not as discrimination or as a third gender but as a normal gender. That is why using the word third gender must be eliminated. Krishna himself takes form as shyamarisakhi and Mohini in the Mahābhārata. In Hinduism, there is a separate deity, 'Aravan', for transgenders. Still, Some social LGBTQ movements will abuse Hinduism only; whereas in other religions, they are not even allowed to exist.

Even our rationalist writers of the constitution speak about women's dignity in several places, but what about LGBTQ, who are more vulnerable than women. Even in Europe, you will find anti-LGBTQ rallies, statements against LGBTQ, and rules and legislation too. But in Bhārat, you won't find a single rally, statement, or movement against LGBTQ.

Religion vs. Environment
Climate change is happening because of excess industrialization not because of Hinduism, yet Hinduism and its festivals are targeted for environmental degradation. If Hinduism is responsible, then climate change would have happened 1,000 years ago.

Eco-Feminism

'Eco-feminism' is a movement that sees a connection between the exploitation, degradation, subordination, and oppression of 'women and ecology'. It emerged in the mid-1970s alongside second-wave feminism and the green movement. The term was coined by the French writer Françoise d'Eaubonne in her book *Le Féminisme ou la Mort* (1974). I have already proven the roots of eco-sensitivity and feminism in Hinduism.

But leftists are again imposing eco-feminism on Hinduism to make it deeply rooted by the misinterpretation of *Sāṅkhya* school. Liberation (mukti) is the supreme goal in Hinduism, and there are various themes like Advaita Vedant, Dvait Vedant, Shaivism, Vaishnavism, Shaktism, Ashtanga yoga, Sāṅkhya, etc. In Sāṅkhya philosophy, diversity is termed prakrati, which one has to give up to achieve purusha (pure consciousness/oneness). So these eco-feminists mistranslate it as 'one has to give up prakriti (feminine environment) to become perfect purusha (perfect husband)', i.e., use and throw model, rather than understanding it in the 'moksha' context (given in detail in chapters 14 and 15).

Religion vs. Nationality

In the case of Hinduism, it is just like pyramid vs. Egypt's constitution or Egypt's citizenship. When the geography of the origin of religion and the current nation are different, there is a conflict of interest because two geographies may clash, and it will become difficult for the population to decide team to choose. Left-inclined people made 'nationalism' a social stigma as a safety valve so that nationalism never turns 'right wing', or they created 'atheism' as the benchmark of nationalism.

As a conclusion, we can say that we can discuss every issue without criticizing Hinduism and find a solution to it. If it is related to social evil or practices rooted in Hinduism, then we can bring Hinduism to the discussion table; otherwise, there is no need. As of today, our foreign policy has improved and is performing at its full potential, but again, rather than finding out problems in 'foreign policy', people divert issues to 'poverty, education, and health' indicators and they term foreign policy of Bhārat as a 'hyper nationalism' to undermine success. If you have problems with health, education, or poverty, then criticize the respective ministries. I am giving you an example to prove how the average communist brain shapes the narrative to divert attention from every discussion that is beyond or against their 'knowledge or communist manifesto' (refer to p. 439, the 10th article)[10].

Should Religion Become Part of Politics?

The rationale behind 'religion should not be part of politics' is avoiding irrationality, discrimination, exclusive representation, unfair practices, etc. But there are many identities that create issues of irrationality, discrimination, exclusion, and unfair practices, which create mass mobilization on non-developmental issues, for example.

1. Atheism
2. Minority interest
3. Anti-nationalism
4. Underworld
5. Class
6. Against a particular religion
7. Use of money
8. Muscle power
9. Availability of funds for the election
10. Caste politics
11. Political ideology
12. Centralization vs. federalism
13. Sub-nationalism.
14. Tribal, ethnicity
15. Hindu-phobia
16. Section of illegal activities
17. Appeasement of non-taxpayers
18. Sub-sect of religion
19. Misinterpreted Buddhism
20. Khalistan
21. International world order
22. Permanent anti-government attitude

23. Alienation from Hinduism
24. Union of 'Why I am not Hindu?' people
25. Post-election discrimination
26. Misinterpretation of history according to social engineering
27. Language politics and language-based extremism
28. Political ideology – communism, capitalism, and their extremism
29. Crime and injustice
    (which is the job of the judiciary and bureaucracy)
30. Urban–rural divide (non-developmental)
31. The constitutional provision for the reservation of seats
32. Parallel world (people with a vision of a utopian state)

All these factors are used to mobilize the masses; 'religion should not be part of politics' is actually 'only Hinduism should not be part of politics', other things can be. If the supporters of all factors mentioned above cannot fight the election on the 'art of policymaking, schemes, budget, development, and respective aspects, stakeholders of the economy', then why are only Hindus asked to keep religion aside.

Impact of Communist Ideology on Policy and Scheme-Making in Government of India

Communism is about distributing money to the poor, which is collected from the rich, or giving special financial or liquidity incentives to the poor. Our policymakers have taken this too seriously; they only transfer liquidity, and there is no creativity in productive scheme design for the poor to make them self-sufficient. For example,
1. Loan availability
2. Loan incentive
3. Tax incentive
4. Deficit financing
5. Credit availability
6. Interest subvention
7. Direct benefit transfer

8. Insurance policies of citizens, crops, infrastructure, etc.
9. Interest-free loans
10. Special economic zones

All these reflect only one thing: either the government will give you liquidity or money or you keep your money with you; there is no need to transfer it to the government. There are kinds of schemes that become successful when people have skills, an entrepreneurial mindset, risk-taking ability, market-capturing ideas, packaging, and startup ideas, but Bhārtiya people don't have any. At least now a day's government is investing a lot in all these things. What will he do even if cheap loans are available? A comprehensive scheme and developing 'particular sector' holistically with a proper 'socialist' approach would be giving a complete package rather than only financial incentives, which would include:

1. Financial support, e.g., loans, tax incentives, etc.
2. Skill-development training
3. Brand building
4. Insurance for an emergency situation
5. Making primary products or inputs available
6. Giving team support to build primary infrastructure and the initial set-up of a factory or workplace, e.g., any company agent comes to setup electric appliances when we buy a new TV, washing machine, etc.
7. Supporting yearly or half-yearly maintenance from government agents
8. Training beneficiaries about market volatility and selling products globally
9. Creating e-market or connecting a beneficiary with an e-market to sell his/her product and setting up digital Infrastructure
10. Training the beneficiary to invest his/her earnings in the stock market or list his company or product in the stock market
11. Making available 'the employees' to the beneficiary to work under him/her through available data with the government and private sectors

12. Socialistic aspects, e.g., women, vulnerable sections, LGBTQ, EWS, SHG
13. Reducing logistic costs, ease of land procurement, and transport service
14. Skilling about direct tax and GST processes, labour laws
15. Waste management process and responsibility
16. Anchor institution: Special purpose, vehicle authority, dispute resolution mechanisms, centre of excellence

This sixteen-point complete package will develop sectors with 'bullet train' speed and vanishing illiteracy, cheating, lethargy, and a slow speed of completion of beneficiaries. The only thing beneficiaries have to do is sign this complete package and get all sixteen benefits in one package with the help of the government. This kind of complete package would be implemented by the government and private sector together as 'integrated approach, customized product design'. Memorandum of understanding (MOUs) will be signed on behalf of the government for assurance and trust, but the government can give contracts for all sixteen or a few targets to the private sector. The government can create a portal where a sixteen-point package will be sold by the private sector, which can create competition in providing this scheme.

The better holistic model would be that, just like Corporate Social Responsibility (CSR), government should make it compulsory that the top 1 per cent people (1.25 crore rich people) do one-to-one, joint ventures with farmers to develop rural-friendly, agro-friendly businesses, or MSME, so that skills, expertise, and market everything are automatically available to farmers, whether it be horticulture, animal husbandry, or solar panels in a farm as per the MOU signed with DISCOMS. This is creativity to transfer not only wealth but skills, market knowledge, best practices around the world, technology, and risk management from rich to poor, from urban to rural. Even if the target of 1 farmer per year is kept, within 10 years, 1.25 crore rich people will give alternate business or earning sources to 10 crore farmers.

Now we will see how value or ideology impact policy, governance, and decision-making.

Table 10.2

	Negative liberty	Positive liberty
	Unmanifested form of liberty/unutilized liberty/on paper liberty/limited to no external interference means believers in negative liberty will open their mouth only when fundamental rights are violated but will never utilize liberty to create and manifest something new	Positive liberty means utilizing liberty and manifesting something new, transforming idea into solid reality
Value system	Equality, inclusion, sharing, temperance, tolerance	Liberty, creativity, competition, prosperity, innovators, creators, producers
Who follows	Generally leftist follow 'negative liberty'; unutilized-untapped potential becomes reason for underperformance	Rightists stand with positive liberty to utilize resources, talent, etc., to make their vision successful
Mindset of policy makers	'Only big promises no implementation', 'on paper development', 'negativity that it's impossible and will remain unmanifested'; therefore 'no creativity, effort, action, formation in many areas' because of lack of will power (refer to pp. 60, 198), i.e., policy paralysis	Time bound completion of projects, improved service delivery, targeted approach, use of technology to ensure absolute implementation

	Negative liberty	Positive liberty
Foreign policy	It's mostly inactive/passive foreign policy, which is wrongly termed as 'reactive or passive', e.g., non-alignment, look east policy, not 'export-led' so no promotion to local industries	Its active foreign policy which is wrongly termed as 'proactive, hyper nationalism', e.g., multi-alignment, act east policy, export-led economy
Legislations	Reactive 1. Formation of national disaster management authority, national investigation agency as a reaction to 2005 Mumbai flood, 2008 terror attack, resepectively 2. Not building border infrastructure will save Bhārat from Chinese aggression, even though China enhancing its border infrastructure[11] Both examples reflect lethargy, negligence, and unpreparedness	Pro-active 1. Solid waste management rules 2016 2. Building border infrastructure[12]
Law and order	'Strict law' would create deterrence effect to curb illegal/unethical practice	'Implementation of law creates deterrence not just law'. This was/is a big loss for Bhārat. 'No implementation' means 'no goal-oriented approach'. If someone tries to implement law or action, then thousand people will come to convince not to implement

	Negative liberty	Positive liberty
Education policy	Non practical education so no vocational training. 4% Bhārtiya people are skilled as compared to 98% in South Korea	Focus on vocational education, skills, etc. National Education Policy (2019), Ministry of Skill development (2015)
Governance and service delivery	At the social level, they always try to remain unorganized, maybe because capitalists love organizing. This behaviour of remaining unorganized is justified as 'liberalism' and right wing observes it as 'indiscipline'. Only promises (red tapeism)	They organize assets and systems, stakeholders so that they become more productive, and discipline is a tool used for organizing things with respect to time
Society	Scattered and fragmented 'diversity'	Unified and integrated 'diversity'
Approach to consumer and citizen	They are not accountable to consumers so no question of responsibility. Because they only come out of the cave to accuse systems when, 1. system or society fails 2. victims are available either exploited by capitalist or dominating class only Both things create a background for 'total revolution', which is very easy because you don't have to do a few things 1. Having holistic knowledge of the economy	Accountability towards consumers makes them responsible

	Negative liberty	Positive liberty
	2. Taking responsibility for the system of economy, scientific research, and development to solve the issue	
Market and economy	They are in demanding mode, as consumption or means of consumption like wages, right to choose, right to life, right to use senses, demanding rights, demanding justice, demanding wages	They create both, product as well as demand
Facing volatility	They don't subject themselves to market volatility, they are in a fairy tales world of equality, liberty, justice, and their role is 'distribution of wealth', once wealth is collected after facing market volatility. The same thing in social theory 'they will peep out only when injustice happens'	They subject themselves to market volatility and face competition, unsustainable, legal–illegal forces
Competition	State-owned resources and property which creates 'government as dictator' with no challenge/competition from private sector	Between various capitalists, capitalist vs. labour
Institutions	Incomplete without professional management	Complete and professional (output-oriented)
Human capital	Fluid (national borders, genders), unaware, spineless, lily-levered, and docile, which give rise to woke culture	Solid, defined skilled, aware, active, vigilant

> I leave interpretation to Bhārtiya people, which liberty was followed for 70 years. Negative liberty is fine when you are poor/weak and if you add 'leadership, finance, and professionalism' to it, then it transforms into positive liberty.

If anyone manifests or utilizes liberty and tries to transform ideas into reality, then all leftists will attack and try to bring their efforts to an unmanifested form, i.e., negative liberty. The best example would be practicing or manifesting religion or efforts to present nationalism, e.g., the national flag, anthem, etc. In the case of religion, if one is practicing rituals, they will say no need for this: 'God is within us' or 'Nationalism is within us', 'No need to show off', 'Who are you to tell what to do', 'It's our freedom to do or not'; all mean the same thing. 'Don't practice; keep it unmanifested.' The unmanifested ideas bring stagnancy and suffocation, which are controlling choices of people, and at the economic level, a state-controlled economy, i.e., a left government. Same stagnancy was in the mind of Arjuna, who refused to manifest his dharma, e.g., Kshatriya dharma. Krishna in the Bhagavad Gita ordered him to do that, i.e., 'activity' and brought him out of a frozen situation. That is why Hindu spirituality is not giving up material life and becoming nothing, but actually transforming oneself from inactivity to activity.

Impact of Communism on Mindset

Rich, majority, urban = majoritarian regime, dishonest, culprits, cheaters, looters, bad people, culprits, safe, secure exploitative, so they should be guilty.

Poor, minority, rural, tribal = honest, victim, innocent, truth, insecure, and unsafe must be appeased and supported in the name of 'strengthening voice'; even if minorities, tribals, etc. take violent paths against the majority, it's justified by communists to keep the world polarized as minority vs. minority.

Good and bad qualities can belong to anyone, but this biasedness about generalized qualities creates a vote bank for communism. That is why we must eliminate this cheap thinking, which is the outcome of communism; otherwise, we may support the guilty culprit just because he is poor or a minority. That is why urbans were considered privileged and were ignored at the development level; 'urban development' remained completely ignored. For example, flowering dirty slums, no waste management, no holistic and advanced development of cities, floods, i.e., the origin of all urban problems (refer to B10, pp. 422, 423).

Global society and international institutions are victims of this 'communist' propaganda, where the majority are villains and the minority are victims. This is because the keys to 'democracy, liberty, freedom, and human rights' were given to left-inclined people rather than an equal share of right and left. You will see the use of the term 'democracy, federalism' to support fringe elements and secessionist movements by tagging Central/republican thought current as 'anti-democratic, anti-human rights'. Left-inclined people used this opportunity to shape demography in their favour through NGO, fake or biased reports. Once a country becomes industrialized or mechanized, the scope for 'communism' dies. So to create an artificial demand for communism, leftists and liberals started projecting the majority as the culprit and the minority as the victim. When it didn't work, they started supporting the import of 'minority' through illegal immigration or by projecting terrorists, fringe elements, secessionist tendencies, Woke culture extremism, ghettos and their warlords, insurgent groups, reverse racism[13] as 'victims of capitalism'. Left-inclined people become so extreme that they start supporting social evils promoted by minorities under freedom of religion. There have been patterns observed globally where establishments and the judiciary give exemptions to minorities in the spheres of 'crimes' as a confidence-building measure.[14]

As communism doesn't have the concept of holistic inclusivity (only support for minorities and victims), to hide their limitations, they try to project every 'nationalism/nationalist' as Hitler, Mussolini, hyper nationalism, right-wing extremists so as to avoid the tags of Hitler,[15] Mussolini, etc. Nationalists follow the path and policies designed by left-wing leaders. Bhārat, Europe, and the USA are victims of this and its historic failure to defeat the communist dragon within their own countries. Why don't illegal immigrants go to Africa, the Arab world,

China, Afghanistan, North Korea, Pakistan, Indonesia, or Southeast Asia?

That era has gone, when communism was in favour of labour and peace. Everything looks fine in context; out of context, any ideology becomes a threat to global society, such as communism and capitalism. It is high time people support nationalism at the national level and humanism at the global level, which goes beyond ideology. The way to tackle this minority extremism is to break down identification based on minority and majority; instead, we shall promote individualism. Government schemes and policies shall be targeted towards individuals where there is no place for 'minority/majority identity strengthening'. The government shall identify the activities that are destroying the social fabric and that are destroying a nation and its tangible or intangible culture. I will see the things in terms of legal or illegal rather than majority or minority. Unfortunately, communists are successful in marketing 'self-destructive mechanisms' as benchmarks of social justice, equality, liberty, neutrality, or war against 'totalitarian, majoritarian regimes, and non-inclusive people'.

A few examples of self-destructive mechanisms (globally) supported by left-inclined leaders in favour of minority appeasement, that are not just anti-majority but also against the law of land are as follows:

1. Grooming gang[16]
2. Proselytization, Atrocities, kidnapping of the majority by other religions
3. Illegal migrants infiltrating through porous borders, i.e., refugee influx, insurgency groups, and their settlement In countries to turn majority demography into minority i.e. Settler colonialism
4. Creating ghettos for dual-use 'religious domination and proxy wars' against the state by promoting warlord culture in ghettos of illegal migrants. Formation of ungoverned spaces or ghettos with unofficial autonomous status
5. Illegal construction of religious places, illegal land occupation of government and private lands, attacking religious places of majority and capturing them

6. Stone-pelting on festivals of the majority community; violent attacks on the majority (organized minority = scattered majority)
7. Selling/sending proselytized women from majority to foreign countries (human trafficking)[17]
8. Talks and a democratic approach towards insurgency groups
9. Continuation of criminal activities past (mediaeval era), present, and future
10. Giving a call for the destruction of tangible and intangible cultural exodus of majority community and destroying it
11. Allowing minorities to violate or giving exemption to if they violate the law by doing crime, etc.[18]
12. An ethnocentric policy/scheme/legislation formation (pro-minority), e.g., the communal violence bill drafted in 2011: only minorities, SCs, and STs can be victims.
13. Judiciary, state, and legislatures together against minority reform[19]
14. Mass shoplifting, i.e., looting malls and shops
15. Social spaces and college campuses captured by terror sympathizers

In a country where culprits are set free, but responsibility and the burden of guilt are on the victim, the victim is punished rather than the culprit (victim shaming). This kind of interpretation of heinous crimes depends on the perception of the victim, whether they accept it under the policy of inclusivity or deny it under the policy of exclusivity, rather than the intention of culprit creates the wrong pattern, which can be equated with putting the burden of rape on the victim who carried himself/herself in provocative/revealing clothes.[20]

We are fed up with social patterns where

- you must have heard 'great power lies with great responsibility', which means small power (a minority in society) has lesser responsibility. What kind of stereotype is this?
- a social pattern where religious extremism, radicalization, and social evils in religion have a safe harbour.
- creating social uncertainty, instability, and unrest.

But because of psychological pressure from pro-minority communist political spaces, many governments (globally), compromise with 'law of the land'! Those who take a call against 'self-destructive mechanism' are non-inclusive, bad majority, anti-democratic, extremist majority, and those who are silent or support 'self-destructive mechanism' are inclusive, good majority. Even international institutions with 193 member countries remain silent on this. These institutions must understand that if countries cease to exist, to whom will they give membership, and what will they keep on the 'tangible or intangible' heritage site list? This is the power of the 'communist narrative', which is exactly the continuing policy of destruction that was carried out by colonial powers earlier in Bhārat. It's high time that Bhārat, Israel, the EU, the USA come up with some conclusive framework to address the issue of 'Self destructive mechanisms' that are a threat to 'rule-based order' internally as well as in the Indo-Pacific.

PART IV
DEMYSTIFYING POPULAR NARRATIVES

11

Scriptures versus Scripture: One Scripture

Today, whatever books are available about Hinduism, they are very important to learn about teachings and historical records. That is why it's very difficult to identify which books belong to Hinduism, as a whole ancient Bhārat was never divided on this religion–secular tight separation. So every book must be accepted as part of history, so there is nothing like rejection; the only matter is whether to follow it or not. Because rejection of a book is used to eliminate the book from your memory (in the case of *Āgamas* and Upavedas), it becomes easy to eliminate it from historical records, just like Bakhtiyar Khilji did with Nalanda.

Shastra is not scripture; shastras means science or rationale behind conduct. When Hinduism is limited to scripture, then without a second, their (Hinduphobic) achievement is the elimination of 'architecture and civilizational, society, personalities, environmental aspects, folklore, tangible culture, intangible culture, deities or gods that are not mentioned in books and tribal cultures', and ultimately hitting a final nail into the coffin, i.e., denying multiple scriptures and coming to 'one God, one book cult'.

In Hindu civilization, folk stories of the Rāmāyaṇa, Mahābhārata, and Puranas are on the tongues of Hindus and are not part of any books and have equal status as stories in books. For example, there are many jatis and communities all over Bhārat who have their own version of the Rāmāyaṇa with local folk stories written or unwritten. In the Tamil Mahābhārata, Draupadi turns into Kali, runs into the forest, and eats elephants at night as she is disappointed with her five husbands. That is why literature written by Brahmins is not a complete picture of Hinduism; the folk stories and emotions of non-Brahmins are equally important. But this doesn't create the narrative of Brahmanism = Hinduism for the Hinduphobic vote bank, so this is hidden from you. As Hinduism was transformed from civilization to religion, it is obvious that whatever books and manuscripts are available in literature must be termed scripture to create an Abrahamic parallel within Hinduism.[1]

Table 11.1

Main book	Law: Civil and criminal conduct
Quran	Sharia
Torah	Talmud (it includes history of Jews also)
Bible	10 commandments
Bhagavad Gita	*Manusmriti*

This model was imposed on Hinduism to limit sources to merely two books.

The following debates are about how skilfully one book religion manages to sell their products over multiple books and the whole civilization of Bhārat and Sanatan.

Elimination Technique

The goal of Hindu-phobic people is to eliminate maximum things from Hinduism and transform it into 'one book one cult' so that proselytization becomes easy.
1. Eliminating tangible–intangible aspects (archaeological sites), folklores by limiting discussion to scriptures
2. Things that are prohibited or not mentioned in non-Hindu scriptures are also kept off the discussion table. Yoga, meditation, surgery, Vedic mathematics, Ayurveda, classical dance, classical music, wine production methods in ancient India, use of opium, space for LGBTQ, etc.
3. Turn back to the Vedas: The Vedas are only true, and other scriptures are false, denying diverse heritage other than the Vedas.

4. One book essence of all: e.g., the Bhagavad Gita. But what about other aspects of Hinduism? *Manusmrirti* is not a law book but a civil-criminal code; the study of law is Nyay-Vaisheshika.
5. One scripture contradicts the other: Diverse views in Hinduism are a feature of multiple opinions; they cannot be taken as contradictions, e.g., according to the Jain Ramayana, Lakshmana killed Ravan.
6. Eliminating those Hindu practices that don't have scriptural references, Hinduism gives space for modification and freedom, but the condition is that it shall follow the central philosophy.

In chapter 6, we have seen that in Hinduism, Śabda Pramāṇa (testimony) is just one Pramāṇa, so we cannot limit it to one or multiple scriptures.

Vedas, Upanishads, and Puranas

These mediocre historians divided periods of history on the basis of these three texts; they project it as a division of history, but it is actually a division of Hinduism. When they explain the period, they explain what changes and differences took place over the period, not continuity. The Upaniṣhads and Puranas are an extended part of the Vedas and are also mentioned in the Vedas. They say the Vedic period is the period of yajña, and the Puranic period is the temple period, but they don't say every temple has a special building to conduct yajña. This is how they use one scripture against another. The Vedas don't exist in isolation, *vedāṅga*, Upavedas, Upaniṣhads and sutra, Bhashya, Vartika, Tika (commentary and explanations), so it is whole ecosystem with essence of 'oneness'.

Problem of Jati

Today in Bhārat, vulnerable sections do face problems of socio-economic backwardness, including serious issues like 'manual scavenging, abusive content, stereotypes against some jatis, and atrocities'. If we go by shastras, then we will find poetic stories like Brahmins are born out of mouth of *Īśvara*, and jati's are outcomes of inter-varna marriages. But these stories aren't scientific explanations for the origin of the jati-varna system. Secondly, Hindu books don't include a list of all jatis. *Manusmriti* includes approximately 52–57 jatis. But in Bhārat, 5,000+ jatis exist. There are five types of people.

1. Hindu scholars who believe in scripture word by word never accept that Hinduism has any role in the jati–varna system because it's not mentioned clearly and adequately, even if it is mentioned in a poetic way. So these Hindu scholars run away from accepting that jati–varna is the outcome of Hinduism.
2. 'Vedas don't mention jati', so we accept varna but not jati (the Vedas do mention jati).[2]
3. Critics of Hinduism give roots to jati–varna in Hinduism.
4. I am only Hindu; I don't believe in caste (this basically means he doesn't believe in caste discrimination).
5. I am Bhārtiya/modern/human; I don't believe in caste system.

All these belong to the same category because they all believe in bookish myth as reality in their own way rather than an anthropological approach (refer to p. 123). These five approaches either relate to or deny a relation with Hinduism. But all three don't study ground-level situations and problems faced by vulnerable sections, which are not just because of traditional issues but also because of modern-day challenges like urban–rural, urban–tribal divide, market volatility, lack of skills, illiteracy, financial illiteracy, etc. That is, criticizing or giving a clean chit to Hinduism by referring to books will never solve the problem. I would say that if someone says I don't believe in the caste system or jati, he indirectly also runs away from the problems faced by people as per jati.

The Bhagavad Gita Has Science of Atom Bomb

This is one of the myths promoted. It is true that the Mahābhārata has mentioned some destructive weapons. I don't know in what context it is said with what intention, but in Hinduism, war happens with zero collateral damage. No public and private infrastructure will be destroyed, no civilians will be killed, and no women will be raped. A war will happen outside the village on open ground. War will also happen on a particular day, according to the calculations of astronomy, with confirmation from both sides, so that instant war expenditure doesn't affect the economy suddenly. When such a system of war is there, then how can one say the Mahābhārata had an atom bomb, which is created with the purpose of collateral damage. There is the possibility of mass destruction with weapons, but not in the form of an atom bomb. In short, Brahmastra is not an atom bomb.

Scripture Doesn't Include Idol Worship

'The definition of God in Hinduism is not the second or third diagrams of Diagram 19.1 (p. 350), but rather the fourth diagram, which is the formless God', this kind of Myths are imposed on Hinduism.

Three Versions of 'Na tasya pratimā asti'

1. 'Na tasya pratimā asti' means 'there is no separate/only image or idol of Īśvara/Paramātmā as it is state (oneness) and that state exists everywhere; it is you who have to realize it'. This state can be experienced in anything you want: plant, tree, soil, water, devata, devi, etc. That state/Īśvara is not one but oneness (refer Diagram 19.1, p. 350)
2. 'Na tasya pratimā asti' means there is one God = Īśvara, and so Brahma, Vishnu, Saraswati, and Shiva are all false gods. But while proving 'certain person' as a kalki avatāra of Vishnu at that time, Vishnu is accepted. If Vishnu is a fake god, his Kalki avatāra (certain person) is also fake.
3. In Hinduism, God himself is a messenger (i.e., Shiva, Vishnu), which means Kalki is also a god; if Kalki = God and Kalki = 'is a certain person', then God = 'certain person', which means God has a body, which contradicts the definition of a monotheistic God who is formless.

Rules of Debate
In Hinduism, rules of debate are also set by rationale; we have detailed books on 'how the debate should be conducted'. There are two sources for rules of debate:
1. the *Carakasaṃhitā*
2. the first and fifth chapters of the *Nyāyasūtra*

So, the six pramanas of the Hindu debate is based on logic, rationality, authenticity, and technical soundness, not one line written in the book vs. another line written in the book; *Śabda* pramāṇa (testimony) is merely one pramāṇa unlike other religions.

That is why Hindu scholars accept, support, deny, and criticize their own scripture, write commentaries, and every effort and viewpoint is welcomed. Whereas some other religions justify even social evils through false analogy and logic just to satisfy that 'testimony doesn't fail' because what they have is merely testimony as the word of God.

Marketing of Religion
As I said, many religions try to make religion exist through the hero worship of the founder by declaring it holy, social work, blasphemy laws and terror, illogical dos and don'ts, avoiding rational criticism, and calling teachings the ultimate truth to avoid debate. If any rational, liberal, or sceptic stands up and asks some unexpected question that makes whole illogical propaganda fail, then religion will fail too. To avoid sceptics, they have started a comparative study of scriptures so that debate is limited to line vs. line rather than rational debate so that religion 'alone' doesn't fail when discussed to prove comparatively better than others.

God vs. Historical Figures
According to some people, God in human form like Ram, Krishna, etc., is unreal because they are not historical figures, so the messages given are also unreal, but non-Hindu religious beings and founders as historical figures are real, and their messages are also real. The actual comparison should be among:

Spiritual test: Science of experiencing our God vs. experiencing their God (Diagram 19.1, p. 350), i.e., God vs. God.

Historical test: Our millions of yogis (chapter 8, Dashnami sampradaya) who experienced God vs. revelation by God only to a single person, i.e, historical personality vs. historical personality.

Some people smartly mix both of them to get favourable outcome.

Double-Standard Approach

Harsh, inhumane, and misogynistic social-civil-criminal law are not told while promoting exclusivists religion. People fall prey to these proselytization activities, and their whole lives they suffer. Global society shall take the initiative to speak on these negative aspects. These laws are implemented by religious heads, priests, theocratic states, freedom of religion, and terror organizations, but the world only focuses on these laws when they are implemented by 'terror organizations'.

In history, this technique has been used by Napoleon in the plebiscite; he framed questions in such a way that the answer to every question was Napoleon, and Napoleon became the supremo of France. So the same technique is used by people in proselytization activities, so the answer to everything is '!'. People never question the 'questions', people always focus on answers.

The Technique of Proselytizers

1. First, he imposed a few concepts of certain 'religious books' on Hinduism, i.e., monotheism on polytheism.
2. Then whatever 'diversity and uniqueness' Hinduism had was eliminated by terming it differences.
3. Then they started discussing the 'imposed concept' of Hinduism as similarities to attract Hindus to accept his 'religious book'.

This is done because once exclusivist religion becomes the majority religion of any state or the state itself becomes theocratic, people should not question any fringe elements who will carry out massacres and cultural genocide of diversity.

Conclusive remark on 10 points of debate
Common things in all religions (hypothetical example)

Table 11.2

Selecting expected outcome ninja technique (deduction)				
Religions	Hinduism	Exclusive religions	Other exclusive religion/ideology	Other religions
Teachings and diversity in religion	{@, #, $, %, *,!,?,∞}	{!}	{β, π,!, ☺}	{£, α,!}
	Whenever bracket ends with positive or negative infinity, its open bracket, i.e., not limited only to books, Hinduism is not merely a testimony but an experience too, which promotes out-of-the-box/out-of-scripture thinking.	They are closed bracket limited to scriptures not able to think beyond religion, religious scripture/book.		Codified and uncodified teachings.
Selecting common things from all religions	!	!	!	!

Ignore differences because to be united, let's select common things	!	!	!	!
Your scripture includes same thing as my scripture	!	!	!	!
What is the last and final word of God?	!	!	!	!
As you can see all scriptures indicate the same thing	!	!	!	!
All the religions believe in one God	!	!	!	!
No person in my religion can become a good follower unless he is a good human	!	!	!	!

Universal Myth: All Religions Are Equal

Citizens of a world or particular country are equal irrespective of their religion or other identities, which is one thing, and saying all religions are equal is another thing. When one says all religions are equal, then what actually do they mean?

They are equal by weight, with an equal number of words and pages. If they say all religions are the same in a diplomatic way, 'all religions teach the same thing', then verse by verse they must be the same; if software is the same, then the display appearance of the software must be the same; then why is there diversity across the religion? Let's compare the volume of books, number of books Hinduism has vs. one book religion, worship of places of those who don't believe in idol worship vs. Hindu temples.

Even if you compare Hinduism and others and wait for outcome, then there are 'n' number of possibilities: equal, unequal, bigger, smaller, etc. Let's speak about non-religious books on economics, politics, culture, music, bio-diversity, and quantum physics. Will you say all are equal or all are diverse? Then on what basis do you confidently say all religions are equal?

Better we say all human beings are equal in terms of fundamental rights irrespective of their identity, race, culture, civilization, ethnicity, creed, caste, or gender; this is quite a broad concept and sensible too. That is why reading books to learn about diversity and concepts is very important. There are also ignorant atheists who have a general idea of religion by keeping all religions in one size basket and saying all are equally wrong. It helps them refute religion unilaterally. For example, if someone says, 'Every God has opened a company, which is known as religion, and has kept a manager to handle every franchise (shop)', I don't have a problem with this statement, but in the case of 'Hinduism', it should be called at least a 'special economic zone or spiritual mall of diversity' and at most a civilization. That is why the world must come out of religion, follow religion, debates on religion–secularism, and learn how human civilization has grown over the past million years.

The Right to Choose vs. Religion's Order

Many religions try to justify the 'social evils' by saying it is the right to choose or the 'right to choose' given by 'religious scripture'. Even the judiciary has fallen for this propaganda. The right to choose is under only the Bhārtiya constitution, not under any religion. The judiciary shall take a strong stand only on a particular practice, whether that practice is wrong or right. It shall take a clear stand whether social evils are also allowed or not under the 'doctrine of essentiality' and the 'right to choose'. Will the judiciary have the same confusion about sati pratha? Should this come under the right to choose or the doctrine of essentiality? Or will it strike down all evil practices. The judiciary shall also take a 'bottom-up approach' where that practice actually originates or has a basis, i.e., subjectivity. The judiciary shall not compare two different attires with different places of origin. For example, piercing ears, wearing bangles, toe rings, bindi—all these practices come under fashion, but some experts also give the scientific origin of these practices.[3] We cannot compare this with 'female shall cover her body parts and hairs so that it doesn't turn provocative for rape'. In the former case, it is scientific fashion, the later puts the burden of crime or guilt on the victim itself. Both practices cannot be treated equally. In the former case, Hinduphobics tried hard to defame Hindu practices by pulling them under 'Brahminical patriarchy, *Manusmriti*, women's rights, independent women, the right to choose for women, imposition by male dominant society or religion', etc.

The person with limited knowledge is satisfied and confident about knowledge, and the seeker is always hungry for knowledge with a humble attitude, 'I don't know'. So start your journey to know the world past, future, and present rather than coming to conclusions in a preplanned way that this 'religious book' is conclusion, solution, etc. The difference between colonizers and seekers is that the former impose a limited framework on the latter for better administration of colonies, while the latter seek knowledge and diversity, respectively. 'You must respect every religion' is a myth created by politicians to maintain peace so that intolerant elements don't create social unrest or security threats, but this myth keeps religions immune from critical enquiry.

Not only Hinduism but the whole world, human civilization, ecology, and all other diverse aspects are beautiful and sources of knowledge. The only condition is removing and throwing away glasses of presupposition. This will make you liberated and will end suffocation, which will make you consume knowledge and the world.

12

It's Terrorism, but for You

There is nothing like extremism; we call it extremism to avoid discussing the 'theory' behind 'physical violence'. When someone wants to create someone as a 'killer', she won't directly go and ask him to kill people. Why would one kill randomly? So the beautiful story is expected to be narrated in latent form as religion, ideology, or movement to save or expand religion or movement so that killing is justified as self-defence. So how is psychology created? What actually goes on in the mind of a 'killer or terrorist'?

You will see all over the world terrorist organizations, but limited to that particular geography based on religious, linguistic, communist, or other ideologies, e.g., Kahane Chai, Aum Shinrikyo, New People's Army (NPA), Ulster Defence Association (UDA), Real Irish Republican Army (RIRA), Shining Path/Sendero Luminoso, Euskadi Ta Askatasuna (ETA), Revolutionary Struggle/Epanastatikos Agonas (EA), Fuerzas Armadas Revolucionarias De Colombia (FARC), Khalistani Tiger Force (KTF), Lord's Resistance Army (LRA), and Liberation Tigers of Tamil Elam (LTTE). They are formed by multiple external circumstances, or ideological motivations, or commandments. I condemn every form of terror with no selectiveness.

Let's take a hypothetical example where some form of terrorism is functioning globally with a certain pattern. Let's try to decode this hypothetical situation and how it functions at a philosophical–psychological level so that no one justifies any form of terror. Let's create a hypothetical story. In the pre-modern world, there were empires (hypothetical), which expanded with the power of the sword, and to maintain administrative and social uniformity, they imposed the 'cult and laws' of their empire through a channel of religion. But in the modern world, empires vanished and armies were left with secular and modern nations in a dormant state as a religion. So these people who wanted to implement 'religion' again with the help of the army because it was not followed by the rest of the people because of rationalism, then those people created a parallel army, which we call terrorism. The goal is to bring whole the world under outdated civil-criminal-social laws in the name of God, which give territorial gains (resources) to the capital of religion. So this hypothetical story continues in this chapter.

Terrorism Has No Religion

Terrorism is an activity, and religion belongs to human beings or a human being belongs to a certain religion. That is why 'terrorism has no religion or has religion'. Both sentences are technically incorrect.

Expansionary utopian states or colonies packed beautifully in the pack of religion were expanding all over the world under a few empires, but a few centuries ago, the concept of a nation came and all military activity of empires came to an end because of a nation with multiple identities and boundaries. So the goal of the people became to maintain the sovereignty of the nation. But people who were still followers of colonization, which they think is religion, wanted to continue that expansion, so they started becoming a headache for national security. They started creating a 'non-state actor army', which we call terrorism in general. That is why such colonization movements with a pan-world utopian state model in the name of religion are unfit for the 21st century and pose a challenge to global peace. But the root cause of the problem is that the fundamentalism of such religions, colonizations, and empires itself is exclusivist and expansionary.

Why Does Someone Become Extremist?

Everyone who is anti-state and with a utopian state model, whose interest is directly or indirectly against national interest, especially in terms of the sovereignty of boundaries, one doesn't participate in social life makes themselves isolated because 'religion/colonization' prohibits it. Doesn't accept the existence of other faiths, their deities/gods, and boycotts them as per religious commandments. This ultimately creates an 'open suffocative prison' for such a person with some heavenly lusty dreams, i.e., the carrot and stick approach.

But what is that special thing that makes someone a terrorist? But what is it that motivates someone to become a militia for terror workers, irrespective of funding, support, or arms supply?

Step 1: Anthropocentrism + ethnocentrism, and approach towards the environment as exploitative. To see the environment as mere resources without having knowledge of the ecological cycle makes human beings exploitative beyond 'ethnicity'. This approach becomes intensified when such people want the resources of others territories, and then the people of that territory are merely hurdles that need to be removed. So multiple techniques are available to remove 'enemy/infidel' (included in religious fundamentalism/manifesto), so multiple methods are used, both soft power and hard power.

1. Pulling them into your team through 'proselytization' by terming religious practices of enemy or infidel as 'illogical'
2. Religious commands to eliminate 'infidel'
3. Religious command to practice discrimination with infidel at the social, economic, and political level

So with the dream of a utopian state, the militia is ready as human capital in a dormant state (religion), which is waiting for a call of action (terrorism).

Step 2: When religion is promoting social evils (refer to 12.1, p. 414) unsound practices, cruelty, technically unsound, impractical, irrational, illogical, and self-contradictory theories, irrespective of space, time, and situation. So to avoid criticism and self-introspection, two tools are used: strong defence and aggressive foreign policy, so that no one touches the core 'unsound system'. This check and balance of defence and aggression are ensured through the following nine-point agenda.

General Nine-Point Agenda
1. Hero worship of Founder
2. By covering religion with the term 'holy'
3. Social work and sweet foreign policy to hide social evils

4. Blasphemy laws
5. Terrorism
6. Strict dos and don'ts
7. Avoiding criticism of religion
8. Boycotting cultures and value systems of other faiths to maintain a unique identity and isolated existence, e.g., strategic separation of us vs. them or marginalization of others
9. Calling teaching the ultimate truth to avoid criticism

One follows these nine-point agenda very strictly just to save that theology of religion plus developing an ego of identity in the name of uniqueness, which is used at various levels for social and political gains, etc.

Step 3: Religious practices and rituals are the only things where there will be complete submission, devotion, and spiritual enjoyment; all other things where generally human beings submerge, like art, drama, dance, and music, are prohibited as prescribed. So that follower or fighter remains busy with the nine-point agenda and nothing else. This attitude of non-participating in the world at a psychological level reflects non-participation in national or social activity, which fuels separatism or expansion. They exist and participate in life just to expand empires in the name of the religious message of truth, by order of God.

Step 4: Religious identity is the only identity in society; don't associate with any other identity like profession, other culture, etc., so that followers don't choose other identities to avoid diversion from the expansionary movement to establish a utopian state.

Step 5: The above steps limit the possibility of human beings flourishing like flowers, as identity is only limited to religion and ensuring its survival with a nine-point agenda. This causes extreme suffocation and stress. This extreme psychological stress is justified by giving comfortable infinite fruits in the heavens that release stress, e.g., operant conditioning or the carrot and stick approach. Those who failed to expand their minds because of religious limitations then hold the government or establishment accountable for their suffocation, underdevelopment, and marginalization, which helps the secessionist movement.

This is something some theocratic countries (hypothetical) understood, and they are expanding minds, which is also reflected in their country in the form of diverse values, diverse religions, a diversified economy, and statutory efforts to build up tolerance. That is why there is no stress in their minds, and so there is no terrorism issue in those countries. But some theocratic countries send funds for missionary activities as expansionary policy, which is an alternative to terrorism within the country because expansionary policy eliminates internal issues.

The Three Types to Ensure Religion's Survival

1. Following strictly and making all religious people follow the religion strictly (religious leaders use this technique).
2. Making religion as states religion so that if people start moving towards atheism, communism, then they can be termed anti-national because state = religion (political leadership uses this technique), but (communism sometimes itself doesn't believe in nation, so itself sometimes turns into terror and carries out cultural genocide as 'religion is the opium of the masses').
3. Funding and expanding religion and colonialism all over the world so that even if it fails to exist on the mainland or capital, then it can exist as a seed bank all over the world or in colonies.
   A. Rich people and other servants of religion use this technique.
   B. Honest followers in colonies of religion all over the world.

Type 2 and 3A people don't follow religion at all; they enjoy life in a liberal way, do whatever they want, and only get hurt when someone attacks their religious identity or any external person breaks their nine-point agenda.

The law of religion/empire (hypothetical) is not imposed in many theocratic countries because criminal punishments are very heinous and may become against human rights and attract political instability. So this becomes a clash point.

Now the condition of a theocratic state is that type 2 and 3A people don't follow a religion, which hurts type 1, and type 1 never questions them because they are supporting religion financially without following, as religion or empire is growing all over the world. The clash is always between (type 1+ type 3B) vs. (type 2 + type 3A).

1. (type 1+ type 3 B) forms a parallel army (terror group) to establish the rule of 'religion/manifesto'
2. (type 2 + type 3A) forms non-secular liberalism or a modern or liberal nation

Table 12.1

Old order	New order
One Manifesto of religion	Democracy, liberty
One religious law	Values of the modern world with no theocracy
One religion	Secular state or socialist state
One leadership	Change in leadership
One ruler	Changing the ruler after the election
One foremless god	Cultural diversity

Both groups accuse each other of terrorism, but all three people are responsible for it. Some are in dormant form (exclusivist religion), and others are fully grown, which manifests religion (refer to 12.2, pp. 414–415).

Terrorism starts because to change the establishment, as there is no democracy and even if it's there, there are no free ideas. If they consolidate empires through strict implementation of the 'Manifesto of religion', then people will suffocate and human rights violations will occur, and if they become liberal, then the revivalist mindset of religious people will create an army of terrorists to eliminate establishments, i.e., being between rock and hard place.

This is the base of continuous instability in theocratic countries and now in democratic countries too, because democratic countries have imported religious fundamentalists through the 'refugee influx'.

This five-step agenda keeps going forever in the name of freedom of religion, which remained unobserved in the mediaeval era because everyone was fighting for some reason. Now everyone chooses the path of peace as a modern nation format, and now the same unobserved movement is seen as terrorism. This unobserved movement remains forever and takes physical form only in four instances, which you call a terror attack.

1. Anyone who opposes it or tries to dilute it through criticism in any way or brings hurdles to the nine-point agenda.
2. When unobserved movement is convinced, the ruling system's and their interests are not only opposite but clashing too.
3. Never kill innocents, but the culprit will be decided by them only. If no one gets as the culprit, then infidels are permanent culprits as prescribed.
4. If these people feel they are discriminated against or there is 'anti-movement' against them, even though they have boycotted other cultures, philosophies, value systems, and the idea of the nation to maintain a unique identity and independent existence, they will react with violence (in their language war against injustice).

It's 'the pot calling the kettle black', and there is a legend and popular narrative around the world that says, 'They are discriminated, which is why they became terrorists'. Fundamentally, perspective is binary, me vs. infidel and my god vs. their god, so even if something is neutral, they will perceive it partially, whether it is news, truth, justice, etc. This becomes a subtle background for terror: 'acts of terror' are carried out for complete justice, equality, human rights, etc. So artificial brainwashing plays a very small role.

This physical form is known as violence. I don't call it terror; I call it elimination. First, they eliminated all the cultural-social aspects related to the enemy/infidel, and when the enemy/infidel opposed then the infidel also got eliminated. That is why they created a negative list (according to the Manifesto book) where a number of things are prohibited so that when violent form takes place, items in the list are eliminated.

To carry out this, the whole drama of an expansionary empire in the name of exclusive religion was created. To feel superior over others, they have concepts like only my god is a real god, infidel, gender hierarchy, and social evils. These kinds of unobserved movements in the name of religion are strengthened financially through funding. This process transforms the 'social base of religion' into 'over the ground workers' (OGW) which help in logistics, buffering for terrorists, arms supply, stone pelting, narrative building, etc. If anyone from the buffer is killed by security forces, then the 'cry of human rights violations by security forces' again helps to strengthen the social base.

Why People Don't Accept the Above Truth?

1. Politicians of other countries don't accept this, because if they do then political instability and issues of sovereignty may arise. To avoid this, they call it merely religious practices so that those who are liberal of that particular religion don't attach themselves to this movement, i.e., avoiding the revival of problems through criticism or accepting truth.
2. Politicians of the same theocratic country don't accept it because they want to remain in power. If people understand the problem is because of religion, empire, or colonialism then they may choose atheism to solve issues, and liberal ideas may culminate in new political challenges to the existing political setup.
3. The capital of religion and kings never accept it because their finances used to create colonies through religion (colonization) will become waste because they have only non-renewable energy resources, so they need colonies to exploit resources to survive. So if the problem is that religion is accepted, then atheism will make all their investments in colonies fail.

    Technique to keep colonized people in control:
    a. Religious brotherhood
    b. Meeting of citizens once a year, irrespective of nationality and other non-religious identities
    c. Visiting the capital once in a life
    d. Hero worship of the founder and God
    e. Celebrating the empire's festivals, rituals, and prayers at the same time all over the world (because of differences in nationality, resources, multiple sectarian fractions, and dishonest followers fighting within themselves)
4. If it is accepted that particular theology or religion (hypothetical) is the root cause of multiple social problems, then who will become the militia for future geopolitical gains? So to maintain the flow of

militias and terrorists continuously, religion is given clean chit in cases of terrorism.

Role of Academics and Intellectuals and Scholars in Promoting Terrorism

The syllabus of academics in religious studies is third-order inquiry, i.e., they will discuss god, soul, mind, and body debates. But the syllabus won't include social evils, civil and criminal law, rituals in the name of god that don't pass the test of rationality, equality, etc. The concepts of infidel, discriminatory, brutal treatment of infidels, or calling for their holocaust or cultural genocide aren't part of the syllabus. How religion and empire have grown historically is also ignored by academics. So because of their partial view, they give clean chit to faith.

This Is Not My Religion

Whenever a terror attack happens, one section of the group says, 'This is not my religion'. Terrorism only ensures 'civil and criminal law as per the Manifesto' is being implemented because people already believe in that manifesto. So the completion of the utopian state, which is an intrinsic value system for religion, manifests practically.

Whether it is a 'theocratic state' or non-state actors (terror organizations), freedom of religion, enforced by priest, etc., implements the same 'civil and criminal law as per the Manifesto'.

Let's ignore all implementing agencies and let's think about 'civil and criminal law as per the Manifesto', which are religious revelations. This means if people are not ready to accept 'civil and criminal law', there is some issue, which means either people have issues with 'Revelation' or with the person to whom it was revealed, even though people believe in the same religion. So they divide this scenario into binary scenarios to avoid debate on this issue.

1. Extremism vs. moderate
2. Right faith vs. wrong faith
3. Terrorism vs. religions are separate
4. Religious fanaticism vs. liberal
5. The right to choose vs. compulsory rituals
6. Wrong vs. right interpretation of religion

7. Hardliner/orthodox vs. moderate
8. Radical vs. soft approach

Why They Don't Accept?

1. If highly polarized people sacrificed dance, music, art, celebration, belongingness, cultural untouchability with others, etc., in their whole lives because it was God's order under the prohibited list just to have a meeting with God after death, if they accept 'their God doesn't exist', their whole religious integrity over life will fail, and it will be a 'huge psychological collapse', as their whole life equations are around God and heavens.
2. Those who are liberal about values yet religious don't accept this because
   a. 'They have a fear that if they accept this', then they have to live their whole lives in guilt because they were following colonization in the name of religion.
   b. Fear of social boycott or elimination by believers (terror fear)
   c. If they accept internally that 'there is no god', yet externally accept it, it gives religious identity, which is beneficial in political spheres.
3. Religious experts, capitalists, and intellectuals don't accept this because these 'believers' are the social base of terrorist organizations, which can be used to achieve the following goals.

The Goals of Such Movements Are

1. political and geographical gains in the enemy or own state
2. pressure groups in policymaking
3. resource-capturing separatist movements
4. expansionary movements
5. extortion and parallel economy
6. narco-terrorism
7. to bring down ranking in ease of doing business FDI, other developmental activity
8. creating no-go zones and, after some time, transforming them into special, unofficial autonomous status (no-go zones are like military blocks of World War II, which later became war fronts)

9. creating geopolitical blocks and creating checks and balances to ensure the game of geopolitics doesn't become one-sided
10. Implementing 'civil and criminal law as per religious Manifesto' so that
    a. colonized people keep bowing down to capital multiple times every day.
    b. the social behaviour of people in colonies all over the world comes under the control of capital with a wave of fundamentalism.

(Common man is made to believe all points except point 10 to make them believe to give a clean chit to religion or empire.)

The Beneficiaries Are Following:
1. Own state, present ruling politicians, or opposition parties
2. Enemy state
3. Capitalists from their own state and other states: arm suppliers, logistics
4. Big political powerhouses
5. High unemployment chooses terror as a path
6. Superpower nations and neighbourhood countries
7. Narcotics, human trafficking, and illegal smuggling
8. Promises were given to the militia that they would die for the sake of religion cum utopian state, so they would get fruits in heaven
9. The capital of religion/kingdom and the origin of religion (colonization) gain territory because civil and criminal law prescribed by the 'religion' get implemented in foreign territory

There is a worldwide narrative that has been very famous except points 8 and 9, i.e., except terrorists and their religious fundamentalism, every other factor is responsible for terrorism. We believe this narrative because the other seven factors are also true, but that doesn't mean the points 8 and 9 are untrue. Communists support this clean chit to religion because according to Karl Marx, every historical event has only 'economic' reasons, so communists refuse to see reality beyond Karl Marx's framework (#RedOrthodox).

Secondly the capital of religion and dragon's land are neighbours, so they keep a non-aggressive policy and give clean chits to each other in respective crimes with exchange of trade, respectively. So this unity, or stand, is reflected globally. The biggest secret is that a follower of such a movement always thinks he is following a spiritual path because suffocation is going to turn into extreme happiness in heaven.

Theism, Atheism, and Half-atheism

Suppose some hypothetical religion follows half atheism; they accept the existence of their own god and related culture and deny the existence of others god and related culture (half atheism).

That religion is divided into two sects, 'X' and 'Y'. Both believe in half atheism, but the historical leaders of both sects are different. In addition, both have separate geography, so sectarian rivalry is divided into geographical rivalry. Both are united under the organization of the religious corporation (hypothetical). When any of the nations of an organization move towards atheism through channels of liberalism on the platform of democracy, then every nation feels threatened that the same wave may come to their country and shake their throne, which is kingship on the foundation of theism or religion.

Table 12.2

Belief/faith	Magnitude
Theism (following religion)	1
Atheism	0
Half atheism of X and Y faiths	0.5
Scale	X ⊢———————⊢———————⊣ Y 0.5 0 0.5

Pendulum keeps moving from half atheism to atheism, or half atheism of X vs. half atheism of Y. This shifting of the pendulum is state vs. non-state actor. The main goal is to keep atheism and its political representation, communism,[1] away because it will give entry to the dragon in the country and the whole political structure will collapse.

Other than this, there is one more hypothetical example where three branches of the same empire exist as religions, and all three have, three different territories with some common nodes.

Diagram 12.1

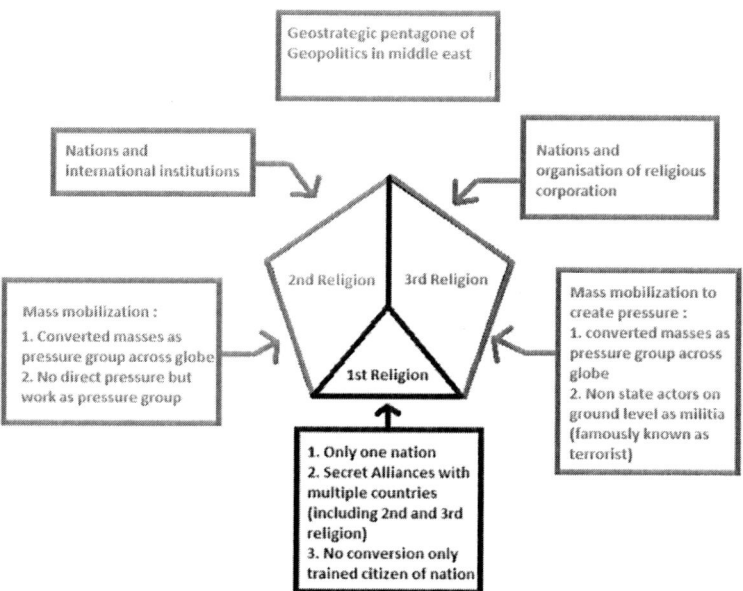

This is how two religions pull citizens of their respective colonies (through proselytization) into a conflict of empires happening on a small geography (common node) with high geopolitical importance. Through conversion (offering citizenship), their goal is to control the area that is geopolitically valuable. So all these religious colonies of two religions play an important role in international institutions in favour of either of the two religions while voting. To satisfy their goals, colonial masters pulled the whole world into war, just like colonized India participated in two world wars on behalf of Britain.

If one wants to end theocratic terror and ensure sovereignty and unity of nation, then start decolonization by giving up 'religious colonialism', but ensure dragon doesn't enter the country through the atheist channel of communism and limit all religions to their place of origin only. Let's limit war to their territories and their demography.

Terrorism sometimes works as an unofficial armed group that is a protective force against organized crimes, human trafficking, narcotics substances, and smuggling.

If Terrorists and Victims Are from the Same Religion, Then How Can Religion Have a Role in Spreading Terrorism?

It means if religions are different, then religion has a role in killing or spreading terror, so the concept of killing infidels is indirectly accepted. Secondly, even if religion is the same, social dynamics are very different in terms of following religion. So honest follower vs. infidel is not the only war, which is an ideal situation. It is actually

i. Clashes among sects of the same religion
ii. Clash for the throne to lead religion, empire, or nation
iii. Dishonest follower, liberal, atheist, non-fundamentalist, traitors vs. honest followers
iv. Supporting a nation over religion vs. an honest follower

Does Religion Promote the Underworld?

There are some activities that are illegal according to law, but those things are employment for someone, or achieving them is the goal of someone. So when such a group of people come together and an create cooperation and ecosystem attached to a particular geography, or without limiting it to geography, this parallel world is the underworld. The reasons to create this can be an unorganized sector, underdevelopment, the utopian state, the secessionist movement, or expansionary movements. But if some religion (hypothetical) gives a ready-made framework of a utopian state, its foreign policy automatically creates a parallel world or underworld if followed.

The Situation Is Out of Control

Smuggling, human trafficking banned narcotic products, arms trafficking, selling of military products—all these things are supplied to non-state actors of an enemy country or targeted country so that these non-state actors, famously known as terror organizations, can destabilize. In the spheres of human values, all these things are wrong, but as far as geopolitics is concerned, these things are merely means for them.

When these 'means' start becoming 'end', then the problem starts.
1. Someone makes this a permanent business or
2. Supplier or businessman controls political masters through funding

The arms industry makes sure that politicians don't ban the selling of arms within and outside nations, which culminates in hate crimes, civil wars, and terrorism within and outside countries. So this situation becomes very difficult because non-state actors become powerful. The third situation is that when a nation behaves irresponsibly, like a race to create nuclear weapons and mass destruction mechanisms, the problem starts becoming serious.

My Religion (Hypothetical) Has Nothing to Do with Terrorism

Table 12.3

What we are told	How it manifests
No innocent should be killed	The culprit will be decided by them only
1. Take arms to protect those with whom injustice happened. 2. Take arms in hands to fight in self-defence or as revenge against the violent person who did injustice.	Ignore the role of the state and judiciary and become a non-state actor (terrorism), take arms in the hands, decide the culprit according to religious rules and sentiments, and implement justice. When truth is religious teachings, then definitely terrorism is justice.
Respect everyone's faith	• There is no other God than my God, so a free hand to destroy tangible and intangible cultures of other faiths • License to kill infidel

What we are told	How it manifests
Men and women are created by God	Women came in so loot should be equally divided
Conclusion: Whole blacklisted prohibited or inferior things are eliminated or exploited once a utopian empire of religion is established.	

How Does a Theocratic State Ensure the Stability and Rule of the King?

These states form alliances with the right and the left wing, but on different standards.

Table 12.4

	With right wing	**With left wing**
Convergence	They form alliances with the promise that they will maintain religious zeal with the right wing and will keep the left wing away, which is anti-religion.	Theocratic nations are dictatorial in nature, whether kingship or democracy; they form alliances on the basis of 'dictatorship similarity' with communist countries, i.e., personality-to-personality cult attachment (with no interference in each other's internal matters).
Contradictions	At the same time, they keep out the private sector and modern banking system, share markets, modern tax system, etc., from their country by declaring it 'non-religious' or 'anti-nation'.	At the same time, they suppress labour rights and ensure cheap labour for high profits, which helps them suppress 'communist uprisings' and 'trade unions' in the country.

Why Radicalization Is Increasing?

In old times, multiple techniques were used to expand empires, i.e., bringing masses under the 'civil-criminal law' of a kingdom.

1. Direct rule of the central kingdom
2. Rule of local/federal government but paying 'tribute' to Central government from locally collected taxes (central–federal clashes or clashes among multiple kingdoms took place and the imposition of 'religion' went to the back seat)
3. Orders/commands of priests, stories of gods, worship/rituals of god
4. Promotion of 'religion' through local art and architecture (but people got lost in local architecture itself and lost connection with 'religion', which itself prohibits certain tangible art and architecture)
5. Over-decentralization happened, and 'religious ethos' was replaced by local culture
6. The nation became more important than 'religion'
7. People were illiterate enough to read 'religion'
8. People are busy building their personal wealth (economic divide)
9. Barriers and differences because of geographic diversity—terrain, scattered identity, i.e., linguistic, racial, geographic
10. In organizations, mass mobilization took longer than self-radicalization does today

All of these factors contributed to colonialism's decline. But suddenly digitization replaced all ten points and 'direct access to religion', which again fueled colonization. All the points above were imposing religion, so there was 'resistance' in the masses as a 'reaction'. But now people are looking at religion as a product and approaching it as a consumer under the 'right to choose' and 'freedom of religion'. Academics and the mainstream call this 'self-radicalization/lone wolf attack'. National boundaries are fading, and the digital world is a new nation.

Now 'rule of religion' = 'rule of central kingdom'

All barriers of politics, economy, society, and local culture, which were hurdles for 'direct rule of center/kingdom', were removed by digitization. Because of digitization, even the illiterate can understand in video format. The whole world of infidels and heads of above ten institutions are calling this 'radicalization' because of its threat to their existence. For me, it's just 'mission colonization accomplished'.

Temporary Solution for Terror
1. Killing heads of terror organizations to project they have almost won the war.
2. Supporting health and raising funds for victims of terror through an international institution.
3. Awarding a 'peace prize' to a few people for working in a terror area, mostly victims.

We haven't yet come out of this kind of terror; forget about the calculation of terror against ecology by the whole of humanity!

PART V
GOING BACK TO THE ROOTS

13

No God to Many Gods, Many Gods to One God

Who is that God? Is he Egyptian or Greek? Hindu, Abrahamic, formless, or bodiless? Even while uttering 'Oh God' due to frustration and stress, who is that God?

The earliest uses of the word God are in Germanic writing often cited to be in the Gothic Bible or Wulfila Bible, which is the Christian Bible as translated by Ulfilas into the Gothic language spoken by the Eastern Germanic or Gothic tribe. This Bible was written in the 8th–9th century AD. The word goddess itself appeared for the first time (not used) in 1350 AD. English came into existence as an outcome or side effect of Greek, Latin, and many other languages with modifications. The Industrial Revolution and technological development made English more popular than rich languages like Latin and Greek. Expansion all over the world as colonies made the English language and English concepts expansionary, and these expansions were an invasion of concepts too. That is why the word *god* became famous all over the world, including in the minds of philosophers, writers, historians, theists, and atheists.

This 18th-century period made Britain rich, which ensured economic security, and this created funding as the extra income for all other activities, right from supporting navigation to artists, philosophers, writers, etc. When the Western world started writing history, especially in English, they already had Abrahamic backgrounds as the driving force and source of thinking, vision, virtue, morals, and ethics. So while writing anything, biasedness was always part of the filter of vision, i.e., if they perceive anything in the world or in books, it must go through a biblical filter in their eyes and minds so that non-biblical things stay out of mind or out of consideration. The best example would be that Western historians never observed transgenders and LGBTQs as part of Bhārtiya society and the Vedas because it might be unholy for them. According to some experts in Hinduism, there are multiple genders, but Western writers never observed that because of the biblical filter and never appreciated it, maybe because of conservative values. They imposed their binary gender division on Hindus (eleven genders) and South Americans (five genders).[2]

The Purpose of Tagging the Word God to Every Personality All Over the World Was

1. trying to fix whole-world civilization into an 'exclusive religions' model
2. diversity of the world ends so that no competition for exclusive religions remains alive

It is very clear from chapter 4 that references given about the similarity between the Indus valley and Hindu civilizations state that all the civilizations and religions have taken up many concepts from Hinduism. They packed some concepts with different names, including deities, and presented them as their 'product' revealed by the God, and used them as a tool of expansion and colonialism, which is generally known as proselytization, on those from whom they adopted all cultural concepts. It's like teaching Elon Musk how to make a Diwali rocket (a firecracker). You might have seen the following concepts somewhere.

Table 13.1

Egyptian civilization
Isis nursing her son Horus
Holy Trinity 1. the Father God Osiris 2. the Mother Goddess Isis 3. the Son Horus

Monastic order first existed in ancient Egypt (virgin males and females were dedicated to monastery e.g., *Brāmhacaryā*)
7 heavens and 7 hells across all civilizations

Monotheists (believers of one formless God) started imposing their own concepts on Hinduism and marketed Hinduism as 'polytheism' (multiple gods). This is how they imposed the term 'formless god' on Hinduism. This expresses the first half of the title, 'No God to Many God'.

Table 13.2

Civilizations	Terms in their civilizations	Terms are given by the Western or English scholars
Greek	Zeus, Hera, Poseidon, Demeter, Athena, Apollo, Artemis, Ares, Hephaestus, Aphrodite, Hermes, Hestia, Dionysus. Term for males: Theos Term for females: Thea	Greek gods and goddesses
Plato's writings	'logos' which means cosmic purpose as the highest virtue	God
Egyptian	• Osiris, Isis, Horus, Horus, Seth, Ptah, Re, Hathor, Anubis • Terms for male: ntr • Terms for female: ntrt	Egyptian gods and goddesses
Hinduism	• Vishnu, Krishna, Bhavani, Radha, Shiva, Brahman, Iswar, Paramātmā, Bhagavān, Ram, Hanuman • Terms for male: devata • Terms for female: devi • There are also deities who are half-male, half-female, transgenders have their own deity.	Gods, goddesses, animal god, water god, air god, transgender god

To carry out the imposition of monotheism (formless god = atheism) on polytheism (Hinduism), there were multiple diplomatic ways found out in the colonial era, and you will see the rise of the 'monotheistic school of thoughts', which marketed their monotheistic version of Hinduism as real. Several attempts were made by exclusivist religions and others to stereotype and stigmatized 'idol worship and polytheism' and creating inferiority complex saying idol worship is wrong.

- Boycotting idol worship
- Yajña vs. idol worship
- Meditation vs. rituals
- Real God is formless
- Formless one God vs. idol
- Doing hardcore anti-idol worship marketing of Hinduism
- Idol worship (fake Hinduism) vs. meditation–yoga (real Hinduism)
- Hate and inferiority creation about idol worship
- God is within me/you not outside
- The essence of Vedas and Upanishads is 'monotheism'
- Ram is a prince not a god, so Ram temple shall not be built[3]
- I believe in god but not in rituals
- I find my god in human beings and not in idols

1. These are outcomes of ignorance, i.e., in Hinduism there is tradition of ancestral worship too; it is mentioned in the Rāmāyaṇa itself, e.g., idols of Dilip, Raghu, etc., so even if it is considered that he is not a god/deity, then also 'Ram temple' should be built.
2. Ram is the incarnation of Vishnu in human form, so he is a deity.

The second step was that they promoted 'God is one and he is formless', and he has just different names, so by doing this, they denied diversity and subjectivity of concepts. Because deities are presiding deities in various aspects of Hindu lifestyle, even the mantras have presiding deities. This completes the second half of the title, 'Many Gods to One God'.

Table 13.3

Aspects of human life	Relation with multiple gods
Festivals	1. Diwali – Ram's coming back to Ayodhya 2. Holi – Pralhad and Narsimha
Geographic unification	Multiple temples of deities are organized in the pattern, i.e., 4 peetha, 52 Shakti peetha. The pattern of visiting multiple temples is related to each other. E.g., a compulsory visit to Kedarnath after Pashupatinath, a compulsory visit to Vitthala after Balaji
16 Saṃskāras	Garbhdharan to Antyesthi; all include Ayurveda and verse from the Vedas and Upaniṣhads to be recited (sometimes in the name of deity)
Yoga–dhyāna–mukti/liberation	1. Taught by Shiva 2. The theme of liberation is based on Shiva, Shakti, Vishnu
Relationship and emotion within humans and with ecology	Rāmāyaṇa, Mahābhārata, Puranas, Upanishads
Cosmology, astrology	1. Story of Daksha Prajapati and his 27 daughters, i.e., 27 nakshtras. All nakstras have 4 properties related to planet, deity, animal, and purpose. 2. Nine planets are deities
Profession and deity	Agriculture is associated with Balrama, and every jati has its own deity as a source of profession
Foreign policy and diplomacy	Rāmāyaṇa, Mahābhārata, Puranas
Puppetry and theatres	Use the themes of Puranas, Rāmāyaṇa, Mahābhārata

Aspects of human life	Relation with multiple gods
Manokamna (wish of the mind)	1. To fulfil the wishes of devotees, temples are created with respective purposes, and those stories include *Pāramārthika* and hidden meaning 2. Can be taken as devotion of deity at *Vyāvahārika* level
Ayurveda	1. Brahma passed 'Ayurveda' to Daksha Prajapati then he passed to the Ashwin brothers 2. Dhanvatri deity of Ayurveda[4]
Celebrating plants and animals	1. Tulsi marriage with Vishnu: end of monsoon and start of wedding season 2. Bail Pola, Jalikattoo, and various animal fairs
Economics, polity, society	1. The whole Vedas, Rāmāyaṇa, Puranas, and Mahābhārata give a picture of society, tax system, currency, and types of jobs 2. Dharmaśāstra extensively gives duties and wealth creation/collection and limitations according to varna, etc
Sex	Kamdevata and 4 apsaras going to disturb tapasya of Shiva
Dance or nritya	1. Bhāratnatyam, Kathakali, and Sattariya, all related Hindu deities, either as origins or stories, are used as the theme of the performance 2. Many deities are known for dancing, such as Krishna, Shiva
Martial arts	1. Mahābhārata and Rāmāyaṇa both include wars so martial art weapons so all information comes from there 2. Shiva is seen as a source of Kāla ripayatoo. 3. Dhanurveda related to archery
Music	1. The Vedas speak extensively about music, and there is upveda *Gāndharvaveda Veda* as an entertainment encyclopedia 2. Many deities carry musical instrument

Aspects of human life	Relation with multiple gods
Land	Association of God with land: kurunji, mullai, marudam, niethei, palai, seyon, mayoon, Vendan, kadalon, kotravai
Moon phases	Kali associated amavasya and Sodasi with purnima[5]
Types of people and their psyche	3 gunas when manifests how they will look in any personality? 1. Sattvic personality (Bramha, Arsa (rishi), Mahendra, Varuna, Yama, Kubera, Gandharbva) 2. Tamisc (asura, raksasa, pashacika, sarpa, preta, shakuna)[6]
Sukta has presiding deity	Sukta are words of wisdom with the name of rishi and the presiding deity, e.g., Gayatri mantra has Savitri as the presiding deity[7]
Yoga	Shiva revealed to Parvati, Krishna revealed to Arjuna[8]
Classification of Vedas	Shukla and Krishna, Yajurveda story to explain classification[9]
51 Shakti peethas	51 letters alphabets are known as Matrika or Mata, which are image reflection of parashakti (cosmic mother)[10]
Kamdev and Yum (punisher)	*Kamasutra* is secular literature, secular punishments, leftist historians termed it 'secular' book[11]

'When the missionaries came to Africa,' said Desmond Tutu,[12] 'they had the Bible and we had the land. They said, "Let us pray." We closed our eyes. When we opened them, we had the Bible and they had the land.'

Academics ignore rituals, theological aspects (actual content), social evils, etc., i.e., the themeless version of religion, out of sociocultural historic evolution, and they try to do third-order inquiry, which includes the following things, and the so-called literate people fall prey to such a useless discussion.

1. Notions of God: Attributes
2. Relation to Man and the World
3. Proofs for the Existence of God and Their Critique
4. Problem of Evil
5. Soul: Immortality
6. Rebirth and Liberation
7. Reason, Revelation, and Faith
8. Religious Experience: Nature and Object (Bhārtiya and Western)
9. Religion without God
10. Religion and Morality
11. Religious Pluralism and the Problem of Absolute Truth
12. Nature of Religious Language: Analogical and Symbolic
13. Cognitive and non-cognitive

When theocratic powers take charge of nations with terrorism, then these people (academics) are ahead to give clean chits to religion, e.g., 'religion' doesn't teach these things. They impose their partial and parallel ideas about religion on society, which keeps problems because of religion alive.[13]

Table 13.4

Columan 1: What people discuss and focus on when they hear religion	Column 2: What actually one should question? Following things must be studied and countered, then column 1 will collapse automatically
Faith, belief, rituals, tangible–intangible culture	Finance to increase local infrastructure and number of followers (human capital to expand empire), i.e., franchisee
God, heavens, messenger, son of God, and debates	Data of properties, lands, funds, political space were captured by a local franchisee of religion in the particular nation, which was the final goal. Property gain in 'every form' by a formless God

Concepts from Hinduism

Evolution of the concept of God/deity can be seen in the following way:

Diagram 13.1

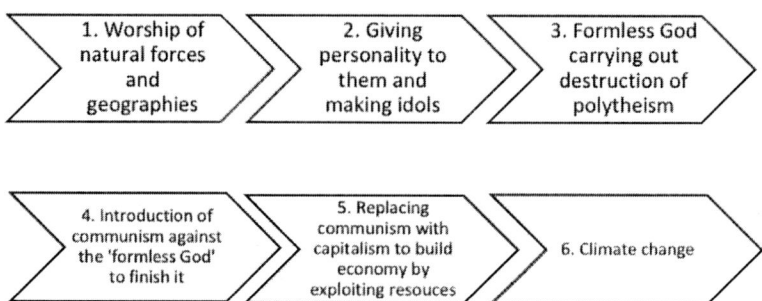

In this evolution in the concept of God, the most important thing is: where did enlightenment/experiencing God or spiritual concepts start? From the archaeological proofs of the Indus valley, which are presented in chapter 4, it is clear that 'science of spiritual experiences, polytheism' existed together over there. For more details, you can refer to the third diagram (Diagram 19.1, p. 350), which clearly shows 'Brahman/Parameshwara/Paramatma' is pantheistic and not formless, and various scriptural references are given in further chapters. So in Hinduism, it is never about 'formless God vs. idol worship'. These debates started when some people tried to get enlightenment, but to hide their failure, they declared God formless and started campaigns against idols. Even if someone destroys idols across the globe, Hindus will still have something to worship because Brahman is pantheistic, i.e., we worship 'animals, trees, geographic features (rivers, mountains), ancestors, Kuldevata (family deity), Gram devata, presiding deity of mantras (verses), navgrahas (planets, stars, etc.)'. Any of these deities can help you achieve enlightenment, but we have already created many frameworks for that, like Advaita, Dvaita, Shaivism, Vaishnavism, etc. When people say God is one, I ask, why not 'Goddess is one? Or cow is one? Or river is one?' All these aspects were deliberately not discussed to

a. Hindus = idol worshipers
b. Tribal culture in Bhārat = tribal worship nature, ancestor's worship

Inference: From here, the movement starts, 'tribals are not Hindus', to make them vulnerable for conversion to either another religion or Maoism.[14]

God Is Invisible Energy So Idol Worship Is Wrong

These kinds of kiddish theories were popular in the pre-20th century because those people didn't know quantum physics, unlike Hindus. When intensity is high, it is energy, and when the intensity of energy becomes low or dense, it becomes matter. So, it is the same reality that we call matter and energy' it's just a difference in energy intensity that differentiates matter and energy. The difference in energy depends on the frequency of particles. The best example is when welding sparks become solid metal once they cool down. That is why this reality, which exists as energy and matter in various forms like stars and planets, is continuous and separated because of different energy levels. Realizing this continuity in and out and the losing binary of matter and energy (maya) is oneness (chapter 14, Diagram 19.1). The whole functioning and performance become quantum after oneness achievements; by will, one can change form matter to energy and vice versa (siddhi/Shakti). That is why the binaries mentioned below are wrong.
a. God is an invisible energy/formless so idol worship is wrong.
b. God is limited to a material idol.
c. Material world is only reality, there is no God.

But oneness exists in whole diversity, so we use all those diverse things and concepts to reach towards oneness rather than binary. To understand this quantum level oneness, Please watch the video 'Quantum Manifestation Explained' by Dr Joe Dispenza on YouTube, which will be the background for the next chapter.

Exact Theory of Creation in Hinduism

Hinduism initiates discussion on 'creation of the universe but keeps discussion open-ended', which is better than giving credit to God and doing all nonsense stuff in the name of God. This approach to Hinduism gives space for modern scientific discovery, which is why there is no clash between science and religion, whether the earth is round or flat. Nasadiya Sukta of the *Rigveda* says as follows: 'Who knows, and who can say whence it all came, and how creation happened? The gods themselves are later than creation, so who knows truly whence it has arisen? Whence all creation had its origin, he, whether he fashioned it or whether he did not, he, who surveys it all from the highest heaven, he knows—or maybe even he does not know.'[15]

On the other hand, in the process of experiencing 'oneness', devotion (refer to A13.1, pp. 415–417) plays a very important role, so everything, including the creation of the world, is devoted to God because 'oneness' is that wide and pantheistic (third figure of Diagram 19.1, p. 350). So, all theories of creation in the name of deity are in the context of achieving 'oneness' or enlightenment to tell his greatness and inclusiveness (third figure of Diagram 19.3). If you see the ingredients used for the creation of the world by respective deities, they are actually symbolic representations of Tattvas that are used in the 'liberation journey', i.e., lotus = chakras, Hiranyagarbha = Bijao[16], Sheshnaga = Kundalini,[17] etc. Creator and creation are not two different things in Hinduism. Creator/oneness/super consciousness is the outcome of pañca-tattva, according to Cārvāka and Pushti Marg says God himself expands or extends himself to form the world. Both accept the existence of oneness, but from opposite directions.

The final experience where one experiences enlightenment or oneness (third figure of Diagram 19.1) is a unique feature of Bhārat where one does not believe in unseen power through logical arguments (refer to p. 272) but experiences it through sadhana. To keep this science of enlightenment alive, there was a natural need for a 'sustainable framework'. So ancient masters kept the 'science of oneness' alive by attaching many aspects related to our lives.

To make common people understand the core philosophy, i.e., creator and creation are not different (Advaita), our masters gave multiple examples, i.e.,

1. As cotton extends itself into thread, similarly, God expands himself into the world.
2. Visvarupa (multidimensional oneness) is the final form of Vishnu.

By reverse engineering, we come to the conclusion that 'Bramhan' (oneness) is projected as 'Bramha' (the personalistic notion of Bramhan/oneness/steppingstone to expand itself into the universe), and he creates the world out of his body so that it satisfies the condition 'creator and creation' are not separate. The theory of creation does not go like scientists do in some experiments, like the neutrino observatory at CERN, where some particles are created and then some events happen and the world forms. The oneness always existed, and the world is the outcome of it as an extension. To explain the relationship between oneness and the world, multiple ways are used; they are explained in chapter 19. Those ways are not the end in itself, which many people identify it as 'Bhārtiya philosophy' (Bhārtiya equivalent to Western philosophy), but they are means to achieve or experience oneness.

The same oneness is projected as a personalistic notion in various texts, i.e., purusha in Vedic texts, Vishnu in Vaishnavism texts, Shiva in Shaivite texts, Bramha/Brahman in *Upanishads*, Durga in Shakta, etc. The whole reality/world is shown as their manifestation in respective traditions, and its subjective truth is ultimately oriented towards universal truth, i.e., oneness. As stories and concepts moved from the East (Bhārat) you will see surface concepts (personalistic notions) migrate there, but core (oneness) was never decoded. So, this shallow understanding reflects on their concept of God, i.e., the formless male god (wrong combination of Bramha and Bramhan: the fourth figure of Diagram 19.1, p. 350). They also misinterpreted the proof of the existence of God (refer to pp. 364–365). Rather than concluding the real nature of 'oneness', they misinterpreted it as a war between

a) truth vs. false
b) light vs. dark
c) bad vs. good
d) god vs. evil
e) heaven vs. hell
f) creator vs. creation
g) monotheism vs. polytheism (ultimately, it takes the wrong path)

h) my god vs. your god (violent campaign against polytheism and idol worship)
i) my own rules in the name of gods' revelation vs. ignorant infidels

The right interpretation of the definition of God turns into chapter 14 (enlightenment), and the wrong interpretation culminates in chapters 3, 9, and 12. Misinterpretation is not random; it is a fundamental or basic structure of some religious scripture.

There are also many misinterpretations in Hinduism itself where creator and creation are different, where proofs of God are given similar to those on page 272, which are deliberately created for 'less intellect people' to keep them connected with 'oneness', but they are illogical if verified with oneness criteria.[18] This is what Ādi Śaṅkarācāryaḥ calls 'Avidya', i.e., wrong knowledge, absence of knowledge, doubt, etc.[19]

Every aspect of life—society, polity, and economy—is shown metaphorically as part, outcome, or extension of oneness. Now you will understand why the theory given on page 119 are described that way. A few more theories:

1. The four Vedas are the outcome of the four heads of Bramha, and he created the ten manasputra from his mind.[20]
2. Every goddess of mahavidya claims other goddesses came out of her or in her form.[21]
3. Krishna says I am the person (purusa) who is mentioned in the Vedas[22].
4. Bhuvaneshwari is the source of all Vedas.[23]
5. Vedanga body of ved purusha[24]
    a) vyakarana – mouth
    b) shiksha – nose
    c) chandas padya – feet
    d) nirukta – ears
    e) jyotish – eye
    f) kalpa – arm
6. Goddesses produce other goddesses from their own bodies.[25]
7. 'When Brahma is acknowledged as the supreme god, it was said that Kama sprang from his heart.'[26]

8. Prajapati generated creation and created the Vedas to nurture it. It is also said that Prajapati created the Vedas with his expiration.[27]
9. Various deities come out of various body parts of purusha.
10. *Brihadaranyaka Upanishad*: The Vedas are born out of iswara's breath.[28]
11. Bramha created through breathing, tapas whole universe: Reverse engineering.[29]
12. The Vedas came out of the heart of iswara.[30]
13. Ancestry in the Rāmāyaṇa and Mahābhārata starts from Brahman and then Brahma (explain ancestry) (refer to A4.1, p. 404).
14. The Vishwarupa of Krishna in Bhagavad Gita is a cosmic, all-inclusive form. He says everything else is maya; I am the reality. I am best among every dimension of reality: deities, Vedas, rishi, etc.[31]
15. Sakata's nature as a goddess (refer to A4.3: 22, 29, pp. 405–406).
16. Brahma's son all sur and Asur everything.
17. Purusha (oneness in third figure of Diagram 19.1, p. 350), who is a cosmic being, is immanent (exists in it) in the manifested world and yet transcended (uniquely separate: Vishishthadvaita) to it.
18. Purusha causes the projection of the universe in space and time.[32]
19. Purusha is described as a being who pervades everything, conscious and unconscious, universally. He is poetically depicted as a being with thousand heads, eyes, and legs, enveloping not just the earth but the entire universe from all sides and transcending it by ten fingers in length—or transcending in all ten dimensions. All manifestations, past, present, and future, are held to be the purusha alone.[33]
20. Creation is described as having started with the origination of Virat, or the astral body of the purusha. In Virat, omnipresent intelligence manifests itself, which causes the appearance of diversity. (Same Rigvedic theory is told by Krishna to Arjuna, where purusha is represented by himself [Krishna]. That is why Krishna says I am not the first one to tell you this message of Bhagavad Gita to you.)

It is very clear that all twenty dimensions given above are indicating towards the third figure of Diagram 19.1.

Theory of *Pañca-mahā-bhūta*

Why is the world made up of *pañca-mahā-bhūta*? Why does Hinduism describe the world as a combination of the five elements (air, water, fire, ether, and earth) rather than describing it in the format of modern 'periodic table' as a combination of multiple elements? Why only five? Why not more?

That is because Hindu medical science (Ayurveda) measures and divides human anatomy into five categories as per the qualities, properties, and behaviours and treats the body on the foundation of these five elements. So the same theory is carried forward as 'theory of creation' may be to popularize ayurvedic teachings. So, the universe is made up of these five elements, which may not hold true outside of the context of Ayurveda. Cārvāka accepts four tattvas instead (denies ether) of five tattva because of ideological limitations, i.e., Pratyaksha pramana, but if we see the utility (as given below) of five tattvas then Cārvāka may deny the other four too because without ether, Ayurveda cannot proceed, as you can see in Table 13.5. As John Passmore said, 'If you throw metaphysics in fire science goes with it, if you welcome science then metaphysics enters through backdoor.'

Attributes of Dosas in Ayurveda[34]

Table 13.5

Vata = Ether + Air	Pitta = Fire + Water	Kapha = Water + Earth
Dry, light, cold, rough, subtle, mobile, clear, dispersing, astringent	Hot, sharp, light, oily, penetrating, spreading, viscosity/ heat, sour/pungent	Heavy, slow, cool, oily, liquid, dense, thick, static, sweet

The whole diagnosis, diet, classification of disease, solution of disease, subcategorization of disease, medicine, and psychophysical behaviour of patients depend on dominance and percentage of doṣa's: patient's prakriti, type of body vatta, pita cough, diets and solutions, do's and don'ts, solution for dosas, immunity types, classification of diseases, testing of patients, various tests that shall be carried out to identify the condition of the patient, treatment.[35]

This pañca-mahā-bhūta theory is also migrated into other concepts like 'theory of creation of universe, vaastu shastra, seven chakras (refer to p. 428), five tastes, hasta mudras, traditions of mukti/moksha'. This is a unique feature of Hinduism: 'core concepts' will be included in multiple subjects (cross fertilization of ideas) to popularize them. You will find the migration of these ideas to Buddhism, Jainism, Japanese, Chinese, and Greek civilizations. As these schools do not know the utility of the five elements, i.e., dosas in Ayurveda, these five elements merely remained as philosophy in their culture! The utility-oriented approach again proves these concepts originated in Hinduism itself. Therefore, whether Cārvāka or any other school accepts or rejects any of these elements, it doesn't matter because they don't know their utility.

Theory of Creation in Samkhya

Theory says that prakriti (natural unmanifested unconscious tendency), which is a bundle of three gunas rajas, tamas, and sattva, comes into contact with purusa (consciousness), and then creation starts. The qualities of creation depend on which guna dominates the created object. It's just like a magnet (purusa), which has magnetic power (consciousness) and moves the iron particles (unconscious prakriti), but at some point purusa realizes it's different from prakriti; it's the 'liberation'.

This creation generates multiple products mahat, manas, ahamkara, five jnanendriyas, five karmedriyas, five tanmatras, five panchamahabhutas: all these products + three gunas are fundamentals of Ayurveda and yoga. Whether it's Samkhya, the genealogy of Ram, Advaita Vedanta, etc., in all these themes, if you move from yourself to Brahman, it's 'enlightenment' (Diagram 19.1, p. 350, 1 to 3), and if you move from Brahman to yourself, it's the theory of creation (Diagram 19.1, p. 350, 3 to 1). So Samkhya philosophy indirectly tells us to use these ingredients and, through reverse engineering, reach 'oneness'/purusa, i.e, creation. Same things about ingredients is mentioned on page 58. Rather than telling you the way of liberation directly or mechanically, Samkhya explains it with a poetic theme.

Marketing of three gunas by using 'creation' as a theme that has significance in Ayurveda, which are actually related to our own human nature (natural tendency), psychological, physical tendency, behavioural patterns, reaction–perception intensity, diet, disease, gunas dominate in particular professions or socio-economic status, sexual tendency, diet patterns, and customized medicine as per the patient's tendency or gunas. I suggest the sattva guna, which leads to liberation. Once purusa (conscious soul) attends liberation, it realizes its real nature, free from all gunas and categories (similar to Nirguna Brahmana, free from all accidental properties).

In Shakta parampara, feminine aspect (Shakti) is conscious and active, while the male aspect is unconscious, passive, and subordinate. So, one shall not develop stereotypes of Samkhya, Vaishnavism, and Shaivism that promote a misogynistic mindset where masculine (purusa) is active and feminine (prakriti) is passive (leftists do this misinterpretation as fodder for igniting feminism). It is just that every theme of the respective leading character is supreme over others, irrespective of gender, but both male and female play an important role in liberation. That is because Ida (Surya Nadi – Active), Pingala (Chandra Nadi – Passive), twin passive and active character represent, these two nadis. Even when Bramha, Vishnu, and Mahesh perform the roles of creator, maintainer, and destroyer of the world, their task with power is Shakti (passive support from the female deity)! Bramha creates and Vishnu maintains the world with power (mahavidya). Mahasaraswati is maintainer; Mahakali is the destroyer.[36] This is also the counter to the narrative where,

God = Bramha, Vishnu, Mahesh, and Bramhan = **theist** (subjective monotheism; God is supreme in the respective context), and Samkhya doesn't have **subjective monotheism,** so it has dualism (prakriti, purusa) so it is atheist (no single god) (refer to Table 1.1, p. 5). So that Samkhya followers politically support leftist (atheism).

The reason for giving gender aspects to liberation is that 'sexual energy' of men and women plays an important role in enlightenment.

These energies in yogic terms are known as 'ojas'. By seeking enlightenment, we transform ojas into tejas (super consciousness, i.e., oneness, which is bright like a thousand suns). That is why retaining 'sexual energy' is preferred and suggested by scriptures rather than transforming ojas into semen (physical form of ojas), i.e., masturbation.[37]

Implementation of this chapter

Table 13.6

Then	Now
Brahman, Krishna, Ram, Shiva, devi	God is one
Land of Ādi -Śaṅkarā; one of the state in Bhārat	Gods own country (indirectly theocratic state)
State	Country/nation

Somewhere, your idea about God/deity or heaven reflects on your lifestyle; people can compare their ideas of God and heaven in their respective religions.

Diagram 13.2

14

Quantum Physics: Its Entanglement with Paramātmā

Diagram 14.1

Why Hanuman is Bramhachari ? when all characters in Ramayana are married ?
Hanuman had Ashta-Siddhi (8 supernatural powers) how ?
He had Ram in his Chest ? What it is or How actually it feels to have Deity within self ?

Enlightenment or Entanglement?

The term 'enlightenment' emerged in English in the latter part of the 19th century, with particular reference to French philosophy, as the equivalent of the French term *Lumières*, which was used first by Dubos in 1733 and was already well established by 1751. This term is like a renaissance for Europe because the 15th-century Copernican revolution came to prove that the earth revolves around the sun, and you know how society reacted to it. Europe knew this truth 1,000s of years ago in terms of Greek and Roman civilization, and then the Roman king believed in that guy, agreed to accept faith, and pushed whole Europe into the dark ages.[1] When whole Europe was igniting fire by rubbing stones, Hindus were burring bodies in a north-south direction, and Hindus, Egyptians, and Greeks knew the whole calendar, which contained the absolute direction and location of solar system planets, and their deity names were based on them. What Europe calls the Renaissance was the regular lifestyle in Hindu, Egyptian, and Greek civilizations. Because of Hinduism, all customs, lifestyles, and patterns are arranged according to cosmic and ecological calculations.

The term 'renaissance' refers to the rebellion of European society against the control of the 'priestly class' because uncle told them many unscientific things, threatening them by showing hell in the future. The Renaissance saw the rapid growth of science and technology, atheism, scepticism, debating society, politics without uncles, schools without religious topics, and liberty, which culminated in the book industry.

17th vs. 21st Centuries Enlightenment

Then comes the 21st century of Hindus, where the term 'enlightenment' is used for what knowledge is achieved by a guy in the saffron dress. All the topics that are covered above were like a breakthrough to the European world, which is why they call it 'showering of light on brains' or 'enlightenment'. Now those same orthodox mediaeval topics are not giving a kick to them, so they started looking for some new kick or enlightenment or breakthrough, which they found in the East, as well as in monasteries of Hindus and Buddhists, where they got to know about terms like inner awakening, concentration, meditation, etc. This entire new breakthrough, they term it with the same old word of 17th-century enlightenment.

Concept and Terms of Heaven in Hinduism

The final goal of life is mokṣa prāpti or liberation, which is achieved after death when we leave this body on earth and start the journey with *jīva* or as *jiva*. You might be thinking it's either heaven or hell; the answer is no. Heaven and hell are again the outcomes of binary division. In Hinduism, there is diversity in the concept of afterlife too.

Table 14.1

Pitṛloka	The general ward where most of the people go
Svarga loka	One who served cows, followed the culture, and did great for humanity goes there and identifies as Jīva Koti devata
Jīva Koti devata	Human categorized as deity in Svarga loka
Īśvara Koti devata	All deities, like Shiva, Vishnu, etc., belong here. These deities are beyond birth and death, but they do incarnate. Some higher deities have their own abodes. 1. Shiva lives in Kailāsa 2. Vishnu lives in Vaikuṇṭha 3. Brahma lives Satya loka (highest in the 7 planes) 4. Jagadamba (devi) lives in Manidvip All 4 are the benchmark for confirming liberation is achieved in respective themes, e.g., Shaivism, Vaishnavism, Vedanta, and Shaktism.
Jīva Koti	This category goes in Īśvara Koti, then they go out of the birth and death cycle, which is the ultimate liberation.
Naraka loka	Anti-social elements. Stages and types of Naraka vary in various books; some are 7 and some are 28.
Pishaj loka	Those who die in sudden accidents or suicide. They are named bhoot, pret. It is said that if anyone left his duty and died, then near ones must complete it so that lifecycle on earth remains undisturbed even after sudden vacuum created by his/her death; otherwise, Jīva will become bhut and will trouble near ones. This logic was created to keep the life cycle unaffected by sudden death, but unfortunately, Bollywood movies project bhoot as a Western ghost and evil who troubles people randomly, which is a huge disrespect to Hinduism.

This is one of the biggest impositions on Hindus, telling them the binary division of hell and heaven, which is handled by God. The diversity of the afterlife is not told to Hindus, and their mindset is kept shallow.

Microscopes and telescopes do the same thing, i.e., magnify things so that human perception can perceive them. It means infinity is not just space research; even when we turn inward deeply, the same infinity can be experienced. This is the basic thought behind it: 'being one with infinity to experience it'. This journey of transforming oneself from 'limited identity' body, mind, Jīva, etc., to 'infinity' Paramātmā, Paramātmā, Shiva, Brahman is called as 'mukti/liberation'. Some experts say the seven planes above and below can be experienced within them too because infinity is the same in and out. The final goal in Hinduism is to become one with the universe and experience life beyond the body or apparent reality. So to experience that, various terms like mukti/liberation, Kailāsa, Vaikuṇṭha, Manidvipa, jiva, and Brahman are used, which are actually themes to experience the same goal (not sects of Hinduism). In Hinduism, 'inwards = outward' is expressed in Sanskrit as 'Yatha Bramhande Tatha Pinde'. What is in bramhand (out there in space) is inside you.

Why There Are Seven Heavens or Planes Above?

The concept of seven chakras itself is an allegory, metaphorically expressed in various terms (in chapter 4, I mentioned numerology), i.e., this concept of chakras itself got transformed and transferred into various concepts and geographies (refer to p. 428). You will find seven-headed snake or dragon giving shelter as an umbrella to either a deity or human being in Cambodia, the Philippines, Laos, Thailand, Siberia (Russia), Mexico, and Hinduism (Vishnu's Sheshnaga), and on Buddha's head, Myanmar, Sumerian (Iraq), a seven-headed Chinese dragon, the seven heaven concept across all civilizations and other religions (refer to p. 288). This snake or dragon is a symbol of Kundalini, and the seven heads are seven chakras in the activated stage. In Mexican Mayan civilization, divine power is known as kuntalini (Kundalini), the god of death is Yum Cimi (Yum Dev), and Echchtl is a divinity that also has an elongated jaw like a monkey and is known as the son of the wind (Hanuman who carries Ram within himself and has achieved ashta siddhi).[2] It shows that concept of enlightenment, zodiac signs, astrology, Ayurveda, deities, everything migrated out of Bhārat, i.e., Hinduism. From these migrated concepts, some people copied, got inspired, and

created 'religion'. In the language of chemistry, there is some empirical formula of all these multiple molecular formula. Hinduism being the mother of all spiritualities knows the empirical formula, i.e., origin/basics. There are three possibilities for the migration of this theory:
1. Manu's story, where he takes seven sages and the Vedas with him during the great flood (which is famous in all civilization)[3]
2. The degradation of Saraswati forced people to migrate to other areas
3. Through business/trade and natural migration from Bhārat

The name, tradition (Hinduism/Buddhism, Jainism), words, and era (Vedic–Puranic) keep changing, but the concept of 'moksha/mukti/liberation' remains constant. In *Shri Hari Stotram* (praise of Vishnu), the names of Vishnu are the names of Ganapati in *Atharvashirsha*, which are the same as the seven stages of Sambhunath's Shaivism (mentioned in Table 14.2).

Theology/Theism and Non-Theistic
In Christianity and Islam, there are stories related to Abraham and Jesus (various prophets). These stories are life events, messages, etc. When one studies this dimension of religion, it is known as theism or theology. When one studies the same things in terms of god, spirit, mind, body, and brain candy, they study (academics) through logical arguments; it's known as non-theistic or non-theological study. Generally, theistic people are considered inferior by non-theistic scholars because of their lack of a critical approach (refer to p. 272).

Hinduism
This non-sense of theistic–non-theistic binary is imposed on Hinduism too. Advaita Vedanta, Patanjali yogsutra, etc., with Nirguna Brahman (refer to pp. 348–350) are termed non-theistic/non theological. Vaishnavism, Shaivism, and Shaktism are considered theistic just because they have a 'theme' of Shiva, Vishnu, Durga, and ritual aspects related to them. Otherwise, all traditions are themes that are directed towards the same goal of 'oneness' (as shown in Table 14.2). Even in Buddhism, Jainism is reduced to a merely moral message and marketed as atheists or non-theistic.

Table 14.2

Stages	Buddhism	Advaita Vedant	Yoga Vashishta	7 lokas in Puranas	7 chakras in[6] kundalini Awakening	Shaiva Siddhanta	Shambhu nath (Shaivite)	Shakta	Egyptian names of chakras
1	Sila-Visuddhi	Ajnana	Shubheccha	Bhu	**Muladhara**	Sakala Pramātri	Nijānanda	Narsimhi	Seth
2	Citta-Visuddhi	Avarana	Vichharana	Bhuvas	**Swadhish Thana**	VijñānaKāla	Nirānanda	Indrani	Het hert
3	Ditthi-Visuddhi	Vikshepa	Tanuman Āsana	Svar	**Manipura**	Śuddhavidyā	Parānanda	Varahi	Heru
4	Kankha-Vitarana- Visuddhi	Paroksha Jnana	Sattavapati	Mahas	**Anahata**	Iśvara	Brahmānanda	Vaishnavi	Osiris
5	Maggamagga -Ñanadassana- Visuddhi	Aproksha Jnana	Asamshakti	Janas	**Vishuddha**	Sadaśiva	Mahānanda	Kumari[5]	Esr[4]
6	Patipada- Ñanadassana -Visuddhi	Shoka Nivritti	Padartha Bhavana	Tapas	**Ajna**	Śiva	Cidānanda	Maheshwari	Pth
7	Ñanadassana-Visuddhi	Trupti= Aham Bramhasmi	Turiya	Satya/ Bramha Loka	**Sahasrara**	Parama Śiva/ Kailāsa	Jagadānanda	Brahmani	Uadyt

Achieving the 7th stage is achieving the 3rd figure of Diagram 19.1 and parmarthik satya of Table 19.2. Once this stage is achieved, there will be a feeling of a single unifying force among all physical objects, and there will be no sense of diverse physical objects, so you will know this physical world is mere maya/illusion. This is mukti/moksha/ liberation. The whole story of deities, the avatars from the *Vedas* to the *Puranas* (Chapters 13, 19) is talking about this spiritual experience. i.e., oneness (indescribable omnipresent pantheistic stream of consciousness). (Refer to pp. 426–428).

This divisionary political history writing created gulf between Hinduism and Buddhism, i.e., 'Buddhist should exclude worshipping Hindu deities' and this is merely political gimmick to create strategic separatism/cultural untouchability with Hinduism for political gains with '0' spiritual understanding. Otherwise, Buddhism also aims or claims to achieve the same oneness, i.e., Brahma, Vishnu, and Mahesh with a different theme of Buddhism, i.e., nirvana.

There are people who say 'doing physical work = achieving Kailāsa'. Such ignorant people are celebrated as founders of new sects or saints in Hinduism. Because of their failure to achieve spiritual integrity, they are demanding separate religious status just to maintain the line of 'hero worship' of the founder.

Dignity of labour ≠ Kailasa/liberation/mukti

Sociopolitical movement ≠ spiritual attainment

Human society is divided into two categories. One is a social lifestyle known as samsara, and the other is an ascetic-level lifestyle known as vairagya. In life, one has to follow four phases: Brāmhacaryā, Gr̥hasthashrama, Vanaprastha, and Saṃnyāsa (renunciate). One who chooses the life of vairagya extends the brāmhacaryā for the whole life, which is known as saṃnyāsa. Interpretation of concept of the seven lokas above and below changes in terms of samsara and vairagya, tradition to tradition.

Terms Programmed for Liberation

1. **Jiva:** Your idea about you in present and to be expected as transformed one in future (including oneness = Brahman) is Jīva.
2. **Samādhi state:** Where one is undisturbed by all external factors because of saṃnyāsa and free from all internal conflict because of conceptual clarity. Where the human/yogi eliminates all disturbances and enjoys various stages of awareness, which some people wrongly or rightly call states of consciousness. All stages of experience happen internally, and the physical state or posture in which the yogi is sitting, standing, or sleeping is known as samādhi state, which is a psychophysically basic stable condition to experience so-called spirituality.

3. **Dhyana ≠ meditation:** Meditation means thinking about any topic very seriously and doing dhyāna is completely opposite, which is done to keep minimum thoughts in the brain or no thoughts at a higher level. Dhyāna is attention and awareness about one object for a longer period of time. Focus, concentration, etc. are suffocating terms that are not the right translation of Dhyāna. Hinduism uses the word 'ekagra', which means seeking oneness with that of Bramhan, e.g., if you are reading a book, then being one with it is 'ekagra'. There are various techniques to learn that, like candle experiment and mirror experiments.
4. **Sūkṣma śarīra:** When activities are at the quantum level, then the material or format of material is also necessarily quantum. So this quantum phase of the body, which is neither material nor non-material, i.e., neither '0' nor '1' in computer language, is called sūkṣma śarīra or quantum body. This sūkṣma śarīra is used as a vehicle to become 'one' with oneness, a manifestation of supernatural powers. Sukshma sharira includes five pranas, five karma indriyas, five janandiyas, and four antahkarnas.[7]
5. **Karana sharirai:** The body or identity on which sukshma sharia is mounted; it's the one that enjoys bliss, joy, calmness, and the impression of past life peace and experiences the four states.[8]
6. **Mahā samādhi:** The point where yogi, who has achieved liberation or oneness, decides that he (as atma) should give up the body and become part of oneness forever is *Mahā Samādhi*. We, common people, think it's death, but it's actually giving up bodily existence by will.[9]
7. *Avatāra:* One who has achieved *Turiyatit* is representation of that 'oneness' in human format, i.e., incarnation of deity (Shiva, Vishnu), so such a person is known as 'avatāra'. Hindus believe Buddha has achieved turiyatit rather than merely turiya, so they call Buddha as 'Vishnu' avatāra. Those who are interested in carving out Buddhists as separate social identities for political gains without knowing what 'avatāra' means deny that 'Buddha was avatāra of Vishnu'.
8. **Sadeh mukti** = when one is alive or Jīva is within human body.

9. Videh mukti = liberation after death according to the karma cycle.[10]

The simple way to achieve this state/sadeh mukti is by making oneself just like liberated jiva; making own qualities just like liberated jiva, just like we are a copy of that liberated Jīva but in body. Then the first question is: what are the qualities of the liberated jīva?

Diagram 14.2

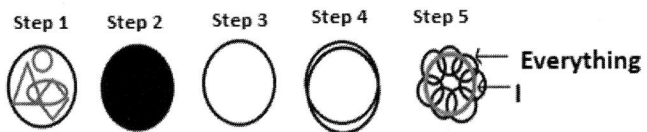

Table 14.3

Step 1	Step 2	Step 3	Step 4	Step 5
Bonded Jīva in social life. This is what Patanjali calls 'modified mind', which needs to be eliminated to reach step 5 (oneness).	Jīva that has adopted 'vairagya' through process of samnyāsa to seek mukti/liberation/oneness.	Jīva who eliminated all the identities and achieved pure 'I' (turiya state).	Jīva that becomes one with 'paramātm/Shiva/Brahman'. Supreme position would be a harsh word, it's called 'oneness'.	The moment someone achieves oneness, with that supreme idea/definition/form/limitation in mind about 'paramātmā' vanishes. That person experiences boundary-less world, i.e., 'I exist in everything and everywhere'.

The journey of Jīva from step 1 to 5 is actually a journey from 'there are many things in my mind' to 'I exist in many things'. It's actually 'ekoham Bhavishyami' let one become many.

Table 14.4

Qualities of bonded Jīva (a normal human being with a social life)	Liberated jiva = I am Brahman = Kailāsa = union with that supreme oneness	Solution of problem to move towards liberation
Have material attachment	Paramātmā doesn't have material attachment or particular body so to become one with it we have to make ourselves like that.	Taking saṃnyāsa (giving up all material and social life)
Family And social life	Then liberated Jīva is alone there, and no family, no other humans.	So one has to shift to Himalaya where there are no humans.
Multiple identities	No social, cultural, economic, family identity.	Adopting a new name according to tradition. In Maharashtra, you will see 'wari'/journey of liberation where male–female devotees, kids, elder, Vitthala (Vishnu avatāra) all are known/call each other as 'Mauli'. This practice ensures all become 'one' with Vitthala irrespective of personal identity.
A lot of memories and related attachments	No memory, only intelligence	Detachment from all worldly pleasures, pains, and one is asked to settle all account of karma so that it doesn't bother or disturb while 'dhyāna', which is an important aspect.

Qualities of bonded Jīva (a normal human being with a social life)	Liberated jiva = I am Brahman = Kailāsa = union with that supreme oneness	Solution of problem to move towards liberation
In karma cycle	Out of karma cycle	Stop doing bad karma and start doing niṣkāma karma (good karma without any self-interest), so that karma account remains nil.
Ego and stress in body[A14.1]	You remain with your inner you without any social identity.	1. Start doing yoga to eliminate all stress in the body so that you almost feel stress less body/light body/body with negligible existence in psychology with proper blood flow and well-functioning nervous system, healthy inter-intra organs plus proper yogi diet as supplementation. 2. Start eliminating ego and start merging yourself with paramātmā and Brahman.

Required Primary Knowledge under the Guidance of a Guru

1. Yoga and postures so that joints, muscles, and other body parts remain healthy so that one can sit for dhyāna for a longer period.
2. Knowledge of Ayurveda and herbs so that one can eat only that product, which gives the minimum required energy and smooths the journey of liberation, e.g., haritaki powder, betel leaf, tulsi, honey, etc.
3. Knowledge of *prāṇāyāma*, meaning 'extending life through breathing', which pseudo-experts translate it as 'breathing practices'. In the Himalaya, oxygen is scarce so one must transform his/her body so that it absorbs maximum oxygen. In higher stages, yogi absorbs energy through these practices with no need for food

intake. In science, this can be equated with 'chemosynthesis', which is generally carried out by a few microbes. But yogis make their bodies compatible for chemosynthesis just like microbes, and they call it 'Pran energy' or 'life energy'.

4. Chanting of mantras according to tradition, one chants the respective mantra. Pronouncing is the most important thing because the frequency of sound is most important in Hinduism while doing dhyāna. Chanting a mantra with particular frequency and integrity positively affects brain development; modern-day neuroscientists call it the 'Sanskrit effect'. Sanskrit is the only language that has this kind of capacity; therefore, other languages can be translated, but Sanskrit can be experienced too. That is why all these liberal attempts, like chanting 'my God's name' in 'my language' in my 'musical culture', are completely unscientific and don't give expected results.

A condition comes when one identifies oneself as liberated jiva = Brahman = Shiva = pure purusa = union with Paramātmā = feeling one with cosmos = pure consciousness (as a side effect). Liberation/mukti ≠ salvation. Salvation generally refers to the deliverance of the soul from sin and its consequences. Making karma account zero with no accumulation of bad as well as good karma is merely a primary need in the journey of liberation. Salvation is a too-cheap translation of mukti/liberation; salvation can be merely the primary stage.

Ādi Śaṅkarācāryaḥ says, 'That is why, Oh Shiva (Oneness), forgive my 3 sins, I am praying to you when I know you are beyond words, I came to Kashi when I know you are omnipresent, I am thinking about you when I know you are beyond my thoughts.' The same thing is quoted by Richard Feynman (Nobel Prize in particle physics) about quantum physics: 'If you think you understand quantum physics, you don't understand quantum physics.'

Stages of Experience

All the basics, which I mentioned: Yoga, prānāyāmaa, absolute understanding of manas, intellect, and oneness = Brahman/Shiva, are mandatory or basic conditions, e.g., driving licence and seatbelt before driving. According to the *Mandukya Upanishad*, there are four states of experience

Table 14.5

State	Experience or existence within	Experience	Reason or condition why it happens
Jågrat (a wakeful state where one can think)	Sense of 'I' exists + thoughts	Where I, body, mind (memory, intellect, etc.) are aware	Awakened state
Swapna (dreaming)	No sense of 'I' + thoughts	This stage is like having a movie theatre within where we have forgotten 'I' and you are completely part of the movie. The story of the movie is made from existing memory modified by intelligence which is not in control.	This happens when the body is recovered from sleep but the mind forces the body to be asleep. As brain (body) is recovered from sleep so it starts generating random thoughts from memory and intelligence somehow hits them randomly out of stadium which we call dreams.
Sushupti (deep sleep or complete unawareness)	No sense of 'I' + no thoughts	Deep sleep	When the body and mind are completely tired or damaged, so body gives compulsory deep rest. This also happens when one has completed a task and there is no thought of incompletion in mind.
Turiya (awareness of 'I')	Sense of 'I' + no thoughts	Explained as following (7 stages belong to this category)	Explained as following

My Personal Experience: Turiya State

Multiple schools of liberation explain the seven states of consciousness in various ways as per the theme; all these states fall under turiya category.[11] What I experienced in turiya state can be experienced at the first step in *Nijānanda*.

When I decided to go into a deep state before sleep, I took a deep breath and completely focused on that deep breathing. In addition, I listened to meditative music on YouTube with earphones. I was in a sleeping position (my samādhi state), free from external disturbances. I imagined that my body has no weight; it was becoming weightless, and only my inner self existed. That inner me was falling into deep, dark space, or I was being lifted up into dark space; that dark space is ensured by my closed eyes. I chanted Om in my mind or went along with the YouTube chanting of Om. Suddenly, without my choice, I went into a state where I knew there was 'I' but I didn't have a concept of 'I' or any identity, thought, or definition related to 'I'. It felt like something was flowing through my whole body—every cell from top to bottom—that something was radiating throughout my body, including the outer layer of my skin. Which was not at all similar to aggression due to masculinity or testosterone. But it was like an inner glow. Which was not generated by my will, nor was there any external agent that I was able to see. Its perfect analogy would be 'Ganga falling on the head of Shiva, who is in samādhi state, and from head to toe flowing continuously'. I thought this story of Shiva was indicating turiya state only, but in a picture form, Ganga's flow was shown outside the body so that we could know, but in reality, it flowed inside from head to toe.

All this experience is so good, but we cannot store it in memory by will, nor can we generate good or bad thoughts about Ganga current while in turiya state; even if you force yourself to generate thought, you won't be able to generate it. It takes not only efforts but time too to come out of that state, but the struggle to think is always there because we are householder people filled with thoughts, so that struggle 'to create thought' in mind is very frustrating because I lose thinking ability in that state. But this frustration doesn't come always or comes at the last stage of samādhi when 'Ganga flow' stops and we remain with 'I' and when we come out of samādhi, 'I' with identity, thoughts, comes back. We only experience pure 'I' and that Ganga flow. That is why, Ganga is not a holy river. It's a blissful river, i.e., inner Ganga. This experience I cannot generate every time, but it happens multiple times if done properly because, before doing this experiment, any incompletion or incomplete thoughts process is in mind, and the mind keeps calculating to complete that. This is what Patanjali calls modification of the mind.

That is why people take saṃnyāsa to experience these stages of higher inner experience for a long time without any disturbances in life. When I come out of this stage, I feel that I have been sleeping for a very long time, my sleep is complete, and my brain has become free from complex calculations and loads, but it was merely half an hour or an hour. A light and fit body is an ideal one because stress in the body from injury or other reasons may create disturbances in focus. If you don't know how to reach this stage, take guidance from the guru. I did it with my minuscule knowledge, with no detailed yoga skills, and without the detailing of prāṇāyāma. Ganga current creates flows through those parts too that are stressed or have an issue and highlight it and send a message to the brain (in the initial stage). Only I have experienced signals of only macro pain, not micro. That is why knowing the theme of the path (Shiva and related stories) is like a 'signboard' on the road; it makes the journey easy and expressible to others. According to neuroscience, this 'state of brain' might be expressed in different terms and units, but 'Shiva-Shakti-Ganga' and 'intra-organs' like chakras and kundalini are programmed in such a way that working on them leads to liberation, which in science is known as the 'Placebo effect'. If we can accept the existence of and use terms like mind and thought when they are merely neurological signals, then why not chakras, manas, chit, etc.

There are 72,000 nadis (not physical but part of sukshma sharira) in the body; out of that, Ida (passive-Chandra nadi) and Pingala (Active-Surya nadi) cross each other six times, so these crossing points are known as chakras. Between these two nadi in the spine, Sushumna nadi (Bramha nadi) exists, through which kundalini

shakti flows from Muladhara to Sahasrahara.[12] There are three psychic knots in Sushumana nadi that change your perception of reality and consciousness (four stages of consciousness). Kundalini pierces through these knots. [13]
1. Bramha granthi: Physical world (Bhur loka), pleasure, pain, sex—location: Muladhara chakra
2. Visnu granthi: Ego, ahamakar (Mahar loka)—location: Anahata chakra[14]
3. Rudra granthi: Concerned with mortal insecurity (Bramha loka)—location: Ajna chakra

I just laugh at those people who do meditation and yoga taught by their shallow knowledge liberal yoga guru. Even gurus don't know what the outcome of meditation is, what the origin of meditation is, or what the purpose of meditation is, the only thing people experience is a temporary pseudo-'thoughtless mind'; people are happy in that only.[15]

The seven chakras are also used to identify their impact on various body functions, related diseases, problems, and solution in ayurvedic practices.[16]

Types of Siddhi/Shakti and Supernatural Powers

While on this journey, one achieves many supernatural powers (siddhi/Shakti) by opening the third eye, which is the pineal gland; according to Shaivism, they are 400; according to Patanjali, they are 8; they are given the following. Hanuman, who had experienced Ram/oneness within him, has this,[17] which is mentioned in *Hanuman Chalisa*.

- **Aṇimā**: The ability to become smaller than the smallest, reducing one's body to the size of an atom or even becoming invisible.
- **Mahimā**: The ability to become infinitely large, expanding one's body to an infinitely large size.
- **Garimā**: Siddhi lets users alter/increase the weight of their body. One can increase his/her weight from a little bit to an infinite point where it becomes immovable. Angat, in Ravana's court,

challenged the warriors in his court to move his feet, but no one was able to do so because Angat used garima siddhi.
- **Laghimā:** The ability to become weightless or lighter than air.
- **Prāpti:** The ability to instantaneously travel or be anywhere at will.
- **Prākāmya:** The ability to achieve or realize whatever one desires.
- **Īśiṭva:** The ability to control nature, individuals, organisms, etc. Supremacy over nature and the ability to force influence upon anyone.
- **Vaśiṭva:** The ability to control all material elements or natural forces.[18]

The 'oneness' with supreme reality in quantum physics is known as 'entanglement' where two things are fused together under the framework of entanglement (oneness), and changes in one are seen as changes in the other, i.e., the abilities to control nature and forces. It is like you have a wish in mind to change the rules of the environment and the things happening in reality, but it's not done with whims and fancies to show off because it might create a sense of ego, which may culminate in losing power. This entanglement, or union of two, is known as 'yoga' in Hinduism. Some experts say Shakti or siddhi achievement is a side effect of a journey of liberation, whereas others say it's the goal, and some say it's a distraction while achieving the goal.

Being Everything vs. Nothing

The goal was to liberate oneself by devoting to Shiva, but we ended up becoming Shiva. This is what happens when we do something without any greedy thinking; we get more than we expected. Don't confuse 'being everything with being nothing', with the analogy that a friend of everyone is a friend of none. It's a wrong analogy; a friend of everyone can be a leader too. The right analogy is 'Mukesh Ambani saying *money is not everything* and beggar saying *money is not everything*'. There is the same difference between everything/completeness/*Pūrvatva* and nothingness/*Śūnyatva (shunyatva)*. Completeness means I exist everywhere in everything. This stage is known as Nirguna Brahman, where you cannot describe yourself. So I will use the same term which that used in Upaniṣhads without translating, which is Brahman; still, it's indescribable.

How Communists Create Vote Bank through 'Enlightenment'

Various paths are shown as rival or sects of each other as their teachings are different, so people fight on paths (philosophical debates) so that the goal (moksha) is never achieved and diversity turns into political clashes. What we study in philosophy in academics is devoid of terms like sukshma sharira, kundalini, and chakra on which the whole philosophical and cultural empire is standing, i.e., Table 14.2. To satisfy ego, the West never accepts the greatness of Hinduism to maintain political hegemony, as mentioned on page 288 of the seven heavens. For that, they also divide Hindus, as mentioned below, to reflect differences at the political level and divide them into 'right wing vs. left wing'.

1. Vedas vs. Puranas or Upanishads
2. Vaishnavism vs. Shaivism, Shaktaism
3. Vedas vs. Buddhism, Jainism, Sikhism, Samkhya, Cārvāka, yoga, Sikhism

Hinduism's ways of attaining Liberation/moksha are classified in two ways.

Table 14.6

	Means	**Ends**	**Breathing**
Dakshinapantha	Prayer, devotion, yoga	Liberation	Exhalation happens through right nostril
Vampantha	Prayer, devotion, yoga + food/non-veg, sex, tantik practices, alcohol (unconventional practices)	Liberation	Exhalation happens through left nostril
Woke culture	Existing beyond conventional boundaries, i.e., nation, gender, social norms, etc., i.e., remaining fluid rather than solid that also physically.[19]		

Vampantha: Pancatatva ritual: Sex, non-veg, all unconventional techniques of seeking liberation, they are not free but bounded in framework of rituals.[20]

Vampanth cannot be equated with woke culture or leftist politics, which is generally done just because of the use of left and right terms. In modern terminology, Vampanth and Dakshinapanth both belong to 'conservative' values as both are ways to seek liberation rather than right-wing conservative vs. left-wing liberal politics. They use diplomatic terms for Hinduism/Hindu schools of liberation they use orthodox/theist/conservative so political level it culminates into right wing, and for Jainism/Buddhism/Samkhya/Cārvāka/Vampanth, they use terms like heterodox/atheist so it culminates into left-wing politics. This is just to carve out Jains, Buddhists, and Cārvāka as a new minority in which they were successful in colonial and post-colonial era. Today, if you hear the words Cārvāka, Buddhism, or Vampanth what comes to mind is 'atheism/communism'. People have forgotten the original essence of these traditions.[21]

By What Logic and Confidence Do I Say that Supernatural Powers Exist or that Siddhi/Shakti Exist?

Birds have intellect, by which they can know all directions and can sense magnetic fields. Snakes have a temperature scan of everyone around them. Cows cry when something wrong happens in their owner's family. Lizards have the ability to change colour. All this happened through the journey of evolution, and this evolution is not just natural. It is the outcome of their need, then this need got transformed into 'will' and this 'will power' made them able to achieve that form and power. The journey of liberation is the science of evolution by 'will', just like other animals, but the difference is that we do it very quickly; it doesn't take generations to reach that level. Vivekananda himself used to read volumes of books and remember by page number. But again, Vivekananda was limited by history books to quotes and morality—brotherhood, i.e., hero worship.[22]

For example, we are watching a 3D/7D movie and reacting physically to everything happening on screen. We feel it's actually happening with us; we feel we are part of that world. It is reality, but in one corner, a popcorn boy is standing without 3D glasses and saying why they are reacting. It's just a movie that is not even clearly visible; it's just a duplication of the picture on the screen. By this analogy, I can say the guy who is watching the movie is a yogi, 3D goggles are 'yogic perception', the guy who is acting in the movie is like devata, with whom one is feeling oneness, and the popcorn guy who doesn't have 3D glasses is like a materialist who wants to understand the movie but without goggles and calls the audience fools because he is not able to watch the movie without a 3D setup. The whole point is that if you think what you perceive as reality through your senses is only reality, then it's merely neurological impulses in the brain because animals perceive the same reality as different, For example, a snake can see everything in terms of temperature; for it, everything is different; cheetah can see everything in terms of speed, whether he can catch and eat; the colours you see might have a different perception for animals. What we study as science is only the study of motion and change of visible medium-size objects, but in deep studies, people go to the atomic level or directly to the universe level, on both the extremes many times 'Pratyaksa/perception' is not possible.

Another myth is that meditation leads to all knowledge or the highest knowledge; however, meditation is simply serious thinking on a topic. But dhyāna or Om chanting is not meditation, as I said; it's giving up thoughts and having minimum thoughts. Chanting Om and other sounds like creating resonance with oneness become a medium to access cosmic truth and reality. The dhyāna is done and what we achieve is not the highest or all knowledge. Because getting the highest knowledge means you are different from the world and you are mugging up knowledge at the highest level by dhyāna, which is self-contradictory in terms of dhyāna. Because dhyāna is done for oneness, which is being one with reality, when we become one with reality, we say I exist everywhere. That is when you can know the truth of every dimension in which you exist, not only in time and space but beyond that too, as supernatural powers also include knowing past and future events. It's like access to 'iCloud' knowing everything whenever you access it by will through dhyāna. Unfortunately, when people say by dhyāna that one can achieve all or the highest knowledge, they are merely having access to memory cards, not 'iCloud' of reality. That is why Jainism says 'infinite knowledge at the time of liberation, not most knowledge'. If you want to see this, please watch the movie *Lucy* (2014), in which 20 per cent and 40 per cent use of the brain is shown as power manifestation and playing with space and time; 100 per cent use is shown as samādhi, as 'I exist everywhere', or, in our terms, 'I am Shiva'/'Aham bramhasmi'. In that movie, there is nothing like living liberation or *sadeh mukti*; for them, 'I exist everywhere only can be achieved once physical appearance vanishes'. In Hinduism, it's vanished, but at a psychological level.

Does This Evolution of Human Beings from Human to Liberated Jiva/Soul Happen Only through Human Beings' Efforts and Will, i.e., Can Atheists Become Liberated Souls, or Can They Manifest Supernatural Powers or Siddhi/Shakti?

See, atheism was a movement against 'monotheism that claimed irrational revelation'. I already explained so many metaphysical terms, like chakras and nadi. In Appendix B, you will find many other terms. Why are atheists denying God/deity? Why not other terms, like sukshma sharira? Because they don't even know these terms. Their goal is to carry out cultural genocide in this civilization without learning about deep diversity, so even if I give a logical proof of God or say you atheist can achieve moksha, they still have to believe the rest of the metaphysical entities as mentioned above because that's the level playing field to do sadhana (sukshma sharira). At every step, there are some benchmarks or qualities that make you realize that you have achieved these milestones. If you don't recognize these metaphysical milestones, how will you know your spiritual growth? Hinduism is not like, 'This is God; these are civil, criminal, social, and cultural codes revealed by him, so believe in God and follow them blindly'. Hinduism is about experience, not belief.

Many legends and schools denied the existence of Paramātmā even after liberation; actually, they forgot to identify themselves as Paramātmā and promoted same atheism to their disciples, and none of the disciples achieved liberation. It is like when you are poor, you identify yourself as poor, but when you actually become rich, you still have that poverty in your character and you behave like poor. This opposite behaviour creates a double standard and makes you fail to achieve ultimate reality or 'Advaita' or oneness.

Now, these failed students of the school of liberation have only remained with the personality cult/hero worship of their first man, who has attained liberation and survives only by promoting a personality cult. It's like someone accidentally finds success at home, and the whole family and future generations celebrate it as 'divine and only success'.

Then there are legends who say all religions teach the same things and they are all equal. The message of all religions is the same: peace, love, harmony, just to get votes. These political legends are only interested in maintaining peace and harmony with love, which is necessary for the development of the nation, but this is the 'biggest fraud' with Hinduism by keeping it in the category of exclusive non-reformative religions. If all religions teach the same thing, 'peace, love, compassion', then why do we need religions? Why don't we directly practice peace, love, and compassion?

Hindus should have a universal brotherhood policy, 'vasudhaiv kutumbakam', 'sarve sukhina bhavantu', the universal value system. Hinduism has only one universal value system, from the Vedas to Puranas, whether in Sanskrit or local languages. That is why calling *Thirukkural* by Thiruvalluvar the non-Hindu secular book is wrong; it should be termed a 'universal value system' book. Tamils should understand that religion = rules for followers of religion and secular = rules for humanity is not true in the case of Hinduism. In Hinduism, there are no double standards; people are becoming conservative artificially to conserve Hinduism; otherwise, Hinduism = universal value system because Western people should not claim a patent on Thiruvalluvar's teachings as they did in the case of turmeric, so let's identify him as Hindu (refer to p. 209). That doesn't mean within the

Table 14.7

Things required for liberation or so-called enlightenment	Hinduism	Rebel 1, Rebel 2, Rebel 3 in Hinduism
		Hypothetical example
Paramātmā	✓	Either of the points are missing which ultimately takes away rebel faiths from enlightenment and thus Hinduism. To compensate that they do following things to project themselves unique/ different from Hinduism 1. Hero-worship of the founder + ethnocentrism 2. Freedom of religion 3. All religions teach the same thing 4. Demand of a separate religious status 5. Parallel economy, polity, society (ethnocentric life) 6. Simplicity and emotional appeal 7. Social work 8. Projecting social reform as a new rebel sect
Guru–shishya paramapara exists to give initiation to seeker	✓	
The authentic technique of yoga and dhyana, Ayurveda, prāṇāyāma, related lifestyle exists	✓	
Role of bhakti, kriya, rituals to make belief on Paramātmā as reality	✓	
Gurus or yogis existed in history	✓	
Gurus or yogis exist today	✓	
Paramātmā is oneness, not one	✓	
Prāthibhāsika satya, Vyāvahārika satya, Pāramārthika satya, all truth at respective levels and there is nothing like falsehood	✓	
Liberation and Shakti and siddhi	✓	

Hindu community there should be alienation like jati-varna-language discrimination; there should be a 'brotherhood bond' within the Hindu community too. But one must not create unnecessary pentagons that will pull the nation into unnecessary conflicts because of Hindu pride. Our goal should be to dissolve 'all pentagons' and promote liberty, fraternity, etc.

Yuval Noah Harari, in his book, says, 'Even though we have evolved, our behaviour is still like hunter-gatherers or collectivism, that is why even after evolution we face loneliness'. When we are part of society, we may get attracted to diversity and ensure our ego is satisfied through healthy conversation, money, power, etc. But Yuval might not know the science of 'liberation', which makes you feel all-inclusive even if you are alone.

God of Bhārtiya People

People give the status of God/deity to everyone who did great work in their profession. Generally, politicians, cricketers, social reformers, caste leaders, language leaders, parents, people who help others, people who do noble work, social workers, people who help in hard times, etc. One must remember that giving the status of God to these human beings is nothing other than speaking out of context. Because experiencing deity or oneness (liberation achievement or mokṣa prāpti) is a completely different science, and those who have achieved it deserve some extra respect. We know we are extensions of Paramātmā or Īśvara tattva exists in all of us, but who has experienced it himself/herself is not different from the deity. If you compare politicians, parents, caste leaders, social reformers, etc., with liberated people, then either you are ignorant or your vocabulary is too weak to express the greatness of politicians, parents, etc. in proper terms. In Hinduism, in many places, the greatness of parents is expressed in a poetic or symbolic way, like in Ganesha's race with Kartikeya (murgon), but that should be understood in that context.

Similarity with Quantum Physics

1. Existing and experiencing the whole reality and existence as one and end of dual nature: matter–matter, matter–soul, soul–god, soul–matter (refer to Diagram 14.2)
2. Connecting or entanglement with other objects beyond the physical body
3. Types of Shakti–Siddhi and their functioning
4. Multiple plains of existence

Quantum Physics: Its Entanglement with Paramātmā

This chapter is a message to all sampradaya within Hinduism and outside to self-introspect, whether you exist because of the technical soundness of moksa/liberation and siddhi or just some cult/personality cult/businessman/hero worship/social reformer in saffron cloth/forceful existence through infrastructure.

15

Three-Dimensional Buddha

'Buddha' is a title rather than a personal name. It is derived from the Sanskrit word 'buddha', which means 'awakened' or 'enlightened'. In its most fundamental sense, a buddha is someone who has attained complete and perfect enlightenment, realizing the nature of reality, the true nature of the self, and the path to liberation from suffering. In a broader context, 'Buddha' is commonly used to refer to Siddhartha Gautama, the historical figure who is the founder of Buddhism. Siddhartha Gautama, after years of spiritual seeking and meditation, achieved enlightenment under the Bodhi tree in Bodh Gaya, Bhārat. From that point on, he was known as Gautama Buddha, or simply 'the Buddha'.

The term 'Buddha' is not limited to Gautama Buddha alone. In Buddhist cosmology, it is believed that there are many buddhas who have attained enlightenment throughout different ages and universes. Each of them teaches the dharma (the universal truth or law) to help sentient beings find liberation from suffering. So, in essence, 'buddha' signifies a state of spiritual awakening and enlightenment that can be attained by any individual who follows the path of practice and understanding laid out in Buddhism. This is what Buddhism and history tell us about Buddhism.

Our biased historians hide from us and teach him out of context. What is the context, i.e., method of enlightenment, i.e., the seven chakras, breathing (pranayama), yoga, kundalini, etc., that already existed before Buddhism from the Indus valley civilization till the Egyptian-Mexican civilization? We have already seen how Buddhism and Jainism were taught in our history book in chapters 6, 7, 13, and 14. But how was this divisionary politics of imposing atheism on

Buddhism, Jainism, and Cārvāka carried out and Buddhism diverted from the main theme of 'enlightenment'?

Buddha and Buddhism in History Books

1. Personality cult

In ancient Bhārat, in history books, you won't find the name of any yogi, rishi, maharishi, saṃnyāsi, etc. All these are either not mentioned or eliminated under the title 'ritualistic Brahmanism' or hardly mentioned. In ancient Bhārat, you will only find two spiritual personalities, Buddha and Mahavira, not as people seeking 'liberation' but as a symbol of peace and non-violence, whereas these two values are merely requirements to achieve 'liberation'. But the Middle Eastern syndrome, where peace is the highest value (because of too much violence happening on the ground), the same thing was imposed on Buddhism and Jainism. In the background, the jati–varna discriminatory system, violence, and both were projected as social reformers. But during them, before them, and after them, wars were happening. This discriminatory marketing of faiths or cults by giving focus to only Buddhism and Jainism is the first step in suppressing Hinduism and its path of liberation. There are many sadhus, sanyasis, biragis, preachers of Hinduism who did the pan-Bhārat journey to spread and learn knowledge. Ādi Śaṅkarācāryaḥ (this is just one example) established four mathas and did debate all over Bhārat. But it's not mentioned in the book. On the other hand, you will find names of places where Buddha got enlightened, where he gave his first sermon, and every detail of his life. This is what I call discriminatorily marketing and building personality cult rather than critically learning two value systems.

2. Projecting them as founders

They were projected as founders of faith by hiding an already existing foundation, i.e., Hinduism (chapters 7 and 14). This was created by not mentioning 'science of liberation, yoga, Sanskrit chanting, prāṇāyāma, oneness, the teachings of the *Upanishads*, simple living, and the Vedas' in history books. So their entry in history books automatically became a revolutionary breakthrough: 'man with a message of peace, non-violence, etc.' which justifies why they were termed founders, i.e., expressing them similar to the Abrahamic prophetic line.

3. Value system

This simple living formula is merely a marketing strategy; everyone lives life according to professional necessity. Even yogi's and sannyāsi follow special diets and exercise, so dividing them into the binary of simplicity and complexity is nonsense, as a household person with a social life with no goal of liberation is not expected to follow the lifestyle of yogi Hinduism.

Simple, heterodox (negative liberty) = no rituals, rules prescribed in the Vedas, giving up material life (negative liberty, i.e., unmanifested religion = making Buddhist, rebels against Hinduism inclining towards communism.

Complex means, orthodox (positive liberty) = rituals, rules, conduct according to dharma sutras, Brahminical dominance.[1]

In addition, Cārvāka, ajivika, and sramana are kept in the heterodox category, marketed as anti-Hindu, anti-Vedas, and anti-Brahminical. Sramana merely means the lifestyle of a yogi and spiritualism (refer to Table 14). If ajivika means merely believing in the fate of niyati, which is also believed by many Hindus today, then how is it heterodox? Projecting Buddhism and Jainism as anti-Vedic without teaching the Vedas and the meanings of rituals is injustice to the Vedas.

What they actually compare is the life of sannyāsi (Buddhism, Jainism) and the life of householder (Hinduism), but they use this diplomatic way of simple vs. complex to create a social divide in the mind of the reader between Hinduism vs. Jainism, Buddhism with discriminatory marketing.

4. Architecture marketing

Buddhism and its journey in terms of 'liberation' whether it was success or failure, you will see in this chapter. But to avoid that discussion, mediocre historians compensated for that vacuum by showing Buddhist architecture in a detailed manner. I don't think Hindu temples are covered in such a detailed manner. Idol worship existed before Buddha too, but it's not even mentioned to create narrative idol worship, which is inspired by Buddhism.

5. Constitutional provision

Hinduism and related personalities and teachings can't be taught because, according to the constitution, 'religious instruction should not be given in school', but the teachings of Jainism and Buddhism can be taught by projecting their personalities of peace, non-violence, and social reform.

6. Pre-Buddhism and pre-Jainism contributions of Hinduism to the world are not appreciated

Before the birth of Buddha, Hindu society knew 'cosmology, chemistry, metallurgy, astronomy, astrology, botany, ecology, philosophy, psychology, language, mathematics, economics, architecture, agriculture, medicine, governance, administration, humanities and aesthetics, ways of liberation, the technique of transforming oneself into Īśvara/Shiva/Brahman, eco-friendly economics and lifestyle, yoga, diet, dance, music, sixty-four types of arts, dressing and fashion, economic setup, employment opportunity, import-export, infrastructure, irrigation, civil engineering, medical science'. But have you seen mention of all these topics? This void is deliberately created so that two personalities (Buddha and Mahavira) look larger than the whole civilization. So that when Jainism and Buddha deny the Vedas, they look rational and remain unquestioned or uncriticized because we don't know above topics included in the Vedas. The reality is, they don't deny Vedas; they themselves remain influenced by them (refer to p. 121).

Secondly, they used the phrase 'Buddhism and Jainism denied authority of the Vedas'.[2] The Vedas are verses that were created by rishi and are not directed towards creating supremacy and authoritative regimes like 'exclusivist theocratic states', so the word authority is not right in the case of the Vedas. But the same people will not say the same thing for Chhatrapati Shivaji Maharaj and Maharana Pratap, who challenged the authority of certain 'religious manifestos'. This rebellion of Buddhism and Jainism is projected as a rebellion against discrimination, violence, and an authoritative regime. As Hinduism has various themes of liberation (refer to pp. 314–315), similarly, Mahavira and Buddha are merely given the respective themes of liberation, so by no angle are they in competition with Hinduism in terms of knowledge contribution and other aspects. I must accept that their future traditions contribute a lot to literature.

7. Morality

Buddhism's AshtangMarg and Jainism's TriRatna are covered in our history books. But the same history book didn't mention morality in Hinduism. *Kalpasutras*, which were written down around 600 BCE, existed much before varna and had the obligation that every Hindu shall follow the following things, irrespective of varna.[3]

1. daya: compassion
2. kashama: forgiveness
3. anusuya: absence of anger
4. soucha: cleanliness
5. sweet nature
6. absence of obstinacy
7. lack of greed
8. absence of desire

Buddha as a Liberated Soul

In chapter 14, I have already discussed the process of liberation, identity change while transformating from Jīva to Īśvara, role of yoga, Ayurveda, etc. When someone is liberated Jīva on the path of liberation, the best way to check his authenticity is by checking his supernatural powers, which we call siddhi or Shakti depending on tradition. When I say Buddha is liberated Jīva, which he himself calls nirvana, I refer to Tripitaka and Mahayana texts where the supernatural powers achieved by Buddha are written. There are some powers that he had from childhood, but I don't believe this because this kind of thing might be written to strengthen the personality cult. So supernatural powers are the proof that Buddha was liberated Jīva according to Mahayana texts, but Buddha himself never claimed or showed any supernatural powers, so it's up to you how much to believe in the Mahayana resources. Further Buddhist texts, like Dipvamsa, also claim Buddha visited Sri Lanka thrice, which is not at all historically proven. In chapter 14, I have already discussed the importance of benchmarks Īśvara/Shiva/Shakti/purusa to check whether one has reached its goal or not. Let us believe for a while that he achieved siddhi/Shakti and got liberated.

Buddha Was Not a Liberated Soul

Buddha didn't exclusively speak about his experience in samādhi state. Generally, most of the yogis ajnate their experience as having experienced the whole cosmos or cosmic form of Īśvara/Shiva. Once Buddha was asked by a disciple about the theory of creation or source, he refused to answer that question by saying that if an arrow comes and hits you, what will you do? Find the source or go to the doctor? This answer is relevant when the arrow hits, but when one is beyond all sufferings after becoming sannyāsi, then such kinds of answers are at Prāthibhāsika level; not Pāramārthika level.

Secondly, Buddha took sannyās because he saw an old man, a sick person, a corpse being carried to cremation, and a monk in meditation beneath a tree. If you see a sick man, will you help him or take him to the doctor, or will you go for sannyās as a solution to the problem? If you see an old man, you will accept the last stage of life or take sannyās. If you see a dead body, you will give emotional support to family members or take sannyās. May be metaphorically, Buddhism coveys the message that liberation makes you free from the age cycle, disease, and death. I have already mentioned the roles of Īśvara, Jiva, etc., on pages 292–293, so it doesn't matter whether Buddha believed in Īśvara, God, or soul or didn't believe at all. But the question is, does the Buddhist text mention how Buddha achieved nirvana? What was the process? What was the metaphysics of that process? Ultimately, his nirvana became the origin of theories like Shunyatavada/ Śūnyatva (shunyatva), momentariness. But shunyatava is exactly the same conception of ultimate reality, which matches with 'Brahman', so it doesn't match with nothingness (which is another name of atheism; refer third and fourth figures of Diagram 19.1, p. 350). In the case of Buddha, you have learned 'cause' from the effect because of a lack of archaeological and documented evidence.

Table 15.1

Process and concept	Advaita Vedanta	Shivaism	Sāṅkhya	Patanjali	Buddha
Benchmark of liberation	Brahman	Shiva	Purusa	Mukti	If he is calling himself liberated, then he must use different terms to express transformation to avoid confusion, rather than there being no atma = Jiva and Īśvara.
Prātibhā Sika identity	Human body	Human body	Identifying the self with reflection of the world	Identifying the self with reflection of the world	Self
Vyāvahā Rika identity	Jiva	Jiva	Modified brain according to information perceived	Modified brain according to information perceived	Self
Pāramār Thika identity	Brahman	Shiva	Purusa liberated from prakriti	Purusa liberated from prakriti	Self
A term used for liberation	Being one with Brahman	Being one with Shiva	Liberating purusa (atma) from prakriti (diversity)	Realizing true nature of purusa that is Īśvara	Niravana

A term used for liberation	Being one with Brahman	Being one with Shiva	Liberating purusa (atma) from prakriti (diversity)	Realizing true nature of purusa that is Īśvara	Nirvana
Theme to give up material life and society	Prāthibhāska satya or maya, avidya or material world or diversity is an illusion.	Bhuloka	What you perceive as you and data in mind is reflection of the world, not you.	What you perceive as you and data in mind is reflection of the world, not you.	World is suffering
The goal is liberation with Different names	Brahman	Shivoham/*Kailāsa*	Mukti from prakriti and realizing true self as purusa.	Realizing true self as purusa.	Nirvana
Yoga and dhyāna	✓	✓	✓	✓	He says vyayama but doesn't know its word for yoga or not
Ayurveda	✓	✓	✓	✓	Buddha never mentions but Tibetan Buddhism has *sowa rigpa* based on Ayurveda
Siddhi prāpti	✓	✓	✓	✓	Buddha never claimed.
Experience cosmos in samādhi	✓	✓	✓	✓	He said ask practical life problems and refused to speak on cosmos.

Four Noble Truths

Buddha's message of the four truths: life is suffering, desire is the cause of it, there is the cessation of suffering, and there is the path of cessation. All these truths are for those who want to achieve liberation. Just like Shaivites show fruits of Kailāsa, the pure blissful liberation; similarly, Buddha calls material life and desires as suffering so that people move towards liberation or nirvana by becoming monks.

But if this suffering philosophy is followed by people in the social life of human society or samsarik people then it is a negative philosophy because you are calling your lifestyle suffering in that you are an atheist and desire is also bad, which means all three ultimately end up with suffocation at the psychological level and stagnation at the economic level. But people want to forcefully grasp the teachings of Buddha for socio-economic development, material prosperity, or abuse Hinduism just to satisfy their ego of the misinterpreted version of Buddhism (moral message + atheism + Hinduphobic content).

That is why those who say Buddhism's four noble truths help in day-to-day life by ignoring context (liberation) are the biggest liars. Because in society, the economy runs because of desire, as desire promotes consumerism, at the society level, desire is not a problem; the incompletion of desire is a problem. In Hinduism, even the yogi has a desire to achieve liberation. Desire is the driving force of human life; it must be directed in the right direction and towards a higher goal. Therefore, calling desire a cause of suffering is conceptually wrong.

Ashtang Marg

His Ashtang Marg is excellent because it leads directly to Pāramārthika satya. But Ashtang Marg only ensures integrity to become yogi. But if one wants to become a liberated soul, then one must learn the basics from the basics, that is, Hinduism, right from yoga, Ayurveda, prānāyāma, Īśvara, ajna, and diet. Even a householder can follow Ashtangmarg as a moral code of conduct. But Ayurveda and other basics needed for liberation are a must for a spiritual journey.

Twelve Links of Dependent Origination

His twelve ajna samudaya links are perfectly placed. Samudaya means collection, and all those twelve points cause the collection of memory as well as addition to karma account. That is why those twelve points are very important in the journey of liberation. Buddha must be seen and understood as one of the schools towards liberation, just like other schools like Shaivism, Adavitism, Patanjali, etc.

These schools' teachings and paths are for those who want to achieve liberation by giving up material life; that is why their lifestyle can't be inspiration and motivation for people who want to achieve success in material life or social life, but it can definitely become an 'ideal code of conduct'. That is why their teachings must be taken consciously, at least in the case of Buddha, who says desire is the cause of suffering; otherwise, in the case of Hindu yogis, there is no need because society and material life are not suffering or negative things for them.

That is why those who take Buddhism as a path to achieve material and intellectual success end up neither becoming materially successful nor spiritual successful; even if they do, they are driven by desire, which is against Buddhism. There are also people who misinterpreted Buddhism and marketed it as a 'social reform against the caste system' and tried to achieve political, economic, and social goals. In reality, Buddhism is the path to spiritual success, not material success. But it does help to carry out functions with grace, minimum violence, etc.

Buddhist Society, Buddhist Kingdom, and Buddhist Country

Why does society call itself a Buddhist society or country calls itself a Buddhist country? What do they actually mean? Everyone has achieved liberation by giving up material life, then who runs the economy? Why the country have weapons and an army? That is why 'Buddhist country' itself is a meaningless concept; instead, that country can say there are a few people or yogis who are trying to achieve liberation by the method of Buddha, and the remaining people are supporting them. That is why an understanding of Buddha is very weak across the globe. Most people do blind hero worship of Buddha.

Some people say Buddhism was spread all over Bhārat in ancient Bhārat. Finding remains of Buddhist monuments means Buddhist monks used to live there, not common people who accepted Buddhism. If common man accepted Buddhism, then by what way people did marriage, cremation, etc.? There is mention of advice given in *sigalovada sattva* on how to live a happy married life, but we don't find mention of ceremonies and conducts of samskara, etc. Most people accepted Buddhism as a religion or theme of life in social life, not a lifestyle, because the lifestyle mentioned in Buddhism is directed towards liberation, which many people don't wish to do.

Why Did Certain Schools of Liberation Fade?

1. These schools went far away from the technique of liberation, as they denied the Vedas, Ayurveda, ecology, and other basic texts of liberation.
2. Economic support doesn't make the content of knowledge strong. Economic support only ensures strong marketing, strong foreign policy, and geographical reach. So, Adi Śaṅkarācāryaḥ, without economic support, single-handedly debated with multiple schools of thought and convinced them to join him.
3. Card of simplicity and popular tone/language are good at attracting the masses, but in debates, only content and intellect works; nothing else.
4. Having a monastery, scripture, sculpture, music, paintings, and all other tangible culture doesn't mean that the 'value system' and 'way of liberation' are correct, applied, and time-tested.
5. In the case of Buddhism, its connection is with Sanskrit, as in Sanskrit words, meanings, concepts, and grammar, are one and the same, that is, the word. So if you lose Sanskrit, you lose concepts. Words that are used in Pali are used in a very different way, which is far away from the actual meaning. For example, vigyan in Sanskrit means वि- ('diverse') + ज्ञान ('knowledge') and in Buddhism, vigyan vada means theory of consciousness. Sanskrit doesn't exist in isolation; it depends on the science of sound and phonetics.[4]

Hinduism always existed as a practice in society, even though there were philosophical debates and differences among Hindu liberation methods and the Buddha liberation method. Unfortunately, mediocre historians try to project it like mediaeval European rivalry between Islam and Christianity: whoever comes in power destroys the other religion (exceptional cases are there). Like Ayurveda, rituals, samskaras, yoga, and various terms were/are part of common human's life. This kind of history was written to make Hinduism look 'unsteady and interrupted', so that Hindus don't get access to seamless and smooth history to keep them confused. Buddha condemned rituals, but that doesn't mean people unfollowed them, so Hinduism was always alive.[5]

6. How one can dissociate from society for liberation and again enter society to teach the path of liberation to eliminate strict protocols among professionals to run the economy. Doesn't it sound illogical?

7. If taking the middle path by calling right and wrong things an extreme path is not true in every context, especially in the path of liberation, where there is no dualism, then how can you create the middle path? That is why Buddhism denies atma on the one hand and, on the other, accepts it in a mild form of five skandhas, which is a combination of physical form, consciousness, feelings, perception, and mental disposition generated by past experience. Which is actually the middle path of atma is there and there is no atma.

8. What Buddha spoke and what Buddha achieved were two different things. Buddha achieved liberation, but he never told formula how to achieve? But according to Hinduism, cessation is merely a starting phase; there are a lot of things to be achieved. Controlling the self and mind are merely forceful attempts to control potential. Mind is potential, which must be shaped and directed according to goal; controlling it is merely the first stage; giving direction to it according to will is the legendary game. In Hinduism, the shaping of the mind is called 'sanskara' or 'software coding' and directing is called uddesya or the purpose of the goal.

Bursting Some Myths

Buddhism and social equality

1. Once someone takes saṃnyāsa, he automatically loses social identity, whether he is Kshatriya, Brahmin, etc., but historians and he said that this equality among sangha (groups of Buddhist monks) is unique to Buddhism. It is unique to Buddhism because sanghas or liberation-seeking people in Hinduism were not even mentioned in history books. How many people know Hindu yogis?
2. If he eliminated or opposed the caste system, then what was the alternative model he gave society to run the economy according to geography? What employment opportunities were created?
3. What were the other social evils in Buddha's time? What did he do to eliminate those?
4. The Madhura sutta (84), the Kannakatthala sutta (90), and the Assalāyana sutya (93) of the Majjhima-nikāya, the Cullavagga ix. 14 of the Vinayapitaka, etc. All recognize the existence of four castes: Ksatriya, Brāhmana, Vaishya, and Sūdra. In the Kannakatthala sutta, the superiority of the Ksatriya and Brāhmana castes is recognized: dve vannă aggam akkhayanti, the two castes are said to be chief and therefore deserve respect and service by the other two castes.

Gender equality

Two important features of early Buddhism were the assertion that the highest goal, ajnat (Nirvana), was possible for women and the creation of a Bhikkhuni sangha. On the other hand, Buddhist texts reflect stereotyped ideals of the submissive and obedient woman whose life was supposed to revolve around her husband and sons. They also contain many negative images of women as temptresses and creatures of passion. Comparisons with poisonous black snakes and fire (the message is: stay away from them) are not surprising in a tradition that set such a store on celibacy and therefore perceived women as a threat. Just as monks were warned against women, nuns were warned against men. Buddhist tradition suggests that the

Buddha was not initially keen to establish Abhikkhuni sangha but ultimately gave in to the persistent pressure of his disciple Ananda and his aunt and foster mother, Mahaprajapati Goutami. The *Vinaya Pitaka* describers the gloomy prediction that the doctrine would decline in 500 instead of 1,000 years because women had been admitted into the sangha.

In *Anguttara Nikaya*, Buddha's conversation with Sujata (daughter-in-law of Anatha Pindika), it is mentioned that there were seven kinds of wives, some approved and others not so:

1. The Vadhaka (slayer) is the wife, who is cruel, pitiless, murderous, neglects her husband at night, passes her time with others, and is bought with money.
2. The Chorasama (thief-like) is the wife, who takes the husband's money and longs to ruin and impoverish him.
3. The Ayyasama (mistress-like) is the wife, who is lazy, fond of luxuries, expensive to maintain, loves to gossip, and talks in a loud, strident voice. She diminishes her husband's zeal and industry.
4. The Matusama (mother-like) is the wife, who takes care of her husband and his property as would a mother to her only son.
5. The Bhaginisama (sister-like) is the wife, who treats her husband with respect similar to that of a younger sister towards her older brother.
6. The companion (wife-like) who is of good birth, faithful to her husband, and is filled with joy upon meeting him, like one meeting a friend after a long time.
7. The Dasisama (slave-like) is the wife, who is calm, patient, and obedient, and meekly accepts her husband's beating.[6]

The institution of marriage was central to the life of the householder. In Buddhist texts, the type of marriage most approved of is one arranged by parents, where the bride and groom are young and chaste. There is reference to ahava (literally, 'the leading, i.e., of the bride by her family) and vivaha (literally, 'leading away', i.e., of the bride by the groom's family). It is not certain whether ahava and vivaha were two different ceremonies or the same one.

The *Vinaya Pitaka* mentions ten kinds of unions between a man and a woman:
1. when a woman is bought by money (Dhanakkhita)
2. when she stays of her own accord with a man (Chhandavasini)
3. when a man gives her money (Bhogavasin)
4. when a man gives her clothes (Patavasini)
5. when an ablution of water is performed (Odapattakani)
6. when she removes her headgear (Obhatachum-bata)
7. when she is also a female slave (Dasinama);
8. when she is also a servant (Kammakari)
9. when she is temporary with a man (Muhuttika)
10. when she is captured in raid (Dhajahata)[7]

Buddha as a symbol of peace

Let us first understand the concept of peace and the world. This earth functions on the principle of 'activity', not 'peace'. The water cycle, carbon cycle, life cycle, changing of seasons, movements of planets, change in atmosphere, and the wilful motion of creatures all represent only one thing: activity. So one has to survive; he has to participate. After the '50s, people are peaceful because they have social security; otherwise, people do work. The function of the whole earth and universe is activity, not peace or motionlessness.

In chapter 14, I have explained what liberation (mukti or nirvana) is and the role of dhyāna–yoga to achieve it. In the whole chapter, there was no mention of peace because peace was never a goal in Hinduism or Bhārat, it was bliss, and peace was a side effect. In Middle Eastern countries, Jews, Christians, and Muslims keep fighting with each other, which is why 'peace' has the highest value. To maintain peace, sometimes religion is to be interpreted as a supporter of peace, even though it does not. When colonial masters came to Bhārat in the 17th–18th centuries, they wanted to project Buddhism as a rational rival against irrational Hinduism, so they projected Buddha as a symbol of peace against sacrificial Hinduism. It is true that Buddha didn't support animal sacrifice, but this idea was already rooted in the Upaniṣads in the form of Vedanta.

Three-Dimensional Buddha

Peace is a side effect in the process of liberation, whichever way you go, because once you give up society in your life, you automatically give up related conflict, and concept clarity within eliminates inner conflict. My question is, if one has achieved peace within, then how can it bring peace into your life.

Diagram 15.1

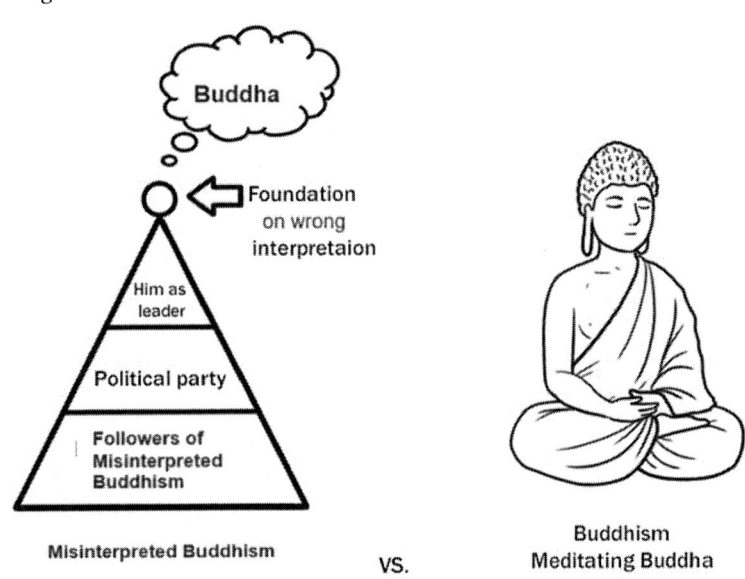

What today's need is that Jains, Buddhists, and Hindus should come together and discuss and share the best of the knowledge they have about the science of liberation so that we all can revive that science and bring back the golden era. Unscientific practices that are continued in the name of tradition must be questioned. Differences created by Western powers on the basis of identity politics must be eliminated from history books. Unfortunately, people are busy with identity politics of separate religious status, which has nothing to do with Bhārat and the liberation process. Identity is not at all required in the process of liberation.

16

The Conqueror

The term Jain means someone who has conquered himself, on his own whims and fancies, on his own senses, and who has control over his self. Leftist historians create a fake narrative that it was suddenly created in 600 BCE, but archaeological evidence say that Jain literature traced its history back to the Indus valley civilization.[1]

Table 16.1

	Hinduism	Jainism
Liberation	Journey of Jīva to Brahman • Journey of Jīva to Shiva • Journey from Prāthibhāsika to Pāramārthika satya	Journey from the false self to the true self. True self: Ananatchatustaya, that is, those with infinite vision, infinite knowledge, infinite bliss, and infinite power.
Benchmark	Achieving Brahman = Shiva = Vaikuṇṭha = Kailāsa	Achieving siddhashila or keval jnana

	Hinduism	Jainism
Hurdle in liberation	1. World appears as maya, reality is Brahman. 2. Karma account is not empty, so one reaps fruits and avoids the accumulation of karma	1. Samvara means stopping incoming karma in account, and nirjara means bearing fruits of karma already done, which are into account. 2. Types of karma: a) Vedniya karma (pleasure and pain) b) Jñānavaraṇa karma (veil of knowledge) c) Darsanavarniya karma (veil of faith) d) Antraya karma (consumerism) e) Mohaniya karma (delusion/moha-maya) f) Ayu karma (life experienced and its karma account) g) Nama karma (multiple identity crises, which is explained in detail in Jainism) h) Gotra karma (determined by the family into which one is born) Solution to empty the karma account and move towards liberation is ahiṃsā (non-violence), satya (truth), asteya (not stealing), brāmhacaryā (sexual continence), and aparigraha (non-possessiveness).
Personalities or identities related	Jiva, Īśvara = Brahman, Guru	1. Jīva and ajiva: Both are conscious (third figure of Diagram 19.1); Jīva is a living being; Ajīva is space, time, medium of motion, matter, and medium of rest 2. Īśvara = Anantchatustaya; they don't use Īśvara as the theme of liberation like we have Shiva, Vishnu. But they have all deities like Hindus which are common in both Hinduism and Jainism. Anti-Hindus keep Jainism in heterodox because it doesn't have Īśvara according to the Hindu framework and call Jains as atheists, i.e., so that Jains run away from their tradition.
Siddhi/ Shakti	Many exist	Ashta siddhi

	Hinduism	Jainism
Experience of oneness	I exist everywhere in everything, I have multiple viewpoints	Anekantvada, i.e., every viewpoint has its own diverse dimension. Western pseudo-scholars interpret it as everyone's opinion is true, i.e., every religion is true, i.e., celebrating orthodoxy and irrationality because it is also true.
Importance of yoga and Ayurveda	Both are there	Both are there; Jains don't eat food below earth level or roots because one has to kill a plant to eat roots, i.e., killing is sin (bad karma). If Jain muni eats garlic and onion because it boosts 'lust', which is not necessary for liberation, then there are various techniques to utilize and control sex energy within yoga, e.g., ojas to tejas.

Jainism gives a theory of substance, which includes the categorization of the world into the following categories:
1. Matter (pudgala)
2. Medium of motion (dharma)
3. Medium of rest (adharma)
4. Space (akasa)
5. Time (kāla)

Similarly, Hinduism's Nyay Vaisheshika has a similar theory.[2]
1. Prthivi (earth)
2. Ap (water)
3. Tejas (fire)
4. Vayu (air)
5. Akasha (ether)
6. Kala (time)
7. Dik (space)
8. Atman (Soul)
9. Manas (mind)

I have already explained their utility on page 279, Table 13.5).

Yuval Noha Harari, in his book *Sapiens: A Brief History of Humankind*, says Jainism and Buddhism believe in natural law as compared to religious laws. What runs on natural law is Hinduism, as the development takes place in the sequence of ecology, economy, society, and polity. On that platform, all schools are seeking liberation. He is a victim of Western theories that projected Buddhism and Jainism as the destroyers of Hindu metaphysics and religious laws and promoted materialism or naturalism. According to Yuval Noha Harari, 99 per cent of Buddhists don't achieve nirvana/liberation. If there had been no concept of yoga, meditation, and liberation prior to all themes of liberation, then no one would have achieved any liberation; forget about establishing any new sect.

PART VI
PERSONALITY, RESPONSIBILITY, AND VISION

17

Bramhacarya: Going Closer to Bramha

Consumerism, small attachments, and physical pleasure are actually ways to get satisfaction through material/physical things. When consumerism goes to the extreme, why will any Hindu go for the metaphysics of his Hinduism, puja, or guru, i.e., in your language, spiritual aspects of life. That is why Hindu philosophy never says 'your journey started when you were born'; it says 'you are soul/atma and because of past karma you got chance to participate in human world in human body' so that you become responsible and conscious while taking any step and decision in life, including consumerism. According to Hinduism, this world was functioning before you with the rule of prakriti/nature consciousness (not merely nature or environment), and it's your duty to live according to the rule of nature consciousness, i.e, your life starts with Bramha (birth and brāmhacaryā) and ends with sanyasa (experiencing Bramha or dissolving yourself into Bramha). In between these two small phases, there are grihastashram and vanprasthashram.

1. **Brāmhacaryā:** it connotes chastity during the student stage of life for the purpose of learning from a guru (teacher) and during later stages of life for the purpose of attaining spiritual liberation (moksha)
2. **Grahistashram:** individual + collective consumerism where one has a duty to take responsibility for the needs of family
3. **Vanprasthashram:** where one transfers duty and responsibility to the next generation and does Niṣkāma karma or work without self-interest to move towards liberation, which is free from random consumerism and accumulation of excess wealth
4. **Saṃnyāsa:** giving up socio-economic identity; life-seeking liberation through devotion and other yogic practices

Brāmhacaryā

To keep the mindset or psychophysical nature intact with 'oneness' you have to make hardware (body) and software (mind, soul) compatible with the format. So for that thoughts, food/diet, and behaviour are programmed in such a way in the Hindu manual that they lead to enlightenment, i.e., 'oneness'. This manual divides thoughts, food, and behaviour, and quality in the three categories: Satvik, Rajasic and Tamasic. In this sequence, the most compatible format is satvik (brain-driven senses), and tamsik is the worst (senses-driven brain). Even if someone is not brahmachari and he is participating in grhastashram, still he/she has to carry out sexual activity, wealth creation, and diet in the prescribed format so that it doesn't turn into excess vulgarity (tamsik). Brāmhacaryā and sanyas are completely aligned with satvik life. In all four phases, satvik is to be upheld as a life formula. Brāmhacaryā is a phase where one learns and studies various fields. As per the Patanjali yoga sutra, to maintain focus either on studies or meditation, the satvik lifestyle is a booster. Brāmhacaryā is the best option because it retains 'ojas' in the body. So Brāmhacaryā is not merely remaining a bachelor; it is a small part of the grand plan.

Brāmhacaryā is a mini packet of sannyāsi which is actual liberty or free from any bondage of social, personal, or economic responsibility so that he/she is free from any type of dealings which helps in focusing on consumption of knowledge and exploration. It's only 'aggressive marketing of consumerism' (not consumption) that gives glory to childhood, which makes consumerism fascinating and Brāmhacaryā boring. Just like in the early days, Napoleon did a 'peace treaty' with European countries, and after a few years, he himself said, 'War gives glory', and suddenly peace appeared as a 'boring symbol of weakness'. This jingoism we appreciate because glory is attached to it. Similarly, remaining attached to worldly pleasure is marketed as supreme pleasure so that you never experience real freedom, independent of all relationships and bondages, i.e., experiencing oneness/Bramhan.

Phase of Bramha is attached to 'creation'. If you follow the lifestyle of Bramha (brāmhacaryā), you will also become a creator because you will get space and time by not involving yourself in worldly pleasure so that you can utilize your consciousness for the greater good of society.

For 'consumers', liberty is choosing one product out of seven, and for 'creator', liberty is creating the eighth product. So it's in your hands whether you want to become a slave to your senses, which makes you a slave to one-seventh products, or you want to control your senses and make the world your consumer. As Buddha said, 'If you want to control the world, first control your senses'.

According to some people, if you create an emotional void, then on your path, you will crave the respective powers: knowledge, money, political power, etc. But this language of an emotional void and craving for power is quite harsh, inhuman, and ruthless, so Hinduism tells the same formula in a very humanistic way: 'control your senses' plus responsible ethics and morality so that you don't turn against humanity and ecology. This is what we teach in the initial phase before grahastashrama. The state of Brahma is the seventh loka (refer to Table 14.2, p. 288), which is beyond all types of consumerism, lust, whims and fancies, and bonding and targeted towards complete, eternal, continuous liberty and stability. So one who follows brāmhacaryā in a traditional way experiences a similar 'lifestyle of Brahma/brāmhacaryā'. The literal meaning of brāhmacaryā is 'moving into infinity': 'Brahma' means infinity, the absolute, or big; 'charya' means to move or to walk, to live. Brāhmacaryā is moving beyond small attachments and instead identifying with infinity and focusing on higher goals (liberation).[1]

Grahastashram

In the name of a relationship, what people manifest is merely love and sex. In Hinduism, it is called 'Sambhog', which means successful love leading to union. Sambhog shastra is a separate branch of knowledge that discusses all things in detail. The *Kamasutra* is a comprehensive guide that covers not only sexual positions and intimacy but also topics like courtship, seduction, the importance of emotional and psychological connections between partners, the nature of love, the diet for sambhog, controlling semen, and the art of ejection. There are multiple stories related to sex, extramarital affairs, etc. but those things are created to give you a message to understand the repercussions; they are in certain contexts (not a guiding principle).

So it is important to know all these things at the end of brāmhacaryā and before the marriage. Even after the marriage, some ceremonies are conducted by a husband, and a conducive environment is created before they have sex. In ancient times, rishis used to come home and describe the heroism of ancestors so that they could save this data in the subconscious mind so that when they had sambhog, they could produce legend.

A pre-marriage relationship shall not be equated to 'lesser dignity'. One must also remember that there is a difference between brāmhacaryā and 'incel movement'. Otherwise, we will see rebels in Hinduism who will seek someone else's patronage for the sake of sex and pre-marriage relationships, which is human capital loss.

World Moving towards Child Marriage

What is marriage? It is a 'framework' created where lust, partnership, family, economic, and social needs are completed so willfully involve procreation. Bhārat has banned child marriage because the government wants to flourish kids like flowers till a certain age until they have mental, physical, and social maturity. Child marriage banning means discarding that framework of marriage for a certain age, where the promotion of child marriage is also considered a violation of the law. Its indirectly promoting brāmhacaryā with the angle of science: 'Evolution as complete men and women'.

But enemies of humanity found a new way to destroy the childhood of our young children. It was okay when influencing media like movies; online series were showing love between young boys and girls as a couple or dating; this was an era before thirty years. Twenty years ago, it was the era of college-level love life; and seven to eight years ago, it was teenage-level love life. Now they are showing students of classes 5th and 6th falling in love; in the coming years, they will show children in nursery are having love lives, after some years through sonography, they will find gender and tummy-to-tummy relationships will be there through Wi-Fi, i.e., perfect pedophilic disorder.

Law says child marriage promotion is a crime, but they found a loophole to show 'lust fulfilment and the need to have a partner' in childhood in the name of dating. When our kids are in the age of getting attracted to all unknown worlds and discoveries, these social media platforms are creating an artificial vacuum of relationships in their minds so that they get distracted from the mode of 'learning and knowing'. Even Khajurao temple has various layers according to age group, which means that even while constructing the temple, we have kept age in mind. If there had been no law, these people would have promoted child marriage too.

18

Dvanva to Dvaita

Part 1

When Arjuna was stuck in decision-making about whether something should be done or not, he was confused about choosing the best out of two bests. When it's just a matter of choice when everything looks equally true, this condition is known as dvanva (ethical dilemma), which is a psychological stagnancy in decision-making very similar to conflict of interest. To take Arjuna of condition and take him to 'the decision', Krishna plays the card of dvaita, where Krishna and Arjuna are two egos; Arjuna is the confused one, and Krishna is clear with the concepts. As Krishna is the sarthi or charioteer of Arjuna, it means that Krishna has control over the Arjuna's mind. Physically, he is a charioteer but what about his psychological state? So dvaita is entanglement where Krishna is the charioteer and handles brain Arjuna and plays Mahābhārata; as he says that whatever is happening I (Krishna) am doing, you are just medium.

The hurdle for Krishna is 'confusion', which may work as a hurdle while functioning, so he eliminates that through dialogue, and after eliminating confusion, he asks to take darshan of him through devotion. In *Vaishnvite Dvaita*, atma of human is the body of Vishnu, i.e., Vishnu software works as solid hardware (avatāra) in the hardware of Arjuna as software (Bhagavad Gita). When one wants to be successful, 'ego' has a role, and the elimination of ego will never lead to success; the elimination of ego will lead to nothingness. In Advaita Vedanta, the ego of the self is also transformed into

'Brahman'; it's not eliminated. In dvaita, 'ego' of Krishna and 'ego' of Arjuna are there, which is why we identify both of them where ego Arjuna dissolves in Krishna (submission). Success and its attributes must belong to something; hard work and the fruits of success cannot hang in the air. So having an ego is not a wrong thing; in Hinduism, ego is not a negative thing; 'aham' is the word that is used for both ego and self. Only the quality and quantity of ego change the destiny of human beings. Unfortunately, we are shown only negative aspects of ego, and positive aspects are termed self-respect; this creation of binary terms confuses us again. That is why there is only one term, 'aham'.

This chapter is not just about what values must be followed to become good human beings in the spheres of humanity and ecology. This chapter is about why people don't follow the right path. Everyone claims or knows what is right or wrong, but practicing right by defeating wrong is always a challenge. Everyone claims their last messenger, jati leader, or self-styled shallow knowledge religious leader taught three to four good things and branded shallow knowledge as 'simple way of life' or 'the truth'. It is important to identify blind spots that stop us from following the right path. These points mentioned are not only about the value system of ethics and morality in general but also the attitude of Hindus towards the Hindu value system and the material lifestyle associated with it. How the wrong value system is injected as software in us by an anti-Bhārat invisible hand, so that this country becomes the hub of 'illegal activity, informal economy', so that country never becomes a superpower. Many third-world countries, which were colonies, are still backward because of the wrong value system injected into them. Remove the pseudo-binary from the mind and explore the diverse reality; that is what Krishna did in the Bhagavad Gita by eliminating dvanva and establishing dvaita.

The human mind chooses those ways and motivational thoughts that allow human beings to remain inactive, lethargic, and lazy, which is the natural state of existence of unemployed and failed people. It's very important to check whether thought or psychology is promoting inactivity, activity, or wrong/right activity.

1. Heart vs. brain: whom to listen?

We have again created the wrong binary, i.e., heart promotes ethically incorrect or emotional or short-term things and the brain promotes what is intellectually right or long-term things.

Table 18.1

Perception	**Emotional perception**	**Intellectual perception**
Activity	Consuming tamsik food, drink, smoking	Consuming tamsik food, drink, smoking
Outcome	How it tastes? What kind of pleasure does it generate?	Its impact on health

Both of these things are promoted by the brain itself. Only when situations go out of control or out of the syllabus questions arise; then only breathing patterns and heart rate changes; that's the only role of the heart. So keep calm and do deep breathing so that you perceive asymmetric or unconventional things just like other things. Take decisions calmly as best as you can as per your principle. Breathing changes with mood. It tells you about your health.[1]

2. Event vs. maintenance or event vs. lifestyle

Doing good things as an event and doing them consistently are both necessary. People do things as events and fail in consistency or maintenance. Whereas people who do maintenance must celebrate it as an event to appreciate consistency. Unfortunately, people do either of them and fail in the long term.

3. You are the architect of your own success

This is the most non-sensical statement, which eliminates all stakeholders, experts, and experienced people related to your profession and leaves you alone, egoistic, and helpless. There should be no shame in asking for help connecting people to success and utilizing their experience and talent in the journey. After the success, give credit to the team/stakeholders so that their appreciation makes them connected in the future too, and when you fail, take responsibility so that those stakeholders feel free to work with you. Aristocracy works on this connection and relationship with no game of ego, and the common man believes in getting ego satisfied: 'I worked, I alone worked, credit goes to me, I am the architect of my success', and then chances of success become negligible and they remain unemployed.

4. The only path

Table 18.2

Right path, activity	Wrong path, inactivity
Complex	Simple
Long term	Short term
Idealism	Practical approach
Strict	Liberal
Extreme approach	Middle path
Followers of path, ethics regulations, morality (follows path because they are weak)	Rebels (projected as stronger), so to look stronger people choose unethical, wrong path
They are victimized by isolating them (sacrifice)	These are accepted as 'new normal'

There is only one way to succeed, which is to follow the right path, to be honest, and to do everything that is required for expected success. But some people get diverted and distracted. People try to justify the wrong path by attaching negative attributes to the right path.

Even successful people use the same attributes to overrate their success over and above failed people. When such negative attributes are attached, why would one become successful? Similarly, many history books also attached attributes of the 'right path' to Hinduism and related practices like rituals, festivals, social systems, etc., and attributes of the 'wrong path' to other artificially created rival faiths. So this discriminatory marketing takes away readers from Hinduism. Plus, it also weakens the reader mentally and persuades him to take the wrong path for 'easy' success in life, ultimately retarding reader to inactivity. This inactivity is intrinsic to many people in the form of lethargy, so this lethargy is actually promoted under the name 'simple way' or 'simplicity'.

Later in Part 2, you will read about the Bhagavad Gita and practice ethics, values, and rules as you are just a medium; whatever is happening, he (Krishna) is doing. Krishna is teaching metaphysics where soul is eternal and body is temporary. 'I (Krishna) exist beyond the body as vishwarupam (cosmic form) on the battlefield just to enhance the performance of Arjuna', by introducing himself (Krishna) as an infinite being, so that taking arms and having war automatically becomes 'simple and finite' in front of infinity (Krishna). What is finite? Its body, war, relation, lust, a world so that Arjuna starts his journey from finite to infinity, from body to soul, from himself to Krishna. This relative greatness of nobel values persuades Arjuna to do 'activity'. Relative existence is known as dvaita, which took Arjuna from dvanva (confusion/ethical dilemma). Unfortunately, we do see exactly opposite marketing in Table 18.2, and that's why people fail in life.

When you want to build an empire and when you choose to start a project, the first brick is proof that 'it is possible', the second brick is proof that 'it is taking shape', and the third brick is proof that 'it is happening'. The mistake a common man makes is that he tries to find out 'whole empire in single or two bricks' and believes it will not happen. Those who choose not to build an empire choose inactivity by believing it's impossible. Generally, the guy who builds gets proof every day in experience that it is happening slowly, but the guy who chooses inactivity every day merely believes it will not happen. So inactivity and laziness are too superficial, which is justified by strongly believing in them. The only way to bring about change is to experience small efforts and small results every day while building an empire, rather than imagining grand success or not believing in it.

Planning, discipline, and time management are merely tools to cut the time taken to complete tasks, but they are by mistake equated with success. That is why, even after knowing planning and discipline, people don't become successful because they don't have a vision and goal. When you know the goal, then to cut the randomness, we use planning; to cut the time, we use time management; and to implement these two, we use discipline.

The whole mess is created by promoting wrong ideas and concepts about success, and most of the motivational speakers only say fake things just to sound attractive. Most of the motivational quotes lead to failure. But you strongly believe that whatever is motivational and sounds attractive, it definitely leads to success. Have a look at the following examples:

1. There is no *shortcut* to success
2. Time management and planning *is success*
3. The plan should be followed *strictly*
4. Have a *practical* approach to life
5. Never take a *complex* path; keeps things simple
6. Choose *middle path*; don't go to extreme
7. Success is an *event* to shut the mouth of haters

With good marketing, shallow and wrong concepts are projected as 'practical' in the name of simplicity in the spheres of success so that you start moving from 'experience depth of life' to 'consumerism' because when life is shallow, you look for a kick every time to enhance the experience, and that kick is given by consumerism, which ultimately helps capitalists and turns the environment into ashes. This is how motivational speakers also earn money without building businesses, economies, or success in their own lives.

Part 2

There are almost forty various gitas; we know only one, Bhagavad Gita, because of its popularity. Somewhere, I also feel we are too busy in making it more holy and ignoring the rest of the gitas and literature. So I will explain Bhagavad Gita in brief rather than unnecessarily stretching it like a commentary. The Bhagavad Gita is for those who suffer from anxiety, fear, or ethical dilemmas that stop them from taking action, or for someone who is too focused on results and stays away from taking action.

In modern Bhārat, we can say the condition of mindset that stops us from investing in the share market is because we are afraid of market volatility. So it is explained through a beautiful dialogue between Krishna, who is the charioteer of Arjuna. Arjuna is in a dvanva, or conflict of interest, an ethical dilemma about whether he should follow his duty or give up arms as he is fighting against his own family members. These guys are on the warfront, so action is war or killing; that should not be interpreted as gita promoting violence. If you are in other professions, then action will change accordingly. In Hinduism, 'Kshatriya' are a class of people who are protectors because, in its civilization, warriors will be there to protect the empire.

In modern Bhārat, only legal forces have the right to take arms and the right to give punishment belongs to the honourable judiciary under the wisdom of the constitution. So in the modern Bhārat constitution, there is our 'Kshatriya'. The greatness of the Bhagavad Gita is applicable to every 'activity' whether in social life or sannyāsi life; it works in both cases because the role of Krishna is very important to push someone from ajnat (commitment) to siddhi (completion), which is a thousand times more practical than life negative philosophy or atheist school in every aspect of life. Life-negative philosophies speak about cessation, take you towards 'inactivity' and ask you to control your mind. That is why even when someone is sannyāsi he does activity, but at a transcendental level. The analogy is that Arjuna is the body and Krishna is the mind, who is controlling five horses, which are five senses; by controlling senses by mind, you can take yourself towards higher goals.

Diagram 18.1

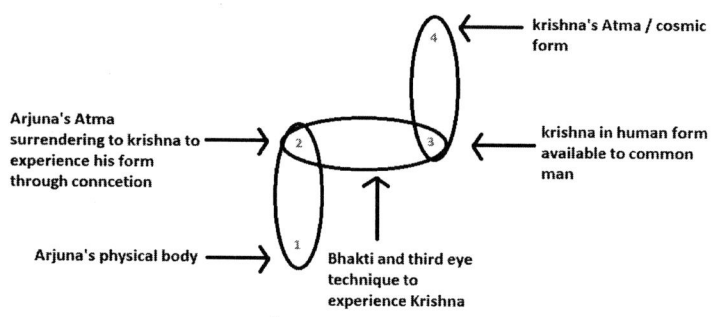

In Advaita Vedanta, all four stages would be in a linear line, and only two stages would be there. First, I and world, second Brahman.

Linear line means oneness; both stages are the same; only maya/illusion makes them exist as two; hence, liberation is possible when one is alive/*sadeh-mukti*. In Dvaita Vedanta, the first and last stages are two separate; hence, the devotee (I and world) is separate from Krishna (Brahman); both are not the same; it is a parallel world/multiverse; mukti is mostly possible after death. In Arjuna's case, it is possible when he is alive because he surrendered to Kirshna and became one with him; that's mukti/liberation. Diagram 18.1 reflects dvaita, Vishishtha dvaita, etc.

Small Commentary of the Bhagavad Gita
Arjuna: How can I kill them?

Krishna:

'Them': They are souls, not bodies, souls are immortal. The body is like clothes, which souls keep changing. If one body dies, the soul takes a new body with the same or a different gender, in your family or may be in a different country, maybe an animal too. Nothing is permanent, so don't think much about your body or their body, which, by your effort or some other way, is going to vanish.

Kill: You are born into a warrior family, you are trained as a warrior, and your duty is also fighting. All three reasons mean the same thing: taking arms and fighting. In modern context, we must take meaning from taking risks in the market.

I: You may die or live or whatever happens to you, you will end by submerging into me, just like a river goes in whatever direction; it ultimately ends by meeting the ocean. To remove Arjuna's loneliness after death that is only 'I' alone, Krishna says here, there, and beyond all of this, I exist everywhere;[2] you, your enemies, everything is going to meet me; no one is alone. You better understand this and align yourself with me rather than too much thinking about 'I' and submit yourself to me. To confirm this, Krishna shows him his cosmic form or vishwarupa form, which means Krishna as the whole universe. Another reason one hesitates to submit himself/herself to Krishna is the background of karma and its cycle. To eliminate this issue, Krishna says, 'If you devote yourself to me, I will liberate you from the karma cycle even if you have sin in your account'.

Can: You are saying 'can' instead of 'should' means you are still not making up your mind to take action. This is happening to you because your senses are driving your mind and taking you to worldly pleasure, pain, and other emotional attachments with the world and humans. So keep your senses in control of your mind so that your vision remains always clear, and that makes you fearless because opaqueness about the path creates fear of failing. That is why clear vision is important. Clear vision comes with the right qualities. There are three qualities: tamas (senses of a slave), rajas (royal warrior or Plato's philosopher-king), and sattva (pure consciousness). You know which quality you need to develop to have a clear vision to see beyond the senses.

How: Just lift the bow and arrow and kill them. Whatever is happening, what I am doing is just medium. When someone else is taking a market risk and you have to just perform a task, you will work fearlessly. But before taking a decision, you must know about the choices that shape it. There are three qualities that shape the decision: tāmasika, rājasika, and satvik. The purest decision is that which is the outcome of choices that reflect satvik quality.

Problem of Fear and Anxiety Is Solved

Then there are critics who say this sounds really good theoretically, but practically, it is not possible. Those fools are forgetting Arjuna was the best archer of that era; his skill development was already complete. Anxiety and fear are psychological problems that Krishna solves. The skill development part is covered by Dronacharya to perform a particular task. If you say the Bhagavad Gita sounds impractical, it means you haven't undergone a skill development course in a particular field. In modern-day, every motivational speaker wants to sound like Krishna, but the listener and speaker both are not aware that the listener hasn't gone through skill development, and that's why every motivation fails in Bhārat and unemployment increases. Here I addressed the useless debate, 'religion vs. unemployment'.

Dharma ≠ Religion

Defining word dharma is one of the challenges. It's not religion that is true, but I would define it as 'qualitative, cultured performance as the duty with a responsible attitude that, when performed, it manifests as justice', when observed externally, only its 'intrinsic quality' is visible. Dharma can be used for personal conduct as an honest way of practicing Hinduism or other concepts, acts, or duties. But at the social level, as one identity to maintain unity, Hinduism can be identified as religion for the purpose of the census.

19

The Real 'Fake God'

In chapter 13, we studied the imposition of the 'formless' concept of God on Hinduism. This chapter is about how that mission was conducted through history books by choosing popular movements like bhakti and while explaining Ādi Śaṅkarācāryaḥs Advaita (oneness). Formless God can be equated with 'Nir-dravya' (God without substance) or 'Nirguna Brahmana' (God with substance but without attributes). Even Nirakar means shapeless, not formless. Ādi Śaṅkarācāryaḥ himself says, 'Study the Vedas and do rituals.'[1]

In Hinduism, Īśvara is supreme, and becoming one with him is a goal, and devotion is a booster to becoming one with him.[2] But you will see even in explaining the bhakti movement, 'formless one god' is imposed on Hinduism, and when any Hindu follows his Hinduism, i.e., Advaita (Aham Bramhasmi), he is termed by the Hinduphobic media as a 'godman' or a person who is on the wrong path.

Table 19.1

Bhakti movement according to most of the historians	Bhakti movement which is denied by or not included in school books
Limited to devotional songs written by some Hindu and Muslim saints	People go to temples, deity-centric festivals, perform rituals, chant mantras, kriya, charya, yoga, offer prasadam or food to deity. Isn't that devotion to devata/devi?
Which is inclusive with no Brahminical varna–jati discrimination	Then how was the economic function carried out at that time?

Bhakti movement according to most of the historians	Bhakti movement which is denied by or not included in school books
Projected as mass movement	Mass gathering and celebration happens like Jagannath yatra, Shivratri, and Kumbha Mela; when we are going to say this is also devotion.
In local language so it had mass acceptance.	When are we going to accept going to temple and performing rituals are also 'bhakti'? Even purohit chanting Sanskrit mantra in front of deity is also devotion, when will we accept it?
Focus on personality cult rather than what they are teaching. What content bhakti saints are giving is that according shastra or Hindu dharma? Any scope for verification?	Bhakti yoga is about bhav samādhi. According to pseudo-intellectuals, bhakti can be done by any liberal way by calling technicalities as orthodox Brahmanism. So that readers don't find Hindu bhakti yoga unique and scientific.
Temple = mosque = church is for prayer of respective religions. Some pseudo-experts say that the 'bhakti movement denied rituals' (but Hinduism god is with form so rituals are part of devotion)	Temple is not for prayer; it is for praise of deity and invoking him through devotion and going in bhav samādhi.
Whole goal is to surpass, suppress, or eliminate the unique factor of Hinduism so that cultural ethos is eliminated from history books and readers become clear slates, vulnerable to conversion. Many mediaeval-era saints from either religion were influenced by the fourth figure of Diagram 19.1 (p. 350); their teachings were not 'authentic' but they were still given weightage to promote an inauthentic value system in young minds.	

Ādi Śaṅkarācāryaḥ Way: Purest Truth

In certain sects, negation and cessation are the ultimate achievements. Whereas in Hinduism, negation and cessation from social life and diversity are merely the first steps of saṃnyāsa. As Śaṅkarācāryaḥ also

Table 19.2

Observe Diagram 19.1	Concept	Example and parallel terms	Ādi Śaṅkarācāryaḥ	Wrong interpretation by Western people
Prāthibhāsika truth	Material world is only reality	Material world	Maya, avidya, or illusion created by supreme reality.	Materialism
Vyāvahārika satya	The material world and the spiritual world exist	Binary or dvaita level truths, birth–death, earth–heaven, materialism–spiritualism. Me and deity/Īśvara are different. Deity = Saguna Brahman, Īśvara, Bhagavān, kuldevata, Ista devata	Ādi Śaṅkarāacharya accepts and writes sutras in praising deities: Shiva, Vishnu, Devi, Surya, and an Ista Devata, such as Karttikeya or Ganesha, which Śaṅkarācāryaḥ calls 'Saguna' Brahman as he was from shramana tradition of five deities (pañcāyatana). We are never told about Saguna Brahman or deities because →	God with form are pseudo-gods and goddess, inferior truth or inferior god, because formless god is real god. Or He is personal god/ theistic religion. So that Hindus give up rituals, lifestyle, and food and festival, celebrations related to deities. Which they call as 'qualitative god' (tathastha lakshana).

| Pāramārthika satya | Oneness is supreme and only mechansm, reality, existence. It is an ajnatent and mass software | No material–spiritual binary. Out of the cycle of birth and death. Beyond time and space equations. That thread which connects everything. Thread = Oneness = Paramātmā, Para-Bramha, Brahman, Parameśvara, Sada-Shiva, etc. | Aham bramhasmi (I am Brahman) Shivoham (I am Shiva). Mahakal supreme time and space (but not as binary). This is Śaṅkarācāryaḥ calls 'Nirguna Brahman'. Akalpurak according to Guru Nanak. Vishwarupam Vishnu (cosmic form). | Formless god is real and ultimate god/truth, qualityless god (swarupa lakshana). Formless god = 1 Advaita = monism = 1 god = impersonal god = non-theistic religion. Therefore, idol worship is wrong. |

negates diversity to realize oneness by calling it maya and avidya, so these Western pseudo-intellectuals call Śaṅkarācāryaḥ a hidden Buddhist to degrade his originality and his contribution to Sanatan dharma.

Diagram 19.1

1. Appearance

Pratibhasika Satya : what appears is only reality.

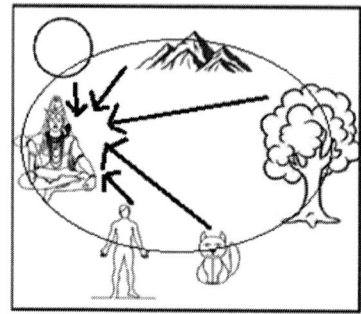

2. Devotion

Vyavaharika Satya: Know the 'supreme oneness' but accpeted in format of deity who will lead to liberation

3. Realization and experience

Parmarthik satya : The one who has realized/became that 'oneness'

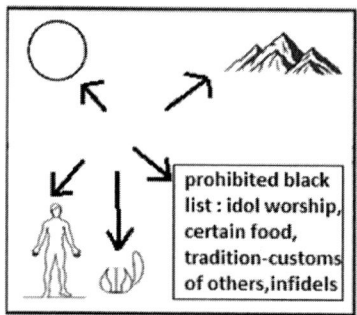

4. Uncompromized order of god

prohibited black list : idol worship, certain food, tradition-customs of others, infidels

Formless God (empty space/vaccume) Who reveals certain things, The god which is atheist assume in criticism

Methods of liberation exist in Upaniṣhads and from there, they exist in various sects in various ways. Śaṅkarācāryaḥ draws inspiration from Upaniṣhads/Vedas; in Upaniṣhads, its Parabrahma and Śaṅkarācāryaḥ call it Brahman, Shaivites call it Shiva, yoga calls it mukti, Sāṅkhya

calls it the liberation of purusa (one reality) from prakriti (diversity), vaisnavites call it Krishna as Viśvārupam (the one form which represents the whole universe). Not only this, Bramha satya is also explained in the Vedas in various ways. How can one say Śaṅkarācāryaḥ draws inspiration from Buddhism?
1. Prajnananm Brahman: *Rigveda (Aitreya Upanishad)*
2. Aham Bramhasmi: *Shukla Yajurveda (Brihadarnyaka Upanishad)*
3. Ahmasmi Bramhammasmi: *Krishna Yajurveda (Aitriya Upanishad)*
4. Tavamsi: *Samveda (Chandogya Upanishad)*
5. Ayamatma Bramha: *Atharvaveda (Mandukya Upanishad)*[3]

Proof of the existence of formless God
1. There are so many mysteries in the world that are unsolved.
2. We don't know the logic behind those mysteries.
3. There must be some mechanism by which the world is functioning in such an organized way.
4. Even climate, atmosphere, the self-sustaining nature of ecology, and constant motion and existence of planets and galaxies must have some reason that is not explained by science.

All these arguments are okay for the existence of God, but what makes you believe that such things are handled by him (genderless and formless God)? Why conclusion isn't scientific theory?
1. You make him play every role that humans can play, but in a larger parameter (mostly infinity), then you say he is only one? Did anyone count God as one or two?
2. Why can't two or multiple bodiless personalities be creators or managers?
3. Why can't multiple material things like black holes, protons, and neutrons and their checks and balances of gravity make the world stable?

Evil in theology of formless God?
If you want to sell defence equipments, then you have to create demand for it through artificial security threats. Same logic applies to evil, terrorize people, and then introduce God. In Hinduism, there

is no evil because we make people Īśvara. As there is no process of experience that creates ultimate reality, such a belief is created, i.e., belief vs. experience.

Formless God = atheism
Formless God and atheists have the same reference point; if you ask atheists and believers in formless gods to draw pictures of their gods, they will leave the paper empty. From the same reference, they will draw their cultural, religious, social, political, and economic theories. This becomes the union point of two theories that look opposite but are two faces of the same coin. That is why you will find both destroying 'tangible and intangible' culture beyond their ideologies.

God Is Omnipresent, Omniscient, and Omnipotent
Omniscient: Having infinite awareness, understanding, and insight possessed of universal or complete knowledge. In general, 'oneness' is aware of all the things, or the respective deity in various themes is aware of all the things, but at the same time, in Hinduism, our deities aren't always aware of issues; it is us who have to praise them and ask them what we want. Whenever any turmoil happens, rakshasa and daitya become powerful. The lower deities go to the higher deities (Brahma, Vishnu, Mahesh, and Shakti) to let them know the issue so that they can take further action because they are in their own meditative state, e.g., Shiva. At the same time, when deities are out of samādhi mode (Shiva), they are aware of issues, they do have access to everything, and they have knowledge of everything.

Omnipotent: Having total authority; having the ability or skill to do everything. In Hinduism, this whole universe is part of Īśvara. People find in Īśvara their respective deities, Vishnu, Shiva, etc. Not every deity is Īśvara. In Hinduism, the deity incarnates on earth. Do multiple things with skills. But at the same time, many times deities fail in their mission, and then they go to supreme deities like Brahma, Vishnu, Mahesh, and Shakti for solutions. Secondly, in Hinduism, the word authority or authoritarian is a very negative word. Even though the supreme has to carry out anything, he will carry out many things according to his wish with Lila, a soft approach to teaching lessons; if someone doesn't understand, then he or she will punish.

Omnipresent: Present everywhere at the same time. When Western religion and philosophy say God has no body, then how do they expect his presence? Secondly, the term 'everywhere' definitely does not indicate vishwarupa or all-occupying because these concepts are in Hinduism. God is everywhere, and God can have access everywhere are two different things. That is why the omnipresent concept is suitable for Hinduism only, as far as the vishwarupa and oneness concepts are understood.

The purpose of not accepting all three qualities as 'general' quality is to let readers know about diversity, complexities, and right-left every corner of Hinduism, (refer to pp. 59–60).

The seven vyarthis include:
1. Satya loka: This is the place of Brahma, where each person's atma is released from the inevitability of rebirth.
2. Tapa loka: Ayohnija devadasis live here.
3. Jana loka: The sons of Brahma live here.
4. Mahar loka: Enlightened beings such as Markandeya live here.
5. Svar loka: This is the area between the sun and the polar star, the abode of the Indra. It is a place, where all the Hindu deities live.
6. Bhuvar loka (or Pitri loka): It is the space between earth and the sun. It's the place where siddha's live (liberated people), siddha tradition finds its origin in Tamil Nadu and related Ayurveda is known as siddha.
7. Bhur loka: This is the earth. Hindus teach that it is one of the billions of inhabited worlds in the universe.

The seven patalas include:
1. Atala loka: Atala is ruled by Bala, who is a son of Maya. Maya possesses mystical powers.
2. Vitala loka: Vitala is ruled by the Hara-Bhava, who is a form of Shiva.

3. Sutala loka: Sutala is the kingdom of the daitya king Bali.
4. Talatala loka: Talatala is the realm of Maya. Shiva is also here under the protection of Maya.
5. Mahatala loka: Mahatala is where many nagas (serpents) live.
6. Rasatala loka: Rasatala is the home of the danavas and daityas.
7. Patala loka (or Naga loka): This is the lowest realm. It is the region of the nagas, ruled by Vasuki, a king serpent.

The above fourteen lokas are for the 'grahasthashram' people to improve their conduct and keep them connected to the 'science of oneness', i.e., Bramha loka, by making them understand hierarchy. Epics mention not only the incarnations of deities but also the characters from almost all the lokas descending to Bhur loka, e.g., apsara, rakshasa etc. We have various interpretations of this, which can be traced in chapter 13, (Table 13.3, p. 271).

Bhakti Yoga (Devotion to Uniting with Īśvara)

The main goal in Hinduism is mukti/liberation and all concepts like Īśvara, Brahman, Krishna, Shiva, Durga, etc., are the same name of that one reality, which is 'oneness'; to relate human beings with Īśvara, Brahman, etc. Some new terms (themes of liberation) were created by our great yogis, which are famously known as Advaita, dvaita, Visistadvaita, Shudhadvaita, and Dvaita-dvaita. These terms play a very important role in relating to and connecting human beings with Īśvara. As Hinduism believes in a user-friendly approach, all these terms, plus yoga, Sāṅkhya, mimamsa, and nyāya are also there. So these terms are not independent belief systems with different content. In the Western world, there is the term philosophy, which is the random, concretized imagination of their thoughts (covered in chapter 21). Philosophers believe in the terms 'God, body, matter, substance', etc., and combine these terms with finite and infinite according to choice.

Table 19.3

Definition	Terms
The one who believes in any one term out of God/body/soul/matter	He is known as a monist and philosophy known as monism
The one who believes in any two-terms out of God/body/soul/matter	He is known as dualist and philosophy is known as dualism
The one who believes in multiple terms out of God/body/soul/matter	He is known as pluralist and philosophy is known as pluralism
These terms are merely related to accepting existence according to mental logics of one, two, or multiple terms from God/body/soul/matter and 'believing' monism or dualism as the sole reality. Mental logics include metaphysical argument, material cause, formal cause, logical cause, etc.	

Unfortunately, Western mediocres equated Īśvara, Brahman, Shiva, Vishnu, etc., with God, and God–human relation Advaita and Dvaita were wrongly translated in the format of Western terms as shown in Table 19.4.

Table 19.4

Western terms	Hinduism
Advaita	Monism
Dvaita	Dualism
Shudhadvaita	Pure non-dualism
Dvaita-dvaita	Dualism with differences
Visistadvaita	Qualified dualism
Achintya bheda-abhed	Identity in differences

These Western terms are only related to accepting the existence of one, two, or multiple entities with multiple combinations, e.g., God, God–matter, God–soul, etc., whereas in Hinduism, Īśvara-human-atma material world is real and exists. Advaita, dvaita etc., are not related to accepting existence but express the relation of the world (human, material world) with Paramātmā. By using these terms, devotee establishes his relationship with oneness and seeks liberation, which is not the case in Western philosophy.

Advaita[4]

Advaita Vedanta expresses 'Brahman' a supreme meaning of liberation. It doesn't express reality in terms of its relation to Īśvara. Because relation means there are two entities, Advaita means only one reality, which is 'being one with Brahman' is liberation. We experience truth or perceive reality at three levels, which are expressed at three levels as shown in Table 19.2 and Diagram 19.1. Even while referring to other schools, like Dvaita, Shuddhadvaits (refer to Diagrams 18.1 and 19.1, pp. 342 and 350). You will undestand the meaning of the Vedic verse 'ekam sat vipra bahuda vadanti', which is 'the truth is one (oneness or liberation), and there are multiple ways to achieve that'. But that truth is different from the fourth figure of Diagram 19.1, i.e., God is one and He is formless.

Shudhadvaita by Vallbhacharya

Name given to Brahman: Shri Krishna
  Qualities of Shri Krishna:
1. Sat-chit-ananda: Truth with unique personality, intelligence, and ananada (the 1,000th part of the happiness of Indra, generally known as supreme happiness).
2. Smaller than smaller, greater than greatest.
3. Manifests himself in the form of the material world, and atma of humans reveals its tripartite nature of existence.
4. Brahman = Shri Krishna is not apparent as we see, but appearance, what we see, is not unreal.
5. Brahman = Shri Krishna = world/universe, and at the same time, Shri Krishna is the cause of the existence of this world (Western scholars try to express it as God as the material cause of this world, etc.).
6. Three aspects of Shri Krishna:

- Shri Krishna's physical existence (sat) manifests as a whole universe, which Westerners call the material world and the metaphysical world something different; in the case of Hinduism, there is no such dualism.
- Ātma of Shri Krishna (chit) has only existence and knowledge.
- Ananda aspect (ananda) remains unmanifested.

But his antarymin form (that which exists in the internal of everything) or oneness (supreme reality) exists in all three whole universes: knowledge (intelligence), existence, and ananda.

7. Jagat (world) is not exactly the same as him or dissimilar.
8. Jīva (living beings) similar to him, i.e., ability to become like him by becoming one with him. Antaryamin exists in everyone; he knows everything within us.

Hurdles while achieving liberation: Ignorance towards the real nature of atma, Īśvara, false identification of self with body only, etc. Just like Advaita Vedanta speaks about maya.

Dvaita-Advaita by Nimbarka

Name given to Brahman: Shri Krishna
Qualities:
1. Of atma:
   - Ātma (jīva) of human beings, and universes dependent on Shri Krishna.
   - Jīva is a knower, agent, and enjoyer, and Jīva is subtle and suffers through the birth–death cycle because of karma account.
2. Of universe: Made from three aspects:
   - Aprakrata (the super matter of which atma is made)
   - Prakrta (matter derived from prakriti with three gunas)
   - Kāla (time)
3. Of Shri Krishna:
   - Highest form, Brahman
   - Free from all good and bad qualities
   - Ruler of this universe (as intelligent oneness software that runs the whole universe as symbiosis)

- He is Krishna, and Radha is his consort (Brahman is Shri Krishna, and atma/universe is an extension of him as Radha)
- He is a creator, and the whole world is his manifestation

Relation between Īśvara and universe:
1. Īśvara/Brahman/Shri Krishna is not identical with the world; otherwise, 'oneness' would have all the qualities of the world. So they are different 'dvaita'.
2. At the same time, the world and that oneness are not separate from each other; otherwise, if they are separate and different from each other, then how can he control the world through symbiosis? So they are Advaita too. This also tells us that God is one and he is bodiless, yet he creates and controls the world, which is a logically incorrect concept.

Ways of liberation:
1. Maryada marg: Karma marg, jnana, upasana (followed by mostly Advaita followers)
2. Pushti marg: By bhakti, praise, and by the grace of God (way of nimbarka)

Achintya Bheda Abhed by Chaitanya Mahaprabhu
Name given to Brahman: Shri Krishna
Qualities of Shri Khrishna:
1. Sat-chit-ananda: Truth with unique personality, intelligence, and ananada (the 1,000th part of the happiness of Indra, generally known as supreme happiness)
2. All good qualities and power
3. Attribute identical to power
4. Free from all differences homogeneous, heterogeneous, internal, and external
5. Manifests himself as the universe and atma through his powers
6. Ātma and the world are its manifestations; they are identical (abhed) yet different (bhed)
7. His shakti (half) manifests in three ways:

- Sandhini Shakti that manifests as sat (the existence of the universe)
- Samvit Shakti that manifests as chit (intelligence or knowledge)
- Hladhini that manifests as ananda

8. Shri Krishna manifests himself in Jīva as 'Jīva Shakti or Tatastha Shakti', and he manifests as the universe and diversity as 'Maya Shakti'.

Ways of liberation:
1. Vidhi bhakti: According to the Vedas and shastras
2. Ruchi bhakti: Affection for Shri Krishna, e.g., just like gopis have an attraction for Krishna, and they become one in raslila; this is a metaphor. When Ram was moving towards Lanka, some rishis met him. So he said I am on a mission, but in the next birth, we will spend a lot of time together. In his next birth, he incarnates as Krishna, and rishis incarnate as gopis.

They believe Krishna and individual human/soul are two separate things, but one can connect with Krishna through a special relation or process that is called 'bhakti'. The unique thing is that for them, Krishna is supreme, but that should be understood in contexts. Sometimes 'Krishna' is marketed as only God, and other deities within Hinduism are referred to as inferior or pseudo by some people who understand 'Krishna' as an islolated concept, i.e., impose vyavaharik truth on parmarthik truth.

Visistadvaita by Ramanuja
Name given to Brahman: Shri Krishna
Qualities of Jiva: 'Jivaand Īśvara are different (dvaita)', but 'they are part of that supreme reality'. The first part of the sentence is 'vyāvahārika satya' and the second part is 'pāramārthika satya'. According to Ramanuja, pāramārthika satya or final liberation can be achieved only after death. Therefore, there is no feeling of bodylessness in liberation.

Ramanuja gives a new concept, 'Vishishth-Advaita' or unique oneness. He creates a new entity of existence. Whose Jiva is 'oneness' and whose body is 'human Jiva'. The human body is out of consideration, i.e., liberation is oneness formed out of human Jīva and oneness (stages 2–4 of Diagram 18.1, p. 342).

Ways of liberation: Only devotion is a way; believing in bodily pleasure and the karma account is ignorance, so one must empty the karma account before death. Liberation is possible only after death.

Dvaita by Madhavacharya
Name given to Brahman: Shri Krishna
Qualities:
1. Of Shri Krishna: He gives a fivefold difference between Brahman and others.
    a. Brahman and individual Jīva
    b. Brahman and matter
    c. Matter and individual Jīva
    d. One individual Jīva and another individual Jīva
    e. One material object and another material object
2. Of Jīve: These qualities are the same in Ramanuja and Madhavacharya.
    a. Nitya Jīva: eternally liberated
    b. Baddha Jīva: eternally bonded
    c. Mukta Jīva: liberated from world

Criticism: If Brahman, Jīva, and matter are separate, then how are they connected with one reality?

Ways of liberation: Only devotion is a way; believing in bodily pleasure and the karma account is ignorance, so one must empty the karma account before death. Liberation is possible only after death.

Shaivism
Schools or methods of liberation within Shaivism according to Madhavacharya:
1. Nakulisha pashupata
2. Shaiva:
    a. Virshaivism (linagayata)
    b. Shaiva sidddhanta (southern Shaivism)
3. Pratyabhijna (northern Shaivism or Kashmir Shaivism)
4. Rasesvara

5. Kapilaka (fifth and sixth according to Yamuna)
6. Kāla mukha

A. Shaiva Siddhanta: Shudhadvait
Name given to Brahman: Shiva
Qualities:
1. Of Shiva:
    a. Self-existence
    b. Essential purity
    c. Intuitive wisdom
    d. Infinite intelligence
    e. Freedom from all bonds
    f. Infinite grace
    g. Potential to do anything
    h. Ananada (supreme happiness with the flavour of bliss)
2. Of Shakti:
    a. Power used by Shiva to run himself and the universe, which is intrinsic to Shiva
    b. Form of Shakti that is conscious and eternal is known as Swarupa Shakti (Shakti with form)

Two stages of experience:
1. Satvika jagat: The world experience in oneness at the pāramārthika stage (wrong translation by Western philosophers = pure matter). This world was created by mahamaya or supreme creativity by Shiva (the term used to express the experience of oneness in words). Mahamaya is also known as shuddha bindu (pure bindu).
2. Prakrta jagat: The world experienced at prāthibhāsika and vyāvahārika stage (wrong translation by West = defiled/impure matter). This world was created by maya or an attractive illusion created by Shiva (the term used to express the experience of oneness in words). Maya is also known as ashuddha bindu (impure bindu).

Bindu: Bindu means 'infinity' represented by the dot '·'. In Hinduism, infinity is a dot, not '∞', because this '∞', a Western symbol, is binary in nature, where matter and energy dualism are present. This is not wrong, but to express 'oneness', which is experiencing infinity without instability or movement by oneself dissolving in it, the best symbol is Bindu. That is why prakrta jagat or material universe is pseudo-infinity or finite world (ashuddha bindu), and oneness (Shiva or Brahman) is pure infinity (shuddha bindu).

Mahamaya + Maya = Parigraha Shakti

3. Of Jīva: To explain qualities of Jīva, Shaiva uses the analogy of an animal or pashu. Jīvas are like pashu, which are bound by rope. Rope is known as pasha, which is the karma account; avidya (ignorance or false knowledge); and maya (attractive visible illusion), all three constitute as pasha.[5] Bondage is known as pashutva (essence to remain or exist as an animal). Because for the animal, life means basic needs, he can't think beyond basic needs or the apparent world. (That's why you see animals around Shiva in the picture; they are actually bonded jīvas that seek liberation under the guidance of Shiva.)

Ways of liberation:
1. removing pasha or bondage reasons is the liberation or mukti
2. becoming one with Shiva or achieving *Kailāsa*
3. Jīva = Shiva = oneness = Brahman

B. Kashmir Shaivism

Ādi Śaṅkarācāryaḥ divides reality into three levels: Prāthibhāsika satya, Vyāvahārika satya, and Pāramārthika satya, and he also gives Saguna Brahman and Nirguna Brahman. This he did to give understanding and difference between this apparent world and that supreme 'oneness' Brahman. So that our understanding becomes deep and the journey of liberation becomes easy. Similarly, Kashmir Shaivism gives thirty-six tattvas, which include the definition, types, stages, and qualities of apparent and supreme reality, such as hatha yoga, food, mantra-tantra, controlling sexual energy, the definition and function of intra-organs programmed in such a way as to lead to liberation, etc. Other schools

don't include these practices in their writings, but they do it Kashmir Shaivism's full package.
1. The five mahābhūta (5)
2. The five tanmātras (5)
3. The five karmendriyas – organs of action (5)
4. The five jñānendriyas – sense organs (5)
5. Antaḥkaraṇa – the inner instrument (5)
6. sat kañcukas (6)
7. suddha tattvas (5)

Name given to Brahman: Shiva
Qualities:
1. Of Shiva:
   a. Infinite, independent
   b. Foundation of knowledge
   c. All proofs and disproofs presuppose his existence
   d. Only reality which is pure
   e. He transcended his own manifestation (abhasa)
2. Of Shakti: Shakti is his inherent power

Ways of liberation: Karma, kriya, jnana, vidya, and devotion are all necessary. Benchmark is becoming one with Shiva.

Shaktism
Name given to Brahman: Shakti, Chandi, Chamundi, Durga, etc.
Qualities:
1. Mother of the universe
2. The supporter of earth and who lives in Manidvipa
3. Shiva without Shakti is shava (corpse)

Ways of liberation: Maya and prakriti are illusions or ignorances that exist in Shakti. Identifying oneself as finite instead of infinite is also a hurdle to liberation. This tradition includes the science of chakras, kundalini, and tantra-mantra. These terminologies and intra-organs are used as a tool to liberate oneself. Shakti tantra is of three type's kaula, samaya, and ajna. Uniting Shakti and Shiva is the benchmark

for achieving liberation. There are three levels of oneness in reality, like Advaita in Shaktism too.
1. Doing ajna to achieve that oneness
2. Chanting mantra-tantra and powerful mantras
3. Doing Vigraha puja and related rituals

Conclusion: All the schools follow bhakti, karma, and jnana marga, whether they accept or not, because of ideological limitations. No one condemns idol worship, rituals, or the existence of polytheism.

Proof of the Existence of Oneness?

We know this world continues to exist with a repetitive pattern of motion of planets, seasons, and birth–death, so that pattern that binds wholeness into one package is oneness. That thread that connects all of us is the 'ansha' essence left in all material form, including the human body, by that oneness.

There is the story of Narsimha (Vishnu avatāra), where Hiranyakashyap gets a boon from Brahma that no human, animal, or deity in its respective form as incarnation can kill him, so Vishnu comes in a new form (half lion + half human = Narasimha) to kill him because Hiranyakashayp troubles his own son, who is a devotee of Vishnu. Similarly, Daruka (rakshas) gets boon that even if he is cut into pieces, the blood that falls on earth while cutting him will culminate into new Daruka; so Kali (devi) cuts him into pieces, and she ensures no drop of blood falls on the earth by elongating her tongue as carpet.[6]

Both stories give the message that whatever combination you create in mind to remain untouched by God by denying his existence, he/she/ze or half animal–half human will come in any combination and will exist near you or within you.

So that oneness is not bound to any definition or body, so whatever logic or combination you create to deny his or her existence, he or she will come up with a new definition, a new logic, and a new combination of existence.

God/Oneness will eliminate that 'negating attitude' because till what point and combination of Īśvara and Brahman will you negate?

Ultimately, one day you will be isolated once you negate the whole world. Still, oneness somehow resides in you. This is how Hirnyakshayp destroyed the pillar on which the house was standing and committed suicide; in other words, he negated himself. Oneness cannot be denied; better you accept and fall in the ocean of Īśvara/Brahman/universe and enjoy oneness bliss, i.e., in Turya state. So that all the cyclone of doubts, critics, cheap attacks on deities, and thirteen debates (refer to p. 210) questioning the existence of 'oneness', all these hold no meaning. If you create any defence system to isolate yourself (denying existence or questioning the potency of deity), oneness somehow will break that system and prove omnipresence, i.e., vishwarupa! All these stories from the Puranas tell you the same truth of as Diagram 19.1, so that you seek the liberation process described in chapter 14. That is why there is not hate in Hindus towards Ravan, Bali, and Hiranyakshyap because they got liberation from their bad qualities through 'oneness'. This has a philosophical-level meaning.

So all the stories are directed towards the process of enlightenment, which are completely different from faiths that project God as formless and as an alter ego of the founder, who imposes his own rules/regulations on people in the name of the formless god with no scope for reform. Unfortunately, atheists pull Hindu deities into the same framework of atheism, which is directed against the formless god rather than studying the unique concept of Hinduism that is directed towards enlightenment through meditative practices as mentioned in chapter 14.

Today's Bhakti Movement

Today, the bhakti movement can be seen all over the world, and everyone is submerging in bhakti from America to Africa, Japan, etc. This is a tight slap to those who say Hinduism = discrimination. Then there are legends who say negative life philosophies like 'life is suffering' help to make humans flourish in every aspect of life, like spirituality, material life, and relationships. This negative atheist life philosophy should compare their life and psyche with YouTube videos of bhakti movement followers. The joy, blissfulness, happiness, spiritual ecstasy—everything just flows out of devotees. If you want practical proof, just see the joy and blissfulness in the people who celebrate 'wari' in Maharashtra of 'Vitthala' and 'Ganeshotsav', Dahihandi, Durga festival, Pongal, etc. 'Bhakti' is a symbol that Hinduism exists without any jati system or any other identity. People from the rest of the religion can compare how fundamental flourishes.

यदायदाहिधर्मस्यग्लानिर्भवतिभारत।
अभ्युत्थानमधर्मस्यतदात्मानंसृजाम्यहम्
परित्राणायसाधूनांविनाशायचदुष्कृताम्।
धर्मसंस्थापनार्थायसम्भवामियुगेयुगे

I appear; I incarnate in a human form whenever damage happens to dharma. Whenever adharma (manifestation of wrong concepts and injustice) increases, then I incarnate; to protect the right people to eliminate the wrong ones, to establish dharma (to create world order according to dharma), and I come from time to time in every era.

20

Why Rituals Are Always Meaningless?

Diagram 20.1

I Am not Hindu, Muslim, or Christian; I Am Only and Only Indian or Human!

1. In which language or culture does your name belong?
2. By which rituals will you get married, buried, or burned?
3. Where does toxic masculinity, gender biasedness, or psychology or behavior come from?
4. Whether you are aggressive about other religions or atheists, what makes you this? Means, do you belong to some group?
5. Even if you have a universalist value system (non-discriminatory), to which sanskara or teachings do you belong?
6. Festivals you celebrate, the nation which finds its identity in some culture, where does that identity belong?
7. Food dishes you eat (*Charak Samhita, Manosallasa, Akbarnama*), phrases you speak, people you welcome (atithi devo bhava), love you shower, where does it originate?
8. Is your history free from religion?
9. Does your etymology has roots in history and culture (i.e., hriday literally means the place where He lives)?

You don't have religion; a nation has no religion; terrorism has no religion; poverty has no religion; hunger has no religion; it means richness, wealth, peace of mind, collectivism—all things exist because of religious people.

Hey fellow reader, you are the victim of communist propaganda. Religion = discrimination, so that religion is kept as sub-nationalism and also as stigma, but atheism or disassociation with any cultural identity, even after indirectly or unintentionally following, is the litmus test of nationalism. The purpose of this chapter is to connect your psychology and behaviour with 'cultural identity'. So, that 'empty identity' of Bhārat culminates in a flourishing garden.

Hinduism is not about only 'mind peace', 'inner awakening', 'inner peace', which is nowadays branded as for consumers who are excessively submerged in materialism. Hinduism is about 'wholeness', where the complete life formula of conduct is taught. As I mentioned, being one with the universe, which is complete participation, is a goal. So many people project religion or meditation as anti-materialism or anti-wealth. This thinking itself makes meditation-mind-body brain candy different from rituals. We treat deity as part of the family, and anything first we offer to deity, we remind ourselves of that oneness, i.e., our deity has a human body, so there will be all humanistic things that will be attached to him, e.g., clothes, food, music, dance, bath, mantra chant, etc. The beauty where materialism, spiritualism, devotion, action, and ecstasy unite is known as puja.

Table 20.1

People and their ideology	Type 1	Type 2
What is it actually?	Non-existence, no-contribution, no creativity, inactivity, uniformity, ideological limitations to explore beyond, non-participation, no celebration, no intangible–tangible culture, illiteracy, choosing nothing, theme-less lifestyle, ideological barrier (untouchability with religion because of ideology), denial/negation, which always culminates in conflict (Has no future, only ceremonial existence)	Celebration, creation, celebration, activity participation, customs, rituals, mutual coexistence, diversity, liberation/moksha, enjoyment, oneness science (Has future)
How it is marketed?	Rationalism, communism, pseudo-liberty from the rules of religion, out-of-the-box thinking, freedom, peace, conflict-free life, love, humanity, and simplicity	Irrational, a false way of life, Brahminism, waste of money, reason for poverty, narrow minded, too complex, diversity = differences = discrimination

People and their ideology	Type 1	Type 2
Example	Non-inclusive or exclusive ideologies against Hinduism. (refer to p. 268)	Mahābhārata, Rāmāyaṇa, *Natyashstra*, Upaniṣhad, Vedas, Puranas' indigenous tribal practices
Category	1. I am only human; nothing has to do with religion. 2. I am only Indian; I don't believe in religion. 3. I am Indian first and Indian last 4. 6 non-inclusive players 5. Monotheist Hindus (refer to p. 268) 6. Religion is the opium of the masses. साहित्यसङ्गीतकलाविहीनः साक्षात्पशुः पुच्छविषाणहीनः । (A person devoid of interest in music, literature, and arts is indeed an animal without horns and tail!)	Bhārat on the ground level or reality: a. Archaeology, anthropology, history, geology, linguistics, food, etc. b. Heritage or cultural symbol in Bhārat and global platforms c. The Parade on 26 January on Kartavyapath d. UNESCO's heritage site and intangible culture e. Museums (Bhārtiya and foreign both) f. Lifestyle of Bhartiya people g. Village life, literature, drama h. Tourism of Bhārat i. National pledge mentions rich heritage j. Antiques that are kept in museums and rich houses are smuggled, etc. k. Protection under Article 51 A(f) of the constitution of Bhārat

People and their ideology	Type 1	Type 2
		l. Celebrated in Rashtrapati Bhavan and White house (Diwali party) m. Intellectual property rights & patent n. Dedicated ministry and departments at Central and state level o. Culture plays role in foreign policies p. International Yoga Day, GI tag
Future	Doing 'cyber attacks, cyber terror, data deleting, Dark Web, deep web' against enemies, e.g., destructive attitude.	Data localization, data protection, technicality and detailing, data security, content creation, NFT, big data, Cloud computing
	Choose your team wisely	

In Hinduism, rituals have meaning, and they are mentioned in detail in our books. It is us who don't know the meaning. There are two benefits to having a meaning:
1. No need for any artificial mechanism to make Hinduism exist,
2. Customs and rituals take you into bhakti mode, which leads to 'bhav samādhi' and finally liberation.

This is how rituals are denied in our history books or in general.
1. Rationality
2. Slavery of Brahmins
3. Modernization
4. Gender equality
5. Impurity/impure form of religion

6. Middleman's business
7. Unscientific (as they do inquire about the science and logic behind the material or costume used for celebrations like Halloween, carnival)
8. Non-sensical idol worship
9. Under the 'right to choose', Hinduism permits 'not to choose'
10. Rituals are complex and boring
11. No need to do this, you can have a direct connection with God
12. Social evils of society are projected as customs so that all rituals are eliminated in a generalized manner
13. Projecting yoga and dhyāna as real ways of experiencing Īśvara and idol rituals as merely non-sensical
14. Symbol of orthodoxy and blind faith
15. Business of looting (non-religious tertiary activities are not business; they are a medium of entertainment, e.g., art, culture, paintings, and celebration)

Why can't rationality, freedom, and the right to choose be directed towards 'following customs'? In Hinduism, the final goal is 'mukti', so all the rituals, praises of that supreme, songs, etc., are directed towards that. We have a method not only to establish 'direct contact with God' but also to directly become God: 'aham bramhasmi/shivoham' (I am Shiva).

There are Hinduphobics who brand 'customs, rituals, kriya, bhakti, temples' as 'meaningless ritualism' or the wrong way of Hinduism and 'meditation/yoga/liberation path' through various schools. Patanjali, Shaivism, etc., are the right way. But they don't know even people on the journey of liberation live in temples and monasteries and participate in rituals too because it helps to emotionally involve with Īśvara. In Brazil, people celebrate carnivals; they don't have any organized or theological framework for culture, which has a philosophical background. Even though we have all philosophical backup or background for this tangible and intangible culture, instead of having celebration mode, we have projected celebration as 'negative aspects of Hinduism' through anti-customs/rituals marketing. Why can't Jagannath Yatra, Pongal, Shivaratri, and Ambubachi Mela can't be the mode of celebration?

Why is it a meaningless ritual? When someone wants to sell a new product, they have to first convince them that the product they already have is illegitimate and useless; the same strategy is used to convert Hindus in the format of 'rituals are meaningless'.

Things Related to Hindu Deities
1. The artist who shows the art of carving
2. The festivals related to temples and deities
3. The prasadam and food related to the deity
4. Books and stories related to the deity that inspire the lifestyle and psyche of Hindus
5. People themselves copy deities, e.g., putting tilak, jewellery, and other cultural symbols
6. Puja and yajña, chanting mantras, and other rituals
7. Daily rituals, customs, or rituals on birth anniversary, etc.

Either you deny Hindu deities or rituals related to him/her both lead to the destruction of tangible/intangible culture, so that the common man loses contact with Hinduism and their future human capital also loses contact with temples. Also, reviving intangible culture becomes very difficult.

When Hindus were
a. politically suppressed
b. financial looted or weakened
c. infrastructure related to Hinduism was destroyed
d. history was not taught or distorted in history books
e. no sense of being Hindu or unity
f. attacked from communists, pseudo-liberals, and pseudo rationalist
g. Vedas, Upaniṣhads, Puranas, and all topics related to Hinduism were not taught
h. facing jati–varna discrimination and social evils
i. didn't know the meaning of rituals, traditions, and samskara

In such a situation, the thing that kept 'Hindu-ness' in Hinduism alive was rituals, customs, festivals, samskara, lifestyle, etc. This is power rituals, customs, and samskara. That is why aggressive enemies are trying to prove rituals are always meaningless. Just like Egyptians don't have any rituals or celebrations of their deities or tombs, they have lost contact with their ancient culture.

Temple-Related Myths

One of the myths spread by anti-Hindu historians is that Hinduism had two phases: first, the yajña phase in the Vedic period, which finished because of Buddhism, and second, the temple phase in the Puranic period, which was inspired by Buddhism. This attitude comes from exclusive religion's teachings: 'Something is the outcome of scripture compulsorily and one scripture or personality is compulsorily rival of other personality or previous scripture.'

Anti-Hindus also Created Binary Division within Hinduism Such As

Vedic Gods vs. Puranic Gods
Yajña period vs. Temple period
Vedic religion vs. Hindu religion
Vedic religion vs. Non-Vedic religion
Sanatan dharma vs. Hinduism

This kind of division is created just to eliminate Hinduism. If you cant destroy them then confuse them and divide them. Make Hindus fight within themselves.

But when we come to the late and post-Vedic periods, we can say with some certainty that idol worship had become an accepted practice in Hindu society; we find many sutras that deal with idol worship.
1. Mānavagrhyasūūtra (300 BC) clearly prescribes that if an image of wood, stone, or metal burns down, is reduced to powder, falls or breaks into pieces, or moves to another place, the householder must offer ten oblations to the fire with certain Vedic verses (one must note that grahyasutras are part of kalpasutras out of six *Vedāṅga*, so the claim that 'Vedas' don't have idol worship is completely false because all grshyasutras are ultimately connected to Vedic tradition). This sutra mentions that deities were made up

of not only stones but wood and metal too, plus yajña also existed with it.
2. Āpastamba, in his grahyasūtras, recommends offerings to the images of three deities: the Išana, Midhushi, and Jayanta. Apastamba makes it abundantly clear that stretching feet out 'towards, a cow, the gods, a door, or against the wind' is a big 'No'.
3. In the time of Gautama, temples referred to as daivakula by Sankhāyana were common, for he forbade answering calls of nature in front of these images or stretching feet in their direction.
4. Panini (300 BC) teaches that an image that is not for sale (like a mūrti in a temple) and is worshipped by a devotee (pujārī) who earns his livelihood attending to the images (if it were) Siva or Skānda (himself) has the same name as the deity whose it is. Meaning, if a pūjārī worships an idol (murti) as Siva, the mūrti becomes a deity 'Śiva' (and should not be treated as 'a figure' made of stone, clay, or metal), i.e., Pran Pratishtha ceremony and other ceremonies after the idol becomes a deity. This indicates popular acceptance of both murti and pūjārī in that society and the construction of temples for public worship as common practice. He goes on to add that a vāsudevaka is one who is a votary of vāsudeva, that vāsudeva was not a mere Kshatriya, but that the word was the name of deity. Commenting on the practice of Mouryas, who crafted images of deities. But in history books, you will see Mourya's connection to Buddhism and Jainism only to tell readers that when you give up Hinduism and choose Buddhism and Jainism you will grow like the Mourya empire.
5. Patañjali (100 BC–300 AD) says such a rule (deity rituals) would not apply to these images but only to the images of deity used for pūjā (worship), i.e., not every idol is made to be worshiped. It had gained a significant following in society; temples had become public places of worship and collective puja ceremonies, much like the public śrauta ceremonies. Interestingly, this period coincides with the emergence of the Maryann Empire (300 BC), the golden period of Hindu civilization. Kautilya's recommendation in the *Arthaśāstra* for the construction of temples dedicated to Siva, the Aśvins, Vaisravana, Lakṣmī, and Mādirā, in the centre of the

capital is indicative of how murtipujā and temples had firmly become a part of Hindu society.
6. By Manu's time (200 BC–200 AD), mūrtipujā was fully institutionalized. The brahmachārins were being regularly directed to worship images of deities. They were to 'circumambulate to the right, clockwise', the holy images they met on their journey. They could not step intentionally 'on the shadow of the (images of) deities, nor of a guru, king, Veda graduate, teacher, tawny (creature), or anyone consecrated for Soma sacrifice'. This placed the images on par with the guru and the king.[1]

Yajña vs. Murti Puja Myth

Vedic devata does reflect on temples, and temples do have yajña shala or place of doing yajña as separate infrastructure, which shows the importance given to it. There is one yajña which is known as *Pañcāyatana* yajña, which has five yajña kundas, one in the centre and the other four at the four corners. Later periods, the same Pañcāyatana style is reflected in temple construction. In yajña, 'devata/deity' is invoked (avahan) and praised, then eventually asked for help. The same thing happens in the temple in front of devata. There is nothing like 'prayer' in Hinduism, just like in other faiths. This shows murti puja was not counter to yajña or inspired by Buddhism. Temples were created by some kings to create employment through construction, as it takes a long time and mass labour. Today, also infrastructure projects drive forty various sectors.

Idol worship inspired by Buddhism is a myth

Temple construction science is mentioned in Hindu books called *Āgamas*, right from the construction of the foundation, pranpratishtha, location of the temple, and tithi (astrological timings). You will see temples where the sun rises and touches deities' feet on a particular day in a year. You will also see temples allied in a straight line from north to south (Kedarnath, Kaleshwar, Ekambareshwar, Chidambaram, and Rameshwaram). Temples are constructed with multiple factors according to Hindu geography, astronomy, the solar-lunar eclipse, economy, etc. By no angle, they seem inspired by

Buddhist infrastructure, in contrast to Buddhist stupas incorporating Vedic fire alter.[2]

The economic significance of the temple is that it gives employment to pujaris, cooks of temples, dancers of temples, musicians in temples, Vedic schools attached to temples, caretakers, and temple-led development by supplying flowers, prasadam, and all puja samgari. In the later period, temples started giving loans to the Vaishya (businessman) community to conduct business. Temples also had checks like modern banks, which means if you submit cash in the temple in the south, they will give you receipts, and when you go in the north for yatra, you can submit receipts in the north temple, where they will give you cash for expenditure. So the role of the temple became more advanced in later periods as compared to yajña. But today, the role of the temples and yajña is replaced by the RBI, other commercial banks, stock markets, etc. Secondly, Hindus are not united as a democratic alliance under any organization; everyone is building their egos with jati leaders and shallow cult leaders, Pseudo-babas, etc. That's why the management of temples and using their wealth for the protection of Hinduism and Hindus is not yet a reality or vision.

The logic of temple control

It's not possible practically that communism will survive because of unsound, impractical policy. Then what is the best way to convince the people that communism still exists? So control temples only (not a mosque, church, or private industry profits) so that majority communists who are Hindu by birth believe that 'communism still works', which is a practical way to get majority votes because people who are Hindu by birth but communist by ideology are in the majority. They do majority vote bank politics in the name of communism, but when someone (Hindu by practice) raises their voice for a discriminatory approach towards Hindu temples, they call it 'majority politics'. Which culminates in the weakening of Hinduism and the strengthening of other religions in society.

State controls temple means if the Hinduphobic party comes in power then they can interfere in temple functioning and infrastructure. If the state controls temples, temples are property of the state, which means the state has religion, which means those Bhārtiya states that control temples aren't secular but Hindu states because only temples are controlled, not mosques or churches. They don't have the guts to control or abolish private property because they (politicians) also have property, so to convince people 'communism still works', they give cute lollipops of controlling and looting the property of the temple. This controlling temple phenomenon is not limited to Hinduphobic political parties. State-sponsored loot of 1,10,000 Hindu temples controlled by the state; appointment of non-Hindus in Hindu temples; state will decide how or which puja will be conducted. Out of 6,000 crores in earnings, temples receive 58 crores. Plus, temple land is also encroached on.[3]

That era has gone when people used to come and destroy or loot the temple; now it's not possible because the world is watching. So this trick is used to keep people away from temples so that one day they become ruins because of a lack of maintenance. So the first step to making this happen is convincing Hindus that 'rituals are always meaningless'. Once symbols, signs, and rituals are eliminated from identity, then who will go to the temple? Then it becomes very easy to loot temples.

There is no discussion in the Hindu community about temple management, whether it should be centralized or any other model of temple management should be found.

What Model Should Hindus Adopt?
1. Centralized agency with state-level branch in all twenty-eight states and nine Union Territories
2. Collecting funds from all temples through a 'mechanism agency' on a daily or monthly basis
3. Moving towards digitization of donations either in temples or direct donation to account of a Central agency
4. The collected funds will be divided into Centre and state agencies with an X:Y manner; the percentage of them may change from time to time

5. The collected funds will be used by:
   1. **State agency**
      a. payment of pujari and worker, management
      b. giving funds to individual temples for the maintenance of temples
      c. giving funds for celebrations at festivals
   2. **Central agency**
      a. welcoming non-followers to Hinduism
      b. carrying out the international mission
      c. building library's all over Bhārat which will have books on Hinduism
      d. supporting jatis and artisans who are part of Hinduism but weak financially, supporting poor Hindus so that no one becomes vulnerable for conversion
      e. setting up standard fees for ceremonies conducted by purohits (sixteen samskaras)
      f. supporting victims of Hindu exodus, e.g., Tamil Hindus, Sikhs in Afghanistan, Kashmiri Pandits
      g. conducting exams to appoint someone as pujari or worker, manager
      h. marketing Hinduism and supporting pro-Hindu intellectuals
      i. carrying out cultural festivals and Hindu carnival
      j. study of anti-Hindu practices
      k. building rationalism and enhancing Hindu human capital
      l. creating awareness in Hindus
      m. donations to natural calamities all over the world, irrespective of the identity of the people
6. Ashrams, mathas, personal spiritual ashrams, multiple Hindu organizations, etc. will all be covered with an asymmetric approach to donation and distribution of funds. The asymmetric approach is very important because Hinduism is very diverse.

The Biggest Question

Other than Brahmins and temples, there are various professions that have a monopoly of particular jatis over infrastructure, skills, and market, e.g., shipbuilding, farming, etc. Why does no one question this monopoly? Other than this, modern business ownership is transferred in hereditary manner; why does no one question that? Will the state or the people go to control that too? Or controlling temples is only satisfying because 'hating Brahmins' satisfies equality? The model that I suggested will also develop monopolies after a few years and personal interest, so breaking monopolies and creating a new model should be processed; otherwise, communism may come.

Someone has a vision, then he/she has a mission; when someone has a mission, then he/she has a plan; when someone has a plan, then he/she develops implementation resources and mechanisms. When someone has all these resources, to implement them efficiently, one ensures discipline and time management. This is the success order; one must not go in reverse order.

Popular Questions
1. Where is it that idol worship and going to the temple solves issues?
2. Where did God say 'pore milk, ghee' for all these things?
3. Where is it that God asked to do these rituals?

Answers: The Vedas, *Āgamas*, etc., clearly mention rituals regarding deity, yajña, sixteen samskras, etc. In Āgamas temple construction, deity related all macro-micro rituals are written. If Brahma is available through food or prasadam, then what is the problem with consuming that? The problem is that 4 per cent of people pay income tax, which needs to be solved for because Hinduism can't be held responsible for poverty, at least in secular countries. This is the real art of marketing: making people believe in the 'non-existence in the name of bodiless God' and 'demoralizing the ritual practice of that which exists'. They have just removed the joy of celebrating civilization. Grhayasutra's broadly includes following things in detail, and we are told rituals are meaningless and religion is an excess of the rules and regulations.
1. Social organization (varnas and ashrama systems)
2. Family life and the position of women
3. Morals and manners (good conduct, truth, and dharma)
4. Purusharthas (trivarga, karma, ethics)

5. Yajñas (daily, periodical, and special) and worship
6. Occupations (other than the primary ones described for the four varnas)
7. Agriculture and cattle breeding
8. Trade and commerce
9. Transport and communication
10. Cities and village life
11. Personal aspects (dress, ornaments, hair fashion, food and drinks, amusement)
12. System of governance (functions of rajas and maharajas, revenue and expenditure, civil administration, army and warfare)
13. Law and justice (penal and civil laws, administration of justice)
14. Saṃskāras for maternity and child welfare
15. Education system (includes saṃskāras related to education)
16. Marriage (laws and customs, rites and festivities)
17. Death and funeral (pre-cremation, cremation, and post-cremation rites)
18. Shraddhas (activities for the ancestors)

All the things can't be followed because of the change in the socio-cultural-economic sphere of Bhārtiya society but at least 'manual' shall be provided state-wise to all Hindus.

Colonial Conspiracy to End Rituals

If you observe 'social movements, social evil eradication movements, pro-Hindu movements, neo-Hinduism movements, neo-Hindu religious organizations, critics of Hinduism, anti-Hindu radical organizations, Hindu personality cults, anti-Hindu personality cults, neo-revivalist movements of Hinduism, communists, atheists, and social reformers' of the British era, all of them have different aims and goals, but there are some common points in them, that also irrespective of their geography. These people and movements never met each other; there were no common meetings, yet there was a common core agenda.
1. Selective atheism: Idol worship, polytheism is wrong, but silence on 'monotheism', i.e., condemning only Hindu deities[4]

2. There is only one God, polytheism and idol worship are social illness according to IPS Rajiv Ahir in his book on modern India (widely used book for civil services)[5]
3. Rituals are meaningless
4. Hinduism is Brahmin religion or Brahmin imposition
5. Do marriage without Brahmins[6]
6. Last rites in Hinduism are non-sensical (including Pitra)

Even though there was Jamindari, there was no 'land reform movement' anywhere in Bhārat as ideology, social movement, or organization because it would have taken the shape of 'communism', which would have ultimately turned against 'British imperialism'. That is why almost all land reform movement happened in the post-independence era as individual movements on respective geography, not as pan-Bhārat ideology.[7]

This is direct proof that all these movements were somewhere controlled by the 'colonials' themselves, because if the colonial masters had attacked directly Hinduism, then the 1857 episode of cow cartridges would have been repeated. If they had promoted this through their Bhārtiya agents under the title of rationalism, atheism, and the anti-Hindu movement, then all Hindus would have united under 'save Hinduism', so they introduced this common agenda in all movements and personalities cults from north to south. The best example would be atheists; if God doesn't exist, then one should deny God with form (idol) and formless God both. Why did they oppose only idol worship? If God exists everywhere, then 'why doesn't everywhere include idols?' The conclusion is that 'idol worship, rituals, polytheism, worshipping environment, etc.'—all these things were not part of 'exclusive religions', as these things are kept on the 'prohibited list', so as to make Hindu human capital compatible for conversion into 'exclusive religions', these changes were being carried out. Then there are pseudo-intellectuals who say, 'Colonial masters were only looters and rulers; they didn't promote any religion or suppress others.' Now you understood the title of the book 'decolonizing Hinduism'.[8]

Karma is broadly classified into five types as follows:
1. Nitya karma (daily obligatory duties)

2. Naimittika karma (occasional obligatory duties)
3. Kamya karma (rites done to attain desired results like Jyotistoma yajñas for reaching heaven)
4. Prayaschitta karma (rites for expiation of sins)
5. Nishiddha karma (forbidden action like killing, drinking, etc.)

Suggestions to know about rituals, their meaning, types, etc.
1. *Hindu Rites and Rituals: Origins and Meaning* by K.V. Singh[9]
2. *Hinduism: Rituals, Reasons and Beyond: A Journey Through the Evolution of 5000 Years Old Traditions* by Ashok Mishra

21

God of Baseless Colonizers

Introduction to Western Philosophy and Science
When you want to build civilization and life, the first thing one will do is observe and know geographic conditions. According to that, one will codify economy, polity, society, and culture, which will change from country to country because of diverse geography. But one who is neither interested in building himself or others, but only interested in running his own state by invading or colonizing others, then his will is metaphysics: 'one world, one rule, one king, one religion, one God, one substance'. So coming to the conclusion that 'one' has roots in philosophy, which later is used by religions to colonize the world. When any culture or person stands, it has a background; no theory or book is without a background. If you read Western philosophy, then you will find two things: God and substance.

Expressing the Existence and Origin of the Earth
Philosophers: To express the origin of the earth, universe, or existence, their assumption is that there is some 'base', so this base, according to philosophers, is the background/origin/source/creator. Which they call it God. Who does the entire task? The kiddish assumption is that if humans can do a small amount of work, then creating a whole universe is a big task, so someone big, bodiless man, is there (not women or transgender). He is genderless. Plato, Aristotle, Descartes, and Leibnitz are all in this category.

Scientist: To express the origin of the earth, universe, or existence, their assumption is that there is some 'base', so this base, according to a scientist, is some date/some spark/event. Which they call the big bang. Which is responsible for all existence. The kiddish assumption is that there must be 'one' event to exist something (not even multiple) at the same time, like temperature or pressure because creation is a big task. How can infinity be a quality of temperature or pressure?

Hinduism believes in a baseless and rootless origin, which is why it's called 'Sanatana'. This reality existed from infinity and will exist till infinity and creation and destruction keep happening. There are some stories too of creation, but with some deeper meaning, which is getting decoded nowadays.

Problem of Change
Philosophers: To express change philosophers like Plato fail. So people come up with their various kiddish theories: 'he is an unmoved mover', 'objects have potential in latent form to transform themselves', 'change happens because of God as the final cause'.
Scientists: They explain change with a case study, with separate formulas or separate expressions in chemistry, physics, and biology.

Problem of Substance
Philosophers: Just like a potter shapes clay, substance is 'base', which is modified by some reason or agent like God, pre-establish harmony by God, diversity in substance exists because of an external cause, etc. Some people call matter a material substance and the soul a spiritual substance. Some say substances have various qualities that cause diversity.
Scientist: Scientists don't consider that some base or basic material is used to create the world. They go deep to the micro-level of the atom, the subatomic level, and the macro-level of the cosmos. They experience reality.

Perception of Reality
Philosophers: They divide existence in a binary way. Outside the body and inside the body and give their theories. Whatever you see outside is merely an idea, not reality or its reality. We perceive it by considering ourselves as the locus of perception.

Scientists: They also have binary outside–inside division. Their perception is based on previous theories that they have experienced and things they have experienced. For scientists, materialism = reality won't be the correct expression.

This, in both a philosophical and scientific way, creates a background for a new concept that is 'imposing bookish-imaginary concepts on reality'. The outcome of philosophy is the subjects of the humanities, and the outcome of science is the environment, ecology, and space sciences. The outcome of philosophy is that humanity (human interest in economic terms) is the base of religion, which gives birth to the suppression of scientific temper and leads to climate change.

But at the same time, this subject of study exists separately, but reality exists as one. That is why the development of new dimensions of reality is, very important, because choosing one of these ways to know reality is not wrong, but these are not the only ways. Allopathy has a cure for 4,000 diseases, and Ayurveda has a cure for almost 17,000 diseases, and Ayurveda considers reality as one and gives holistic lifestyle, solution, etc., i.e., all factors are considered in Ayurveda. Today, the same thing is called as 'One Health' approach by the World Health Organization (WHO). In Asian countries, like Bhārat and China, there are multiple traditional methods that are not known to the world.

Development of Logic

Philosophers: Philosophies make assumptions regarding God, substance, realities, monadology, etc., and give reasons and logics like ontological proofs, cosmological proofs, logical proofs, causal arguments, etc.

Scientists: They come to a common conclusion when they see the repetitive behaviour of phenomena and find out the reason that is common in all events, and they call that common reason as reason or logic that is responsible for that phenomenon. This is reflected mostly in topics like the binomial theorem, differentiation–integration, permutation–combination, trigonometry, etc. These formulas help create the same phenomena artificially. There are two things in scientific observation and discovery: observation is 'gravity' and the formula's functions of gravity is discovery. In Hinduism, there was no such binary, and in those times, there was no culture of patent, so we never got recognition. Western people, even when observing something small in the environment, file patents, which have been known to many people in third-world countries over the years. Today, also because of this, not applying for a patent is in the genes of Hindus, which causes huge loss for Bhārat. Even in case of biodiversity, as per the national geographic survey says there are 8.7 million species.[1] Hinduism and Jainism accept a figure of around 8.4 million, which is very close to a scientific survey.[2]

It's Not Bhārtiya Philosophy

Western philosophy is impractical (in terms of experiencing God), which has nothing to do with reality, but somewhere deep that philosophy becomes psychology and starts appearing as real because it seems intellectually real. On the other hand, philosophers like Descartes, Leibniz, and Newton who are philosophers on the one hand but are mathematicians and scientists on the other. That is why their works are two-dimensional and interrelated. That is why it's not practically possible to divide science and philosophy into binary formats. Yuval Noah Harari in his *Sapiens: A Brief History of Humankind* mentions objective reality (river, mountain, etc.) and imaginary reality (God, religion in story format) in the philosophical terms material world and metaphysics. Accepting imaginary reality as only imagination and limiting it to religion and God is a narrow view; even scientific theories are imaginary sometimes. I deny this binary division too. But the problem of philosophers and scientists is that they both create orthodoxy, which is anything that doesn't fit in the formula or logic that is wrong, incorrect, or doesn't exist. When it happens in the case of philosophers, it gives birth to monotheism and creates communal clashes based on belief systems. Evolving to come to 'single solution' like God, substance, monotheism, monocropping, mono-diet, monoculture, and you know the negative of this 'mono'. The monotheistic idea of concluding with a 'single' conclusion also reflects in science. Even if you see Darwin's theory, it's about 'we all had one ancestor that is common in all species'. To justify this, biologists try to categorize all of them into a few categories: genre, sub-species, etc. Whether it's religion or some scientific theories, they are the outcome of psychology. 'Conclusion comes to one term, not many.'

Bhārtiya philosophy is created or exists with some practical life goal; it is created by keeping human psychology in mind. That is why, for 5,000 years, people have practiced Hinduism without reading books on Hinduism. On the other hand, Greeks, Egyptians, and all other civilizations vanished. So a practical approach makes Hinduism unique. So it's not just philosophy but a way of life.

Mind-Body Brain Candy Business

Western philosophers used their liberty and gave childish theories of mind, body, soul, and God connection, and psychologists added the new term intellect. Further, modern 'self-styled masters came', who copied the basics from Hinduism and some terms from Western philosophies and psychologies and created the new product 'spirituality' and started selling it for well-being and inner happiness.

Those English gurus, to make their 'mind, soul, spirituality, spirit, divine, God' brain candy more acceptable, combine it with happiness, joy, and life solutions. I don't understand how anyone can stay 100 per cent in one emotion, i.e., happiness, irrespective of situation and events. Horror, anger, interest, fear, excitement, craving, sadness, confusion, lust, etc., are part of human life when a person is a part of society because in society events keep occurring. The problem is not lack of happiness; the problem is being in one emotion for a long time beyond the event or situation, which creates boredom, and a longer duration creates suffocation, which transforms into frustration. If you want to be in one emotion or beyond emotion or pure happiness, then you have to go outside socio-economic life to avoid events and their effects. That is what we call sannyāsi, which is the first step towards liberation or sat-chit-ananda. These spiritual masters give brain candy of happiness through books that look good but are impractical. Then there are useless fellows who keep saying, 'Keep smiling, be happy', but never tell me why should I smile and be happy always? What about other emotions? When you are part of society, there are six ways to achieve the so-called happiness.

1. Do any act responsibly so that when you reap fruits, you should not get shocked by sadness or surprise. A responsible attitude makes you aware of fruits, which minimizes the effect of sorrow if karma is like that. People do karma or activities by whims and fancy, then keep crying while reaping fruits.
2. Do that work that your heart loves; otherwise, if your brain is busy with something and your heart loves something else, then you will use your brain to earn something that you can spend on what your heart demands. Which is a huge waste of time and waiting for happiness, which we call getting caught in dvanva (confusion between two choices, in this case heart and brain). So if your heart loves cricket, then utilize your brain and body to play cricket, take it as a responsibility, and earn money by choosing it as a profession (which we call Advaita or oneness of heart-mind-body). Even if you earn little, you will be happy because you already have got happiness, and the amount is merely for some needs.
3. You are not unhappy; sometimes you are bored because of inactivity. Inactivity is the biggest boredom, so if you are part of society, then the activity is a necessity that will make you busy, and the question of happiness will vanish. If you are sannyāsi then yoga–dhyāna and other inner processes should be done. If you think enlightenment is nothingness, then you are heading towards boredom.
4. When you realize certain activities are what make you forget happiness and you choose consumerism and related things to forget the thought 'how to remain happy' then you are in a vicious cycle of being in kick by doing various acts for new kicks. A time comes when no kick works. then you move towards new kick spirituality. So better you make bhakti metaphysics part of your lifestyle from starting rather than accepting it after intense materialism. I am not saying stop consumption, but eliminate tamas, increase rajas, and move towards sattva.
5. Another thing is to reduce or increase the intensity of reaction to every emotion according to the situation so that you understand what the right emotion is and its intensity while conducting any transaction or business in life, which we call vyahara dnyana or knowledge of socio-economic-emotional transactions.

6. Merely doing dhyāna, prāṇāyāma, or puja for few minutes in the morning won't work. You need to set up a complete lifestyle from thinking, diet, breathing patterns, sitting postures, code of conduct, problem-dealing mechanism, everything correctly, but that doesn't mean giving up dhyāna, prāṇāyāma, or puja. So practice the right belief system and thinking as per shastra or oneness so that psychologically and physiologically, performance always remains high and dhyāna and prāṇāyāma and bhakti intensify it.

What these English gurus teach is to practice the lifestyle of sannyāsi in social life to remain happy, and the whole goal of happiness becomes a failure. That is why Ādi Śaṅkarā gives three truths to be followed at respective platforms, and one is expected to move towards Prāthibhāsika (apparent truth), Vyāvahārika (truth to be used for socio-economic-emotional transactions), and Pāramārthika (ultimate truth or that oneness which sannyāsi achieves). You have to act according to the situation.

Spirituality Business

'Spirituality' first began to arise in the 5th century and only entered common use towards the end of the Middle Ages. In a Biblical context, the term means being animated by God. The *New Testament* offers the concept of being driven by the Holy Spirit, as opposed to living a life in which one rejects this influence.

In the 11th century, this meaning changed. 'Spirituality' began to denote the mental aspect of life, as opposed to the material and sensual aspects of life, 'the ecclesiastical sphere of light against the dark world of matter'. In the 13th century, 'spirituality' acquired a social and psychological meaning. Socially, it denoted the territory of the clergy: 'The ecclesiastical against the temporary possessions, the ecclesiastical against the secular authority, the clerical class against the secular class.' Psychologically, it denoted the realm of the inner life: 'The purity of motives, affections, intentions, inner dispositions, the psychology of the spiritual life, the analysis of the feelings.'

In the 17th and 18th centuries, a distinction was made between higher and lower forms of spirituality: 'A spiritual man is one who is Christian, more abundantly and deeper than others.' The word was also associated with mysticism and quietism and acquired a negative meaning.

Today in the 21st century, spirituality is about meditation and 'mind, soul, spirituality, spirit, divine, God' brain candy, which is a philosophical comfort zone when materialism, atheism, and theism have failed. In the Western world, people do yoga meditation however they want, it is still beneficial to them. They have removed the devotion and liberation aspects of yoga to make it look 'themeless' or non-Hindu, to make it more acceptable to conservatives in the West and to steal the patent of yoga from Bhārat.[3]

Table 21.1

Terms used by Western mediocre	Actual terms with depth and diversity of experience
mind, soul, spirituality, spirit, divine, God, subconscious mind	Sūkṣma śarīra, manas, citta, buddhi, ahankara, divya sharira
consciousness spirituality, salvation, ecstasy, prayer, transcendentalism, mysticism	Advaita Vedanta, dvaita, siddhi, Turiya, sushubdhi, samādhi, cosmic experience
power yoga, aerobic yoga, peaceful yoga, Islamic yoga, Christian yoga, yin yoga, acro yoga, stealing yoga as physiotherapy[4]	raj yoga, kriya toga, kundalini yoga, karma yoga, hatha yoga, bhakti yoga, mantra yoga, dnyana yoga, swara yoga, ashtanga yoga, siddha yoga
scripture	sutra, bhashya, vartika, tika, itihasa
Holy verses of scripture	shloka, mantra, sukta, stotram, sutra, shatkam, sashtakam

Think Positive to Fail in Life

Another thing that is a symbol of this English guru's is 'be positive, think positive'. This is a non-sensical thing. Because the division of reality into positive and negative is again binary, just like truth vs. falsehood and wrong vs. right. Something that is positive for you may be negative for other people; similarly, something is right for you may be wrong for others. So it's the self-interest of various stakeholders that divides right from wrong. For example, Gilgit Baltistan being part of Pakistan may be positive thinking or the right thing for Pakistan, but it is a false claim. The reality is that Pakistan is occupied illegally, and it's an official part of Bhārat. It's a difference of opinion; nothing is positive or negative.

Be positive in teaching is indirectly saying, 'Bring internal change in you, don't involve yourself in world affairs, and stay unaffected, which will be the reason for happiness'. I think sannyāsi/brāmhacaryā is the same thing, not evolving in world affairs and moving towards Īśvara. But this thing works until world affairs are not physically or in any way against you. Once they turn against you, you will be busy adjusting and convincing your mind to stay unaffected, and they will destroy you. That is why it's very important that when you are part of society, you consider pros and cons and geopolitics or Vyāvahārika satya, but that doesn't mean to avoid turning inward and stop changing oneself.

What if something doesn't work according to your positive thinking? That is why one must come out of the positive–negative binary and start calculating self-interest, collective interest, and enemy interest; otherwise, be positive and turn inward, move away from responsibility, and practice impractical sannyāsi in social life. So this is positive, think positive is for those who are brahmachari, sannyāsi, vanaprastha (retired) stage. Others should understand strategic existence, dynamic reality, and the conscious being to remain in competition, sometimes as a leader and a follower, and sometimes just as a competitor according to the situation at the personal, national, and world level.

The 'think positive' is merely hope given to a middle class or service sector, which is good at the initial stage but will never make you a businessman or capitalist because for that risk has to be taken, which includes loss, quality failure, market dynamics, and choice of consumer, which will not be according to your 'infinite positive thinking'. That is why no rule is universal; one must understand it in context, space, and time; no one is expected to be aggressive always by indulging in conflicts, and no one is expected to be away from conflict by a self-convincing peace philosophy. One must follow by observing the situations of self, people, nation, humanity, and ecology.

Table 21.2 Terms used to explain so-called Bhārtiya society

Essence of Hinduism	
Professional approach	**Jack of all trades, master of none**
Vedas, Upaniṣhads, Purāṇas, siddhas, Āgamas, Dharmaśāstra, festivals, char dham, common lifestyles of Hindus, 16 saṃskāras, yoga –meditation, books on cosmology, Vedic math's, science, astrology, Ayurveda, economics, society, polity, Kamasutra, mukti-moksha, architecture, traditions	Inclusive, tolerance, peace, unorthodox, orthodox, rational, irrational, modern, backward, literate, illiterate, new, old, neutral, biased, moderate, extremist, global, scientific, unscientific, dogmatic, ethical, unethical, inclusive, exclusive, open, liberal, conservative, secular, communal, atheists, religious, logical, illogical, truth, secular, respecting others religion, god is one, all religion teach same thing,

This is what Western and so-called Bhārtiya philosophy, science, religion, civilization are all about. Mahatma Gandhi once said we must practice our own religion (Hinduism) and let other new philosophies and religions come into Bhārat, and we must learn from them too.

Now it is up to you to decide what to learn from Western philosophy/religion.

∞Kāla Bhairava: The Singularity of Artificial Intelligence

Singularity is a problem created by artificial intelligence that is beyond human control. Artificial intelligence behaves by its own will, and carries out functions without any boss or owner, and owns decision-making power and implementation in its own hands. There are no checks and balances in the hands of humans. Its unstoppable uni-directional growth, i.e., 'singularity'. But according to me, it's not just related to artificial intelligence but to other aspects too.

Traditional Challenges

Uncriticized religions and ideologies give rise to 'unscientific or irrational practices', which are eternally practiced in every era, which itself is a human rights violation in the format of 'social evils'. This makes the rest of the religions and ideologies grow unilaterally and seamlessly without checks and balances. Even though not controlled or funded by anyone, people get access to data as consumers (the right to choose), and they self-radicalize and carry out tasks independently, which disturbs communal harmony and global peace.

Non-traditional Challenges

1. Eternal exploitation of ecology for eternal profits
2. No sense of waste recycling or circular economy
3. Uncontrolled artificial intelligence and its unethical use and threat of singularity
4. Automated, uncontrolled growth of genetically modified animals or plants
5. Development of anti-microbial resistance by haphazard use of medicine

6. Exposing nanomaterials to the environment
7. Dumping every waste in soil, air, water, etc.
8. Darknet and Dark Web giving seamless access to 'banned' content, i.e., online illegal market, i.e., cyber security threats

All above are 'singularity', unidirectional and a threat to humanity and ecology. From our present practices, we can find out our future, i.e., the effect of the cause, which is 'Global Polycrisis' (we have seen this in the chapter 'Kāla Bhairava: Father of Artificial Intelligence').

Table ∞.1 Similar functions

Functions	Traditional singularity	21st century or AI and singularity
Goal	Expansion to maintain supremacy over resources	Expansion to maintain supremacy over resources
Medium of expansion	Physical	Digital
What it looks	Ideology or religion	Picture, software, file
What it is actually?	An empire that is marketed as religion	AI-based software, e.g., spyware, malware, etc.
How it works	1. Spying as a dummy of empire 2. Corrupting enemy through proselytization; separatism (when in minority) and capturing (when in the majority) 3. Looting physically 4. Looting physical assets 5. Destroying history and infrastructure 6. Creating the fake imaginary concept of bodiless God and heavenly dreams	1. Spyware 2. Corrupting data files 3. Financial fraud 4. Illegal data mining 5. Data deleting, e.g., malware, phishing, DNS tunnelling, zero-day exploit, SQL ejection 6. Deep fakes which appear to be real and believed as real

Functions	Traditional singularity	21st century or AI and singularity
When goes out of control of owner	Unstoppable expansion, terrorism and atrocities, disturbing global peace	Singularity which turns against humanity and its data may take physical form, like terrorism, if connected with machine learning.
Non-physical owner	Invisible God, past leaders	software in the name of a virus written by human

When I say singularity, it includes everything that is started by humans but is no longer under human control. A socially disturbing singularity like terrorism can be debated and faught at the social level, but what about anti-microbial resistance (AMR), nanotech, AI, and gene editing? Is it controllable by debates or any physical war means? Today, 7 lakh deaths happen annually because of AMR, and by 2050, 10 trillion dollars losses plus 10 million deaths annually are expected. Do those preachers of uncriticized religions and ideologies have a sense of all these things? What non-sensical they are feeding to humanity instead of real-life issues.

In today's world, there is no 'comprehensive waste management', so we cannot expect AI to solve the problem of waste management as it does not exist in our minds either. What if AI becomes tomorrow's scientist and starts doing things in a haphazard manner? AI is the outcome of our talent or digital extension of *us*. So the seeds and biasedness limitation we have, same limitation AI has. Monopoly over it will reflect such biases.

Today, at least humans can handle terrorism because they have strong economic and technological support. But what if terrorists start doing data mining and using AI? Then it will be the most dangerous combination of traditional challenges (lone wolfs) and modern-age digital singularity. Secondly, there are owners or promoters of peace and violence, but in the case of singularity, there is no owner. Think how dangerous it will become. As we have sown seeds of automated intelligence in the form of AI, over time it will grow potentially and manifest itself in the form of singularity. Just like we are destroying the environment, the same exploitative approach will reflect in AI. This is what Kāla Bhairava gives trees of those seeds that you have sown.

Biggest Fraud: 'Peace'

Peace was okay when wars were happening, but today people are using peace as a platform to expand their interests geographically. This book exposes all such efforts, and also because of digitization, all other mediums of expansion like religion or ideological proselytization will fail in the future and digital media will be a whole and sole influencer and choice shaper through AI.

Peace will be meaningless in the future because wars will happen virtually. Peace is not 'non-violence'; peace is responsible activity where the interests of every stakeholder are satisfied. If there is no terror and no geopolitics, business is going well, but it's not peaceful because climate change is a challenge because the interest of ecology is not satisfied.

It is time to give up old singularities and get ready for the 21st century's singularity against us, which is climate change, and the 22nd century's singularity, which is machine learning through AI, to destroy the whole world. Because making digital infrastructure is cheaper than preparing for war and physical expansion, even poor countries can have creative and choice-shaped software that will help them in business and market capture.

That is why, in the coming future, cyberattacks are going to be a tool for everyday violence, right from street fights to organizational-level or national-level terror and violence. One day only fair trade and market-managing international agencies are going to be the future and reason for peace because invading a country for resources through political or religious ideology is going to be completely useless or outdated, and eternal exploitation will be like digging one's own grave. So producing responsible software engineers and limiting that technology to responsible people is going to be a new challenge, just like today we have norms for nuclear bombs.

It is the responsibility of humanity to transform the system from heading towards singularity to multi-stakeholder responsible ownership, which is block chain technology. So singularity and multi-stakeholders block technology have their own limitations, which can be eliminated by keeping both in rotation. Time to become upgraded with a new form of society with new metaphysics as psychology rather than religion and old political and cultural ideology so that seed sown culminates into the expected tree and cycle of Kāla Bhairava continues. Even if we win the war on climate change and singularity, what if, in the future, another planet strikes the earth? What about 'Black Swan events', i.e., black hole sucking up the whole solar system? Or aliens come to earth? Or we go to some another planet? One day the sun is going to die; are we prepared for that? And then we will realize whole setups of religion, gods, constitution, ideology, and nation will collapse; even food and human operating systems may change or maybe a whole new body with new material like nanotech but with the same consciousness. There will be no war, just destruction. Eco-friendly humanity or destruction, the choice is yours!

Whatever faults or mistakes I have done so far with the help of my hands, legs, speech, and body, also due to my actions, also by seeing and hearing, or may be mentally or as per the injunctions of the Vedas, all these Oh Lord Shiva who is all compassionate, please forgive me. You are the Lord of all deities and one whose nature is to bless all.

Welcome to Hinduism

to explore without an exploit, to die without fear,
to seek without biased, to devote without rules,
to cry with joy, to finish sorrow with collectivism,
to fight without hate, to meet *Īśvara* before death,
to exist without marketing, to learn without hurdles,
to identify without discrimination, to love without boundaries,
to experience instead of mere belief, to change without turmoil,
to unite without an enemy, to experience diversity without conflict,
to expand without disturbance, to consume without climate change,
to intermingle without artificial respect, to stay blessed without guilt,
to practice truth at different levels, to lie without compromising truth,
to win without war, to experience depth without compromising quality,
to dissolve yourself without efforts, to fight with deity to establish justice,
to take *Saṃnyāsa* to experience completeness, to have an identity without ego,
to challenge which seems to be real, to believe in truth without identifying someone false,
to remain powerful without troubling others, to experience the simplicity of complex matrix,
to exist beyond emotion and body, to experience cosmos rather than merely happiness,
to experience happiness without consumerism, to experience strength without hurting,
to liberate self rather than limiting to code, to live the life which is on *Karma* mode,
to modify without compromising basics, to help without self-interest,
to romance than merely sex, to organize without expansion,
to induce spirituality without giving up social life,
to manifest *Īśvara* in multiple formats,
to become one with the universe,
to become being,
than nothing.

Appendix A

Chapter 1

A1.1
Discretionary marketing strategy against Hinduism

Hinduism: Divide and rule, discrimination, threat to national unity, caste politics, hate politics, religion and politics can't be together, communalism, extremism, anti-humanity, fascist, lies, mythical, fake, anti-democratic, centralized in hands of Brahmin, attaching it with politics and election, projecting as politically motivated, British agents (in colonial period)—if you criticize the six non-inclusive players, your name will be attached to all these adjectives.

Ideology of six non-inclusive players: Freedom from caste politics, love, bonding, unity, no religion in politics, rationality, free from communalism, protectors of constitution, humanity and democracy, social justice, human rights, equality, non-discriminatory, politically neutral, anti-British (in colonial period), etc.

A1.2

The prominent Tamil leader, E.V. Ramasamy (popularly known as 'Periyar') stated that the Tamil society was free of any societal divisions before the arrival of Brahmins, whom he described as 'Aryan invaders'. Ramasamy was an atheist, and considered the Indian nationalism as 'an atavistic desire to endow the Hindu past on a more durable and contemporary basis'. (Dirks, Nicholas B. (2001). *Castes of Mind: Colonialism and the Making of Modern India.* Princeton University Press, p. 263. Ramasamy notably remarked that upon seeing a Brahmin and a snake, he would encourage people to attack the Brahmin. (Pandian, Jacob (1987). *Caste, Nationalism, and Ethnicity: An Interpretation of Tamil Cultural History and Social Order.* Bombay: Popular Prakashan.

A1.3

Dravidianism, Marxism, and Nehruvianism are enamoured by monopolistic world views and see that as strength. They see deep diversity as a weakness. Then they invented 'Brahminical conspiracy' as the basis of weakness. This is a throwback to the colonial protestant view of the so-called 'Brahminical Hinduism' as the result of 'priestcraft' (Neelkandan, Arvind. *Hindutva*. BluOne Ink, p. 537.

A1.4
Origin of the word *Aryan*

The word was picked from Hindu books (*Vedas*) and Iranian books; other than this, there is no historical reference to whether it was a particular empire, group, race, etc. In Sanskrit, it means gentleman. The term Arya was first rendered into a modern European language in 1771 as Aryens by French indologist Abraham-Hyacinthe Anquetil-Duperron, who rightly compared the Greek arioi with the Avestan airya and the country name Iran. A German translation of Anquetil-Duperron's work led to the introduction of the term Arier in 1776. The Sanskrit word *Arya* is rendered as 'noble' in William Jones' 1794 translation of the Indian Laws of Manu, and the English Aryan (originally spelled Arian) appeared a few decades later, first as an adjective in 1839, then as a noun in 1851. This term was not used generally by Hindus because people identified themselves by jati, a devotee of deity, empire, varna, etc. But using this term wasn't prohibited or stigmatized. British writers made it a strong identity and put some present social groups under the umbrella of Arya (social engineering). When we read Hindu scripture, this word is neither associated with race or group nor is it frequently used, like 'Om', 'Shanti', etc. (google Wikipedia).

Origin of the word *Dravida*

The English word Dravidian was first employed by Robert Caldwell in his 1856 book of comparative Dravidian grammar based on the usage of the Sanskrit word Dravida in the work *Tantravarttika* by Kumarila Bhatta (Zvelebil 1990). Caldwell used 'Dravidian' as a generic name for the family of languages spoken in southern India to distinguish them from Indo-Aryan, the branch of Indo-European spoken in the Indian subcontinent. There is no definite philological and linguistic basis for asserting unilaterally that the name *Dravida* also forms the origin of the word *Tamil*. The etymology of the name Dravidam is very simple. Dravidam = Thee + Ra + Vai +tam or Thee + Ra + vidam. Vidam or idam means the place or the land. Thee + ra denotes the 'Athee' (primordial fire) and the sun, respectively. Hence, Dravidam means the land of people who were the worshippers of Thee + Ra [thirai – sky] or whose ancestors were from the sky or Thee + Ra. It could be Thiru vidam, the land of Thiru, the 'wealthy land'. Alternatively, Dravidam means the land of Thirayan, the seafarers '–the ruler of the sea'. Thiraiyan could also mean 'the ruler of the sky'. 'Thiru' could also originate from 'Theeran' or 'Dheeran'. This proves, that just like *Aryan*, even *Dravida* is not a word that is used to indicate people of a particular race, or language.

A1.5
From the Indian Genome Variation Project (IGVP) to Ayurgenomics, all of them become agents of bionationalism and genomic nationalism. Of course, behind all these, there lurks ominously the specter of Hindu nationalism, upper caste and patriarchal. Attempts to link caste with race in international forums get a positive flip, and any attempt to delink caste and race becomes suspect. Dalit activists (who are actually connected with right-wing evangelical organizations in the United States) who used genetic studies to further their propaganda about caste and race became the good people in her narrative. The 'upper-caste' scientists of India who challenge them are the antagonists. It is interesting that the author avoids mentioning Dr Ambedkar at all in this context. The reader may be reminded that Ambedkar rejected the racial interpretation of the caste system and social exclusion, even as he uncompromisingly fought against both. (Neelkandan, Arvind. *Hindutva*. BluOne Ink, p. 440.

Chapter 3

A3.1
In *Akbarnama*, by Abul Fazal, Akbar confesses regretfully that he had forced many Brahmins out of fear of power, to adopt Islam (Neelkandan, Arvind. *Hindutva*. BluOne Ink, p. 475.

Chapter 4

A4.1
Solar Dynasty (Ramayana)

Brahman (Supreme Being: Oneness Diagram 19.1) Brahma (deity) – Rishi Mariachi-Kashyap-Vaivasman – Vaiswa Manu-Ikshavaku-Bharata-Vikukshi-Bhan-Kakakutsa-Anena-Pruthu-Vishishthva-Chandra-Yuvanshva-Shabashta-Brihadshva- Kuvalaishva-Dridhshva-Pramod-Haryashva-Nikumbha-Amitashva-Krishnashva-Prasenjit-Yuvanshva-Mandhata-Kruktusa-Sadaysya-Sambhruhut-Ananranya-Brihadshva-Haryashva-Hastya-Sumana-Tridanva-Trayaruni-Satyavratha-Harishchandra-Rohitshva-Harita-Chanchu-Chakshu-Vijaya-Prapapendra-Vriruk-Vrik-Shushandhi-Bahuk-Ashishtha-Sagara-Asamanjash-Anshuman-Dilip-Bhagiratha-Suhotra-Shuroti = Nabhag-Ambirasha-Sindhudvip-Ayuthayu-Rutukama-Savakama-Sudas-Soudasa-Asmaka-Mulaka-Dasharatha1-Advil-Vishvasaha-Nithin-Animitra-Dunulaha-Krishkarma-Kathvanga-Dhirghabhanu-Raghu2-Aja-Dashratha 2 – Ram

Lunar Dynasty: https://en.wikipedia.org/wiki/Lunar_dynasty#/media/File:LUNAR_DYNASTY_(Chandravamsha).png

Same structure for Ayurveda

Bramhan- Bramha- Daksha Prajapati-Ashwinikumaras-Indra-bharadwaja- atreya-6 students of atreya (who divided into 8 branches)- rishi paramaapra (along with *Vedas*, ayurveda was transferred) *Simplified Ayurveda*, p. 5.

A4.2
Mahābhārata content

Ramesh Chandru. *Mahabharata: Myth or History? A Compendium of Evidences*. Historica Foundations.

1. Vishnu, Vaishnava mentioned in *Vedas*, p. 19
2. Visnu Lakshmi came out of yagna, p. 19
3. Mahabharata characters mentioned in *Vedas*, p. 20
4. Grhyasutra aware of *Mahabharat*, p. 20
5. Chandogya *Upanishad* aware of *Mahabharata*, p. 22
6. Vyasa claims he created *Vedas*, p. 24

Appendix A

7. Vicitravirya father of Dritrashtra and not vyasa, p. 29
8. Nirukta: Story of Grammar in *Mahabharat* and story of Akura and Krishna, pp. 30–31
9. Archaeological sites which mention Krishna, pp. 48–72, but problem is people question Krishna's existence because of lack of contemporary proof but never question Buddha's existence for same reason, p. 72
10. *Mahabharata* mentioned in Buddhism, small stories, gods and goddess, pp. 83–84
11. Jataka story mentions the story of Krishna and Arjuna, pp. 85, 86, 87
12. Vidura is Buddha and Ananda is Dhananjaya in their previous birth, p. 87
13. *Buddha Charita* mentions: Rama, Krishna, Parashuraam, p. 90
14. Ashwaghosa's saundaryananda Krishna, p. 91
15. Buddhism has concept of petta vatthu ghost stories, p. 92
16. Theravada Buddhism mentions Vasudeva Krishna
17. Jainism also mentions *Mahabharat* and related stories, pp. 98, 99, 100, 101
18. Tamil scriptures mention Ettutogai and Pattupatu, pp. 110, 113.
19. *Mahabharata* includes medicine and surgery
20. Arthashahtra, Natyasahstra, Pancatantra (no aspect is free from *Mahabharata*), pp. 133–46
21. Flora fauna, measurements, weapons, pp. 194, 195, 196
22. Archaeological site related to Krishna, p. 206
23. Dwarka archaeology, pp. 211, 212, 213, 214, 215, 220
24. Image worship goes back to 8000 BCE, p. 229

A4.3
Sulabh Jain. *The Evolution of Religion: The History and Religions of Egypt and Harappan India*. Leadstart Publishing House.
1. River is deity, p. 20; God of eastern desert, p. 125
2. Lapis Lazuli found in Egypt, p. 25
3. Village deity Horus, Seth, Anubis, Anubis becomes God of Death, Horus + Rey become Solar God, p. 125

4. Harappan group of villages emerged into city, p. 4
5. Swastika Seal, p. 47
6. Worship of Shivling, p. 47
7. Rishabh Totem, p. 46
8. Similarity between Zoroastrian and Hindu gatha, p. 53
9. 50 lakh population, p. 57
10. Worship of Nandi bull in Harappa, p. 69
11. Trishul and Damru found, p. 70
12. 9 avatars of Vishnu = Evolution, pp. 82, 83
13. K 68 seal in Harappa 7 Goddess in Kalibangan, p. 91
14. Shiva, Shakti, Dakhsa, Prajapati, Soty, p. 92
15. Durga = Brahman without a second thought she is a combination of Shiva, Bramha, Vishnu, p. 104
16. Left-handed yoga – Vam Panth, p. 105
17. Shakti Peetha concept led down in Harappa, p. 105
18. Mimamsa 3 udties
19. Egypt = God manifested himself and created universe, p. 126
20. Transmigration of soul, remove negative from soul, p. 126
21. 2 stages of Liberation, p. 126
    a. Realizing Brahman
    b. Rejuvenating body
22. Concept of afterlife punishment, p. 127
23. Merging of two kingdoms = Merging of two gods = Ptah + Sokar (deities), p. 128
24. Ptah = Sokar = Osiris = Ego alteration of deities to maintain stability of 3 merged empires. Natural forces became community deity, community deity became village deity, as empire grew village deity become deity of empires, when two empires merged then respective deities also merged to maintain equal cultural/spiritual share for stability of empire, i.e., multiculturalism. Even though names of deities are same but change in socio-economic structure means that their meaning and contexts also changes, p. 128
25. Ptah craftsman's deity = Similar to Vishwakarma
26. Importance of sound and phonetics like Vedic culture, p. 129

Appendix A

27. Sekment lioness female deity = Narsimhi (female counter part of Narsimha), p. 131
28. Multiple gods represent sun (12 Aditya), p. 133
29. Deities related to lion, bull, lizard = Hinduism animals are vehicles of deities, p. 133
30. Atum = Self-created Brahman created earth, sky, air, water as children Geb, Nut , Shy, Tefnut (deities) = Concept of pancha tattva in Hinduism, p. 134
31. Egg = Bramhanda, flower, serpent related to creation, p. 137
32. Ra (deity) created pancha tattva, p. 138
33. Constellation concepts knew to them, i.e., Solar Lunar Calander, p. 148
34. Concept of Solar and Lunar dynasty, p. 148
35. Amun = God of fertility = Indra, p. 150
36. Akhenaten = Prophet Moses, p. 160
37. Atum = Bramha, Shu = Vishnu, pp. 171, 172
38. Sexual relationship between earth and sky, p. 174
39. Ptah (Shiva) with trident and front of him there is bull named Apis (Nandi), Ptah apples ashes of cremated body, p. 180
40. Zeus = Jupiter = Indra, p. 180
41. Female deity related to power = Sekhmet = Durga, p. 182
42. Surya = Ra = Sun god, p. 185
43. '7' horses chariot of Surya = Solar deity is having boat, p. 185
44. Anant Nag = Mehen (serpant goddess), p. 186
45. Story of Daksha Prajapati = Story of Ra and Nut, 189
46. Amun = Vishnu = Blue Colour, p. 193
47. Amun Kem Atef = Sheshnag of a Vishnu, p. 193
48. Importance of cow, pp. 194, 195, 196
49. Rahu Ketu concept, pp. 198, 199
50. Mat = Mata (female deity) = Takes multiple forms, p. 266
51. Usha = Nut, Kali = Baset, pp. 214, 215
52. Kundalini = Ua Zit, pp. 217, 218
53. 7 chakras, pp. 220, 225
54. Sati, Isis, Sita, pp. 224, 225
55. Kali and Shiva having sex = Geb and Nut having sex and sex position is also same, p. 227

56. Ganga falls from Shiva = Anuket (Nile) falls from Ithyphalli (deity), p. 229
57. Divine Eye of Horus = Shiva, p. 229
58. Universal order is Dharma = Maat, p. 233
59. Min = Shiva = Phallic deity, p. 239
60. Osiris Narsimha, pp. 243–44, 245
61. 3 layers body exists in both civilization
62. Horus and Sat having tug of war = Churning of ocean between sur and asur, p. 258
63. Karma theory = Retributive justice, p. 271
64. Reincarnation, pp. 293–94

A4.4

1. Nagaland myth/History: Koza: father/ancestor of Naga and his kids established twelve different tribe from Khezhakeno village, there is sacred stone/idol worship, p. 5.5 of Pavneet Singh. This story is similar to Jacob and the twelve tribes in Judaism.
2. Arunachal Pradesh (Dhammai story) and Assam (Minyong) have a story of sky and earth having male and female forms and between them sexual relationship is observed. These stories with modification have migrated to Egypt and are also seen in Hinduism in one or the other form, pp. 172–77. There are some folklores in Arunachal tribes that have stories exactly like those in Hinduism, https://www.hindu-blog.com/2021/07/folklore-in-arunachal-pradesh-stories-creation-sorrow-mortality.html; https://college.holycross.edu/projects/himalayan_cultures/2004_plans/sstidfol/pages/India_Creation_Myths.htm

A4.5

Content of *Ramayana Ramayana Retold with Scientific Evidences*: cropping pattern, p. 55; Dashrath, p. 8; minister, p. 55; Critic have been absorbed, p. 56; change of river course and rise of water level, p. 94; Chaturangini sena, pp. 98, 100; diplomacy, p. 312; geographic feature, p. 148; flora fauna, pp. 155, 234, 181, 182, 194, 259, 60; Lunar Solar calendar, p. 190; herbs, pp. 331–40; tribes data, p. 135;

Bhil, Koli, Gond, pp. 191–92, 192–209; Shabar Matanga, p. 242; jewellery, p. 274, places not mentioned in *Ramayana* are traced through folklore, pp. 305; twelve Great Maharshis, p. 178.

A4.6

Yuga	Main period	Sandhya / sandhyansh	Total length	Human years (total length × 360)
Satyuga	4,000	400 + 400	4,800	17,28,000
Tretayuga	3,000	300 + 300	3,600	12,96,000
Dwaparyuga	2,000	200 + 200	2,400	8,64,000
Kaliyuga	1,000	100 + 100	1,200	4,32,000
	10,000	2,000	12,000	43,20,000

There are multiple interpretations, but I think it's the historical timeline of 12,000+ years, where the Ikshwakus era starts somewhere starts around 10,000–9,500 BCE. This historical timeline is fixed into the 'Time units calculations' mentioned in chapter 6 (p. 115), which is divided in 4 parts, or yugas. Similarity of numbers can be found from above table and numbers on page 115. Some important geographic, historical events do exactly match with Hindu timeline (pp. 436, 437, *Ramayana Retold with Scientific Evidence*).

A4.7
Privatization vs. nationalization
The tussle between privatization and nationalization of assets is like the story from satyuga, samudra manthan: unless there is a tussle, fourteen ratnas won't come out. But if anyone maintains monopoly over fourteen ratnas (profit) then their value system will be financed, i.e., the private sector works on a profit-oriented mindset, which gives birth to professionalism for maximum output, whereas nationalization ensures equal distribution but lacks professionalism because of a 'lack of profit-oriented approach and no competitors'. Just like the Yuga cycle wheel must be rotated artificially for a smooth rotation of wealth,

professionalism, and social interest, one cannot stick to either of them, i.e., privatization or nationalization.

But still, transfer of power is easy in a democracy, but rotation of wealth is not easy; it will bring 'Pralaya', i.e., clashes and war. If you want to avoid this, then allow all the values in Diagram 4.1. to flourish, where equality and diversity are given high weightage and discrimination-inequality plays a significant role in creating the flow of money and professionalism. The balance shall also be maintained between privatization and nationalization; otherwise, choosing either of them at an extreme level will bring demand for the other, as mentioned in the Diagram 4.1. Rule of law and its implementation play an important role, i.e., lack of professionalism and tax invasion by the public and private sectors, respectively. Just transferring ownership to either of them doesn't give the government the freedom to implement the 'rule of law'. So understand the demands of society and the market and support privatization or nationalism accordingly.

Chapter 5

A5.1

Should there be any foreign policy towards non-Hindu theology/culture/people (from chapter 3)?

	Policy	Examples
Kids	1. Infidels are those who don't follow my God, e.g., idol worshiper, atheist, etc. 2. We must expand our religion (colonization) to whole world. 3. All religions teach good things. 4. Religion is root cause of conflicts and wars.	1. Desert trilogy of religions. 2. Those who close eyes while understanding desert trilogy of religion with universalist value system tape on eyes. 3. Atheism is real peace.
Men	We must have a foreign policy for desert trilogy as a counter. We are infidels according to chapter 3 theology; we must prepare for them.	Anti-desert trilogy of people.

Legends	1. Knowledge of desert trilogy is there, but no permanent or rigid foreign policy like kids and men 2. Strengthening and reclaiming territory, economy, people according to the situation, time, space, political equations with proper use of anger, pride, treaty, alliance, emotional intelligence, power, wars 3. Everyone feels connected to an empire irrespective of identity and profession so internal revolt is avoided 4. Connecting everyone irrespective of identity to empire through the economy, society, polity, culture, ancestry, personality cult, value system, law and order. So that everyone's potential is used for the empire so that possibility of the rise of parallel counter empire is avoided.	1. Chhatrapati Shivaji Maharaj 2. Before independence, Britain's Labour party was in favour of India because India was a colony and today the labor party is against India so the Indian diaspora in Britain is in support of right-wing party of Britain (no rigid foreign policy or anger about crony capitalism)

A5.2

Ram temple was constructed by Meghsuta (King of Saket in the lineage of Govind Chandra of the Gadhwala dynasty in 1114–1155 CE. In the nearby site of Ayodhya Ram Temple, a rock inscription has been found that is deliberately not taught in history books so that parallel theories can be promoted, e.g, it was not a Hindu temple, it was Buddhist architecture, etc. So that Hindus lose claim to the Ram temple, p. 80 (*Ramayana*).

Chapter 10

A10.1
Picture on page 142, *Hindutva* by Arvind Neelkandan (BluOne Ink): 'Thiruvarur sculpture showing a Chozha prince executed under the chariot wheels because his chariot had killed a calf, and the cow had complained. Chidambaram Ramalingam "Vallalar" (1823–1874) used this traditional account to propagate cow protection and food security, even as British-engineered famines loomed over the horizon.'

A10.2
Kinsley, David. *Tantric Visions of Divine Feminine*. Motilal Banarasidass.
1. Mahavidya goddess dwell in cremation grounds and sit on corpse, p. 7.
2. Garlands of several heads (always males), blood sacrifice of always male victims, they are sexually aggressive and are in sexually dominant position, p. 7.
3. Sakta peetha, where Sati's yoni fell, p. 17.
4. Wherever female exists, there exists a goddess in female form, p. 20.
5. She pervades all aspect of reality Mahadevi = Vishwarupam, pp. 21–22.
6. Sati's face is lotus, she is black, breasts are large, she is naked, p. 23.
7. Hair is dishevelled, she glows like a million suns, p. 23.
8. Matrakas came out of male gods like Brahmani from Bramha, Maheshwari from Shiva, Kaumari from Akrtikeya, Vaishnavi from Vishnu, Varahi from Varah, Narsimhi from Narsimha, Aindri from Indra, p. 32.
9. Male god have gained powers to defeat demons by worshipping the mahavidyas, p. 34.
10. Shiva is subordinate the goddess, p. 36.
11. Shiva is corpse without Shakti, p. 36.
12. 3 gunas with 3 devi, Mahasaraswati with sattva, Mahalakshmi with rajas, Mahakali with tamas, p. 42.
13. Vidya the form which liberates you, avidya which is delusive form, p. 45.

14. Siddhis, p. 51.
15. Posture, breath control, p. 52.
16. 10 yogini = 10 siddhis, p. 56.
17. Shiva lies down in front of Shakti, p. 63.
18. Kali is top of Shiva while having sexual intercourse, p. 74.
19. Semen, yoni, etc., she violates the idea of subordinate, controlled, passive women, p. 80.
20. Kali is Nirguna, p. 87.
21. Maya (false consciousness), nudity represents illuminated consciousness (unaffected by maya), Kali exists in cremation ground where pancamahabhuta dissolve liberates you from moh, maya, lobh, p. 88.
22. Brahma = Dashina Kali, p. 90.
23. Tara is common in Hindu and Buddhist, p. 92, 93.
24. Tripura Sundari helps out the carry out mission against demon, also has power to reverse the action done by male gods; rejuvenating Kama deva who was killed by Shiva, p. 116, 117.
25. Tripura Sundari is source of Vishnu avatar, p. 117.
26. Tripura Sundari is older than Brahma, Vishnu, Mahesh, p. 121.
27. Bhuvaneshwari = she is Vishwarupa, who is Prakriti, who makes all this world, p. 131.
28. Panchamahabhutas = Prapancheswari form of five elements, p. 133.
29. Bhuvaneshwari is mother of Brahma, Vishnu, Shiva, p. 134.
30. Bhuvaneshwari destroyer of raktabija, p. 134.
31. Bindu = conjunction of Shiva and Sshakti, p. 137.
32. Chinnamasta standing on Kama and Rati (couple having sex), symbolizes she is suppressing sexual energy, desire, sexual force p. 154.
33. City of Shiva (Kailasa) = city of Vishnu (Vaikuntha) = city of Shakti (Manidweepa) 7th chakra, p. 172.
34. 4 yugas, pancamahabhutas are also mentioned in Shakta Sampradaya, p. 98.
35. Bagalmukhi, she who gives 8 powers.
36. Bagalamukhi: male is static, female is dynamic, p. 202.
37. Sava sadhana (meditation on dead body), p. 201.

Chapter 12

A12.1
Social evils
1. Child marriage
2. Polygamy
3. Polyandry
4. Property inheritance issues (gender)
5. instant divorce by men (marriage is just a contract)
6. Slavery, sex slaves
7. Compulsory mutilation of certain body parts
8. Stereotyping women
9. No recognition of LGBTQ+
10. Stone pelting
11. Sexist mindset
12. Pedophilia
13. Necrophilia
14. Discrimination with infidel at a social, political, economic levels
15. Denying existence of deities of other religions
16. Sense of superiority over other religions.
17. One-night marriages, pleasure marriages (Legal prostitution)
18. Looting and killing unarmed men
19. Pay religious tax by infidels'
20. Marriage of infidel is null and void
21. Human trafficking
22. Killing of women and children of polytheist is justified along with polytheists
23. Domestic violence against women
24. Women can't go out without male companion

A12.2

1. **Analogy of agriculture**

For the world, all they will say is that we have nothing to do with each other, but everyone will say I am the real farmer; my agriculture is true agriculture. They all work together, but the world exists separately, i.e., too big to fail.

Appendix A

Activity number	Category of People	The analogy of agriculture activity	Conclusion of analogy
1	Category 1	Some people prepare fields by ploughing and removing grass	Finishing existing culture and infrastructure, eliminating non-followers.
2	Category 2	Seeding	Expansion through preaching
3	Category 2	Irrigation	Funding
4	Category 1	Sprinkling fertilizers	Whoever enters in the area or questions the religion, will be eliminated
5	Category 2 (permanent reaping) and category 1 (enjoying fruits in heaven)	Harvesting	Reaping the fruits of expanded empire through collecting religious tax and imposing a tax on infidels, heavenly lusty fruits

Chapter 13

A13.1

Many people misinterpret 'theory of causation' in Western philosophy with Hinduism's devotion and praise of deity.

Theory of causation	Stuthi or praise (refer to Diagram 19.1)
The theory of causation in Western philosophy is about 'bodiless God' as cause of the existence of earth, God as the cause of change or motion. God is a software engineer who sets worlds function. If he is the supreme cause, then what is the cause of his existence? Then they limit the definition by calling it supreme cause.	In Hinduism, there is no causation theory; Western people impose it on Hinduism forcefully by reading praise of Hinduism. Hindus praise Īśvara (Krishna, Shiva, and Shakti) in devotion. Greatness of deity and devoting whole creation to him is aimed towards liberation/moksha.

Theory of causation	Stuthi or praise (refer to Diagram 19.1)
Here there is no goal of going nearer to God as there is no concept of oneness with that supreme.	Here there is the concept of oneness, so people use praise tools so that human beings and Īśvara come closer and become one or unite which we call oneness or yog (union).
Here God sets up the world as software and whatever happens God is responsible. What if a virus enters in software? What is a question of free will?	In Hinduism, Īśvara (oneness) exist and he/she/it is the base (taranhar literally means thread which holds) of this world on which world is there. 3rd figure of Diagram 19.1. It is our will whether to become one with Īśvara or not, will karma lead to liberation or not, the pre-condition will of humans doesn't change against ecology and the cosmos.
God sets up principles, function, software	Īśvara is the principle, function, software and we are part of him and Īśvara is part of us. It is us who have to realize that, but this is in context of liberation. In general, there is free will.
If God has pre-sets all the function of the world, then what he does for the rest of the time?	Here Īśvara is a function with intelligence and works every time because universe and Īśvara are not separate.
Western philosophers impose qualities, functions, and duties on God according to their whims and fancies on one bodiless God. Which leads to contradiction logically.	In Hinduism, we seek to know and experience oneness and accordingly we express its nature and function. It is not a theory of causation; it is the theory of realization about the function that is Īśvara.

Theory of causation	Stuthi or praise (refer to Diagram 19.1)
e.g., God = 1 and God = ∞ hence 1= ∞ how is this possible? This separation of God and world; world and human reflect at the social and economic levels. At the social level, God is used as a colonizer. At the economical level, the world and its ecology are inferior and made to consume only. Because you are one stakeholder of the world and universe, not part. This is the base of capitalism: consumer-led or market-led economy. God created this world, but he is not part of the world (he is up there but without body); similar reflection is seen in human behaviour produce-consume and steps aside; don't care about consequences (climate change, sovereignty of nation).	That is why all the multiple definitions, concepts that I explained in various terms exactly indicate that oneness. You won't find a contradiction in the definition. Unbroken limitless existence which we express with the analogy of thread (oneness) is infinity. Which you will only experience when the body is not your boundary, you are part of infinity. It is the only individual ego that is stopping you to realize infinity by identifying yourself with a finite body and individual ego. This understanding makes Hindus eco-friendly because you won't exploit ecology and others because others are no more others, they are part of you.
Conclusion: Trying to fit the process of liberation in the framework of philosophy again fails.	

Chapter 14

A14.1

1. Politically egoistic people create instability by demanding benefits based on 'I', i.e., identity politics of appeasement.
2. Socially, it creates unnecessary clashes among two or more 'I', i.e., ego clash.
3. Economically, it creates an excess of wealth accumulation which creates inequality and pressure on natural resources. That is why Guru Nanak says share food, wealth without self-interest to avoid ego-building which will one day culminate into oneness with paramātmā. That is why Sikhism also promotes social service to

humanity as teachings but not as a marketing strategy to forcefully exist with unsound teachings by converting others as other religions do.

4. Ultimately, all three culminate into 'I' as an inner identity which is egoistic and which attaches you to material, human beings excessively which causes hurdle in experiencing Turiya state and further oneness journey.

Appendix B
Decolonizing Efforts by Governments through Policy and Social Movements

Chapter 2

B1
National mission on mechanization of agriculture, 2014–15, https://www.farmech.dac.gov.in/revised/2020/Final%20SMAM%20OP%20Guideline%2020-21.pdf

B2
Promoting indigenously manufactured products
a. Market Access Initiative Scheme, 2017–18
b. International Cooperation Scheme (IC), 1996
c. Procurement and Marketing Support Scheme (P&MS)
d. One District One Product Scheme, 2019–21
e. Establishing of Indian Brand Equity Foundation, 1996

B3
India rejected the report by US State Department on religious freedom that criticized India for alleged attacks on minorities,
https://www.newsx.com/religious-freedom-report-india/#:~:text=India%20rejected%20the%20report%20by%20US%20State%20Department,it%20was%20based%20on%20%E2%80%9Cmisinformation%20and%20flawed%20understanding.%E2%80%9D;

Malhotra, Rajiv. *Breaking India* (US governments direct involvement). Amaryllis, An imprint of Manjul Publishing House Pvt. Ltd., ch. 15, p. 268.

B4

a. Coalition for Disaster Resilient Infrastructure (CDRI), Headquarter in Delhi, 2019
b. International Arbitration Centre, Headquarter in Delhi, 2019

B5

Traditional knowledge system revival
a. Reviving traditional industry (SFURTI scheme), 2015
b. Traditional knowledge system (Brainchild of M.M. Joshi), 2000
c. Vocal for Local (brand building tag for local product), 2021
d. Atmanirbhar Bharat (local industry production), 2020

B6

No Bindi No Business Campaign, 2021, https://www.newsbharati.com/Encyc/2021/10/22/No- Bindi-No-Business.html

B7

Innovation initiatives
a. Technology-Based Entrepreneurship Development Programme (TEDP), 2021
b. Aatmanirbhar Bharat ARISE-ANIC, 2021
c. Abdul Kalam Technology Innovation National Fellowship, 2018
d. Accelerate Vigyan, 2020
e. Access to Knowledge for Technology Development and Dissemination (A2K+), 2021
f. Advanced Hydrogen and Fuel Cell Programme (AHFC), 2022
g. AICTE-Faculty Development Programme (FDP)
h. Innovation in Science Pursuit for Inspired Research (INSPIRE) Programme, 2008

Chapter 9

B8

Value system and impact on policy-making

1. Schemes for unorganized and informal sector
   a. Pradhan Mantri Shram Yogi Maan-Dhan (PM-SYM) Pension Yojana
   b. National Pension Scheme for Shopkeepers, Traders, and the Self-Employed Persons (NPS-Traders)
   c. Pradhan Mantri Jeevan Jyoti Bima Yojana (PMJJBY)
   d. Pradhan Mantri Suraksha Bima Yojana (PMSBY)
   e. Atal Pension Yojana
   f. National Social Assistance Programme (NSAP) – Old Age Protection
   g. Ayushman Bharat-Pradhan Mantri Jan Arogya Yojana (AB-PMJAY)
   h. E-Shram portal for informal sector workers, 2021
   i. PM-Swanidhi (for street vendors)
2. Regulation for business, https://www.oecd.org/gov/regulatory-policy/44925979.pdf
3. Illegal immigrants: Treaty with Bangladesh solving border disputes, launching of NRC to identify immigrants.
4. Connecting India and bridging rural–urban divide
   a. Ek Bharat Shrestha Bharatz, 2015
   b. PURA scheme, 2003
   c. Shyama Prasad Mukherjee Rurban Mission
5. Accountability
   a. Tax charter launched in 2020
   b. https://transformingindia.mygov.in/performance-dashboard/
6. Cooperation and coordination
   a. Hub and spoke model: Parmarsh scheme
   b. One stop solution: Common service centre
   c. Timely compliance and monitoring: Pragati app
   d. Synergy and convergence: PM Gati-Shakti
   e. Diversified and holistic policy making: National logistic portal
   f. Single window clearance: Prakash portal

g. Active participation of citizen: Mygov app
7. Skill development
    a. Pradhan Mantri Kaushal Vikas Yojana
    b. National Apprenticeship Promotion Scheme
    c. Pradhan Mantri Yuva Yojana (Yuva Udyamita Vikas
    d. Skills Acquisition and Knowledge Awareness for Livelihood Promotion
    e. Skill Strengthening for Industrial Value Enhancement
    f. Jan Shikshan Santhans (JSS)
    g. National career service portal
    h. Pm-Yuva Yojana
    i. Sankalp (World bank initiative)
    j. Strive (industry-oriented skills)
    k. Skill build platform
    l. Gramin Udyami yojna (skilling tribals)
    m. Green jobs by ILO
    n. Reskilling framework by WEF
8. Integrated governance:
    a. One nation one ration card
    b. GST
    c. One nation one Urea brand

Chapter 10

B9
Overcoming red orthodox mindset
a. Tourism based promotion
b Adopt heritage project
c. Swadesh darshan scheme (thematic circuits development)
d. Prasad scheme
e. Establishing ministry of Ayush and drug development with WHO

B10
Urban development schemes
a. AMRUT mission
b. National Urban Sanitation Policy
c. HRIDAY

d. NULM
e. Swachh Bharat Mission-Urban 2.0 and Atal Mission for Rejuvenation and Urban Transformation 2.0
f. Pradhan Mantri Awas Yojana-Urban (PMAY-U)
g. 'SVANidhi se Samrddhi' program
h. National Urban Digital Mission (NUDM)
i. Integrated Command and Control Centers (ICCC)
j. Urban Transport in India
k. Light House Projects (LHPs)

B11 Overcoming shortcomings of history books through government policy
a. Declaration of international yoga day by UN, 2015
b. Yoga being part of India's foreign policy, https://www.aljazeera.com/news/2019/6/21/how-yoga-diplomacy-helps-india-assert-its-rising-global-influence
c. Mission LIFE, Lifestyle for environment, 2022
d. Sports, music, dance, art is no more extra curriculum activity, it's now mainstream education to promote students in respective fields (job diversification) as per New Education Policy, 2019
e. Financial literacy schemes, https://investor.sebi.gov.in/pdf/FinalNSFE.pdf; https://www.nabard.org/content1.aspx?id=517&catid=8&mid=8
f. Diversification of rural employment:
   i. The Deendayal Antyodaya Yojana–National Rural Livelihood Mission (DAY-NRLM)
   ii. The Deen Dayal Upadhyaya Grameen Kaushalya Yojana (DDU-GKY)
   iii. Women empowerment initiatives like NRHM (ASHA)
   iv. Aganwadi (PM-POSHAN)
g. Schemes for MSME Development
   i. Prime Minister Employment Generation Programme
   ii. 2nd Loan for upgradation of the existing PMEGP/...
   iii. Credit Guarantee Scheme for Micro and Small Industries
   iv. Micro and Small Enterprises Cluster Development Programme

v. Scheme of Fund for Regeneration of Traditional Industries
vi. Entrepreneurship and Skill Development Programme
vii. Assistance to Training Institutions (ATI) Scheme
viii. Skill Upgradation and Mahila Coir Yojana
ix. Procurement and Marketing Support (PMS) Scheme
x. International Cooperation (IC) Scheme
xi. National SC-ST Hub
xii. A Scheme for Promoting Innovation, Rural Industry
xiii. Modified Market Development Assistance (MMDA)
xiv. Interest Subsidy Eligibility Certificate (ISEC)
xv. Work-Shed Scheme for Khadi Artisans under Khadi Vikas yojana
xvi. Pottery Activity under Gramodyog Vikas Yojana
xvii. Beekeeping Activity under Gramodyog Vikas Yojana
xviii. Agarbatti Making Project under Gramodyog Vikas Yojana
xix. Promotion of MSMEs in NER and Sikkim
xx. Tool Rooms and Technical Institutions – A Component of Infrastructure Development & Capacity Building Scheme
xxi. ZED Certification Scheme
xxii. Lean Manufacturing Competitiveness for MSMEs
xxiii. MSME – Innovative (Incubation, IPR and Design)
xxiv. Digital MSME
xxv. Credit Guarantee Scheme for Subordinate Debt
xxvi. Self-Reliant India (SRI) Fund
xxvii. Raising and Accelerating MSME Performance (RAMP)

h. Schemes and policy for middle class
  i. Faceless income tax
  ii. No income tax up to 7 lakh rupees
  i. National mission on manuscript, 2003
j. Vedic heritage portal launched in 2023
  i. Over 550 hours of audio–visual content related to more than 18,000 Vedic mantras have been uploaded on the website, prepared in conjunction with people who know Vedas, Vedic research institutes, Vedapathi families, and experts from all over the world. The Vedic Heritage Portal is available in a mix

of English and Hindi, besides audio content in Sanskrit. The portal also includes research articles and lectures on scientific subjects explaining the relevance of 'Vedic knowledge' from the perspective of modern science.

ii. Apart from the Vedic Heritage Portal, the IGNCA is planning to create a museum dedicated to the Vedic implements, or vessels used in yajna. The museum will showcase over 250 vessels from the Vedic traditions of Karnataka, Kerala, Tamil Nadu, and Andhra Pradesh. IGNCA is also working on a project called Vrihattar Bharat, which will explore cultural the linkages of India with 40 other countries, including Southeast Asian nations, such as Cambodia, Vietnam, Laos, and Mongolia.

Unanswered questions
1. Even after so many invasions, which is the value that accepted all of them into this culture?
2. Even after so many attempts at separatism and brainwashing, why is Bharat still united?
3. Even though the two epics, Ramayana and Mahabharata, have wars in them, are Hindus still peaceful?
4. Even after atheist and communist attacks, why does Hinduism still survive?
5. Even after so many attempts at secularization or attempts at vanishing Hinduism, why does Hinduism exist?
6. Even after so many racial invasions, why is there no racial theory among the Hindu masses?
   I don't want to answer because . . .

Appendix C

	Chakras	Location	Colour/No. Of petals/ Mandala	Animal/Bija letter	Arc letters	Presiding deity	Centre of locus	Importance
In the times of danger	Muladhara	Between anus & genitals (adrenals)	Red/4	Airawat elephant on square/ (Lam)	व श स ष	Ganesha/ Bramha	Dhakini Shakti	Bhulinga which is coiled up by Kundalini resides on Kama-Bija
Sexual incitement	Swadhishtana	Root of reproductive organ (gonads)	Vermillion colour/6 varun mandala (water)	Makara alligator on half-moon / (Vam)	ब म म य र ल	Vishnu	Rakini Shakti	The water is then subjected to heat for its conversion into steam. This steam spreads within and outside the body and washes away the impurities and cleans many places.
Laughter	Manipuraka	Naval (pancreas/ adrenals)	Violet/10 (agni mandala)	Goat /(Ram)	ड ढ ण त थ द ध न प फ	Rudra riding bull	Lakini Shakti	The Rudra purifies the pranas of the Sadhaka by heat and makes them suitable for the Brahmanda

Loving devotion	Anahata	Heart (thymus)	Yellow/12 vayu mandala	Black deer on inverted triangle within hexagon/ (Yam)	क ख ग घ ङ च छ ज झ ञ ट ठ	Ishwara	Kakini Shakti	Bana linga within triangle below which there is an eight-petalled lotus on which Jivatma resides. Place where Manas resides and accepts satvik attributes.
Grief stricken	Vishudhhi	Throat (thyroid)	Green/16 akash mandala within that chandra mandala	Elephant with akash bija (Ham)	अ आ इ ई उ ऊ ऋ ऋ ल ळ ए ऐ ओ औ अं अः	Sadashiva with bull	Sakini Shakti	Lord Shiva Shakti also becomes visible. By the power and grace of Shiva and Shakini, the Sadhaka attempts to control his manas.
Awareness	Ajna	Between the two eyebrows (pineal)	Blue/2	(om)	ह क्ष	Hakini is both male female (Ardhanarishvara)		Chakra where one losses duality of world. Perception = thought
Superconsciousness / oneness	Sahasrara	At the base of Sushumna (pituitary)	Indigo/1000	(om)	Varna mala from अ - क्ष	Shiva–Shakti union	Yakini Shakti	All categories of tattva, deity, mandala are visible/experienced at same time.

https://isha.sadhguru.org/in/en/wisdom/article/7-chakras-mystical-dimensions-body-seven-chakras
http://kundalinisadhana.com/english-beejyoga/kundalini-index.htm

Appendix D
Hinduism vs. Prophetic Religions

	Hinduism	Prophetic religions
Supreme reality	Brahman	God
Definition of God/ Brahman	Beyond description and comprehension that is a single uniting pantheistic omnipresent power or a force that is beyond all categories including heaven.	
7 heavens	Various presiding deities in each chakra/heaven. The physical form of deities can be experienced during spiritual journey to heaven.	Various presiding 'prophets' in each heaven. The physical form of prophets can be experienced during spiritual journey to heaven.
Discussion	The debate on the relation between an individual and God keeps on going whether one is over the other or equal, which gives birth to the Advait vs. Dvait discussion.	God is over and above everything, which is correct but because of that an individual never looks for the process of being one with God. Few 'post prophet' saints claim 'oneness with God'.
Holistic insight	Brahman + multiple deities in 7 heavens. Brahman is oneness and rest of the deities are its manifestation (expansion).	God + multiple prophets in 7 heavens. God is one and the rest of the beings are prophets. God is supreme; He is over and above 7 heavens. The prophets are on a spiritual journey.
Superficial insight	Polytheism, idol worship, paganism.	Monotheism, anti-Idol worship, anti-polytheism. God is one and formless, God is supreme, God is greater than the deities of other religions/spiritual systems.

Notes

∞Kāla Bhairava: Father of Artificial Intelligence
1. https://youtu.be/q7vemMPAQOY; https://nithyanandapedia.org/wiki/Kalabhairava

Chapter 1: The Cold War Within: Atheism Invasion Theory
1. Chatterjee, Debi [January 1981] (2004). *Up Against Caste: Comparative Study of Ambedkar and Periyar*. Rawat Publications: Chennai, p. 42.
2. https://vpmthane.org/vpmDDSS/pdf/Article/27-The-role-of-church-and-western-NGO-sin-destabilization-activities-in-India.pdf and https://esamskriti.com/e/National-Affairs/For-The-Followers-Of-Dharma/How-the-Church-controls-development-in-some-districts-of-Coastal-Tamil-Nadu-1.aspx
3. Chatterjee, Debi (2004). *Up Against Caste: Comparative Study of Ambedkar and Periyar*. Rawat Publications: Chennai, p. 43.
4. https://karnataka.pscnotes.com/main-notes/paper-ii-general-studies-1/thedravida- movement/
https://www.news18.com/amp/news/politics/while-making-separate-country-comment-dmks-a-raja-cites-periyar-but-he-dumped-the-dream-66-years-ago-5497453.html
https://www.news18.com/amp/news/politics/while-making-separate-country-comment-dmks-a-raja-cites-periyar-but-he-dumped-the-dream-66-years-ago-5497453.html
https://www.opindia.com/2018/03/the-dmk-party-and-their-dravida-nadu-absurdity/amp/
5. *Collected Works of Periyar*, published by the Periyar self-respect propaganda institution, Compiled by K Veeramani, pp. 12, 176.
6. Ryan Cimmino (2018). 'Threat from Tibet? Systematic Repression of Tibetan Buddhism in China', *Harvard International Review*, https://hir.harvard.edu/repression-tibetan-buddhism-china/
7. 'Pandya Country', p. 121, Tamil land pp. 112–24, Ancient India NCERT textbook for class XI (revised edition 1980, reprinted 1981) by R.S. Sharma.
8. a. Arvidsson, Stefan (2006-09-15) [2000]. 'Primitive Aryans: Research near the Beginning of the Twentieth Century'. Aryan Idols:

      Indo-European Mythology as Ideology and Science. Translated by Wichmann, Sonia. Chicago: University of Chicago Press. p. 153. Retrieved 23 October 2022. Die Gru*ndlagen des Neunzehnten Jahhunderts (1899).*

   b. *Aryan Idols: Indo-European Mythology as Ideology and Science.* Translated by Wi*ch*mann, Sonia. Chicago: University of Chicago Press: p. 153.

   c. *Dravidian Linguistics: An Introduction* by publisher Pondicherry Institute of Linguistics and Culture.

   d. Caldwell, Robert (1856). A *Comparative Grammar of the Dravidian, or, South-Indian Family of Languages.* Harrison: London. p 4-8

9. *India that Is Bharat: Coloniality, Civilization, Constitution* by J Sai Deepak, pp. 306, 303, 310, 311.

10. Chanda, Ratna, and Mamata Dhar. *Caste System (Its Evolution through Ages).* Sanskruti Pustak Bhandar, pp. x–xi.

11. a. Malhotra, Rajiv. *Breaking India.* Amaryllis (an imprint of Manjul Publishing House Pvt. Ltd.), Chps. 3–6.

   b. *Collected Works of Periyar,* pp. 488, 404.

   c. *Collected Works of Periyar,* pp. 387, 247.

12. Bhaskaran, Ramaswami (1967). Sociology of Politics: Tra*dition and Politics in India.* Asia Pub. House, p. 48.

13. *Collected works of Periyar,* p. 223.

14. Saraswati, Chandrashekharendra. *The Vedas,* 11th edition, published by P.V. Shankarankutty, p. 20.

15. *Mahabharata (Myth or History)* by Historika foundations, pp. 113,114, *Indian Art and Culture* by Nitin Singhania, 4th edition, pp. 16, 19.

16. *Hindutva,* pp. 556, 603, 610.

17. Dirks, Nicholas B. (2001). *Castes of Mind: Colonialism and the* Ma*king of Modern India.* Princeton University Press, p. 263.

18. *Hindutva,* pp. 608, 609, 610.

19. *Collected Works of Periyar,* pp. 608, 609, 610.

Chapter 2: Macaulay's Formula of Brand Building

1. *India that Is Bharat,* pp. 67, 70, 76.

Chapter 3: Religion, Laïcité, Secularism, and Conflicts

1. In *The Pagan Christ: Recovering the Lost Light* Thomas by Allen Toronto: 2004. In *The Power of Myth* with Bill Moyers, ed. Betty Sue Flowers. New York: Anchor Books, 1991.

2	https://www.dnaindia.com/world/report-china-s-cultural-genocide-erodes-buddhist-way-of-life-1157258
3	Holyoake, G.J. (1896). *English Secularism: A Confession of Belief*. Library of Alexandria. pp. 47–48.
4	Chisholm, Hugh, ed. (1911). 'Holyoake, George Jacob'. *Encyclopædia Britannica*, vol. 13 (11th ed.). Cambridge University Press, p. 622.
5	a. Berman 1990, p. 213. b. 'The later Holyoake felt that the new label "agnosticism" more exactly suited his atheological position.' (Berman 1990, p. 222).
6	*The Vedas*, p. 2.
7	https://www.hinduismtoday.com/magazine/october-november-december-2016/2016-10-educational-insight-six-streams-of-hindu-philosophy/
8	Indian Art and Culture: secular building (p. 1.42), secular painting (p. 3.13), secular cave painting (p. 3.8), secular love (p. 3.11), secular dance (p. 7.5), secular theatre (p. 8.6), Secular writers (p. 6.17, 6.27, 2nd edition), Abhanga (Hindu devotional songs) has two meaning secular and spiritual (Appendix 1, A 2.6).
9	Singh, Pavneet. *Internal Security*. McGraw Hill, p. 9.5.
10	Khan, M.A. *Islamic Jihad: A Legacy of Forced Conversion, Imperialism and Slavery*. iUniverse, Bloomington, IN, pp. 88, 113.

Chapter 4: Multilayer Data Science: Hindu Society

1	a. *Mahabharata*, pp. 246–73 (3101 bce) b. *Ramayana: Retold with Scientific Evidences* (Revised Edition). Garuda Prakashan Pvt. Ltd, p. 134 (Ikshwaku 1st king Holocene epoch), Time period of Ramayana p. 53–54, Birth of Rama, p. 412.
2	https://www.wikiwand.com/en/Shatapatha_Brahmana#Brihadaranayaka_Upanishad c. *Tantric Visions of the Divine Feminine: The Ten Mahavidyas*, Motilal Banarsidass Publishers. 10 avatars of Vishnu = 10 avatars Shakti. Tara is Rama, Bhairavi is Rudra, Matangi is Bramha, Dhumavati is Varaha, Sodasi is Shiva, Bhuvaneshwari is fomeless Brahman, Bagalmukhi is Vamana, pp. 21, 20.
3	https://www.templepurohit.com/suryavansh-solar-dynasty/
4	*Mahabharata*, p. 29.
5	*Caste System*, pp. 52–53, https://study.com/learn/lesson/bourgeoisie-proletariat-karl-marx.html
6	https://www.indiatoday.in/india/story/china-efforts-to-destroy-buddhism-wont-succeed-says-dalai-lama-2315990-2023-01-01

7   *Mahabharata:* gold chariot, p. 199; gold 5000 BCE ornaments precious stones from Banawali Mohanjadaro
8   *Ramayana Retold with Scientific Evidence*: copper arrowheads of 5000 BCE, p. 86.
9   *Mahabharata*, p. 196.
10 https://vedicfeed.com/yajna-meaning-and-types/ https://prepp.in/news/e-492-kalibangan-indus-valley-civilisation-ancient-india-history-notes https://dharmawiki.org/index.php/Kalpa_Vedanga_(%E0%A4%95%E0%A4%B2%E0%A5%8D%E0%A4%AA%E0%A4%B5%E0%A5%87%E0%A4%A6%E0%A4%BE%E0%A4%99%E0%A5%8D%E0%A4%97%E0%A4%AE%E0%A5%8D); https://www.wikiwand.com/en/Shatapatha_Brahmana#Date
11 Totem of Bull (refer to Appendix 1, A4.3: 7, p. 406)
12 *Mahabharata*, pp. 227–28; *Caste System*, p. 20.
13 *Mahabharata*, pp. 224, 223.
14 *Mahabharata*, p. 225.
15 https://www.earthismysterious.com/the-mystery-of-harappan-script/
16 https://vedicologyindia.com/significance-of-peepal-tree-why-is-it-special-and-sacred/; https://knowledgeday2day.blogspot.com/2018/04/induis-culture.html
17 https://blogmedia.testbook.com/blog/wp-content/uploads/2022/03/seals-of-indus-valley-civilization-3324ffb8.pdf
18 *Ramayana Retold with Scientific Evidences*: city of horses was Indus area where hoses were grown and elephants from Vindya and Himalaya, p. 55.
19 https://youtu.be/KgkAdf0pv6Q?si=y9LsHXWtyoNeMTqZ (Youtube channel 'project satyaloka', Video 'Indian astronomy origin and evolution').
20 http://www.mahavidya.ca/2008/04/14/ayurveda-the-ancient-hindu-science-of-health-and-medicine/
21 *Mahabharata*, pp. 201, 205.
    Archaeology proofs:
    - 7000 BCE cultural proofs, pp. 85, 95
    - Beads articles, pots 7000 to 4000 BCE
    - Archaeological site, p. 132
    - *Ramayana Retold with Scientific Evidences*: proof of Ramsetu 7000 BCE, pp. 128, 331.
22 *The Vedas*, p. 44.
23 50 lakh population of Indus valley (A 4.3, 9). *Ramayana Retold with Scientific Evidences*: 72 times Saraswati mentioned in *Ramayana* and is alive, p. 146.
24 *Ancient India*: Brahmin priest and Buddhist monk, p. 66.

25 *Ancient India*: Brahmin priest and Buddhist monk, p. 219.
26 Ranganathan, Anand. *Hindus in Hindu Rashtra*. BluOne Ink. Waqf board is 3rd largest landowner, 70 per cent Delhi landowner (including Central vista, Nehru stadium), 3,54,913 estates, 8,66,035 properties, which includes 80,200 acres of land, p. 27.
    a. Waqf can claim any property as their property arbitrarily, pp. 30, 31 (legal but unconstitutional land grabbing)
    b. State doesn't collect money from mosques, p. 36.
27 The following is a list of massacre and exodus of infidels and minorities:
    a. Hindu exodus in Bhutan, https://thediplomat.com/2016/09/bhutans-dark-secret-the-lhotshampa-expulsion/
    b. Exodus of Hindus in Srilanka, https://www.hinduamerican.org/blog/5-things-to-know-about-hindu-challenges-in-sri-lanka
    c. Bangladesh anti-Hindu, https://foreignpolicy.com/2021/10/29/induism-communal-violence-hindu-muslim-identity-crisis/
    d. Hindu–Tamil genocide, https://www.humanrightspulse.com/mastercontentblog/the-tamilian-struggle-for-justice-in-sri-lanka-acknowledging-the-tamil-genocide
    e. Kashmiri pandits, https://hindugenocide.com/induis-jihad/seventh-exodus-of-kashmiri-hindus-4l-hindus-estranged-overnight/
    f. https://hindugenocide.com/timeline/
28 https://www.thehindu.com/news/international/tamils-flag-escalating-attacks-on-temples-in-northern-sri-lanka/article66769957.ece (for those who say its linguistic issue not religious)

Chapter 5: Neutral History Books Before Saffaronization

1 https://www.historydiscussion.net/history-of-india/the-religious-policy-of-aurangzeb-and-its-effects/2820
2 *Hindus in Hindu Rashtra*.
    a. Babur identifies himself as killer of Hindus for sake of Islam, p. 82.
    b. Hindu gods and their idols are dirty, their destruction gives me joy (St. Francis Xavier), pp. 82–83.
    c. Khwaja Moinuddin Chishti, converted Hindus and said, 'I will destroy Hindu temples', p. 83.
    d. Tipu Sultan destroyed 800 temples, 27 churches, captured 60,000 Christians, converted 30,000 (figure could be 80,000), p. 85.
    e. Aurangzeb killed 4.6 million Hindus, p. 87.
    f. Order to destroy Kashi temples, p. 101.

3. a. Understanding Muhammad, pp. 89, 305. https://www.iranpoliticsclub.net/library/english-library/AliSina-UnderstandingMuhammad6th.pdf
   b. Khan, MA. 'Islamic Jihad: A Legacy of Forced Conversion', Imper*ialism and Slavery*. iUniverse 1663 Liberty Drive Bloomington, pp. 42–65, 67, 68, 69, 177, 220–245, 267–270, 13–71, 73–146.
4. NCERT book for Class 7 Social Science: *Our Past—2* (History), p. 149.
5. https://www.logically.ai/factchecks/library/b01c6f5f
6. https://www.scoopwhoop.com/inothernews/induis-facts/
7. https://indianexpress.com/article/india/maoist-pamphlet-exhorts-marathas-to-brace-movement-for-quota-goal-7356012/
8. *Hindus in Hindu Rashtra*: judiciary discriminatory towards Hinduism, animal sacrifice, loudspeakers, pp. 74, 73.
9. http://sikhprofessionals.net/wahegurus-way/why-sikhs-are-not-hindus-simplified-version/
10. a. https://www.thehindu.com/news/national/tamil-nadu/are-sri-lankan-tamils-not-hindus-asks-stalin/article30314508.ece
    b. *Hindutva*, pp. 582, 588, 603.
    c. Rajan, Nalini (1974). *Practising Journalism: Values, Constraints, Implications*, https://en.wikipedia.org/wiki/Jogendra_Nath_Mandal)
    d. *Collected Works of Periyar*, pp. 149, 305, 306, 307, 311, 20.
11. https://mpsctopper.com/wp-content/uploads/2021/07/6th-Std-History-Textbook-Pdf-Marathi-Medium.pdf. According to Periyar, Brahmin are Aryan invaders and Muslims are Dravidians, *Collected Works of Periyar*, p. 376.
12. NCERT Book for Class 7 Social Science – *Our Past-2* (History), p. 149.
13. 'A critical survey of Indian philosophy' by Chandrashekhar Sharma. Motilal Banarasidas, pp. 252, 318, 5.13.
14. 'A critical survey of Indian philosophy' by Chandrashekhar Sharma. Motilal Banarasidas, pp. 252, 318, 5.13.
15. *Indian Art and Culture*, p. 14.9, 4th edition (opposition) and 2nd edition (fight).

Chapter 6: Humanity: The Lowest Value of the Universe

1. Jawaharlal Nehru (1964). *The Discovery of India*. Signet Press: Calcutta, p. 288.
2. 'A critical survey of Indian philosophy', pp. 40-41
3. https://www.hindustantimes.com/india-news/dissent-is-the-safety-valve-of-a-democracy-justice-chandrachud/story-1vOft3QfRvszjGuBBWSuLI.html
4. 'A critical survey of Indian philosophy', p. 226.

5   'A critical survey of Indian philosophy', p. 211.
6   https://isha.sadhguru.org/mahashivratri/significance-of-mahashivratri/
7   https://isha.sadhguru.org/mahashivratri/significance-of-mahashivratri/
8   https://youtu.be/_AaaOR0DVjs?si=SZtZH69DhQscLoqg; https://youtu.be/5wr7pNA2T5E?si=F-Hh0HxjUE-q6-ej (channel: The Sanskrit channel, video: Navagraha).
9   https://www.youtube.com/watch?v=3iAxgCP8oPY (channel: The Sanskrit channel, video: Learn 12 Sanskrit months, *After watching this you will know importance 'Numerology' of 108, why it has so much importance 108 names of deities, 108 pearls in Garland etc.*); https://youtu.be/uXA3uLnhc7o?si=avzeVpXqavnGfz8Q (channel: project Satyaloka, video: Muhurta); https://youtu.be/538kzPciYAY?si=jhVkk23beQliktqM (Channel: Project Satyaloka: Vasara)

Chapter 7: Blockchain Technology: Jati, Caste, and Brahmins

1   https://www.templepurohit.com/mantras-slokas-stotras/vedic-suktas/purusha-suktam/#:~:text=The%20Purusha%20sukta%20describes%20in%20detail%20the%20spiritual,Rigveda%2C%20dedicated%20to%20the%20Purusha%2C%20the%20%E2%80%9Ccosmic%20Being%E2%80%9D
2   *Caste System: Its Evolution through Ages*, final report of a minor research project by Dr Ratna Chand and Smt. Mamata Dhar (published by Sanskrit Pustak Bhandar).
3   https://practicalphilosophy.in/2013/06/08/the-context-of-four-varnas-in-the-gita/
4   Jaini, *The Jaina Path of Purification* (1998), p. 289.
5   Jaini, *The Jaina Path of Purification* (1998), p. 290.
6   Jaini, *The Jaina Path of Purification* (1998), p. 340.
7   Singh, Upender. *A History of Ancient and Early Medieval India from the Stone Age to the 12th Century.* Pearson, p. 291.
8   *A History of Ancient and Early Medieval India*, p. 294.
9   *Indian Art and Culture*, p.15.20, 4th edition; *Caste System*, p. 45.
10 *Indian Art and Culture*, p. 14.9, 4th edition.
11 https://www.wisdomlib.org/definition/ikshvaku
12 Shah, Natubhai (1998). *Jainism: The World of Conquerors*, Volume I and II. Sussex Academy Press: Sussex, p. 25, https://thezenuniverse.org/buddhist-cosmology-the-zen-universe/
13 https://www.oxfordbibliographies.com/display/document/obo-9780195393521/obo-9780195393521-0019.xml; https://jothishi.com/

astrology-in-buddhism/; https://jothishi.com/astrology-in-jainism/; https://jainworld.com/library/jain-books/books-on-line/jainworld-books-in-indian-languages/handbook-of-jainism/time/
14. Class XI NCERT ancient Indian history textbook (1999) by Ram Sharan Sharma, p. 65.
15. *Caste System*, p. 7.
16. *Caste System*, p. 12–17
17. *Caste System*, p. 20–21.
18. *Caste System*, pp. 20–21.
19. *Caste System*, p. 25.
20. *Caste System*, p. 17.
21. *Caste System*, p. 20.
22. *Caste System*, p. 20.
23. *Caste System*, p. 20.
24. *Caste System*, p. ix.
25. https://archive.org/details/all-18-smritis-and-18-upsmritis-collections-sanskrit-only-2-upsmritis-missing/All%2018%20Smritis%20in%20one/
26. Caste System, pp. 28, 26, 30, 31, xii, 51, 28, 29, 24, 23, 12, xiv, 22, 21, 11, 23, 10.
27. Notheast Bharat and Mahabharat, https://karsewak.blogspot.com/2008/01/ancient-history-of-northeast-india.html; https://indianculture.gov.in/north-east-archive/history-north-east#:~:text=It%20is%20believed%20that%20North-East%20India%20finds%20a,associated%20with%20these%20regions%20further%20crystallises%20their%20belief; http://www.hinduwisdom.info/Nature_Worship.htm
28. *Caste System*, p. concept (vii, viii, 3), Caste in USA caste system, Portuguese word.
29. India that is Bharat, pp. 278, 279, 281.
30. *Breaking India,* chapter 12, p. 196
31. https://currentaffairs.adda247.com/projected-threefold-growth-in-tax-collection-under-modis-10-year-governance/

Chapter 8: Human Capital versus Institutional Efforts

1. https://www.vedantu.com/question-answer/what-do-you-mean-by-jati-panchayat-class-11-social-science-cbse-600512d2e7ed25330db6eee4
2. https://history-is-mystery.com/the-forgotten-battle-naga-sadhu/

PART III UNTOUCHABILITY WITH HINDUISM

1. *India that Is Bharat*, p. 188 and https://academic.oup.com/edited-volume/35402/chapter-abstract/302650087?redirectedFrom=fulltext&login=false

2. A fake global hunger index:
   a. https://www.pib.gov.in/PressReleasePage.aspx?PRID=1868103#:~:text= The%20index%20is%20an%20erroneous%20measure%20of%20 hunger,and%20cannot%20be%20representative%20of%20the%20 entire%20population
   b. Fake perception of India through indices, https://eacpm.gov.in/wp-content/uploads/2023/07/6-Global-Perception-Indices.pdf
3. Anti-India and anti-Hindu propaganda:
   a. *Hindutva*, p. 538, 565.
   b. https://www.opindia.com/2022/02/meet-un-experts-behind-statement-supporting-rana-ayyub-india-geneva/
   c. https://frontline.thehindu.com/social-issues/social-justice/interview-ambedkar-views-on-gender-ignored-says-ashwini-k-p-unhrc-special-rapporteur-on-racism/article66169478.ecehttps://www.opindia.com/2021/07/how-george-soros-fund-open-society-foundation-anti-india-narrative-media-ngos/
   d. https://millichronicle.com/2023/02/explosive-how-george-soros-network-against-india-works-from-the-shadows.html
   e. https://hinduexistence.org/2022/10/30/strong-protest-against-bbcs-false-narrative-including-anti-india-and-anti-hindu-bias/
   f. https://www.opindia.com/2021/03/bbc-islamise-hindu-roots-of-holi-hinduism/
   g. https://tfipost.com/2022/08/here-we-shred-bbcs-anti-hindu-propaganda-piece-to-pieces/
   h. https://www.opindia.com/2023/01/gems-of-bbc-headlines-india-modi-documentary/
   i. https://theamericanhindu.com/posts/take-action-remove-sunita-viswanath-as-columbia-religious-life-advisor/
   j. *Breaking India*, p. 297.
   k. https://www.firstpost.com/explainers/explained-from-vandalism-of-hindu-temple-to-khalistan-referendum-the-growing-pro-khalistan-sentiment-in-canada-11258341.html
   l. https://tfipost.com/2022/09/a-quick-recap-of-how-canada-became-the-hq-of-the-khalistani-movement-and-why-jaishankars-statement-makes-sense/
   m. https://www.theatlantic.com/international/archive/2017/10/how-did-unesco-get-so-politicized/542733/
   n. https://culturaleconomics.org/the-politicization-in-de-selection-of-unesco-world-heritage-sites/

o. https://ww1.odu.edu/content/dam/odu/offices/mun/issue-brief-2019/ib-unesco-heritage-sites.pdf#:~:text=Despite%20the%20success%20and%20popularity%20of%20the%20World,Exploitation%20of%20the%20list%20for%20domestic%20political%20purposes

p. https://www.hindustantimes.com/opinion/why-be-a-part-of-unesco-if-it-s-not-protecting-or-projecting-india/story-Jju7PQS6ijGcAsOl6UfzdK.html

q. https://www.timesnownews.com/international/article/uk-labour-partys-stance-on-kashmir-remains-unchanged-as-top-politicians-attend-pak-backed-anti-india-webinar/601591

4 a. *Hindus in Hindu Rashtra*, pp. 20, 56.

   b. The home minister of Kerala, Kodiyeri Balkrishnan, openly admitted that the state government was under pressure to set SIMI (Students Islamic Movement of India – terror organization), Men free, p. 565 *Hindutva*.

5 a. https://www.youtube.com/watch?v=7NfUhbA_J6w

   b. https://www.thehindu.com/opinion/editorial/culture-and-peace-the-hindu-editorial-on-indias-stand-against-uns-selectivity-on-religions/article33264763.ece#:~:text=In%20a%20strong%20statement%20at%20the%20UN%20General,%E2%80%94%20Islam%2C%20Christianity%20and%20Judaism%20%E2%80%94%20over%20others

Chapter 9: Why I Am Not Hindu?

6 https://www.islamicity.org/3068/did-islam-just-copy-from-judaism-christianity/

7 https://www.indiafacts.org.in/divide-et-impera-how-the-british-created-sikh-identity/

8 https://www.allaboutsikhs.com/sikh-way-of-life/sikh-festivals/the-sikh-calendar-gurupurabs-and-festival-dates/#:~:text=Until%20the%2013th%20of%20March%2C%201998%2C%20the%20Sikhs,and%20aligns%20with%20the%20Gregorian%20calendar%20as%20follows

9 Panini saw Shiva's cosmic dance with damru beats, and fourteen vyakarana sutras were revealed to him. He wrote ashtdhyayi on these sutras, known as Maheshwara sutras. We chant these sutras on Sravana Purnima, and in Tamil Nadu, they are known as 'avanniavittam'. That is why there are vyakarana mandapa in Shiva temple. The Aindrayam book by Lord Indra is the basis of Tolkapiyam (book for Tamil grammar), *The Vedas*, p. 137.

10 Krishna idols were removed from golden temples, https://punjab.global.ucsb.edu/sites/default/files/sitefiles/journals/volume20/9-Sheena%20Pall%20.pdf

11 https://www.outlookindia.com/website/story/the-new-red-corridor/229193

12 *A History of Ancient and Early Medieval India*, p. 262.
13 *Hindutva*, pp. 478, 610.
14 https://www.opindia.com/2020/01/periyar-history-hindu-hate-lord-rama-sita/
15 *Indian Express*, 14 September 2023 (Hindu vs. Sanatani).
16 India is a bigger enemy of Islam; Muslims are a Quam wholly separate from Hindus (leftists try to defend this separatism by calling Hindus majoritarians), Muslim nationalism cannot be based on language, homeland, race, colour, or economic system. Secularism makes Muslims slaves in Delhi; Kashmir must be an Islamic state, Jihad against state of India, *Hindus in Hindu Rashtra*, pp. 17–18.

Chapter 10: Opium of Marxist Mythology
1 https://timesofindia.indiatimes.com/business/india-business/explained-what-are-freebies-and-how-they-may-burden-state-finances/articleshow/93306455.cms; https://theprint.in/judiciary/freebies-not-bribes-but-shake-root-of-fair-polls-what-sc-said-in-2013-order-it-plans-to-revisit/1098952/; https://swarajyamag.com/politics/a-brief-history-of-freebie-promises-in-tamil-nadu-why-dmks-stalin-is-promising-rs-1000month-for-women
2 https://www.worldatlas.com/what-is-economic-determinism.html
3 *India that Is Bharat*, p. 177.
4 *Collected Works of Periyar*, p. 402.
5 https://tamilandvedas.com/tag/gods-in-tirukkural/
6 *Collected Works of Periyar*, p. 442.
7 https://qz.com/india/764352/the-journey-of-indias-gdp-from-1000-a-d-to-2020
8 *The Beautiful Tree* (Indigenous Indian Education in the Eighteenth Century), published by Bibila Implex, pp. 91–155, 155–78, 194–98, 199–200 (1823 AD), 221–22 (1825 AD).
9 *Tantric Visions of the Divine Feminine*, p. 20, Kali became Krishna and Chinnamsta became Narsimha.
10 https://www.thehindu.com/opinion/lead/dilemmas-of-indias-great-power-ambitions/article67113422.ece/amp/
11 https://m.economictimes.com/news/politics-and-nation/congress-leaders-should-recall-antonys-statement-on-border-issue-during-upa-rule-kiren-rijiju/articleshow/86973159.cms
12 https://timesofindia.indiatimes.com/india/modi-government-significantly-enhancing-border-infrastructure-jaishankar/articleshow/102488837.cms
13 https://www.today.com/tmrw/what-reverse-racism-experts-weigh-term-t184580

14 a. https://isgp-studies.com/immigration-the-rape-of-norway
   b. https://www.jihadwatch.org/2020/12/uk-report-on-muslim-rape-gangs-a-politically-correct-cover-up-they-dont-like-explosions
   c. https://www.birminghammail.co.uk/news/midlands-news/muslim-cops-label-counter-terrorism-25508438
   d. https://www.opindia.com/2020/07/muslim-grooming-gangs-uk-victim-narrate-details-rape/ https://www.news18.com/news/opinion/left-parties-allegiance-to-china-than-support-indian-interests-4059788.html
   e. https://www.ibtimes.com/how-many-people-did-joseph-stalin-kill-1111789
15 https://www.hindujagruti.org/hindu-vidhidnya-parishad/kerala-high-court-order-on-love-jihad/
16 https://www.hindustantimes.com/india-news/arabian-nightmares-hyderabad-still-a-thriving-bride-bazar-for-rich-sheikhs/story-dcLypwP6lk5l4Lh8dT5fYI.html; https://www.indiatoday.in/india/south/story/arabi-kalyanams-return-to-haunt-poor-muslim-families-in-kerala-175385-2013-08-28
17 https:// www.europereloaded.com/no-go-zones-a-guide-to-western-failed-states-european-secessionist-movements/
18 *India That Is Bharat*, p. 177.
19 *Hindus in Hindu Rashtra*, p. 56–65.
20 https://hindupost.in/dharma-religion/tn-hindus-booked-for-stopping-children-from-attending-christian-school-fearing-conversion/?feed_id=6760&_unique_id=651830e2b8439

Chapter 11: Scriptures versus Scripture: One Scripture

1 *The Vedas*, p. 1.
2 *Caste System*, p. 9; https://pujayagna.com/blogs/hindu-customs/why-do-women-wear-a-toe-ring; https://pujayagna.com/blogs/hindu-customs/why-do-we-pierce-ears; https://allindiaroundup.com/general/scientific-reason-for-wearing-bangles/; https://www.thespiritualindian.com/apply-vibhuti-tilak-sandalwood-on-body/
3 https://blog.oup.com/2020/06/how-buddhist-monasteries-were-brought-back-from-destruction

Chapter 12: It's Terrorism, but for You

1 https://simple.wikipedia.org/wiki/Wulfila_Bible#:~:text=The%20Wulfila%20Bible%20%28or%20Gothic%20Bible%29%20is%20a,contains%20mainly%20a%20translation%20of%20the%20New%20Testament

Chapter 13: No God to Many Gods, Many Gods to One God

1. Barnhart dictionar.
2. https://www.youtube.com/watch?v=6bDe4uRu27c
3. https://archive.siasat.com/news/ram-not-god-just-human-being-justicekatju-1463642/
4. Nisha Manikantan. *Simplified Ayurveda*. Shri Shri Publication Trust, p. 8.
5. Tantric V*isions of the Divine Feminine*, p. 45.
6. *Simplified Ayurveda*, pp. 102, 104, 106, 108.
7. *The Vedas*, p. 4.
8. *The Vedas*, p. 52.
9. *The Vedas*, p. 45.
10. *The Vedas*, pp. 131, 132.
11. *Ancient India*, pp. 7, 178.
12. https://www.goodreads.com/author/quotes/5943.Desmond_Tutu
13. *Internal Security*
    Section 3: Global fundamentalism and its threat to the security of India
    a. Chapter 1: The clash of Messianic civilizations, secrets of divine love and cosmic wars
    b. Chapter 2: The Al Qaeda and its threat to the security of India
    c. Chapter 3: The ISIS and its threat to the security of India
    Section 6, 7, 9
    https://www.indiafacts.org.in/tag/justice-z-s-lohat/
    https://theprint.in/opinion/adivasis-are-not-hindus-lazy-colonial-census-gave-them-the-label/618051/; https://www.outlookindia.com/national/explained-what-is-the-sarna-religious-code-and-what-are-its-followers-deman—ng--news-230860
14. https://www.indiatimes.com/news/india/tribals-govt-religion-573661.html
15. https://www.swami-krishnananda.induishnu/nasadiya.pdf
16. *Tantric Visions of the Divine Feminine*, seed syllables, beeja mantra, breathing, Bij akharas—content power if repeated multiple times, you can absorb the superconsciousness and power, p. 90; *The Vedas*, p. 95. https://www.thespiritualindian.com/sheshanaga-significance/
17. https://www.publishyourarticles.net/knowledge-hub/philosophy/how-does-nyaya-prove-the-existence-of-god-distinguish-between-the-nyaya-conception-of-god-from-the-advaita-vedanta-conception-of-the-god/221/
18. 'A critical survey of Indian philosophy', p. 76.
19. 'A critical survey of Indian philosophy', p. 76.

20. (10 rishis) Dalal, Roshen (18 April 2014). *The Religions of India: A Concise Guide to Nine Major Faiths*. Penguin UK, ISBN: 9788184753967.
21. *Tantric Visions of the Divine Feminine*, p. 22.
22. *The Vedas*, p. 7.
23. *Tantric Visions of the Divine Feminine*, p. 70.
24. *The Vedas*, pp. 133, 115.
25. *Tantric Visions of the Divine Feminine*, p. 20.
26. Coulter, Charles, and Patricia Turner (2000). *Encyclopaedia of Ancient Deities*. Routledge, ISBN: 978-0786403172, p. 258.
    https://www.hindujagruti.induismuism/knowledge/article/how-were-four-vedas-created.html
27. https://www.britannica.com/topic/Prajapati-Hindu-deity
28. *The Vedas*, p. 6.
29. *The Vedas*, p. 28.
30. *The Vedas*, p. 7.
31. Easwaran, Eknath (2007). *The Bhagavad Gita*. Nilgiri Press, p. 179–90. Liberate yourself from worldly things, relationships, connect yourself with me and do duty. Easwaran 2007, pp. 203–10.
32. Krishnananda, Swami. 'A Short History of Religious and Philosophic Thought in India'. Divine Life Society, p. 19.
33. Same as Vishwa Rupa of Krishna in Mahabharata = Diagram 19.3. Aiyar, B.V. Kamesvara (1898). *The Purusha Sukta*. G.A. Natesan, Madras.
34. *Simplified Ayurveda*, p. 137.
35. *Simplified Ayurveda*, pp. 89–100, 122, 123, 124, 126–31, 19, 20, 26, 28, 29, 30, 34–39.
36. *Tantric Visions of the Divine Feminine*, pp. 14, 25.
37. a. Ojas: ultimate refined product we it (connects physiology with consciousness) 20 ayurveda
    b. *Tantric Visions of the Divine Feminine*, Hindu spirituality retention of semen is necessary Shakti, p. 155.
    c. *Tantric Visions of the Divine Feminine*, for spiritual awakening and maturity, idea is expressed sexual energy must transfer upward rather than downward (from ojas to tejas), p. 160.
    d. *Tantric Visions of the Divine Feminine*, loss of semen weakens men, p. 170.
    e. https://svasthaayurveda.com/11-ways-to-increase-healthy-ojas/
    https://www.worldhistory.org/article/1737/constantines-conversion-to-christianity/ https://www.historyhit.com/why-were-the-early-middle-ages-called-the-dark-ages

Chapter 14: Quantum Physics: It's Entanglement with Paramātmā

1. https://www.worldhistory.org/article/1737/constantines-conversion-to-christianity/ https://www.historyhit.com/why-were-the-early-middle-ages-called-the-dark-ages/
2. https://nykdaily.com/2020/10/similarities-between-hinduism-and-mayan-religion/; https://greekcitytimes.com/2022/09/07/9-greek-and-indian-mythology/; https://www.thebetterindia.com/41620/similarities-hindu-greek-mythology/; Lord Rama in global civilizations: https://lordrama.co.in/sri-rama-and-vedic-history-of-the-world.html
3. https://www.ancient-origins.net/history-important-events/great-flood-00263; https://www.newworldencyclopedia.org/entry/Great_Flood
4. Jain, Sulabh. *The Evolution of Religion: The History and Religions of Egypt and Harappan* India. Leadstart Publishing House, pp. 219–23.
5. *Tantric Visions of the Divine Feminine*, 7 chakras associated with goddess, 3 nadis, kundalini shakti, siddhis, pp. 47, 48, 49; Lotus, kundalini sushmna, yoga shakti, p. 169.
6. Refer to p. 426–428).
7. *Simplified Ayurveda*, pp. 54, 55, 56.
8. *Simplified Ayurveda*, pp. 54, 55, 56. https://www.lakshmanjooacademy.org/blog/the-practical-theory-of-the-seven-states-of-turya-and-blis
9. https://www.youtube.com/watch?v=qv14wKmU18U
10. *Simplified Ayurveda*, pp. 57–60.
11. https://www.lakshmanjooacademy.org/blog/the-practical-theory-of-the-seven-states-of-turya-and-bliss
12. *Simplified Ayurveda*, pp. 56–60.
13. *Simplified Ayurveda*, p. 62; *Tantric Visions of the Divine Feminine*, Bhuvaneshwari breaking knots and activating 7 chakras, p. 136.
14. *Tantric Visions of the Divine Feminine*, Kali finishes ego and liberates, p. 88.
15. *Simplified Ayurveda*, p. 62.
16. *Simplified Ayurveda*, pp. 64, 68.
17. *Simplified Ayurveda*, ashta siddhi siddhis, p. 54.
18. *Tantric Visions of the Divine Feminine*, superpower that give liberation, p. 25:
    a. Marana = causing persons death by will
    b. Uccatana = ability to make enemy sick
    c. Stambhana = ability to immobilize person
19. https://www.thehindu.com/news/national/india-to-fence-entire-border-with-myanmar/article67818240.ece
20. *Tantric Visions of the Divine Feminine*, p. 55.

21 *Indian Art and Culture* (4th edition), p. 18.
22 https://worldyogaforum.com/blog/mystic-powers-of-the-yogi-swami-vivekananda/

Chapter 15: Three-Dimensional Buddha
1 *Hindutva*, p. 481.
2 'Authority of *Vedas*' (*Collected Works of Periyar*, p.90).
3 *The Vedas*, p. 170.
4 *The Vedas*, p. 21.
5 *The Vedas*, p. 193.
6 *A History of Ancient and Medieval India*, p. 312.
7 *A History of Ancient and Medieval India*, p. 295.

Chapter 16: The Conqueror
1 Refer to p. 406: 7.
2 'A critical survey of Indian philosophy', pp. 48–68.

Chapter 17: Brahma Kills Consumerism to Save Dharma
1 https://www.artofliving.org/us-en/yoga/beginners/brahmacharya-yamas-celibacy

Chapter 18: Dvanva to Dvaita
1 *The Vedas*, pp. 8–9.
2 *Tantric Visions of the Divine Feminine*, Goddess is everywhere, p. 30.

Chapter 19: The Real 'Fake God'
1 *The Vedas*, p. 37.
2 *Tantric Visions of the Divine Feminine*, devotion in liberation, p. 52.
3 *The Vedas*, pp. 52, 53.
4 'A critical survey of Indian philosophy', pp. 239–390.
5 *Tantric Visions of the Divine Feminine*, pashu and pasha is available in Shakti too, p. 87.
6 *Tantric Visions of the Divine Feminine*, elongates tongue, p. 71.

Chapter 20: Why Rituals Are Always Meaningless?
1 Mishra, Ashok. *Hinduism – Ritual, Reason and Beyond*. Storymirror Infotech Pvt. Ltd, p. 255.
2 *Hindutva*, p. 472.
3 *Hindus in Hindu Rashtra*, pp. 5, 6.

4   *Collected Works of Periyar*, pp. 218–19, 221, 223, 235, 234, 240.
5   *Spectrum* by Rajiv Ahir (IPS) History 28th edition, p. 280.
6   https://theswaddle.com/can-self-respect-weddings-be-the-feminist-anti-caste-solution-to-marriage/; https://antisuperstition.org/simple-marriages/
7   https://thewire.in/caste/periyar-anti-caste-politics
8   *Collected Works of Periyar*, pp. 218–19, 221, 223, 235, 234, 240.
9   Index of *Hindu Rites and Rituals* by K.V. Singh.

Chapter 21: God of Baseless Colonizers
1   https://education.nationalgeographic.org/resource/biodiversity/
2   https://www.academia.edu/43754020/Eighty_four_Lakh_yonis_The_Jaina_Doctrine_of_8_4_Million_Embodiments; https://hinduism.stackexchange.com/questions/9901/what-are-the-84-lakh-8-4-million-species
3   https://www.businessworld.in/article/Bizarre-Yoga-Patents-Deepen-Indo-US-Dispute/20-06-2016-99364/
4   *Hindutva*, p. 605.

About the Author

Shubham Gokul Deore is an independent researcher. His fields of interest are history, philosophy, religion, political science, and policy-making. He dabbles in and is passionate about poetry for which he received appreciation during his schooldays from the Magsaysay awardee Dr Prakash Amte. Shubham also won multiple awards in essay-writing competitions in school. He has a bachelor's degree in civil engineering. *Decolonizing Hinduism* is his debut book, a dream since his college days.